The Book of The
REVELATION

The Book of The
REVELATION

by

WILLIAM R. NEWELL

"The Revelation of St. John was for a long time a shut book to me. I did not cease to long for a time when an insight might be granted me into its wonderful depths. Several years ago I was visited with a heavy season of affliction, which obliged me to discontinue for some months my official duties. I looked about for rod and staff that might comfort me, and soon lighted on The Revelation. Day and night I pondered on it, and one difficulty vanished after another. At the period of my recovery, there was scarcely a point of any moment respecting which I did not think I had obtained light."

HENGSTENBERG.

MOODY PRESS

CHICAGO

ISBN: 0-8024-7305-9

Printed in the United States of America

THE BOOK OF THE REVELATION

1. The only *prophetic* book in the New Testament, therefore the only *divine* and *accurate account of present and future things.*

2. *Closes God's Book,* therefore peculiarly important as is Genesis which opens God's Book.

3. A book *not sealed,* therefore can be understood if Scripture is compared with Scripture.

4. *Special blessing promised* its reader and hearer. Special blindness follows its neglect, for neglect of it grieves the God who gave it.

5. *Simple belief* of its statements is the only proper approach to it.

6. *Its method (visions* given to John, the beloved disciple) is the *very best way* of securing the confidence, awaking the interest, impressing the mind and arousing the conscience of the reader.

7. *Is addressed to Christ's servants,* therefore such will be blessed by it.

★ ★ ★

Romans, Ephesians and Hebrews should be known *before Revelation.* Romans, justified forever by faith; Ephesians, our calling, one with the Risen Christ; Hebrews, our Great High Priest, Who makes continual intercession for us, and leads our worship in heaven.

REMEMBERING that the Father hath committed all judgment, and also the authority to execute it, unto the Son, "because he is a son of man," we shall expect *Christ* to be seen as *the Judge,* in each judgment scene in The Revelation; and also that He will have a *special character* towards *each stage* of judgment.

I. The part concerning judgment will include:

First, judgment of *the assemblies* (churches) as God's house on earth; for judgment must "begin at the house of God" *(I Peter 4:17).* This judgment *Christ carries on as risen, glorified Son of God,* in His priestly character, but as a priest dealing *judicially.* Church testimony on earth is finally rejected. Chapters 1 to 3.

Second, the scene is removed to heaven, where is seen the Throne of God as holding *the whole earth* in responsibility. *Christ, as the Lamb slain, takes the sealed book* of the divine counsels of earthly judgment. The seals, trumpets and vials follow. Chapters 4 to 18.

Third, Christ Himself comes as King of kings and Lord of lords in the Great Day of Wrath; *sets up on earth His iron-rod judgment rule of 1000 years,* at the end of which, Satan being released and man rushing again to his banner, the *world's affairs are closed* up, and *heaven and earth pass away.* Chapter 19.

Fourth, all moral, responsible beings (except Christ's own) are called to the judgment of *the Great White Throne,* which has nothing to do with earth or with dispensations, but with *eternal destinies only.* Chapter 20: verses 11-15.

II. Then we have the New Creation: a new heaven, a new earth,—"all things new"; with the new Jerusalem the home of God and His saints; the Throne of God being established therein.

It is for this new heaven and new earth wherein righteousness is at home, that the Spirit, through Peter, declares the saints are looking.

CHRIST IN THE REVELATION

We find our blessed Lord directly named in seven chief characters:

1. He is the *risen, glorified Son of God* among the churches as the lightbearers of this present age, judging their state by His Spirit *(chapters 2 and 3)*.

2. He is *the Lamb in heaven* (after the rapture of the Church) publicly invested with authority to carry out the determined preliminary judgments upon men before His personal arrival on earth as Judge and King *(chapters 4 to 19:10)*.

3. He comes to earth as *King of kings and Lord of lords* in the Great Day of Wrath *(chapter 19:11-21)*.

4. He is *Christ*, reigning with His glorified saints on earth, during one thousand years *(chapter 20:1-6)*. He is *then* "King over all the earth" (Zechariah 14:9).

5. He is *the Judge upon the Great White Throne*, with the holiness, righteousness and truth of deity absolutely and finally unveiled in judgment (chapter 20: 11-15).

6. He is *the Lamb, upon "the throne of God and of the Lamb"*: through whom, though subjected willingly to the Father *(I Corinthians 15:28)*, the glory and love of the deity will be expressed forevermore (chapter 21: 22, 23; 22:3, 4).

7. He is *"I Jesus . . . the root and offspring of David, the bright, the morning star,"* to His own, His beloved servants (chapter 22:16). He is the Coming One, expected and longed for by His real saints, the Bride, the true Church, who are under His grace continually. The Revelation's last words are, "The grace of the Lord Jesus Christ be with the saints. Amen." We must study this book *in the light of this verse,* and of Revelation 1:5: "Unto him that *loveth us,* and *loosed us* from our sins by his blood!"

Whatever judgments fall, they do *not* fall on the saints, the Body of Christ!

THE VARIOUS JUDGMENTS

1. Of the Church's earthly history—chapters 2 and 3.

2. Of the rebellious nations—especially the Beast-worshippers—chapters 4 to 16.

3. Of the system of earth idolatry called "Babylon"—chapters 17 and 18.

4. Of the Beast, the False Prophet and the Kings and armies of earth at Armageddon—chapter 19:19-21.
   (This is the Great Day of Wrath.)

5. Of the devil's permitted career on earth, for 1000 years—chapter 20:1-3.

6. Of the spared nations, in enforced righteousness, justice and peace, during the Millennium—chapter 20:4-6.

7. Of the rebellious earth, upon Satan's release—chapter 20:7-9.

8. Of Satan himself in the Lake of Fire forever—chapter 20:10.

9. Of the unsaved, at the Great White Throne—chapter 20:4-15.

◆◆◆◆◆◆

We repeat over and over that our Lord is not seen in the book of The Revelation as the Head of the Body, the Church. This description belongs wholly to Paul, who unfolds in his epistles the character, calling and destiny of the Church of God. In The Revelation we are not studying the calling of the Church as the Body of Christ, as risen and heavenly.

But The Revelation does deal with *outcomes*: (1) of the earthly church testimony, for as a witness for God the church is proved unfaithful and removed from the scene: the real Church taken to heaven (4:1), and the false, destroyed by the Wild Beast (chapter 17). (2) Then the nations, under responsibility to occupy and govern the earth, are judged and desolated. (3) Jerusalem, "the holy city," is seen as "Sodom and Egypt" (except for a remnant). The nation is handed over to the delusions of Antichrist. (4) Finally, the rebellious of the race of Adam and the earth they chose and claimed, following Satan's captaincy in their final testing, are destroyed, and new things are brought in.

CONTENTS

Part One—JUDGMENT—Chapters 1-20

Part Two—NEW CREATION—Chapters 21, 22

Author's Note

THE TEXT used is in general that of the Revised Version, which is much more accurate than that of the Old Version. At times it is necessary to render literally; and, in several instances to paraphrase, to make clearer the meaning.

CHAPTER I

OPENING MESSAGE

Revelation 1

The Revelation of Jesus Christ: which God gave Him.
This expression is the true title to the book. It is a communication or unfolding of the details' of future things by our Lord Jesus Christ. These opening statements are startling: (1) God *gave* Jesus Christ this *apocalypse,* or "revelation." (2) It was that He might show it unto *His servants* (literally bondservants). (3) Jesus Christ communicated it *"by his angel."* (4) It was *"His servant John"* to whom it was communicated. (5) John faithfully "bare witness of the word of God, and of the testimony of Jesus Christ, even of all things that he saw."

We have, first, God; then Jesus Christ; then, His angel; then, His servant John, and finally Christ's *servants,*—to whom the Revelation *comes.* Furthermore, we note that John bears witness to two things:

(1) *"the word of God,"* and (2) *"the testimony of Jesus Christ."* "The word of God" is evidently God's word to Christ in which He communicated to Him this *apocalypse,* or revelation; and "the testimony of Jesus Christ" is our Lord's faithful communication of what God gave Him to tell us.

First, there can be no doubt, that Jesus Christ is the Second Person of the Trinity. The Father, in Hebrews 1:8, addresses Him as *God,* saying, "Thy throne, O God, is for ever and ever." Our Lord claimed worship, and plainly says that "all should honor the Son even as they honor the Father" (John 5:23). And in a comparison of Revelation 1:8 with 22:13, all doubt vanishes.

But, secondly, we must remember and believe Christ's own words in Matthew 24:36: "Of that day and hour knoweth no one, not even the angels of heaven, neither the Son, but the Father only." Compare Mark 13:32, and also His parting words after the resurrection, in Acts 1:7, "It is not for you to know times or seasons, which

1

the Father hath set within his own authority."*

Again, in Hebrews 10:12, 13, "He . . . sat down on the right hand of God, henceforth expecting till his enemies be made the footstool of his feet." The word here used means, "to await from the hand of another." Taken in connection with the preceding verses, it indicates a state of constant *expectancy:* certain of the *event,* but leaving the *time* in the hands of the Father. When our Lord came to earth, we read (Philippians 2:7) He "emptied himself." He left His glory, His wisdom, and His power, absolutely in the hands of the Father. This did not subtract an iota from His Deity, but placed Him where He could say to the Father (Psalm 22:9, 10), "Thou didst make me trust when I was upon my mother's breasts. I was cast upon thee from the womb." So He spoke on earth, "The Son can do nothing of himself, but what he seeth the Father doing." Now, of course, our Lord has entered into His glory, and all authority has been committed unto Him in heaven and on earth.

Nevertheless, these plain words are before us as we enter upon The Revelation: "The Revelation of Jesus Christ, which *God gave* him." This revelation must have been communicated to Him after His ascension to heaven, by the Father who has "set within his own authority" times and seasons. We believe:

(1) That the times and seasons are yet within the Father's authority—of course by the glad consent of the Son.

(2) That the book of The Revelation contains the details of the carrying out of the divine decree· that all Christ's enemies should be put under His feet—all things, save the Father, subjected unto Him (I Corinthians 15: 24-28).

---

*This word *authority* (often translated "power" in the old version) is the Greek word *exousia,* used first in Matthew 7:29, "He taught them as one having *authority,* and not as their scribes"; again, Matthew 21:23, "By what authority doest thou these things?" and again, Matthew 28:18, "All authority is given unto me," etc. It is used 21 times in The Revelation, its last occurrence being in 22:14, "Blessed are they that wash their robes, that they may have the right (*exousia*) to come to the tree of life," etc. "Power (*exousia*) means authority to do a thing" (Liddell and Scott). That seems to me to be the primary meaning of this word in Scripture.

(3) That the Father has not revealed "the day and the hour," so that we are waiting and watching and expecting, along with our Lord, the Father's giving Him His Kingdom, which He "went into a far country, to receive . . . and to return" (Luke 19:12).

Our Lord said in Gethsemane, "Thinkest thou that I cannot beseech my Father, and he shall even now send me more than twelve legions of angels? How then should the scriptures be fulfilled, that thus it must be?" (Matthew 26:53, 54). He left it to the Father to grant Him, as He pleased, weakness, shame and suffering, or resurrection, power, and glory. And this was perfect obedience!

Christ will, of course, occupy the eternal throne, for He is God, yet it will be "the Throne of God and of the Lamb," an infinitely beautiful and gracious arrangement. For our Lord will not retire from us into the Godhead, although He is and will continue to be, "God blessed forever": but He will be a man, and as such will reign on "the Throne of God and of the Lamb" forever!

To show unto his servants (literally bondservants). This revelation is written not exclusively to the Church, but to all willing *subjects of Christ*. This will include the spared remnant of Israel, also those among the nations that attach themselves to them in the awful time of trouble; in fact, all companies of God's saints. Although written "for the churches" (Revelation 22:16), the book of The Revelation is not addressed to the Church, the assembly of God, the Body of Christ, *as such,* as are Paul's Epistles. The Revelation is a prophecy, testified *to* the churches, for their information as to "the things that are to come," and for warning and correction.

No wonder, then, that those not subject to Christ should find difficulty with the book of The Revelation! It is a remarkable fact, that although our Lord Jesus said in the upper room, "No longer do I call you servants; . . . but I have called you friends"; and although Paul tells the church saints, in Galatians 4:7, "Ye are no longer bondservants, but *full-age sons:*"—nevertheless all the apostles in their writings call themselves *bondservants of Jesus Christ!* If we are having difficulty with this blessed closing book of God's holy Word, let us surrender ourselves to Jesus Christ as His servants. *The book was written to bondservants.*

The things which must shortly come to pass. "The *things*,"—this is definite. It describes events. Do not then look for vague "symbols." *"Must* come to pass"— here is *certainty, necessity.* Man dreams of "development," "progress," "achievement." God says, "The rulers of this world are coming to nought" (I Corinthians 2:6). *Believe* God; *doubt* man. Satan is the prince of this world and the God of this age. He deceiveth the whole world. Let us not be deceived. The things we are about to study in The Revelation "must come to pass," and, "shortly."

"Shortly" surely indicates imminence. We have the same Greek expression in Romans 16:20, "The God of peace shall bruise Satan under your feet shortly" (Greek: *en tachei).* He is not yet bruised, but we are expecting it! The same phrase is used in Revelation 22:6, "The things which must *shortly* come to pass." This shuts out the "historical" interpretation of the book,—that is, making the seals, trumpets, vials, etc., apply to the events of the past church centuries. In fact, the strictly prophetic part of The Revelation does not begin till the churches are out of the scene,—that is, after chapter 4. I firmly believe that unless we reject utterly the idea that this part of The Revelation has been "gradually fulfilling itself" in the present age, we shall miss the meaning of the book. Remember Paul's explanation of the doctrine of the Jewish remnant in Romans 9:27, 28, "The Lord will execute *his* word upon the earth, finishing it and cutting it short." The present dispensation must not in any sense be confused with God's future dealing with the Jewish remnant after the true Church has been taken to heaven. Strictly speaking, the true Church has nothing to do with the present age, any more than it has to do with this world. Judgment for her is past; her citi-

zenship is in heaven; she is one with Christ; she is indwelt by the Holy Ghost, and may be caught up *at any
moment*. Although she is *informed* in Revelation about
"the things which must shortly come to pass" on earth,
she will not be *in* them; even as Enoch was taught of
the Lord's coming and judgment (Jude 14), but yet was
not to pass through it; and as Abraham was taught concerning the destruction of Sodom, while he himself dwelt
on the mountain away from the place of judgment.

It is absolutely necessary for us to distinguish, as
members of the Body of Christ, between what is said
about us (in the epistles), and what is told *to* us, as
friends, by our Lord, in The Revelation.

"Shortly," moreover, not only means imminency, but
also *rapidity of execution when action once begins*.
"Things which in their entirety must soon come to pass"
—in God's speedy time, although He seems to delay; for
the same Greek expression is translated "speedily" in
Luke 18:7, 8.

**He sent and signified (them) by his angel unto his
servant John; who bare witness of the word of God,
and of the testimony of Jesus Christ, even of all things
that he saw.** The manner of the communication of
The Revelation to John by Jesus Christ is remarkable. He
"sent and signified by his angel."* This angelic agency of

---

*Many other angels are seen besides this revealing one whom our Lord
calls "mine angel": the whole "innumerable company" in 5:11 and 7:11;
four in 7:1; "another," 7:2; the seven trumpet angels in 8:2; "another" in
8:3; "another strong angel," 10:1; six successive special angels in chapter
14; seven angels with the seven last plagues, chapters 15, 16; another
heralding Babylon's final destruction in 18:1-3; the "strong angel" who
illustrates that destruction, 18:21; the "angel standing in the sun," who
invites the birds to Armageddon, 19:17; the angel that binds Satan, 20:1-3;
and the scene of 21:9.

We know that after Satan is bound and the millennial kingdom brought
in, the "inhabited earth" will not be "subjected to angels" (Hebrews 2:5).
Therefore we do not find angels ruling after the binding of Satan. Of course,
it is by angelic operation that the kingdom of the 1000 years is cleared of
all those opposing it. See Matthew 13:40-43, remembering that it is "the end
of the *age*," not the "world," seen there.

It is quite astonishing to study this direct interference by the Lord of
hosts through the "angels of his power," even in the preliminary judgments
which precede this public manifestation, as well as at that manifestation,
II Thessalonians 1:7. Even evil angels, like those "bound at the great river
Euphrates," are made use of. See also 9:1, for the "star" there is evidently
a fallen angel.

How little do the "wise" of this "modern" age dream, in their "grass-
hopper-visions," of these marvelous beings, the "mighty in strength." *One*
of them slew 185,000 men in one night in Hezekiah's day!

course does not refer to the title and introduction (1:1-8);
nor to the great personal vision of Christ (1:9-20); nor
to the messages to the seven churches (chapters 2, 3).
Also the thrice repeated "I come quickly," and the "I
Jesus have sent mine angel," are spoken directly by the
Lord. Indeed chapter 22:6-10, and again 10-20 may well
have been spoken by the Lord Himself; while the closing
verse, like the opening of the book, is the Spirit-inspired
utterance of the apostle. Like 1:4-7 it is more apostolic
than seer-like in form, and so, more *intimate* to our
hearts.

The manner of angelic communication to John, like
other phases of inspiration, is beyond our faculties. Much,
indeed, like John, Daniel "heard a man's voice between
the banks of the Ulai, which called and said, Gabriel,
make this man to understand the vision" (Daniel 8:16).

The Revelation concerning, as it does, *governmental*
matters on earth, which are in angelic hands until the
Millennium, is committed largely to direct angelic ministry.

John speaks of **"all things that he saw."** Speculation
upon inspiration is vain. God tells us it was "in divers
manners" (Hebrews 1:1). John, in The Revelation
writes much as Daniel wrote. Both deal with God's
government of this world. We may know the whole is
authoritative. We shall find here "what the Spirit saith
to the churches," and also the awful tribulation time itself, the Holy Spirit reminding us by His especial witness, that all is taking place according to God (Revelation
14:13); and, at the end, Jesus Himself speaking, *attesting* all (22:16), although it had been testified by His
angel: "I Jesus have *sent* mine angel."

Blessed is he that readeth. This is directly contrary
to the attitude toward The Revelation which very many
Christians have. A special blessing is pronounced on
the readers of this book, also on **they that hear the
words of the prophecy.** *Living oracles* give and support life (John 6:63). Note that it is the *words* that
are to be read and heard. God is *especially particular*

concerning this one prophetic book of the New Testament, as we shall note at its close (22, verses 7, 9, 10, 18, 19). Doubtless the *public* reading and hearing of this book of The Revelation to the assembled saints is especially in view. "Give heed to reading," is Paul's command to Timothy (I Timothy 4:13); and this was public reading. It ought to be practiced everywhere.*

And keep the things that are written therein. Now the sense of the word "keep" is its primary one of "watching over," "guarding as a treasure," as well as its secondary one, "to give heed to." We cannot "keep" a prophecy as men might "observe" a law. The prophecy will be fulfilled, *whether we pay attention to it or not.* But there is *divine blessing* if we give heed to it and jealously *guard its very words!*

For the time is at hand. No dates are set for this "time of patient grace," this "day of salvation," the "acceptable year of the Lord," in which the Church finds herself. And although from Revelation 4 onward, the Church is to be on high, we must remember that the whole book of The Revelation is included by our Lord in 22:16: "I Jesus have sent mine angel to testify unto you these things for the churches." "The time is at hand" should be in the heart of every believer, every day! "Prophecy annihilates time, and all intervening and even opposing circumstances, and sets one down on the threshold of accomplishment," (W. Scott). The first use of the Greek word translated "at hand" should instruct us. Compare Matthew 24:32, 33, *"nigh," "near."* The words are repeated in Revelation 22:10, which see. In John 11:54, 55 you have "near," of *place;* and "at hand," of *time;* and note in this latter verse that the Jews were getting ready for the event! Despite all the arguments of those who have said, "My Lord delayeth

---

*Dean Alford, himself an English churchman, says: "If the words are to be understood as above, they form at least a solemn rebuke to the practice of the Church of England, which omits with one or two exceptions the whole of this book from her public reading. Not one word of the precious messages of the Spirit to the churches is ever heard in the public service of a church never weary of appealing to her scriptural liturgies. Surely it is high time that such an omission should be supplied."

his coming," the only attitude of obedience is, to *"watch"*: for we *know not* the day nor the hour! They are no friends, but deadly foes, who put this and that "event" between the believer and his Lord's coming.

John to the seven churches that are in Asia: Grace to you and peace. First, regarding the writer of this book: it was John, the beloved disciple. There is no real doubt that John the apostle was the writer.

Fausset well says, "John—the *apostle:* for none but he (supposing the writer an honest man), would thus sign himself nakedly without addition. As sole survivor and representative of the apostles, and eye witness of the Lord, he needed no designation but *his name,* to be recognized by his readers."

John writes as a *Seer* more than as an Apostle in Revelation. There is no speaking with personal apostolic authority (except in this *salutation* of 1:4-7; and the *benediction* of 22:21) as Paul in his epistles, and Peter, and John himself elsewhere. Instead of speaking authoritatively in the Spirit, we find John falling at the feet of the glorified Son of God in this chapter. He is hearing His voice as Judge, and seeing visions of Him as such, for the Father hath committed all judgment unto the Son, whether it be in the present house of God on earth, the churches; or toward the elect nation, Israel; or toward the earth's peoples and nations. John in The Revelation is merely the *writer.* Twelve times in this book he is told to *write.* Therefore we need to give the more earnest heed to The Revelation. There are those who seek to evade (to their own sorrow) the authority with which Paul was invested. But there is no way of evading the direct words and actions of the divinely-appointed Judge, Christ Himself, here at the end of God's Book.

The "seven churches" indicate representative assemblies, both as to history, and as to spiritual state. Other important assemblies (like the Colossians within a few miles of Philadelphia and Laodicea), are not mentioned, although doubtless John was familiar with all of them and had labored among them. Let us, therefore, at once take these seven churches as representing all the assemblies of the Church's *history;* even as Paul writes to seven cities of the Church's *calling* (Romans, Corinthians, Galatians, Ephesians, Philippians, Colossians and Thessalonians).*

Note the blessed announcement to *us,* "*Grace* . . . and *peace.*" As our Lord so lovingly speaks at the close (22:16), "I Jesus have sent mine angel to testify unto you these things for the churches." Let us see that we keep the sweet taste of grace and peace as we read of the bitter things that are coming upon the earth. If at any point throughout the terrible things which you read in these Revelation chapters, you cannot stop and look up with perfect confidence saying, "I am *under grace,* and God has announced peace to me," then you are falling into unbelief. Flee to the eighth of Romans, and to the second of Ephesians, where you belong! Your Lord will have His servant John write many things *for* you which are not *about* you. Paul is *your* apostle. Any of you who are believers are not appointed unto wrath— any kind or degree of wrath. Israel and the nations will experience wrath; but you, who are in Christ, are already *glorified* (Romans 8:29, 30)!

From him who is and who was and who is to come. This is the Eternal One, the self-existent Source of all being, and the One to whom all moral beings are responsible. How different this name of God from Paul's greetings: "Grace to you and peace from God our Father," for Paul's task was to set forth our *sonship* and its blessed privileges. Or, as John himself writes (I John 1:3, 4): "That which we have seen and heard declare we unto you also, that ye also may have fellowship with us: yea, and our fellowship·is with the Father,

---

*The teaching of some that the seven churches of Revelation 2 and 3 represent Jewish assemblies in tribulation times arises from Satanic delusion. It is always coupled with other fantastic and heretical dispensational doctrines (as Bullingerism with subtle denial of eternity of punishment). Govett well says, "These seven churches were prophetic of the things which ARE, not of the things that *were* to be."

and with his Son Jesus Christ: and these things we write, that our joy may be made full."

The Revelation is not dealing with the unutterably glorious standing of the Church as the Body of Christ and of the saints as full-grown sons of God, and of our heavenly calling and walk. These things are not to be forgotten for a moment by the believer who reads The Revelation. The Revelation is "obviously distinct from the other parts of the New Testament, in that God is reverting a great deal to the principles on which He had acted in Old Testament times."

It is at once manifest that God is spoken of here as "the Administrator of the world,"—indeed, of all creation; and the third and second Persons of the Deity are likewise connected here with government, rather than salvation. It is of the highest importance to see this.

We read, consequently, of the Holy Spirit, not as "the one Spirit" dwelling in all the members of the one body, but, **from the seven Spirits that are before his throne.**

There is, of course, but one blessed Spirit: yet He is spoken of here as seven-fold; for He is the executive person of the Godhead, and acting in The Revelation in a purely *governmental* way. In this character His place is "before the throne of God" in heaven, as we read in Revelation 4:5: "seven lamps of fire burning before the throne, which are the seven Spirits of God." Now if we turn to Isaiah 11, we find that upon our Lord's return as King, upon the throne of David, the Spirit rests upon Him in His governmental offices in exactly a seven-fold way: first, as to His Deity—"the Spirit of Jehovah"; second, of wisdom; third, of understanding; fourth, counsel; fifth, might; sixth, knowledge; seventh, "the fear of Jehovah" (begetting that fear). And also in Zechariah 3:9 and 4:6, 10, we again read of the governmental operation of the Spirit of God: "Not by might, nor by power, but by my Spirit, saith Jehovah of hosts" . . . "these seven shall rejoice, . . . the eyes of Jehovah, which run to and fro through the whole earth."

We find our Lord Jesus Christ, although the second person of the Trinity, mentioned *last,* in Revelation 1:5, for God desires immediately to emphasize certain things concerning Him; and it is He who is to rule on earth.

And from Jesus Christ, the faithful witness. He was that, first, when He was on earth, as Paul says in I Timothy 6:13, "Christ Jesus, who before Pontius Pilate witnessed the good confession;" or, as our *Lord* says in John 7:7, "The world . . . me it hateth, because I testify of it, that its works are evil." But He is evermore the witness to the truth, as we shall see in His searching messages to the seven churches, covering the present time, as well as when He afterwards carries out faithfully what is written in the seven-sealed book of judgment on the world.*

Next He is called **the firstborn of the dead.** Others who were raised, like Lazarus, were brought back into this earthly life merely to die again; Christ, into "newness of life," in eternal victory over death. The Greek word for firstborn *(prototokos)* is a most important one to lay to heart, indicating, as it does, the fact of His divine personal dignity and precedence. This is the explanation of the same word in Colossians 1:15, "the firstborn of all creation"; which does not for a moment mean that our Lord was a creature, but that He is the head, object and heir of all creation. The very next verse declares that "all things have been created through him, and unto him"! And inasmuch as the book of The Revelation is to reveal all things actually *subjected* to Him, we must connect Psalm 89:26, 27, 37, with our Lord. God the Father speaks of Christ thus: "He shall cry unto me, Thou art my Father . . . I also will make him *my* firstborn, The highest of the kings of the earth";—just

---

*"He was the *faithful witness* because all things that He heard of the Father He faithfully made known to the disciples. Also because He taught the way of God in truth and cared not for man, nor regarded the person of men. Also, the truth which He taught in words, He confirmed by miracles. Also because the testimony to Himself on the part of the Father, He denied not, even in death. Lastly, because He will give true testimony of the works, good and bad, at the day of judgment."—Richard of St. Vincent, 12th century.

as the very words, "the faithful witness" are found in verse 37 of this great Psalm!

This leads us to the third designation of Christ in Revelation 1:5: **the ruler of the kings of the earth.** *Ruler,* not prince: our Lord is not one of the princes of the earth, but the ruler of them all, as will be brought forth in The Revelation.

This characterizes the whole book of The Revelation. Our Lord Jesus Christ is not seen in His work of redemption—that is Romans; nor in His office as High Priest and Advocate on high—that is Hebrews and I John; but the first great question in The Revelation is, *Who shall rule,—Satan and man? or God by Christ?* Keep this in mind through all our study.

But ere we enter upon Christ's stern offices of judgment, John is given to speak a most tender word to our very hearts: **Unto him that loveth us, and loosed us from our sins by his blood.** Remember,—do not forget!—the words of John 13:1: "having loved his own that were in the world, he loved them unto the end." Jude, after a brief story of the apostasy of Christendom, stands at the portal to The Revelation and speaks, as we are about to enter this great book, "beloved . . . keep yourselves in *the love* of God." Note in Revelation 1:5 that the *loving* is in the present tense, and the *loosing* in the past (aorist). The loosing was done once for all at Calvary; the loving goes on forever!

And he made us to be a Kingdom, to be priests unto his God and Father. Notice again that John does not here speak of us as the Body of Christ, and members one of another—which of course we are—but as a *kingdom.* It is unfortunate that the old version here calls us "kings." The word in the Greek is in the singular number, "kingdom." The reference to us as *a kingdom* is entirely consistent with the whole book of Revelation. We must connect this passage with Revelation 5:9, 10, where the four living ones and the four and twenty elders sing a new song concerning Christ, who has just taken over the seven-sealed book: "Worthy art thou to take the book, and to open the seals thereof: for thou wast slain, and didst purchase unto God with thy blood out of every tribe, and tongue, and people, and nation, and madest them . . . unto our God a kingdom and priests, and they reign upon the earth." Both these passages, of course, look forward to the millennial reign of chapter 20, after which *the earth* will *pass away.*

Notice that we have been made priests unto *Christ's* God and Father, for Christ is the heir, and we inherit through and in Him. It is intensely interesting, and solemnly instructive also, that we are not only a *kingdom,* but *priests.* Of course, all believers have this priestly function *now,* as in Ephesians 2:18: "through him (Christ) we have our access in one Spirit unto the Father"; and we are today those to whom God looks to pray "for all men; for kings and all that are in high place" (I Timothy 2:1, 2), as well as for one another, for all saints, and for the salvation of others. We are also to be offering up "a sacrifice of praise to God continually," through our Great High Priest in heaven (Hebrews 13:15). But The Revelation looks forward to the exercise of royal priesthood! When our Lord Jesus shall return to earth to reign, the full Melchizedek priesthood will come in: "He shall be a priest upon his throne" —and we with Him!

No wonder, then, that John utters the adoring words, **to him be the glory and the dominion unto the ages of the ages. Amen.** He speaks thus of Christ, who is God. Otherwise the words are blasphemy. It is deeply solemn to note that the *first* of the many ascriptions of praise in this wonderful book of The Revelation is given to Christ, who "loveth us, and loosed us from our sins by his blood." Let us be forever rejoicing in it. Also the first use of God's great particular designation of eternity, "unto the ages of the ages," is in thus ascribing eternal glory and dominion to Christ.*

---

*This remarkable phrase, first used by Paul in Galatians 1:5 (Greek), occurs 21 times in Scripture, 14 of these being in The Revelation (including 14:11, where the definite article is omitted, because it is there *introduced* as connected with eternal judgment; whereas in 20:10 it is included, as denoting what has already been introduced).

And now we come to what we may properly call the *first* great TEXT of the book of The Revelation: **Behold, he cometh with the clouds; and every eye shall see him, and they that pierced him; and all the tribes of the earth shall mourn over him. Even so, Amen.**

We call it a *text,* or *theme,* because all preceding our Lord's glorious advent to this earth in chapter 19 leads up to that event. Next, He reigns on earth 1000 years. And, after the last judgment, the New Creation is seen, and we have in 21:5, the *second* great TEXT: "Behold, I make all things new." But note that in the last chapter of The Revelation, our Lord will three times emphasize His *personal coming* as the object of all thought and hope: "Behold, I come quickly!" "Behold, I come quickly!" "Yea: I come quickly!" (Revelation 22:7, 12, 20).

Those who understand the place our Lord's personal return to this earth holds in Scripture, find The Revelation unfolding itself to them. To others it is merely a "book of symbols"—vague, objectless.

Now it is not the rapture of the Church, when we shall be "caught up in the clouds, to meet the Lord in the air," that is seen in Revelation 1:7, although doubtless that rapture is involved and included. It is rather the public *revelation,* or *epiphany to the whole world* that is referred to, because that event brings in *the kingdom* toward which The Revelation looks.

The Greek word, *"parousia,"* beginning with Matthew 24:3, is used sixteen times in the New Testament as a general term for Christ's *presence* as against His *absence* now in heaven. *"Parousia"* is the opposite of *"apousia,"* (absence). Both Greek words appear in Philippians 2:12, —"not in my presence *(parousia)* only, but now much more in my absence *(apousia)*." Compare the same word in II Corinthians 7:6, 7; 10:10.

However, the term *"parousia,"* applied to our Lord's coming, covers His arrival in the upper air, His taking the Church up thither, according to I Thessalonians 4:13-

18; our each appearing before His *bema,* or awarding-seat there (I Corinthians 3:12, 15; 4:5; II Corinthians 5:10), and the marriage of the Lamb of Revelation 19:6-10. During this period we are spoken of as *"tabernacling in the heavens"* (Revelation 13:6).

During this time we shall find chapters 6 to 16 under fulfilment, including The Great Tribulation, which will cover the last three and a half years before our Lord's public coming spoken of in Revelation 1:7.

This public manifestation is called in II Thessalonians 2:8 "the manifestation of his coming": literally, the *epiphany (epiphaneia)* of His *parousia,*—so vividly translated by Rotherham: "the forthshining of His arrival." Our Lord arrives in the upper air first, taking up His saints; then, after the terrible events on earth culminating in The Great Tribulation, we read in Matthew 24:29, "Immediately after the tribulation of those days the sun shall be darkened, and the moon shall not give her light, and the stars shall fall from heaven, and the powers of the heavens shall be shaken: and then shall appear the sign of the Son of man in heaven (the revelation of Himself to the spared remnant of Israel according to Zechariah 12:10) ; and then shall all the tribes of the earth mourn, and they shall see the Son of man coming on the clouds of heaven with power and great glory." This is the great, manifested coming of Revelation 19:11-16.

This *public manifestation* is that phase of our Lord's coming with which The Revelation deals. The rapture of *the Church* is secret, instantaneous, "in a moment, in the twinkling of an eye."

Furthermore, the Lord must have come *for* His saints in order to come *with* them. For we read in Colossians 3:4, "When Christ, who is our life, shall be manifested (this is public), then shall ye also with him be manifested in glory."

It is of the very first importance that we distinguish the rapture of the saints from their manifestation at

Christ's revelation. To be caught up in the clouds to meet our Lord and the joy of His presence is certainly different from "the revelation of the Lord Jesus from heaven with the angels of his power in flaming fire, rendering vengeance" (II Thessalonians 1:7, 8).

"Behold, he cometh" is the one vivid point, the common expectation. It is motion from a place to a place. As Paul says in I Thessalonians 4:16, "The Lord himself shall descend from heaven." He is now the Man, glorified, at the right hand of the Father. *"From thence he shall come."*

Now, this advent, or arrival, of Revelation 1:7, is an exact fulfilment of the promise given the disciples in Acts 1:11: "This Jesus, who was received up from you into heaven, shall so come in like manner as ye beheld him going into heaven." There, in verse 9, "as they were looking, he was taken up; and a cloud received him out of their sight." He went up with a visible, tangible body. He went up in their sight, a cloud covered Him from vision. Exactly thus will He be manifested.

But note quickly that this coming with clouds of Revelation 1:7 is not describing the rapture of the Church *essentially.* We are, indeed, to be caught up into the clouds to meet the Lord, but He is the Lord *from heaven,* and we, "accepted in the Beloved," being one with Him and seated with Him in the heavenlies, are not connected with clouds or earth; therefore the rapture will take us as heavenly ones into the presence of our heavenly Lord, into the midst of the clouds with which He will afterwards come, and we with Him.

Every eye shall see him, and they that pierced him; and all the tribes of the earth shall mourn over him— that is, the whole earth and especially the Jewish nation. Zechariah's prophecy (12:10), and John's words (John 19:37), prove this. See also Matthew 24:30.

"Every eye" shall see His public manifestation as Son of man, beheld from the earth's surface. It is not the rapture of the Church, when "we shall see him even as he is," and "be like him" (I John 3:2). There is no mourning there! It is, however, the exact fulfilment of Matthew 24:27, 29, 30: there is the darkening of the sun, moon and stars, just before; then the sudden bursting on the scene "as lightning" of the arrival, the presence *(parousia)* of Christ, His holy angels, and all His saints! "And then shall appear the sign of the Son of man in heaven: and then shall all the tribes of the earth mourn, and they shall see the Son of man coming on the clouds of heaven with power and great glory."

First, black night—the withdrawal of all creature light; next, the sudden appearance of the Son of man, but, as "the sign," for He must be *seen* by the remnant of Israel and the "sign" is this vision of Himself, when "they look on him whom they pierced." Then comes the most utter "mourning of sorrow" ever known on earth, for this nation who crucified Him.

We must remember that it is *back to the Mount of Olives, whence He went away,* that He will come. Just before His feet "stand upon" that mountain (Zechariah 14:4, 5), He will make Himself seen in His glory, yea, in His love, to Israel, beleaguered by the hostile nations of earth. Read Zechariah 14:1, 2. Jerusalem will be taken —half made captives, the residue spared. Then comes Christ: "And his feet shall stand in that day upon the mount of Olives, which is before Jerusalem on the east." "And Jehovah my God shall come, and all the holy ones with thee." There must be, however, a little space for this *mourning* (Zechariah 12:10—13:1). It is at that time that "a nation shall be born in a day." Israel, like Thomas, must see before they believe, but they shall see! So the weeping of the spared of Israel will be penitential grief over this Messiah whom in their blindness they pierced. But the fountain "for sin and for uncleanness" will at that time be opened to them (Zechariah 13:1), and they will cry, "Lo, this is our God; we have waited for him" (Isaiah 25:9).

But what about the tribes of the earth?* Their mourning will be because of utter loss, despair and terror. "And
men shall go into the caves of the rocks, and into the
holes of the earth, from before the terror of Jehovah, and
from the glory of his majesty" (Isaiah 2:19); for "the
day of the Lord" shall come upon them "as a thief,"
"suddenly as a snare" (I Thessalonians 5:2, 3; Luke
21:34, 35). That day is "the death knell of the world's
gayeties and pleasures, the turning of their confidence to
consternation, the conversion of their songs to shrieks
of horror and despair."

Even so, Amen. Here we have the Greek word *"nai,"*
which means "entire assent," *"yea!"* and the Hebrew
"Amen," which means, *"be it done."* Both words are
found in II Corinthians 1:20, and also in the next to the
last verse of The Revelation. In Revelation 1:7 they are
in the apostle's mouth, and should be in the mouth of
every believer, Jew or Gentile, as a response to the prophecy of our Lord's coming. In Revelation 22:20 the *"nai,"*
meaning "yes," "yes indeed," "truly," is in the mouth of
Christ; the response, *"Amen,"* meaning, "let it be so,"
"I consent from my heart," is in the mouth of His apostle,
representing us all!

And now we come to Revelation 1:8, where God sets
His own seal upon this book of The Revelation; and
we beg deep consideration of this great verse. God as
the great I AM is *attesting* this last book in a most
unusual and solemn way.

**I am the Alpha and the Omega, saith the Lord God,
who is and who was and who is to come, the Almighty.**
It is evident that God speaks here *as God*. Our Lord
Jesus Christ takes the same titles in Revelation 22:13:
for He is the second person of the deity. Yet it is fit-

---

*We must read "earth," instead of confining the term to the land of
Israel. See all the occurrences of the Greek word *gē*, beginning with the
first verse of the Bible (Septuagint). Of some 260 occurrences of this word
in the New Testament, none, perhaps, but Luke 21:23 indicates Palestine in
anything like an absolute way, and this not really so in view of "Jerusalem"
in verse 20, and "Judea" in verse 21; while in the same chapter, verses 25,
33, and 35, the meaning of *gē* is evidently *the whole earth*. Always when
indicating Palestine, the word *gē* is modified,—as, "land of Judah," "land of
Israel," Matthew 2:6, 20; "land of Canaan," Acts 13:19. So also we see
"land of Sodom," "land of Egypt" (Acts 13:17).

ting that here in chapter one, after the announcement of our Lord's coming, and of the general contents of The Revelation (in view of the character each Person of the Trinity takes), there should be a *solemn seal upon all by God as GOD.* It is fitting also that this seal should cover the revelation made of Himself to men in connection with earth in all the former Scriptures.*

Alpha and Omega, the first and last letters of the Greek alphabet, call attention instantly away from every *creature-claim*—God is *all!* The expression "From *aleph* to *tau*" (first and last letters of the Hebrew alphabet), was used by the Hebrew rabbis to signify *completely, entirely.* Men dream of "evolution"—that is, a beginning *without God.* It is Satan's lie *in toto.* They also dream of "development," that is, "progress" *without God;*—even prating of "eternal advancement," though they "die like gnats." God, the I Am, declares Himself to be the Alpha and the Omega: not a beginning and an end, but the only One: "the everlasting God, Jehovah, the Creator of the ends of the earth . . . I, Jehovah, the first and with the last" . . . "I am the first and I am the last, and besides me there is no God" . . . "from the time that it was, there am I." Take a tonic for spiritual anaemia from the forties of Isaiah!

"The Lord God." Here we have two names of God from the Old Testament. *Adonai* is the title of absolute authority, as "Lord of lords, the great God," in Deuteronomy 10:17; or Micah 4:13, "the Lord of the whole earth"; or, Lord also of heaven's hosts, Isaiah 10:33. God's children know and acknowledge His *lordship.*

Then "God." This is "El" or "Elohim": the mighty One, beginning with Genesis 1:1.

Then we have the *Jehovah* name of self-existence: "who is and who was and who is to come." See Exodus 3:13-15.† But it is not mere self-existence that is seen

---

*We do not find the name *Father* in this great verse, for that name was revealed to and is held by the *Church,* which is not connected with earthly government, but is altogether heavenly in calling, character, and destiny.
†Scofield has an excellent note on the name Jehovah. See his comment on Genesis 2:4, in his "Bible."

here: it is God in absolute present existence,—"who *is*"; but looking back to His former revelations of Himself and His purposes,—"who *was*"; and also able, and ready, and about to, make good all in the future that He has been and spoken in the past,—"who is to come."

It is striking that when the dispensation changes and God, after the trumpet of the seventh angel, takes His "great power," manifestly to *reign,* the twenty-four elders worship God as the One "who art and who wast" (11:17): for at that moment they have entered into eternity, so to speak; they are with God, and God at last begins to rule in public righteousness, which, of course, will be forever. So the words "who is to come" are no longer needed.

"The Almighty." There is nothing more profitable than to meditate upon the names and titles of Deity. Although the name Jehovah seems to have been known and called upon even before the flood (Genesis 4:26), even the patriarchs did not understand its meaning as Jehovah revealed it for Israel. It was by the name Almighty He asked Abram and the patriarchs to walk (Genesis 17:1): "I am God Almighty; walk before me, and be thou perfect." Exactly the same counsel is given by Paul in II Corinthians 6:17—7:1. All power is in God, not in the creature.*

It is necessary for us to become thoroughly acquainted with God's introduction of Himself in this book of The Revelation, for it characterizes Him throughout the book. The little son of a presiding judge might sit in a court room, and when the judge enters, delightedly exclaim, "That's my father!" but he would have no desire to in-

---

*Scofield's note (Genesis 17:1) on the "Almighty God" is as weak and dangerous as his note on "Jehovah" is excellent. To be the "all-sufficient" One *involves,* indeed, almighty power. But such verses as Job 21:20; 37:23; Psalm 68:14; Isaiah 13:6 and Joel 1:15 do not easily reconcile with so limited a definition as "all-sufficient, the nourisher and satisfier of his people." It is significant that Paul, in II Corinthians 6:18, calls "the living God" of Hosea 1:10 "the Lord Almighty" (Greek, *pantōkrator*); and it is also in connection with His tender attitude to them as "a Father," toward His "sons and daughters." It is this word *pantōkrator* that is used eight times in The Revelation. It is too bad that so excellent a commentator as Dr. Scofield should say, "The primary name *El* or *Elohim* sufficiently signifies all-mightiness." It plainly *does not;* or God would not have used the more specific and most awe-inspiring Hebrew name, *El Shaddai,* Almighty, or its Greek equivalent, *pantōkrator*. The other occurrences of "Almighty" in The

terrupt the proceedings! Indeed, he would glory in the pronouncements of his father as *judge;* and in the judge just because he was his father.

So with the saints: they are willing, yea, they rejoice, that judgment should begin even at the house of God, as it indeed does do in the seven churches.

And now we come to the first of the three great visions of Christ in the book of The Revelation: the first is as the risen, glorified Son of God judging during the present age the spiritual state of the assemblies—"churches" —on earth, as His light-bearers. The second is as the Lamb in heaven "as it had been slain" taking the book of government and judgment from the hand of God on the throne. The third is as the King of kings and Lord of lords returning to earth in the Great Day of Wrath to establish the millennial kingdom. May God especially help us, for we are on holy ground here:

> I John, your brother and partaker with you in the tribulation and kingdom and patience which are in Jesus, was in the isle that is called Patmos, for the word of God and the testimony of Jesus. I was in the Spirit on the Lord's day, and I heard behind me a great voice as of a trumpet saying, What thou seest, write in a book and send it to the seven churches: unto Ephesus, and unto Smyrna, and unto Pergamum, and unto Thyatira, and unto Sardis, and unto Philadelphia,

---

Revelation are 4:8; 11:17; 15:3; 16:7, 14; 19:15; 21:22. Present limitless power, the majesty of it, and the worship it deserves, accompany this name throughout Scripture, and especially in The Revelation.

After writing this note, I found to my horror, but I confess not to my surprise, the following: "In order to corroborate the doctrine (of sex in deity) just mentioned, certain Theosophists have invented a new derivation for the Hebrew *Shaddai,* which in our versions is correctly rendered 'Almighty.' They suppose it to be connected with a word *shad,* which signifies a woman's breast. But such a derivation is impossible, and, so far as we are aware, has never been proposed by an unbiased scholar. More than one Christian scholar has taken up this Theosophical derivation of *Shaddai,* and explained the word as meaning first 'full-breasted,' and then 'bountiful.' The irreverent use of one of the grandest titles of the Most High should have checked them." (Pember: THE CHURCH AND THE MYSTERIES. Page 413.) The Babylonian doctrine of "the motherhood of God," source of all abominations, is what is subtly brought in here. The true derivation of *Shaddai* is Hebrew, שׁדי from root שׁדד to be *strong, mighty:* in adjective form used only of *God (Gesenius).* To miss this meaning of *The Almighty* is to endanger the consent of our hearts to *His righteous judgments.*

and unto Laodicea. And I turned to see the voice that spake with me. And having turned I saw seven golden candlesticks; and in the midst of the candlesticks one like unto a son of man, clothed with a garment down to the foot, and girt about at the breasts with a golden girdle. And his head and his hair were white as white wool, white as snow; and his eyes were as a flame of fire; and his feet like unto burnished brass, as if it had been refined in a furnace; and his voice as the voice of many waters. And he had in his right hand seven stars: and out of his mouth proceeded a sharp two-edged sword: and his countenance was as the sun shineth in his strength. And when I saw him, I fell at his feet as one dead. And he laid his right hand upon me, saying, Fear not; I am the first and the last, and the Living one; and I was dead, and behold, I am alive for evermore, and I have the keys of death and of Hades. Write therefore the things which thou sawest, and the things which are, and the things which shall come to pass hereafter; the mystery of the seven stars which thou sawest in my right hand, and the seven golden candlesticks. The seven stars are the angels of the seven churches: and the seven candlesticks are seven churches.

I John. These words are used in 22:8. Compare "I, Daniel," Daniel 8:15, 9:2, 10:2. As Daniel was known throughout the Babylonian and Persian empires, among both Jews and Gentiles, and took this for granted, so John, the last of the apostles and well-known of all Christians, takes for granted the intimate knowledge of himself and affection for himself that history and tradition assert, especially in the very region to which the Church epistles were addressed.*

---

*"The time of John's death lies within the region of conjecture rather than of history; and the dates that have been assigned for it range from A.D. 89 to A.D. 120." McClintock and Strong, quoting Lampe.

Your brother and partaker with you in the tribulation and kingdom and patience which are in Jesus. Again we remark that John writes The Revelation not as an apostle exercising authority, but as a Seer, unfolding that unveiling of the future which Christ gave him. How humble and loving is his attitude. There is absolutely no "ecclesiastical dignity" here! Note the order: trouble and trial—tribulation—first; then the kingdom assured to us, and then the patient waiting for that kingdom's manifestation. Compare Acts 14:22: "through many tribulations we must enter into the kingdom of God;" II Thessalonians 1:4, 5: "your persecutions and in the afflictions which ye endure . . . to the end that ye may be counted worthy of the kingdom of God, for which ye also suffer." (Note here it is not The Great Tribulation, but the ordinary trials of Christians.) We are in *Christ* as to our risen life, standing and fellowship; but that life becomes the life "of *Jesus*" when manifested in our body; and is hated of the world; so that we are "delivered unto death for Jesus' sake, that the life also of Jesus may be manifested in our mortal flesh" (II Corinthians 4:10, 11).*

Was in the isle that is called Patmos. Where The Revelation was written, we cannot say. Irenaeus says in Ephesus, but the visions were received on a small, rocky, barren island in the Aegean Sea, fifty or more miles from Ephesus, probably in the reign of the Emperor Domitian, A.D. 81-96, who had banished John thither.

For the word of God and the testimony of Jesus. The "word of God" is the larger term setting forth that insisting upon God's claims on men and warnings to them to which all the prophets bear witness. The testimony of Jesus is the gospel, John's peculiar message being that "Jesus is the Christ, the Son of the living God"—dying, rising, interceding and about to return as Lord over all.

---

*If we "learn Christ" and hear Him, as those that are taught in Him, it will be "as truth is in Jesus," separating us utterly from the "manner of life" of this world, and therefore incurring their hatred. See Ephesians 4:20-23. The common loose quotation, "the truth as it is in Jesus," wholly misses the truth!

"Art thou a king, then?" asked Pilate of Christ. For saying "yes" our Lord was crucified. For witnessing the same, His apostles and martyrs suffered. It is striking that John mentions the kingdom ("tribulation, *kingdom* and patience") in verse nine. The early Church for 300 years looked for the imminent return of our Lord to reign, and they were right!

I became in the Spirit on the Lord's day. Now, first, as to the "Lord's day." It was the first day of the week, in which, although banished, John had spiritual fellowship with the believers who gathered on that day to remember the Lord (Acts 20:7, I Corinthians 16:2, John 20:19-26). The words do not mean "the day of the Lord," in the sense of His advent and 1000 years' reign, as some teach. First, the adjective form is the same as in the words "the Lord's supper" in I Corinthians 11:20; and, second, it is too early in the book to refer to "the great and terrible day of the Lord"; and third, the church age is directly addressed in the letters to the seven churches in 1:19: "the things which are."*

"I became in the Spirit." The reading "was in the Spirit," as if denoting simply a devotional state or even a conscious "communion of the Holy Ghost," is impossible here, as also in 4:2.†

And I heard behind me a great voice, as of a trumpet. Compare 4:1, where the same voice speaks again after the same manner. "It is important to apprehend that the general object of this book is the revelation of the relations of God, as *ruler,* with the world, viewed as intro-

---

*Alford's trenchant note (Gr. Test., in loc.) should dispose of all objections. Whatever originates in Germany (Wetstein) with "modern interpretation" and is spread in other lands needs to be thrice inspected!

†"Not merely 'I was,' but *I became* in the Spirit, that is, in a state of spiritual ecstasy or trance, becoming thereby receptive of the vision or revelation to follow." (Alford)

" 'I was,' Greek, *I came to be, I became,* in the Spirit,—in a state of ecstasy; the outer world being shut out, and the inner and higher life and spirit being taken full possession of by God's Spirit, so that an immediate communication with the invisible world is established." (Fausset)

" 'I became in the Spirit on the Lord's day': 'in the Spirit' is a state into which he *entered.*" (Darby)

See also Winer. Dean Alford protests further: "They must be bold indeed who can render it, 'I was transported by the Spirit *into the day of the Lord's coming,*' in the face of the absence of a single precedent in the universal usage of the early Church!"

ducing into it Jesus as *heir*. It will be seen how much of difficulty this removes" (Darby). It is the same blessed *person* who said, "Come unto me," and who took young children in His arms; upon whose loving bosom John himself leaned his head at the supper; but the *circumstances* are absolutely different. *The trumpet* accompanied divine manifestations and commands—Exodus 19:13, 16, 19. It emphasized *authority*, whether for solemnity, alarm, or gladness—Numbers 10:1-10; Leviticus 25:9; Zechariah 9:14; Matthew 24:31; I Corinthians 15:52; I Thessalonians 4:16. We *must* recognize the *lordship of Christ*. Note that it is Christ's voice in Revelation 1:10, "*as* of a trumpet."

Saying, What thou seest, write in a book and send it to the seven churches: unto Ephesus, and unto Smyrna, and unto Pergamum, and unto Thyatira, and unto Sardis, and unto Philadelphia, and unto Laodicea. Note that the book is to be sent to *each church individually*. There was then no "synod," "convention," "conference," or "diocese" of Asia! What follows, then, belongs to this church age, represented by these assemblies. The churches addressed were then existent. We have not therefore come to the part of the book which deals either with Israel or the earth or the Day of the Lord. Our Lord indeed will be speaking to these churches with trumpet authority; yet it will be "what the *Spirit* saith to the churches," and it will be "as many as I love, I reprove and chasten."

And I turned to see the voice that spake with me. The Lord spake behind His servant. John was evidently wrapped in thoughts of communion, of that "fellowship . . . with the Father, and with his Son Jesus Christ" which he constantly had, and desired all saints to share (I John 1:3, 4). But the Lord has other plans for His servant on *this* Lord's day! Note that it is the *voice* he turns to see. Our Lord is ever the *Word* of God.

I saw seven golden candlesticks (literally, *lampstands*). John is about to learn how the Lord judged of that which bore His name on the earth. There are seven—not seven in one, as with Israel (Exodus 25:31-40). Each church is *independently* responsible to the Lord although all are governed by Him and addressed by the one Spirit. "The candlestick is not light, but the bearer of light. The light is the Lord's, not the Church's; from Him she receives it." Moreover, the candlesticks are of gold, which in scripture types stands for the glory of God, which the churches were set to maintain.*

In this wondrous vision of the glorified Lord in the midst of the candlesticks, the churches, mark how all the description sets forth His *Judgeship,* which is His character until the New Creation comes, in chapter 21.

And in the midst of the candlesticks one like unto a son of man. How infinitely precious to the heart is His appearance as connected with *us,* although glorified with the glory which He had "with the Father before the world was!" Yet *Paul* never calls Christ "son of man": He takes that name only when He claims what is due Him on *earth.*

Clothed with a garment down to the foot. This is the robe of the priest and of the judge. Also, it is the aspect of the priest, not in priestly services, but in *judging* character. It was the high priest's business to see that the candlestick was "kept in order" in the old sanctuary through the night,—"from evening to morning" Leviticus 24:3, 4.

These candlesticks (Revelation 1:12), all bear light, for they are the churches or assemblies of saints still recognized by the Lord, and consequently still having the right to the oil of the Holy Spirit, and to Christ as light. Nevertheless, our Lord's attitude is in the dignity of priestly judgment rather than as Intercessor, or even

---

*"The candlestick of the Jewish sanctuary was the one only—its six branches set into the central stem,—and it spoke of Christ, not of the Church. The seven candlesticks (of The Revelation) are for lights, not in the sanctuary (where Christ alone is that), but in the world. And while there is a certain unity, as representing, doubtless, the whole Church, yet it is the Church seen, not in its dependent communion with Christ, but historically and externally, as 'churches.' Each lampstand is set upon its own base, stands in its own responsibility." (Grant)

using the "snuffers," with which the high priest kept bright
the lamps of the Jewish candlestick. Here in The Revelation He is judging each church's *use* of its light,—that
is, dealing with the churches according to *their responsibility to burn brightly,* rather than seeing to it from His
side that they do thus burn.

Girt about at the breasts with a golden girdle. The
correct rendering of Isaiah 11:5, is, "And righteousness
shall be the girdle of his waist, and faithfulness the girdle
of his *loins.*" Our Lord in The Revelation scene is girt
about at the *breasts* with a golden girdle. The girdle
at the loins means service. When Christ returns to reign,
as in Isaiah 11, it will be both in majesty and in service:
therefore the *double* girdle. But in The Revelation He is
not serving, but stands as a priestly judge: therefore the
girdle at the waist only; and it is of gold, setting forth
His divine glory. *Contrast.* John 13:4, 5. Jesus "girded
. . . to wash the disciples' feet." This is the same Lord,
for He keeps cleansing us yet, but in an entirely different office than portrayed in The Revelation.

**And his head and his hair were white as white
wool, . . . white as snow.** Here is the Ancient of Days
of Daniel 7:9, 10, 13, 22. Notice Daniel says that the
Ancient of Days sat on the throne, and also that the
Ancient of Days *came.* As we find in Revelation 5:6, 7,
"in the midst of the throne . . . a Lamb standing, as
though it had been slain, . . . he came," and took the
book, etc. All must honor the Son even as they honor
the Father.

White,—the color of deathlessness and of eternity as
well as of holiness. John seems to have been given to
see His head and hair and eyes at first with some with-
holding of the forthshining of His brightness, in order
that he might distinguish them.

His eyes were as a flame of fire. Not yet *a* flame
of fire, as in 19:12, in the great and terrible day, for it
is yet the dispensation of grace; but they are none the
less searching.

His feet like unto glowing brass,* as if they had been made fiery in a furnace (literal translation). The only metal I ever looked upon which absolutely dazzled my sight was a piece of fine brass. Brass is a composite metal, produced through fire.

His voice as the voice of many waters. Here is resistlessness, the effect of the multitude of the attributes of deity! It is not the trumpet sound, calling to attention, so much as the infinitude of the *voice*. Read Psalm 29.

He had in his right hand seven stars. In the midst of the overwhelming glory of Christ's presence the seven stars are thrust upon John's attention. "In his right hand"—the place of power and authority, as well as possession.

Out of his mouth proceeded a sharp two-edged sword. This is His *word,* the word of God at Christ's mouth: living, active (Hebrews 4:12). It is peculiarly through this word, spoken by the Spirit, that He will judge and administer among the churches.

His countenance was as the sun shineth in his strength. Now the Seer is given to look fully upon the face of the glory of Christ, and we read, "when I saw him, I fell at his feet as one dead." So also Isaiah (Isaiah 6); Moses and Aaron, often; Joshua (Joshua 5); Job (Job 42), and all to whom it was given to view God's glory. Let all who deny the Deity of Christ behold His beloved disciple at His feet "as one dead,"—at one sight of Him glorified. It is also to be noted that having seen Christ thus, John is no more afraid,—not even of the throne in heaven!

And he laid his right hand upon me, saying, Fear not;—the same grace yesterday, today and forever! He is the One who evermore speaks to His own, "It is I; be not afraid."

---

*The Greek word here rendered "glowing brass" is the despair of scholars—*chalcolibanus.* Alford simply transliterates it, as some others also do. *Gold* would stand for the glory of God, silver for redemption. "His feet like unto glowing brass" indicates wrath-judgment upon sin by the holiness of God, by which route—Calvary—our Lord overcame. He stands here among the churches on earth. He is gracious, but He must judge according to the glory which He died to secure for God.

Now follows a three-fold utterance that should banish all our fears forever:

(a) **I am the first and the last, and the Living one.** These are the words of *God!* Or the Jews were right, "He blasphemeth" (John 10:33-38; 8:58, 59). Again in Revelation 22:13:—He is the Eternal One, the Self-Existent One. He is *God,* though He is *man.*

(b) **And I became dead, and behold, I am alive unto the ages of the ages** (literal translation). Peter writes, "the God and Father of our Lord Jesus Christ . . . begat us again unto a living hope by the resurrection of Jesus Christ from the dead." For forty days after His resurrection He had been with the disciples, not yet glorified, even eating and drinking with them, again and again (Acts 10:40, 41). To know by His own word from out that glory in which He now stood that the One whom John had seen dead and pierced was alive forevermore, —*"this same Jesus,"*—would be comfort unutterable to His apostle's heart! He speaks first as the deity. Secondly of His death as a divinely ordained event,—"I *became* dead"; and thirdly of His humanity for all eternity! "Alive" is used in the New Testament only of those in the body. It is supremely important that we hear our Lord announcing His being *alive* in His risen *body,* "unto the ages of the ages," whether as "the Lamb" in heaven, "the King" coming in the Day of Wrath, "Christ" reigning with His saints, Him who sits on the Great White Throne (John 5:22, 27), or the Lamb "on the throne of God and of the Lamb" forevermore!

(c) **And I have the keys of death and of Hades.** Death held the bodies and Hades the spirits of men in Old Testament times. Since Christ's resurrection death briefly holds the bodies, though Hades* does not hold the spirits, of God's saints.

Hades is literally, " the unseen": yet it is a *place,* with gates. It is in the *heart* of the earth. Matthew 12:40. It is the Hebrew *sheol;* as we see by comparing Psalm 16:10 with Acts 2:27. Men went down into it—Genesis 37:35, R. V. Spirits, not bodies, went there,—except in "the new thing" that God did in the judgment of Korah, Numbers 16:30-33, R. V. There was "a great gulf" there, fixed by God, separating His own from "the pit wherein was no water": for Christ had *covenanted* to shed His blood for *His* "prisoners,"—

Christ's words should banish fear. One who has the keys of all is speaking, commissioning "his servant John" with His tender hand still laid upon him, but in the character of the eternally Living One now alive unto all the ages, and having the keys!

Our Lord has a character, an office, to maintain, of which many Christians think lightly, or not at all. He is the One ordained of God to be the Judge of the quick and dead; for God "will judge the world in righteousness by the man whom he hath ordained; whereof he hath given assurance unto all men, in that he hath raised him from the dead" (Acts 17:31). It will not do to forget this, or we will lose that fear of God which is "the beginning of wisdom." We have been commanded to "have grace, whereby we may offer service well-pleasing to God with reverence and awe: for our God is a consuming fire" (Hebrews 12:28, 29). We are indeed in a dispensation of grace, God "not reckoning trespasses," and gladly accepting all who believe. But God has seen fit to give this revelation, this apocalypse, to Jesus Christ, that He might show it unto His servants, and if you or I neglect or slight this one great prophetic book of the New Testament, who can say where we will end? Unitarianism, Universalism, and no-hellism are rolling like tidal waves over the land. "Blessed is he that readeth" The Revelation, and keeps its every word inviolate!

Write therefore. You see it is in view of this vision of the glorified Christ, the Son of God, of Revelation 1, and of those declarations concerning Himself which we have just been considering, that John is to write: "Write therefore." Judgment, like salvation, is connected

which made them "prisoners of *hope*"; and God promised Christ He would "render double" unto them,—not only delivering them from the *pit*,—as was Lazarus, in Abraham's bosom as a child of faith delivered,—but also bringing them up from the "stronghold," in which they waited. See Zechariah 9:9, 11, 12. When Christ ascended, after the three days there in "the lower parts of the earth," He led up His "captives,"—the Old Testament saints,—in His ascension (see Ephesians 4:8-10) so that they are now "spirits of just men made perfect," in their proper place in heaven, awaiting the Lord's second coming and the resurrection. It is blessed, and sad, to reflect upon the *countless hosts* waiting with *eagerness* our Lord's coming: and the prattling ones who "do not believe in it,"—and the frightful terror awaiting them!

Note that our Lord's words in Matthew 16:18 refer to the *gates* of a literal *region*,—in this earth's center: into which gates the saints of the *Church* were never even to enter.

solely with the person of Christ. I beseech you, study The Revelation with this before you: God is *bringing* again the firstborn into the earth, and that as *the Heir* (Hebrews 1:2, 6). It will be vain to become occupied with "sevens," "hundred-forty-four-thousands," "six-sixty-sixes," the restoration of the Roman Empire, the person of the Antichrist, the two wild beasts, the "millennium," or even the new Jerusalem; unless, along with God the Father, who has subjected all things unto *Him, Christ* is ever before our eyes! No doubt, having put down all enemies, "then shall the Son also himself be subjected to him that did subject all things unto him" (I Corinthians 15). That does not mean that *the throne of God and of the Lamb* will cease, for *it* will be forever and ever and ever!

We now have our Lord's own outline of the book of The Revelation. Let no one misunderstand it (for it is very simple and plain); nor dare dispute it; nor think to substitute for it his own vain thoughts!

The Lord's outline: 1. The things which thou sawest—that is, the vision which we have just beheld of Christ Himself. **2. The things which are** (are on). 3. **The things which shall come to pass after these things** (literal translation). This last has but one possible meaning,—those things which succeed in time the things that are now on, or the Church things.

We shall have occasion to recur from time to time to this divine division of the contents of this book.*

The mystery of the seven stars which thou sawest in my right hand, and the seven golden candlesticks. A mystery (Greek, *musterion*) denotes not what is beyond our understanding, but simply what must be *revealed* to be understood: it signifies a hitherto hidden truth, veiled perhaps, under a symbol, but now revealed. "The correlative of mystery is revelation."

The seven stars are the angels of the seven churches: and the seven candlesticks are seven churches. We

---

*We shall remark again and again that the word "hereafter" is no real translation at all of the Greek phrase *meta tauta* which closes verse 19 and opens and closes 4:1. The phrase means, "after these things."

have seen that these seven churches were chosen by the Lord to represent assemblies of the whole church age. Seven is completeness: they represent all the assemblies and they are fully in Christ's control. Not only is He "head over all things to the church, which is his body," the real Church, but also all local assemblies, and whether faithful or not, they lie in His direct and exclusive ownership and dominion.

There has been much discussion of the meaning of the *angels* of the churches. "Angel" (Greek, *aggelos*) signifies "a messenger"; "apostle" (Greek, *apostolos*), "one sent forth." Paul (II Corinthians 8:23) calls Titus and those travelling with him "the apostles of the churches, the glory of Christ," (literal translation).

In the sense of our Lord's words, "their angels do always behold the face of my Father" (Matthew 18:11), the meaning is evident. Their *representatives* (in this instance, actual heavenly beings) are called "angels."

Stars in Scripture stand for those having authority and leadership; also for teachers, both faithful (Daniel 12:3), and false (Jude 13). Inasmuch as the name "angel" is our Lord's interpretation of the symbol star, the name "angel" cannot be itself *another* emblem. It must be the actual name applied by the Lord to certain persons definitely responsible for the state of the churches addressed. Now the Greek word *aggelos,* translated "angel," is used of *men,* in Luke 7:24—"the messengers *(aggeloi)* of John." In 7:19 we read of these same men, "John calling unto him two of his disciples sent them to the Lord . . . and . . . they said, John the Baptist hath sent us unto thee, saying," etc. That is, they were the representatives of John, just as in the same chapter (verse 27) the same word *(aggelos)* is used concerning John himself, in his relationship to Christ: "Behold, I send my messenger before thy face."

Again, in James 2:25, the word *aggelos* is used to describe the spies who came to Rahab: "she received the messengers" *(aggeloi)* etc.; just as we read of "the angels of God" meeting Jacob in Genesis 32:1; and, in the third verse, of Jacob himself sending "messengers" (the same Hebrew word both times—*malahchim*). Indeed, this word is used by Moses in Numbers 20:14, "And Moses sent messengers from Kadesh unto the king of Edom," while in verse 16 of the same chapter we read, "He heard our voice, and sent an angel," the Hebrew word being the same. Again, in Judges 6 the angel of the Lord is mentioned seven times, and the angels, or messengers, Gideon sends, twice—the same word. Sennacherib's representatives are called "messengers" in Isaiah 37:9, 14; and in the same chapter, verse 36, we read of the "angel of the Lord"—the same word.

Now we know from Daniel 12 that Michael the archangel stands for the nation of Israel. There is no hint, however, that angelic beings bear any such relationship to or responsibility for, the assemblies of God in this dispensation. Indeed, the very contrary is implied in Colossians 2:19. Christ is the only Head of the Church, and the Holy Spirit the only Administrator of her affairs on earth. But men are held *responsible*. Paul (Acts 20:28) said to the Ephesian elders (and Christ begins with the Ephesus assembly in The Revelation): "Take heed unto yourselves, and to all the flock, in which the Holy Spirit hath made you bishops"—(*episkopoi,* that is, *over-watchers*). Peter also: "The elders . . . I exhort . . . tend the flock of God which is among you, exercising *the overwatching* willingly . . . neither as lording it over God's heritage, but making yourselves examples to the flock" (literal translation).

We read in II Corinthians 8:19 and 23, of those sent forth with Titus, that they were the messengers (Greek, *apostoloi,* apostles) of the churches; they were "the glory of Christ," while in II Corinthians 11:13-15, concerning Satan and his ministers, that they fashion themselves *into apostles* of Christ: "for even Satan fashioneth himself into an angel of light."

Therefore the angels of these churches (Revelation 2 and 3), are those appointed by the Lord, and this appointment brought about by the Holy Spirit, to represent and be held responsible by Christ for the condition of each assembly. Such "angels" may or may not be recognized or appointed by men: they are often despised by men. But they deal with the Lord directly concerning the assembly which each represents. They are capable of receiving personal, spiritual communications from Christ concerning the assembly, and are responsible to Him alone to carry out His directions.

We shall see in these seven epistles that the invasion of overlording ecclesiasticism made no difference in the relationship of the "angel" of any church to Christ. He was still able to address the church through the angel, despite Balaamites and even the woman Jezebel, and all obstacles.

As Hengstenberg says, "They were called 'angels of the churches' because they were sent of God to the churches to be guarding them." He compares Matthew 18:10, concerning the "little ones": "in heaven their angels do always behold the face of my Father who is in heaven." Thus, so long as it has its lampstand at all, the "angel," or spiritual representative of an assembly, is a "star" in the Lord's hand.*

Now, in this dispensation, the Church is God's house.† I Timothy 3:14.

Now there are in general three forms of iniquity judged in The Revelation.

First, there are the common sins of "mankind" which take the forms of idolatry, lust and violence. They are distinctly seen in Revelation 9:20, 21 (compare the two great commandments of the law given to Israel, Mark 12:33).

Second, there is the awful atheistic blasphemy of the wild beast of Revelation 13, sustained by Satanic power.

---

*Note that the lampstand (Greek: *luchnia*) which represents the churches, is an entirely different word from the "torches," or "lamps," of chapter 4:5, which is in Greek, *lampas*. The former are to hold a light, but the Spirit *is* light. Furthermore the lampstands of the churches were to lighten the darkness of this world; but the *throne of God* needs no illumination. The seven "torches of fire" in 4:5 are for searching, judging power, "sent forth into all the earth."

†The *Church* here is the assembly of God, the people, not the building! The Most High in this dispensation "dwelleth not in temples made with hands." (Acts 7:48.) No building or location in Christendom is *in itself* holy above any other.

But, third, there is that which makes possible the first, and provokes into being the second—that is, the corrupt ecclesiasticism or clerisy of an apostate church. This, of course, precedes the other two.

Man awaits the permission of religion to indulge himself in the sin he loves. There is too little consideration given this awful fact. Even in professedly Christian institutions of "learning," a course in "comparative religions" is calmly prescribed! Now God declares that "the things the Gentiles sacrifice, they sacrifice to demons and not to God"; and also that Satan is "the god of this age," and "the prince of this world"; and that we true believers "are *of God,* and the whole world lieth in the evil one" (I John 5:19).

That the devil hates the Church of God with a deadly enmity goes without saying, for the saints confess and serve the Lord Jesus Christ under whose feet the God of peace will shortly bruise Satan.

Real believers, moreover, have been raised up with Christ and made to sit in the heavenlies with Him, being united to the lowly One who now is "far above all power and dominion"; and whom Satan so fears that he will *flee,* if resisted in faith by saints subject to God. It is that bringing on the scene of the direct power of the Lord Jesus through the Holy Ghost (the Christian's proper warfare, Ephesians 6:10-14), which the enemy so dreads and against which he is so desperately malignant.*

Therefore we will be foolish indeed not to look for the history of Satanic opposition in this account of the churches. And we may expect the professing church to be tempted along the same old lines,—first, of pride and self-assertion; secondly of fleshly indulgence, lust and license; thirdly of that hateful ruse called *idolatry* by which man seeks to hide from himself by "religious" rites his real spiritual state, while he indulges his evil propensities.

Let us study these seven messages in view of the several parts of each.

---

*Satan is named eight times in The Revelation, five times in connection with the *churches*—six times if we include the name *devil* in Revelation 2:10.

CHAPTER II

THE SEVEN LETTERS

Revelation 2, 3

About one-eighth of the book of Revelation is taken up with these seven messages. The true student of God's word learns to give most attention to what God most emphasizes. Therefore we beg the reader not to pass lightly over these seven solemn messages from the Lord Himself concerning our own days, nor to be in undue haste to get over into the distinctly prophetic and more spectacular part of The Revelation, beginning at chapter four.

Some one truly says, "There is always a tendency in the human heart to become occupied with the dispensation in which we are *not.*"

The things that are, the messages to the churches, search us out in a most peculiar way. "Most interpreters pass over this portion of the book slightly." (Alford)

"In his latter days, Bengel strongly recommended to those about him careful meditation in these messages to the churches. He said, 'Scarcely anything is so fitted to affect and purify us.'" (Hengstenberg)

I EPHESUS

First Love Left

THE ADDRESS: **These things saith he that holdeth the seven stars in his right hand, he that walketh in the midst of the seven golden candlesticks.**

This address is *general,* including all churches: for it was at Ephesus that believers were by Paul entirely separated from connection with Judaism (Acts 19:8, 10).

Moreover, Christ is seen judicially walking about (Greek, *peripateo*) among them.

Ephesus had a great beginning! (Read Acts 19.) Paul, and Timothy, and all truth (Acts 20:20; I Timothy 1:3).

But now the Lord must declare to her her present state in *His* eyes.

CONDITION KNOWN: **I know thy works.** This word, "I know" is repeated seven times, once to each church. It is inexpressibly solemn, and we cannot avoid the truth that the Lord is directly cognizant of every detail about *every* assembly of His on earth.

COMMENDATION: Now, there was much to commend in Ephesus. It would be a flawless church in the eyes of many! **Thy toil and patience.** They were a working church, and they went steadily on. *Patience* is mentioned twice: in connection, first, with service; and second, with suffering. **Thou canst not bear evil men.** There was holiness there—a precious character! To permit men known to be bad to be in *fellowship* or even in *office,* is common today, but is treachery to Christ—whom the Church represents. Further, it is deadly wrong instead of kindness, to the unsaved and evil, to have them in "fellowship." Some day they will curse you for such unfaithfulness!

Didst try them that call themselves apostles, and they are not, and didst find them false. "Ministerial courtesy" had no place at Ephesus! Plain scripture tests are given. The saints have "an anointing from the Holy One." They may know, if they will, false teachers, those who are "abiding not in the teaching of Christ." We are not to receive them into our house, and we are to give them no greeting (II John 10); much less are we to suffer them to preach and teach in our assemblies. Ephesus had both the discernment and the spiritual energy to reject those whom she "found false."

Thou hast patience and didst bear for My name's sake, and hast not grown weary. To suffer steadily is harder than to serve sturdily. Not growing weary was certainly a mark of vigorous life.

CONDEMNATION: **But I have against thee, that thou didst leave thy first love.** Note, the word is *"leave,"* not *"lose."* To love lies in the power of the will, otherwise it would not be commanded. Now the love of Christ and the Church is that of bridegroom and bride. You cannot judge by what you see in the lukewarm churches today of *the intense devotion to Christ's Person* into which such assemblies as Ephesus were brought by the Holy Ghost. You may see it in the martyr days, sometimes today on the mission field, and in supremely devoted souls like Samuel Rutherford, Fletcher of Madeley, Madame Guyon, Brainerd, Payson, McCheyne, and Cookman. We regard such cases of devotion as unusual; no, we should say they are *normal.* Christ has immeasurable love, and that continually, for every redeemed one; and *love yearns for love.*

Consider newly-married people. Their life is one continuous story of affection—delight in one another. Service is not service, but gladness, for such a bride. Two New England girls worked in a textile factory. Mary went away on a visit of several months. Returning, and meeting her friend on the street, she asked her,

"Maggie, are you working at the same old factory?" "I'm not working at all," burst out Maggie: "I'm *married!*"

Doubtless such a one was busier with her housework than ever she had been at the factory! But she toiled unconscious of the work as such—it was for *him.* She parted from him with an embrace as he went to work in the morning, and she prepared the evening meal ever looking out at door or window for his coming. As he neared home, she went to meet him. All her labor was a mere circumstance, swallowed up in her devotion to her husband.

But days, weeks, months pass, and she becomes occupied with the details of her housekeeping, of her own life. She prepares just as good meals, keeps the house in as good, perhaps even better, order; but she has gradually changed her habit of watching for her husband at night, or going eagerly to meet him. She calls, "Goodbye" from somewhere upstairs in the morning, instead of holding *him* fast every moment she can.

Now this was Ephesus; and this was *the departure from first love: while Christ, the Bridegroom, has love in all its freshness, and will evermore have, for the Church.* It was Ephesus, leaving that devoted pouring out of *response to His love* that grieved His very heart!

This is the beginning of that decline which ends in Laodicea, and Laodicea's awful state: "I have need of nothing," yet loathsome, in poverty, wretchedness, misery, blindness, nakedness! Men that question the very virgin birth, and the deity of Christ, and His physical resurrection, are suffered today! The "Christian religion" has taken the place of personal devotion to the Bridegroom.

LOVING COUNSEL: **Remember therefore whence thou art fallen, and repent.**

"Fallen"! With all their earnestness and activity, the leaving of their first intense love made them a *fallen* assembly! "Remember—repent—do first works!" Recalling, even with severe effort and anguish, our moments of greatest devotion to our Lord, the hours when we felt most deeply His tender love, and our own response—to *remember* such times—this is our first task. Thus His love, His goodness, will lead us to *repentance*. Repentance is not mere sorrow (though godly sorrow works repentance—II Corinthians 7:10); but repentance is a changed state of soul. It is "the judgment we have passed, in God's presence, under grace, upon ourselves and all we have done and have been." In this case especially it will be "the goodness of God that leadeth us to repentance." Christ's unvarying, undiminished affection for us, even through our coldness and neglect, will break us up. If not, *nothing* will!

And do the first works. Instantly let us say, this is *not* a call to *"Christian service"* or "renewed activity." Ephesus had toil, patience, intolerance toward evil, patience in suffering,—*everything*. But the "first works" are the goings forth of *affection* to Christ, freely, devotedly, as in our first love. It is the story of the bride of the Song of Solomon (Song of Solomon 5:2-16). Her slowness caused His withdrawal, and it caused her much trouble; but it brought her at last to cry, "My beloved is the chiefest among ten thousand; he is altogether lovely!" "First works" with her, were, *finding* again Him whom her soul loved! Most Christians—yes, real Christians—let Christ go, when He "makes as if He would go further." This, those walking to Emmaus did *not:* "They constrained him, saying, Abide with us." And He went in with them. In Laodicea we shall find Him standing *without*. Astonishing! Outside of the Church when His place is *in their midst!*

PROPHESIED ACTION: **I come to thee, and will move thy candlestick out of its place, except thou repent.** The words "I come to thee," correspond to the judicial, personal visit of the Lord to Sodom ere its destruction (Genesis 18). These words do not signify operations by the Spirit, but an act of Christ, who is head over all things to the Church, and who is judging over each assembly. The fatal visit would not be recognized by the church, but it would definitely occur. After the Judge's visit there would be no more assembly there in Christ's eyes. The Spirit would be withdrawn, and darkness and desolation follow. So it happened at Ephesus, and, alas, to how many thousands of other careless "Christian" assemblies in the centuries since! No longer a lampstand!

This "coming" is not His coming again at the rapture, to receive His own; but His special, necessary, judicial action toward an assembly persisting, after much light, and blessing, in neglect of *Himself*. Alas, the lampstand *removed!* The priceless privilege of setting forth such a Christ before a dying world, gone forever. I have before me a picture of the Ephesus of today—a ruined archway, a Moslem dwelling, and a forbidding castle, 'midst desolate hills. No lampstand for Christ where once Paul labored three years, night and day with tears!

But this thou hast, that thou hatest the works of the Nicolaitans, which I also hate. What Nicolaitanism was, let us consider under Pergamum, the third church. We only stop to note the tender consideration of Christ: He cannot refrain from noting Ephesus' common feeling with Him in the matter of a certain terrible evil. "This thou *hast*": if we have the least jealousy of love for our blessed Lord, He notes it. Let this comfort us.

CALL TO HEAR: He that hath an ear, let him hear what the Spirit saith to the churches. This is most solemn. Evidently not all the Ephesus assembly is meant; but only those who had gotten life by hearing —hearing the voice of the Son of God (John 5:25); for "belief (faith) cometh by hearing, and hearing by the word of Christ" (Romans 10:17).*

Moreover, those who can discern when the Spirit is speaking—being born of the Spirit and led by the Spirit

---

*One of the most solemn studies in the whole Bible is that concerning *the hearing ear*. At the end of the forty years in the wilderness Moses tells Israel that although they had seen all the mighty miracles, Jehovah had not given them, as a nation, eyes to see and ears to hear! (Deuteronomy 29:4.) Neither did they hearken in the land to God's messengers, the prophets; and Isaiah was commanded judicially to "make the heart of this people fat, and make their ears heavy, and shut their eyes; lest they see . . . hear . . . understand . . . turn . . . and be healed" (6:10). Jeremiah cries, "O foolish people, and without understanding; that have eyes, and see not; that have ears, and hear not." The Lord Jesus preached openly at first, (Matthew 4:17, with 13:3): then He turned to *parables*, "because seeing they see not, and hearing they hear not, neither do they understand . . . for this people's heart is waxed gross (literally, 'grown fat', from prosperity), and their ears are dull of hearing (literally, 'hearing heavily,' that is, sluggishly and imperfectly), and their eyes they have closed" (Hebrew, "smeared over"). "This citation (from Isaiah) gives no countenance to the fatalist view of the passage, but rests the whole blame on the hard-heartedness and unreadiness of the hearers, which is of itself the cause why the very preaching of the word is a means of further darkening and condemning them" (Alford).

Jehovah said to Ezekiel (12:2), "Son of man, thou dwellest in the midst of the rebellious house, that have eyes to see, and see not, that have ears to hear, and hear not." There is nothing more awful than to be hearkening to God's words with an unopened or uncircumcised ear! Hearing without response brings the fatal delusion—the ability to *forget*, of James 1:22, 24. "They would not give ear" is God's continual complaint through the prophets.

Our Lord even says to the disciples in the boat (Mark 8:17, 18), "Do ye not yet perceive, neither understand? have ye your heart hardened? Having eyes, see ye not? and having ears, hear ye not? and do ye not remember?" Divine truth enters by the *ear:* and that act of the will which receives it, is called *hearkening*, which sometimes involves *inclining* the ear (from all else).

Now, seven times in the gospels, and eight times in The Revelation—seven times to these churches!—comes this eternally vital, open, yet *private* call to any *opened* ear: "He that hath an ear let him hear."

Know you not that the most of the readers and hearers of the book of the Revelation will not really HEAR, in the sense in which the Lord means—a personal, separating word to "sink down into their ears"?

Seiss remarks, "Fishermen and taxgatherers, by listening to Jesus, presently find themselves in apostolic thrones, and ministering as priests, and rulers of the dispensation, wide as the world and lasting as time."

(all God's real saints being "not in the flesh but in the Spirit," though they do not always walk by the Spirit, sad to say)—know the Spirit's voice in the Scriptures. They are not Sadducees,—"Modernists." To such, even Christ's *servants,* are the messages of The Revelation really addressed. These only have "an ear."*

In emphasizing this, let us note how to Ephesus, Smyrna, and Pergamum, "he that hath an ear" is addressed to the whole assembly; while after Jezebel is admitted as a prophetess (Thyatira), "he that hath an ear" comes still *more* privately, at the *very end of the letter.*

PROMISE TO OVERCOMER: **To him that overcometh, to him will I give to eat of the tree of life, which is in the Paradise of God.** There are those who overcome, and there are those who *are* overcome. These latter are lost (II Peter 2:20). They give up Christ's words (I Corinthians 15:2, Colossians 1:23, Mark 8:38). We note two classes—and only two—in Revelation 21:7, 8. The tree of life (not a symbol, but a reality) is seen in Revelation 22:2. When the first Adam sinned, we were shut out from the Garden (Genesis 3:22-24) lest we should "live forever" in this sinful state. This tree, under divine wisdom, sustained humanity in physical *immortality,* i.e., invulnerability to bodily dissolution. Now, in the last Adam, we already have eternal life as to our *spirits* (John 3:6); but we look forward to *bodily* immortality and incorruptibility; for redemption of the body is part of our salvation in Christ: I Corinthians 1:30.†

II. SMYRNA

The Church in Suffering

ADDRESS: **These things saith the first and the last, who became dead, and lived** (literal translation). How fitting a title! The church at Smyrna was troubled, poor, and blasphemed by false Jews, and some were

---

*I have again and again looked the New Testament through for it, but I can find *no Sadducee saved!* Can you?

†One of the great proofs of the *pagan ignorance of the Word of God* that obtains everywhere in so-called *Christendom,* is the readiness of tens of thou-

to be martyred. But Christ speaks as having endured the same thing and risen triumphant over all, even death itself!

CONDITION KNOWN: **I know thy tribulation, and thy poverty.** How blessed that Christ keeps saying, "I know"; no matter what the troubles and the poverty. He had no place to lay *His* head. **But thou art rich**—spiritual riches: they had the "gold refined by fire" which wretched Laodicea so woefully lacked. Riches in grace come when patience has its "perfect work" in trial (James 1:2, 4).

And the blasphemy of them that say they are Jews, and they are not, but are a synagogue * of Satan. Terrible words! Satan early entrenched himself against Christ and His gospel in Judaism,—"those who pretended to have the legitimate, hereditary claim to be God's people." They were the *not Jews* who were Jews "outwardly" (Romans 2:28, Matthew 3:9). In John 8:44, our Lord said to the Messiah-rejectors of His day, "Ye are of your father the devil." Believers today need to be faithfully warned regarding their attitude to the Jews: (a) not to join at all in that Gentile envy and hate lying at the root of "anti-semitism"; and (b) not to give special place to Jews, even Jewish believers, as such; but (c) to glorify God for the "remnant according to the election of *grace*," among them, now being saved; and (d) to remember that the most of the nation is to be cut off as apostate before the Millennium sets in; (e) to believe that God's words in Romans 3:22, 23, and 10:12 are true *today:* "There is no distinction . . . for all have sinned"; and, "there is *no distinction* between Jew and Greek: for

---

*Contrast "synagogue,"—a *gathering together*, the Jewish thing—with "ecclesia," the *called-out-from*, away-from, which is God's word for the Church: "called out" from *Judaism* and all earthly *religion*, as well as from the world.

---

sands to listen to *Eddyism*, talking of "mortal mind"! The Bible *never* applies the word "mortal" to either spirit or soul, but *to the body only.* See for yourself. The Greek *thneetos*, mortal (liable to death), is used six times,—Romans 6:12; 8:11; I Corinthians 15:53, 54; II Corinthians 4:11; 5:4; and the word for *immortality* (not liable to death,—Greek, *athanasia*), three times,—I Corinthians 15:53, 54, and I Timothy 6:16; and *incorruptibility*—Greek, *aphtharsia* (not possible of *corruption*), eight times,—Romans 2:7; I Corinthians 15: 42, 50, 53, 54; Ephesians 6:24; II Timothy 1:10; and Titus 2:7.

the same Lord is Lord of all . . . that call upon him."
Jewish sinners, Irish sinners, American sinners, Hottentot
sinners, Hindu sinners, English sinners, Scotch sinners:
no difference at all! *Just sinners, all!*

But alas, the early Church speedily became *Judaized.*
There is great appeal in a visible *temple,* gorgeous *ritual,*
an accredited *priesthood* ready to assume *responsibility
for you* in divine things. And when all this was yoked
to such a mighty *past history* as had the Jewish nation;
and,—most potent of all, *the possession of the Old Testament oracles,* which all Christians accepted as inspired
of God,—the influence of these *lying Jews* may easily be
imagined! Especially so (and alas!), because of the
wealth Judaism could, and did display, to make con-
temptible the "little flock" of Christ!

These false Jews are called *liars* twice by the Lord,—
once as to their *claims,* and once as to their *character*
(Romans 2:9 and 3:9). They were liars because they
denied the truth of the absolute *deity* of *Christ;* because
they perpetuated the lie that Christ did not rise, but that
His disciples stole His body away; because, further, they
said that His miracles had been wrought by Satanic
agency; because also they rejected all the mighty works
wrought after Pentecost in *the Name,* Jesus of Nazareth.
The Lord stamps their very claim to *be* Jews as a *lie.*
He only is a Jew who is one *inwardly,* and circumcision
is *inward,* not outward in the flesh (Romans 2:28, 29).
There are not many Jews in God's sight. You have *seen*
very few! Most of the so-called Jews are "chaff and dross,"
and the "liberal" Jew is worst of all. The fact that some
preachers make up so easily with liberal Rabbis labels
both!

Yes, Judaism is more acceptable to the flesh than faith
in an *unseen Lord;* an earthly "religion" is more attrac-
tive to a carnal heart than a *heavenly walk!*

Christ, whom these Jews at Smyrna had rejected, calls
their opposition to His Church, also their *daring* to sub-

stitute their *synagogue* for the *assembly* that owned His Name, one simple, awful word—*blasphemy*. And so it is today!*

LOVING COUNSEL: **Fear not the things which thou art about to suffer.** Count up Christ's "fear nots": they include everything. The world is always in fear—of disease, of disaster, of death. God's saints should not be so. The Captain suffered: so shall the soldiers; but (unlike Mohammed's deluded followers) fullness of joy awaits them.

> "Ye fearful saints, fresh courage take!
> The clouds ye so much dread
> Are big with mercy, and shall break
> In blessing on your head."

Therefore fear not! Remember Hebrews 2:14, 15.

The devil is about to cast some of you into prison, that ye may be tried. But, "the God of peace shall

---

*The ancient account of the martyrdom of Polycarp, Bishop of Smyrna, in A.D. 168, eighty-six years after his conversion, is very definite, that the Jews "joined the heathen in clamoring for his being cast to the lions; and, when there was an obstacle to this, for his being burned alive; and with their own hands they carried logs to the pile: the Jews being most desperately forward, as is their custom, to render this service."

Having lost earthly power under Nebuchadnezzar, the Jews felt nothing was left them but their religious preëminence, which meant their self-righteousness. Now, religious righteousness will do anything, as history fully reveals. For this, "the Jews . . . killed the Lord Jesus and the prophets, and drove out us (the apostles), . . . and are contrary to all men; . . . forbidding us to speak to the Gentiles that they may be saved; to fill up their sins always" (I Thessalonians 2:14-16). The Jews are unchanged—except the "remnant according to the election of grace" (Romans 11:5). If missionaries to the Jews would pursue Paul's method of "provoking them to *jealousy*" by boasting of a Savior they had nationally rejected, instead of offering them the "Messiah" (which God is now not doing!) they would quickly find the same deadly enmity and persecution and violence which Paul suffered. When the opportunity offers, the majority of the Jews will go over openly to Antichrist, as we well know from Daniel 9:27, Isaiah 28:14, 15, and many other plain prophecies. We do well to have "great sorrow" for them as did Paul in Romans 9; to remember that nationally they are "beloved for the fathers' sake"; and to labor to reach them. But it is folly to close our eyes to their blinded, deadly state! The nation that crucified Christ, stoned Stephen, and most bitterly hated and opposed the gospel of grace preached by Paul, *remains unchanged.* The fountain for sin and for uncleanness is not yet open for them nationally, nor will it be until "that day" of Zechariah 12:10 to 13:1, when, beleaguered by all the hostile nations of earth, and in despair, they at last "look upon him whom they pierced," and fall into such mourning as has never been known! They will not believe until they *see.*

Today Laodicean lukewarmness admits Rabbis, Swamis, Unitarians, and "modern" Bible disbelievers—*infidels*—to its "religious platforms." Nevertheless, "synagogue of Satan," our Lord's awful name for the Jews that opposed the gospel (that is, the deity, virgin birth, blood atonement and the physical resurrection of our Lord), still remains.

bruise Satan under your feet shortly" (Romans 16:20). The binder shall be bound (Revelation 20:1-3). Do not stumble because the adversary is still permitted to oppose you. He opposed your Lord, but only brought out your Lord's supreme choice of holiness and His Father's will. "The trial of your faith worketh patience."

Ye shall have a tribulation of ten days. Be thou faithful unto death and I will give thee the crown of life. How good it is to know that "God is faithful, who will not suffer you to be tempted above that ye are able." Every trial is measured by the heart of infinite love in a hand of infinite care!

The early Church did indeed have just ten great persecutions under the Roman emperors, beginning with Nero and ending with Diocletian, whose last persecution, and probably the most terrible of all, *was just ten years long!* Nero, Domitian, Trajan, Marcus Aurelius, Severus, Maximum, Decius, Valerian, Aurelian, and Diocletian, were the ten principal Pagan persecutors. However, there was constant, though not always general, trouble until Constantine's edict of toleration.

"Faithful unto death." This means to the point of *martyrdom:* It does *not* mean "holding out to the end" of our lives, according to the old expression. In that sense, many who have failed have been saved—I Corinthians 11:30, 32. The *crown* of life is "the special prize promised to the faithful." James 1:12 shows this crown of life to be a special mark of approval after a saint's enduring the Lord's prescribed trials through love to *Him.*

CALL TO HEAR: **He that hath an ear.** Not all would hear in the days of terrible trial, so they needed the words of their loving Lord. Like Israel, "they hearkened not unto Moses for anguish of spirit, and for cruel bondage." It is our profound conviction that not only in Russia and Germany but in other countries there are *terrible days of trial directly ahead* for the Church of God. It is *our* proper portion—all the day (of grace) long are we to be *killed,* counted as sheep for *slaughter.* Therefore, remember the exhortation of Peter (who at the first, fled and denied, but later was crucified for his Lord): "Forasmuch then as Christ suffered in the flesh, arm ye yourselves also with the same mind," or "thought," "intent," "resolution" (I Peter 4:1), that is, with the same *"expectation,"* when necessary.

He that overcometh shall not be hurt of the second death. There is a double negative in the Greek— *"not at all* be injured." The saints may have to bow their heads to those who execute the *first* death—who "kill the body"; but over these, we read, "the *second* death hath no authority" (Revelation 20:6). No real believer is coming into *judgment.* See John 5:24, R. V. Believers' *works* will be examined, but not as *sin: that* is gone forever, borne on the cross! Hebrews 9:28: "so Christ . . . shall appear . . . apart from sin."

It is striking to notice that the name *Smyrna* is simply the Ionic Greek for *myrrh,* a fragrant gum in common use. So, "perfumed with myrrh." Note Song of Solomon 3:6 and 1:13 with Matthew 2:11; Psalm 45:8; and, especially myrrh as used at our Lord's burial—John 19:39. The Smyrnan church represents the *martyrs,* and the fragrance of their affection *fills the whole house of God, even today!* Have you read, "Foxe's Book of Martyrs"? The Bible and Foxe's book were all John Bunyan had! I beg you, read the story of the martyrs. *You will need it.*

III. PERGAMUM

Idolatry and Clerisy Arising

ADDRESS: **He that hath the sharp two-edged sword.** The sword is Christ's *word* in its stern, judging character. Therefore in Pergamum let us expect *evil* to be dealt with. In Ephesus, first love was left; in Smyrna came chastening—the fires of Satan's opposition: if perchance there might be recovery; but it proved unavailing. The Pergamum period may well be looked upon

as beginning with Constantine's "embracing Christianity"*
in 313 A.D., when the Church settled down in the world.
The enemy's plan now was to *favor* the faith he had
fought and defile what he could not destroy. The Christian "religion" became that *of the Empire that had slain*
the Lord!

CONDITION KNOWN: **I know where thou
dwellest, even where Satan's throne is.** The Devil is
not yet "in hell," nor even shut up in the abyss (Revelation 20:1-3); but he is the prince of *this world,* the god
of *this age.* He walks up and down in *the earth* (Job
1:7), where he yet has his *capital* and also his *throne,*†
whence he directs the principalities, the powers, the world
rulers of this darkness, the spiritual hosts of wickedness in
the heavenlies. (Compare Ephesians 6:12.) When Israel
was owned of God, when the Jerusalem temple stood,
Satan's great opposing city was Babylon, on the Euphrates.
See notes on Revelation 17 and 18. "Pergamos (properly
called Pergamum), was a sort of a union of a pagan
cathedral city, a university town, and a royal residence,"
says Blakesley. The title, "chief temple-keepers of Asia"
was held by its inhabitants, showing "the supreme importance of Pergamos to heathendom." When the Babylonian cult of the Magians was driven out of Babylon,
they found a haven at Pergamum, and Pergamum's king,
Attalus III (B.C. 133), willed his kingdom and title into
the hands of the Romans (Justin p. 364, Strabo). The
title of the Magian high priest was, "Chief Bridge
Builder," meaning the one who spans the gap between
mortals and *Satan* and his hosts. In Latin, this title was
written, *Pontifex Maximus.*‡ •

---

*That this Roman Emperor was ever truly a *believer* one doubts. Fisher
(History of the Christian Church) says: "He was never fully weaned from
the cultus of Apollo. There were occasions on which he ordered the Pagan
soothsayers to be consulted. That he did not receive baptism until the day
before his death, was not due, however, to a lack of faith (!) but to the current
belief, in which he shared, that the holy laver washed out the guilt of all previous sins." (Faith in a "holy" vessel, and "water" *is not trust in Christ's
blood.)*

†Observe carefully that the true reading is *thronos,* "throne," not "seat."

‡In the bloody conflict for the bishopric of Rome, Damasus, one of the
Babylonian priests or Magians, in 366 A.D., secured the office, and finally
was conceded from the emperor, the title *Pontifex Maximus.* According to
Zosimus, Constantine had assumed the title in 325, as the heathen emperors

COMMENDATION: **And thou holdest fast my name, and didst not deny my faith, even in the days of Antipas my witness, my faithful one, who was killed among you, where Satan dwelleth.** Five of these seven cities "contended for the privilege of worshipping the emperor," and that Pergamum was the most prominent in this; yet the church there as a whole held fast Christ's name as the deity, and His work alone as the object of faith, and that even amid most terrible persecution. Antipas' name was dear to Christ, as is the name of each who suffers for His sake. Let us see in this scene anew the *absolute* present enmity of this world toward Christ!

CONDEMNATION: **I have a few things against thee, because thou hast there some that hold the teaching of Balaam ... idols ... fornication. So hast thou also some that hold the teaching of the Nicolaitans in like manner.*** Over against the faithfulness of the martyrs of Smyrna and Pergamum, stands the beginning of actual *tolerated evil.* "Thou canst not bear evil men" was written of Ephesus, but of no other church. You know the history of Balaam, the mysterious prophet of Numbers 22, 23, 24, who, prevented from cursing God's nation Israel, counselled the king of Moab to entice Israel into Moab's heathen idolatry, with its obscenities and abominations (Numbers 25), bringing death by plague on twenty-four thousand Israelites! Satan, failing to overthrow the church by persecution in Smyrna days, snares the Pergamum church into idolatry and fornication. To "eat things sacrificed to idols," in the sense of Revelation

---

before him had appropriated it, "because it contributed to exalt at once the imperial and the episcopal dignity, and served to justify the interference of the emperor in ecclesiastical counsels and in the nomination of bishops." Gratian was the last emperor to whom the title was applied. The medals of Constantine and his successors, down to Gratian, and the inscriptions relating to them, gave them the title of Pontifex Maximus. Thus was Babylonianism, begun by Nimrod, perpetuated in that which had the name of the Church!

*A good deal turns on the position of the last word *homoiōs* in the original. It seems to me that the peculiar emphasis in the first part of the sentence on Pergamum's *having,* that is, *permitting,* these Nicolaitans, might be strong enough to attach this last adverb to the *fact* that she suffered them, rather than to *what* they taught. Otherwise, we must conclude that the Balaamites and the Nicolaitans taught and practiced the same things: viz. idolatry and license. Whereas, it *seems* probable that the *name* Nicolaitans, as we say elsewhere, holds its own interpretation:—laity-bossing *clerisy.*

2:14, is to engage in idolatrous worship, feasting in the idol's temple. Outside, "in the shambles," saints could buy whatever they pleased, even though it had been previously offered to idols (I Corinthians 10:25). In Pergamum, however, they sought to "drink the cup of the Lord and the cup of demons," and thus "provoke the Lord to jealousy" (verses 21, 22). "Idolatry" is here to be taken literally, as is "fornication." It is astounding how early was the invasion of idolatry into the Church, and the *defense* of it, even by some so-called "church fathers"!

Idolatry was always accompanied with utter fleshly license and often nameless abominations, just as with Israel at Sinai and in Canaan,—just as is religious idolatry today, both Romish and that of heathen countries.

Those who would make the idolatry and fornication of this "teaching of Balaam" mere worldliness, should be more careful in their study of church history, and more observant of what idolatry has brought to every nation (see notes on chapter 13).

II Peter 2:10-15, 18, 19, and Jude 4-11, show how literal is to be our interpretation of our Lord's words to Pergamum concerning the teaching of Balaam! All through the Church centuries, we find such as the Mormons of today, or the "House of David" associating with Christ's Name the very abominations He denounces.

Now, as to the Nicolaitans, their *works* Ephesus had, but hated; Pergamum had not their works only, but also their *teaching*. Moral energy is waning. "Ye that love Jehovah, *hate* evil." Literally, in Revelation 2:15, it reads, "Thus you are having—*you!*" The emphatic expression indicates the astonished, indignant, grief of the Lord.

Again, regarding the Nicolaitans: who were they?

1. The old writers tried to connect them with Nicolas of Antioch,—but unsuccessfully.

2. There is really no known record, except in The Revelation, of any sect by this name in the early Church.

3. It is not the manner of Scripture to compel its readers to obtain wisdom for its interpretation from outside history. Therefore, if we do not find a direct Bible

allusion, as in the case of Balaam, we may look for the meaning in the structure of the word, as, for instance, in the name Melchizedek, "king of righteousness," from the meaning of his name; and "king of peace," from the city (Salem) he rules.

4. We would in this way find "Nicolaitan" derived from *nikao,* to conquer; and *laos,* people; and the meaning, *rulers of the laity,* indicating that dire clerisy which very early sprang up. A priestly caste was formed, corresponding to the priests and Levites in Judaism.

5. That no notice should be taken by the Lord of this particular evil, which, beginning in Ephesus, ripens so fully in Thyatira, the next church, would be almost inconceivable. It is not the Lord's manner to denounce evil fruits without having remarked upon the tree.

6. Inasmuch, also, as the Lord selected these seven churches to represent all the assemblies of the church dispensation, He would scarcely choose an assembly in which two "teachings" of practically the *same* moral corruption, existed.

LOVING COUNSEL: **Repent therefore.** This call is directed to the whole assembly, as if recovery were yet possible for the whole. The deeper the evil, however, the more difficult the self-judgment!

PREDICTED ACTION: **Or else I come to thee quickly, and I will make war against them with the sword of my mouth.** This "coming," like that of verse 5, is not our Lord's second advent, but His entering *personally* and that *quickly,* upon their affairs *judicially:* affairs which otherwise would continue unchanged under the ever-present, although grieved and vexed, Spirit. "War . . . with the sword of my mouth," brings to mind at once the angel of the Lord standing with his sword drawn against the mad prophet, Balaam, in Israel's days! The targets of Christ's sword would be chiefly those practicing these evils,—"against *them.*" The exact way in which Christ would use the sword of His Word against these corrupters, He does not explain. However, we know Christ's words to the Jews, "if I had not come and

spoken unto them . . . but now they have no excuse for
their sin." And we know that Paul and his company
were "a sweet savor of Christ unto God, . . . in them
that perish . . . a savor from the death unto death"
(II Corinthians 2:15, 16), as well as the opposite to those
being saved. Doubtless faithful preachers minister death
to as many as they save—*perhaps many more.*

CALL TO HEAR: The Spirit is still speaking, and
"to the churches," that is, to all of them throughout
this church age: **let him hear!**

PROMISE TO OVERCOMERS: **The hidden
manna.** "Hidden" is a reference, perhaps, to the wilderness manna preserved for a memorial in the ark of
the covenant (Exodus 16:32, 34; Hebrews 9:4). There
was an especial reason for the Lord's setting before the
mind of these Pergamean believers that secret and blessed
relationship into which the heavenly saints are brought
by the Spirit while on earth, and, more wondrously, at
Christ's coming; because of the *hidden things* taught
and gloried in by the Babylonian system of idolatry, and
the "mysteries"* taught its initiates, there at Pergamum,
"where Satan's throne was."

**A white stone and upon the stone a new name writ-
ten, which no one knoweth but he that receiveth it,**
was promised. Christ is infinite in His excellences; and
each member of His Body sets forth what no other member could. Also there is a *personal* character in all trials,
through which the overcomer (that is, the true believer),
will be brought to know the Lord in a peculiar way
shared by no other. Dean Alford beautifully comments:

"These very terms (*a new name written*) seem to
require that it should be the recipient's *own name,*—a
new name, however; a revelation of his everlasting title,
as a son of God, to glory in Christ, but consisting of, and
revealed in, those personal marks and signs of God's
peculiar adoption of *himself,* which he and none else is
acquainted with. If the heart 'knoweth its own bitter-

*See the subject of "mysteries" in Hislop's "Two Babylons," or Pember's
"Church. Churches, and Mysteries." (The latter securable second-hand only.)

ness, and a stranger intermeddleth not with its joy,'
(Proverbs 14:10), then the deep, secret dealings of God
with each of us during those times by which our sonship
is assured and our spiritual strife carried on to victory,
can, when revealed to us in the other blessed state, be
known thoroughly *to ourselves only.*"

IV. THYATIRA

The Papacy in Power

ADDRESS: **These things saith the Son of God,
who hath his eyes like a flame of fire.** Here we have
Christ in the most searching and terrible aspect of any
He assumes toward the churches. He is "the Son of
God," the *Deity.* He is also the Son of man, but His
eyes as "a flame of fire" search *this* church—the holy
jealousy of infinite love. We remember the words of the
Song (8:6):

> "Love is strong as death;
> Jealousy is hard as Sheol;
> The flashes thereof are flashes of fire,
> A very flame of Jah."

And his feet are like unto burnished brass. They
stand to judge in Thyatira according to His own glorious holiness. For there sin is *tolerated.* And not only so;
but an *authority* permitted that supplants Christ!

CONDITION AND COMMENDATION: **I know
thy works, and thy love and faith and ministry and
patience, and that thy last works are more than the
first.** We have come with Thyatira to the *papal period*
of church history, and before our Lord brings this hateful system before us, mark how He cherishes such
devotion (and it was, here and there, very great), as
marked this dark time. Notice that "love" here comes
before "faith," as if it were only those in whom intense
love for the Saviour burned, who had faith to outlast
those days. Then "ministry,"—and we remember with
tender hearts the amazing, self-denying lives of many
who, having not much light, yet *loved:* i.e., Bernard of

Clairveaux, Mechtilde of Helffde. How well the reader of church history remembers their patient endurance and increasing works!

CONDEMNATION: **I have against thee that thou sufferest the woman Jezebel** (literally, "thy wife," as Jezebel to Ahab). This reference in the local assembly, was undoubtedly to a literal woman whom the Lord calls by the hated name of the seducing queen of Israel of long ago.*

Who calleth herself a prophetess. Now to do this was to take the place of the Spirit, who indeed spake "not from Himself," but "what He heard" from the Lord in glory. This is exactly Romanism. The Word of God teaches that "pastors and teachers" are given to the Church: that is, *she must herself BE taught!* Rome's doctrine is that the Church *is* the teacher. "The Church is your mother," "You must hearken to her," "She alone knows the voice of God," etc., etc. THIS IS *NOT TRUE*. It is the denial of all divine truth. *Rome holds no doctrine unleavened with error.*

The same rebuke Christ gives Thyatira applies to all who turn to *human* authority, rather than opening the ear to hear what the *Spirit* says to the churches. *You* may be thinking of "Christian Scientists," and their "Mother Church"; of the Mormons, with Joseph Smith and Brigham Young. But *the Lord* may be thinking of *you*, devoted as you are to "Doctor So-and-So," or to "*my* church." An old Puritan preacher used to say, "I want to hear but two things: First, does *God* speak? Second, what does *God* say?" Unless we have this attitude, we place ourselves in Thyatira.

---

*This name "Jezebel," applied to this Thyatiran, is proof again that God expects us to read from Scripture the deep meanings of the names He uses.

"Jehu answered, "What peace, so long as the whoredoms of thy mother Jezebel and her witchcrafts are so many?" (II Kings, 9:22).

So she wrote letters in Ahab's name . . . saying, "Proclaim a fast, and set Naboth on high among the people . . . and stone him to death." (I Kings 21: 5-10; 18:4, 13).

Whoredom, witchcraft, religious fasts,—and *murdering God's prophets,—* this was Jezebel. *Is not this also Rome?* Jezebel also supported a *horde of idolatrous priests* of her own—Babylonians all. See *Baal* in "The Two Babylons," Hislop, and "Great Prophecies," Pember, pp. 138-139.

"Thou *sufferest* the woman Jezebel": here was the cause of blame. Whether from sympathy with the evil, or lack of moral fibre to resist it, it is all the same: they *suffered* it. Today the so-called Protestant is as weak as, weaker often, than the Romanist, because he *suffers* some "great" denomination to hold him in its clutches, though he knows sects are directly contrary to the Word of God (I Corinthians 1:11-13). "Be loyal to your denomination" is mere whip-cracking over you. Their shallow pretentious "educational" systems; vast anti-Scriptural *debt*-incurring "church" building plans; their huge, bossed organizations, and ecclesiastical wire-pulling, keep their votaries in spiritual babyhood. "Our standards" are more to them than direct Bible study. The "Federation of Churches" (??) conceived and controlled by "modernism," (which is Tom Paine infidelity in a pulpit coat*), is *"suffered,"* despite the methods by which it procures godly but simple-hearted speakers to place on its platforms beside its trusted "modernist" deceivers. (Thank God, some have revolted from this self-appointed "Federation." If you would know the *real* "Federation," read Col. Sanctuary's *"Tainted Contacts."*)

Now you may say that in speaking thus we are departing from exposing the direct evils the woman Jezebel brought into Thyatira—idolatry and fornication. True: and we shall note those evils; but we have spoken as we have lest any one might think that in escaping these particular sins he had not *suffered any* "Jezebel" system.

And she teacheth and seduceth my servants to commit fornication! This, of course, in Thyatira's case, was literal, and in Rome's case is literal. The confessional teaches children to discover and speak of the lowest abominations of the human heart; the result of which is to familiarize them with such things, stifle conscience, and finally open the flood gates to .indulgence of the flesh, especially with Rome's Babylonian priests, with

---

*See "The Deadly Parallel," G. W. Dowkontt, where Fosdick's and Paine's beliefs and teachings are compared, column by column, with Paine preferable!

whom to sin, is, by their teaching, no sin.*

In the face of the revealed corruptness of the history of the confessional, and its results in Catholic lands, the Vatican's plea against the terrible evil of divorce, is seen to be a "play to the galleries." The papal decree "Ne Temere" (warning against *adultery!*) of Pope Pius Tenth, in which honest marriages, blessed by God and by years of marital uprightness, happiness, and fruitfulness, are declared to be nothing more than adultery because between a Catholic and a Protestant, shows up real Jezebel deceitfulness.

Next, as to idolatry: note the order is changed from Balaam's teaching, verse 14, where entering upon the idol worship was first, and the licentiousness followed. In Thyatira, fornication is first, then idolatry. I quote from McClintock and Strong's Encyclopedia:

"Images were unknown in the worship of primitive Christians, who abstained from worship of images because they thought it unlawful in itself to make any images of deity. By the steady pressure of the heathen ideas and habits upon Christianity, emblems such as the dove, the fish, the anchor, vine, lamb, etc., formed the first step; then, paintings representing great Biblical events, saints, martyrs, which were placed in the vestibule of the church. Yet this practice was unfavorably regarded by the synods of the fourth century. When, however, in the same century, Christianity was proclaimed (by Constantine) the religion of the state, the use of painting, sculpture and jewelry became general for the decoration of the churches, resulting in the adoption of a regular *system* of symbolic religious images. The teachers of the church became gradually more accommodating in their relations with the heathen, allowing them to retain their old usages, while conforming to the outward forms of Christianity. Thus the worship of images became so general that it had to be repeatedly checked by laws. In the sixth century, it had grown into a great abuse, especially in the East, where images were made the object of a special adoration: they were kissed, lamps were burned before them, incense was offered to them,—in short, they were treated in every respect as the heathen were wont to treat the images of their gods. The same arguments now used by the Romanists to defend image worship were rejected by Christians of the first three centuries when used in defense of image worship. The heathen said, We do not worship the images themselves, but those whom they represent. To this Lactantius (third century A.D.) answers, 'You worship *them;* for, if you believe them to be in heaven, why do you not raise your eyes up to heaven? Why do you look at the images, and not up where you believe them to be?' Thomas Aquinas, a Roman Catholic (13th century), declared, 'A picture, considered in itself, is worthy of no veneration, but if we consider it as an image of Christ, it may be allowable to make an internal distinction between the image and its subject, and adoration and service are as well due to it as to Christ.' Bonaventura the Franciscan, said, 'Since all veneration shown to the image of Christ is shown to Christ himself, then the image of Christ is also entitled to be prayed to.' Bellarmine, Rome's principal authority in dogmatic theology (1542-1621), writes, 'The images of Christ and the saints are to be adored, not only in a figurative manner, but quite positively, so that the prayers are directly addressed to them, and not merely as representatives of the original.' " *De Imaginibus.*

---

*I defy any sincere one to read McGavin's "Protestant," or "Fifty Years in the Church of Rome," by Father Chiniquy (F. H. Revell & Co., New York), or the writings of Liguori, the Roman Catholic "theologian," and deny that Rome teaches, as well as seduces, to fornication and immorality, *in the confessional.*

Idolatry, the worship of images, is a primary teaching of Romanism. "Jezebel" then, which truth-enlightened men acknowledge to stand for Romanism, introduces uncleanness through the confessional first; then the adoration of images, and thus a proceeding ever deeper into idolatrous superstition; for idol-worship ever degrades its devotees (see Revelation 13 and 17).

I gave her time that she should repent; and she willeth not to repent of (literally, out of) **her fornication.** The chief hold, after all, of false religion, is the liberty it gives to the lusts which the heart loves. Repentance, which is God's way out, the human heart hates.*

Behold, I cast her into a bed. "Will change her bed of whoredom into a bed of anguish: so most commentators." (Alford) The Lord often deals thus with wicked leaders; He was even more abrupt and condign with Ahab's wife (II Kings 9:30-37). (He will yet deal effectually with the female *leaders* "suffered" in our own day, who center attention upon *themselves,* and pose more and more as *prophetesses,* using all sorts of meretricious showmanship to hold the poor people spellbound.)

And them that commit adultery with her into great

Hear the testimony of an earnest lad:
"When I had confessed all the sins I could remember, the priest began to ask me the strangest questions on matters about which my pen must be silent. I replied, 'Father, I do not understand what you ask me.'
'I question you on the sixth commandment' (in the Bible, the seventh).
Thereupon he dragged my thoughts to regions which, thank God, had hitherto been unknown to me.
I answered him, 'I do not understand you,' or, 'I have never done these things.'
Then skillfully shifting to some secondary matter, he would soon slyly and cunningly come back to his favorite subject, namely, sins of licentiousness.
His questions were so unclean that I blushed and felt sick with disgust and shame. I was so filled with indignation that, speaking loud enough to be heard by many, I told him: 'Sir I am very wicked; I have seen, heard, and done many things which I regret; but I never was guilty of what you mention to me. My ears have never heard anything so wicked as what they have heard from your lips. Please do not ask me any more of these questions; do not teach me any evil that I do not already know.' "—"Fifty Years in the Church of Rome," pp. 26-27.

---

*Mr. H. A. Ironside well says, "Romanism is Christianity, Judaism, and Heathenism joined together; and the Lord abhors the vile combination. God gave her (Rome) space to repent, and she repented not. Go back to the days of Savanarola in Italy, Wickliffe and Cranmer in England, John Knox in Scotland, Martin Luther in Germany, Zwingle in Switzerland, Calvin in France—all those mighty reformers whom God raised up throughout the world to call Rome to repent of her iniquity, but she repented not. If she had had any desire to get right with Him, she would have repented in the 16th century." *Lectures on The Revelation.*

tribulation, except they repent of her works. Here is a most terrible threat! We know of The Great Tribulation; and I cannot avoid the conclusion that this warning points to it. For we read in Revelation 17 that the Babylonian harlot is to be hated and made desolate by the Beast and his ten kings (Revelation 17:16).

Please note at once that these last four churches look *toward the end*—that is, to the *closing* of church testimony to give way to the *kingdom.* Thyatira, impenitent, is threatened with the *tribulation;* Sardis, with Christ's coming *as a thief*—that is, (after the true Church has been raptured) they will be "caught" like the *world*—I Thessalonians 5:2, 3; Philadelphia, faithful though weak, has the promise of *the Rapture,* to escape all the trouble of the awful "hour" that is coming; while Laodicea is spued out as lukewarm, irrecoverable—ending the history of the Church as Christ's earthly witness.*

And I will kill her children with death. Jezebel's punishment is distinct from that of her proper *adherents* (not those who *suffer* her, but those who are *begotten* of her). "There is a transition from literal to spiritual fornication, as appears in these verses" (Fausset). Some commentators believe that the whole passage refers to "spiritual fornication," that is, union with the world. Others, and I can but agree with them, insist that a prominent, gifted, strong-willed, evil *woman* was permitted in Thyatira (as such are often today "suffered"). Her "children" are evidently those whom she seduced subtly into the wickedness described, and who clung to her. These the Lord threatens to kill with *death,* which seems to me spiritual, eternal—"except they repent of *her* works." The "death" was to be so evident that all the

---

*Seiss well calls the attention of those who question whether the seven churches of The Revelation stand for the entire Church in its whole history, to the words of Victorinus, bishop of Petavium, martyred in 303 A. D., and the first church commentator on The Revelation known to us: "Paul first taught us that there are seven churches in the whole world, and that the seven churches are the one entire Church. Paul wrote 'Ad Romanos, ad Corinthios, ad Galatas, ad Ephesios, ad Thessalonicenses, ad Phillipenses, ad Colossenses'; and John, obeying the same method, has not exceeded the number seven."

churches shall know that I am he that searcheth the reins and hearts.*

Note, *"all* the churches," not these seven representative ones merely. How dull our spiritual perception, not to understand why candlesticks have been removed, and personal judgment executed, before our very eyes! David's child by Uriah's wife was publicly smitten and slain by Jehovah (II Samuel 12). The "angel" of the Thyatiran church was good, personally; but he "suffered" his wife to teach and practice fornication,—even to bearing adulterous seed. These would be *slain* by the Lord: and the woman herself be fittingly dealt with. And she would become a *warning,* as did both Lot's wife and Jezebel. But the evil would go on into a *system,* to be judged finally (Revelation 17) as a great whore that corrupted the earth!

And I will give unto each one of you according to your works. Here is judgment, certainly—whether to Jezebel herself, to her children, or to those real servants of the Lord who *suffered* her either in Thyatira, or now, as a system: to each, a just dealing. None of Christ's own will be lost; but responsibility in church life on earth is solemn: for the Church represents *Christ.*

To you I say (the godly ones who will really hear) **to the rest that are in Thyatira, as many as have not this teaching, who know not the deep things of Satan, as they are wont to say.** The Magians from Babylon continually spoke of their *"deep* things," their "inner knowledge," just as the Theosophists, Christian Scientists, Spiritualists, and "Unity" devotees do today (simply ancient Gnosticism revived!). The Lord sees through all the enemy's delusions and "mysteries"; they are not "deep" to *Him.* His real saints are simple-hearted (blessed simpleness!). It is no sign of spirituality to be familiar with Satanic psychic or demonic "depths."

I cast upon you none other burden,—quoted from the

---

*Grotius well says, "Through the *reins* (Latin, *renes*) the *desires* become known; through the *heart*, the *thoughts.*"

decision of the council at Jerusalem (Acts 15:28, 29).
"This act of simple obedience (keeping from idolatry and
fornication) and no deep matters beyond their reach, was
what the Lord required of them."

LOVING COUNSEL: **Nevertheless that which ye
have, hold fast* till I come.** How easy to let truth and
devotion slip in *Jezebel* surroundings! Christ's sure and
imminent personal coming again is *the tonic for faith*!
"Hold the fort, for *I* am coming!" We shall see that from
Thyatira on, our Lord's *return,* and *not* the recovery of
the Church to her first estate, much less the conversion of
the world, is *the only object of hope.*

PROMISE TO OVERCOMERS: **And he that
overcometh, and he that keepeth my works unto the
end.** "It is not enough to deny Jezebel in doctrine and
works, but 'he that *keepeth* unto the end *my* works' is
crowned at the end: '*my* works,' evidently in contrast to the
works of Jezebel, verse 23. *Her* works were unholy; His
works, holy."—Scott. **To him will I give authority
over the nations; and he shall rule them with a rod of
iron, as the vessels of the potter are broken to shivers;
as I also have received of my Father.** Here is the first
definite view in The Revelation of the coming millennial
kingdom to be established by the Lord at His return to
the earth (Revelation 19:15; 20:4-6). The papacy has
ever grasped at "temporal power." She wants to rule
the world *now,* before Christ comes—thus *proving* herself false; not a *church,* but *Babylon.* God's saints, with
their Lord, await expectantly the Father's time (Hebrews
10:13, Psalm 2:7, 8). Those who learn Christ's *patience*
become trained and fit to rule. Recall, "He that ruleth
his spirit is *better* than he that taketh a city" (Proverbs
16:32); although man despises this path (Luke 22:25, 30).

And I will give him the morning star. When the
Millennium comes, it will be broad day—the Sun will have

---

*" 'Hold fast'—aorist: more vivid and imperative than would be the present,
setting forth the renewed, determined grasp of every intervening moment of
the space prescribed until the time when 'I shall come': the aorist gives an
uncertainty as to when the time shall be, which we cannot convey in our language." (Alford)

risen, with healing in His wings (Malachi 4:2, 3)—but now it is night. And, although we know "neither the day nor the hour" of our Lord's coming, yet into the heart of the faithful believer comes that wondrous *expectancy* of His coming, which John elsewhere describes as having our "hope set on him" (I John 3:3). This is the experience of the believer who awakes out of sleep (Romans 13:11), who by the grace of God hears His voice when He says, "Awake, thou that sleepest, and arise from among the dead (ones), and Christ shall shine upon thee" (Ephesians 5:13). To such, Christ becomes indeed the Morning Star, the harbinger of the glorious coming day, though the night be yet all around us. Just as the multitude lie physically asleep, while here and there one, watching all night, or risen very early, sees the blazing beauty of the morning star, so these spiritually awakened or aroused find Christ's coming arising as the day-star in their hearts (II Peter 1:19).

Nowhere in church history appears so intense a devotion to the person of Christ in a time of great deprivation of a free Bible and preaching, and the so-called "means of grace," as in the dark ages Thyatira stands for. All around was *night,* in the world and in the Church; the threat of death was over all, but *Christ* was known, loved, served and sung. He was the only light; but He was enough!*

CALL TO HEAR: **He that hath an ear, let him hear.** Note the *change in place* now! Jezebel and her "children" will go on as they are (Rome's motto is *Semper Idem*—"Always the Same"), but "the rest," the remnant, will hear.

---

*Concerning this De Wette says, "Arriving at full conviction of the certainty of the coming of Christ."

Luther: "Two degrees of the Christian life: in the first, faith rests upon outward evidences; in the second, on inward revelations of the Spirit."

Jonathan Edwards: "When Christ was going to heaven, He comforted His disciples with the thought that after awhile He would come again and take them to Himself, that they might be with Him."

And again: "I have sometimes a sense of the excellent fullness of Christ whereby He has appeared to me far above all, the chief of ten thousands. Once, as I rode out into the woods I had a view that for me was extraordinary of the glory of the Son of God. The person of Christ appeared ineffably excellent with an excellency great enough to swallow up all thought or conception—which

V. SARDIS

Dead "Protestantism"

ADDRESS: **These things saith he that hath the seven Spirits of God, and the seven stars.** This is the designation of the Spirit as before the throne in heaven (Revelation 1:4, 5). We have noticed that it is not as the indwelling Comforter (although He is such to all believers), that He appears in Revelation. The Spirit is subordinate to the Son, as the Son to the Father, in the divine creative and redemptive arrangements, although all are equal in the fact of Deity. Christ now begins *anew,* as it were: He has the seven stars, as in Ephesus, but He has also the seven Spirits of God. There will be utter searching, which is here emphasized (Zechariah 4:6-10).

We have, in Sardis, what has often been called a *new beginning.* God leaves the Jezebel corruption and the ecclesiastical hierarchy behind, with Thyatira; and takes up what is known as "Christianity" *since the Reformation.*

CONDITION KNOWN: **Thou hast a name that thou livest, and thou art dead.** Nothing could describe "Protestantism" more accurately! As over against Romish night and ignorance, she has enlightenment and outward activity: the great "state churches," or "denominations," with creeds and histories, costly churches and cathedrals, universities and seminaries, "boards," bureaus of publication and propaganda, executors of organized activities, including home and foreign missions, even "lobby" men to "influence legislation" at court! You and I dare compare the Church with no other model than the Holy Spirit gave at Pentecost and in Paul's day! And compared to *that*—it has a *name,* but is *dead*—not to speak

---

kept me the greater part of the time in a flood of tears and weeping aloud." And his seraphic wife thus testifies: "Mr. Sheldon came into the house about ten o'clock and said to me as he came in, 'The Sun of Righteousness arose on my soul this morning before day'; upon which I said to him in reply, '*That Sun* has not set upon my soul all this night: I have dwelt with Him in heavenly mansions; the light of divine love has surrounded me; my soul has been lost in God and has almost left the body.'" (See *Memoirs* of Edwards, in his Complete Works.)

See Samuel Rutherford's Letters, Finney's Autobiography, especially his last meetings in Boston. See also the hymns that came out of the darkest papal times. These all had *The Morning Star!* (Appendix I.)

of being "filled with the Holy Spirit," "admonishing one another with psalms and hymns and spiritual songs." Pass through the churches of Christendom and ask one question: Are you born again? Are you a new creature in Christ Jesus? Like the Philistine-yoked Jews of Nehemiah's day: "I saw the Jews that had married women of Ashdod, of Ammon, of Moab: and their children spake half in the speech of Ashdod, and could not speak in the Jews' language, but according to the language of each people" (Nehemiah 13:23, 24). So with church-membership of our day, yoked with the world by marriage, by lodge-fellowship, by narrow sectarian bigotry and crass ignorance of the Word of God and even of the gospel of salvation. "Thou art dead." Awful state! Given to recover the truth at the Reformation in the most mighty operation of the Spirit of God since the days of the Apostles, Christendom has sunk into spiritual *death!*

LOVING COUNSEL: **Be thou watchful, and establish the things that remain, which were ready to die: for I have found no works of thine perfected before my God. Remember therefore how thou hast received and didst hear; and keep it, and repent.** Notice here first, "no works . . . *perfected.*" Neither in *doctrine* nor in *walk* did the Reformation go back to the early days of the Church. In doctrine they did teach (thank God!) *justification* by faith apart from works. Luther's "Commentary on Galatians" is in many respects the most vigorous utterance of faith since Paul. Yet the Reformers did not teach Paul's doctrine of *identification,*—that the believer's *history,* as connected with Adam, *ended* at Calvary: that he died to sin, federally, with Christ; and died to the law, which gave sin its power. All the Reformation creeds kept the believer under the law as a rule of life; and "the law made *nothing* perfect." Whereas, Scripture speaks of a *perfect* conscience, through a *perfect sacrifice;* of faith being *perfected;* of being made *perfect* in love; of *perfecting* holiness in the fear of God.

Of course, there is no perfection in the flesh, but Paul distinctly says concerning believers, "Ye are *not in the flesh* but in the Spirit, if so be that the Spirit of God dwelleth in you"; and, "if ye are led by the Spirit, ye are *not under the law."*

Furthermore, the Reformed creeds did not get free from Rome* as regards what they still called "sacraments,"— a Babylonish term. For *sacramentum* was the Latin word for a *mystery* of the pagan religion. "The grand distinguishing feature of the ancient Babylonian system was the Chaldean *mysteries,* that formed so essential a part of that system" (Hislop, p. 4). "Even in the prayer-book of the Church of England, the Lord's Supper is called 'these holy mysteries'! But such a term for it is unknown in the New Testament, and was subsequently introduced merely because the *initiates* (of Babylonish idolatry) fixed upon the Memorial Supper as the one thing in Christianity which they could most easily metamorphose into a *Mystery,* or *Sacrament.* Then, associating Baptism with the bath which preceded (pagan) *initiation,* they called it, also, a Mystery, or Sacrament,—though they often dropped all disguise, and spoke of it plainly as *initiation."* (Pember)

Consequently neither is the *walk* perfected. Not knowing that they died with Christ and are risen ones, their walk is pitifully short of Paul's: some, worldly and wholly shallow; some, even sincere souls, using man-made prayers by rote, and even man-made festival days, which belong to Paganism or Judaism; regarding really devoted souls as fanatics,—especially those who live in view of, and speak of, the imminent return of the Lord, as did constantly the early Christians!

Note *watchfulness,* that hardest of spiritual tasks to a

*J. A. Froude, the historian, says, "Protestantism has made no converts to speak of in Europe since the sixteenth century. It shot up in two generations to its full stature, and became an established creed with defined boundaries, and it has come about that the old enemies have become friends in the presence of a common foe (anti-churchism and atheism). Catholics speak tenderly of Protestants as keeping alive the belief in creeds, and look forward to their return to the sheepfold, while the scarlet woman on the seven hills, 'drunk with the blood of the saints,' is now treated by Protestantism as an older sister, and a valued ally in the great warfare with infidelity. The points of difference are forgotten; the points of union are passively dwelt upon; the remnant of idolatry, which the more ardent European Protestants once abhorred and denounced, are now regarded as having been providentially preserved, as a means of making up the quarrel and bringing back the churches into communion."

drowsy soul, is enjoined by the Lord that "the things that remain"—those few "fundamental" doctrines still known and preached, may not be wholly lost, but established. "Remember": like Ephesus, they must go back to the beginning. Protestantism *did* receive, and *did* hear. In the Reformation days, all Europe was stirred concerning divine truth. People crowded halls for four or five hours at a time to listen to discourses and debates upon Scripture. Alas, the deadness, the ignorance, the coldness and the carelessness today! *"Keep* it and *repent":* to recover truth once lost and especially the love of it, so as to hold the truth fast, is a deadly difficult task! Protestantism—Christendom—is *giving it up.*

PREDICTED ACTION: **If therefore thou shalt not watch, I will come as a thief, and thou shalt not know what hour I will come upon thee.** Notice three things: watchlessness, visitation, and ignorance. To the Sardis church, unheeding, the words, "I will come as a thief" meant, not our Lord's second coming, but visitation in judgment like that to Ephesus in 2:5, and Pergamum in 2:16. The *processes* of divine judgment we cannot by any faculties given us discover; the only thing for us to do is to receive divine *warning.* Now a *thief* takes away secretly our property—what belongs to us: so would Christ come suddenly, secretly, and remove *everything of value* from the Sardis assembly. So He *did,* for *that* assembly is gone—the very *place* of it!

But there is a wider application: to Protestantism, with its "name to live, but dead," Christ threatens that aspect of His coming which really belongs not to His saints but to the world. *"Ye,* brethren, are not in darkness that that day should overtake you as a thief . . . ye are all sons . . . of the day" (I Thessalonians 5:4, 5). To be *overtaken,* then, and *judged as the world,* is *the doom of dead Protestantism,* just as the tribulation was the destiny of Romanism in Thyatira.

PROMISE TO OVERCOMERS: **But thou hast a few names in Sardis that did not defile their garments:**

**and they shall walk with me in white; for they are
worthy.** Here we have the faithful remnant—"a few,"
—like "the rest" in Thyatira. Faithful preachers know
them in every assembly. They *hearken.* They are *separate
from the world.* They *pray, go to prayer meetings, work
for their Lord, and love the Word.*

Note that this remnant were not "defiled." "They are
not in contact with the spiritual death around them which
is here counted defilement, as in the Old Testament was
considered the touch of a dead body." (Ottman.)

"With me in white." Here it represents manifested
victorious righteousness. Compare the white robes of
Revelation 6:11; and that public association with Christ
of Revelation 19:14. Note rejection of defilement constitutes "worthiness," (Christ *Himself* of course being our
only *righteousness*).

PROMISE TO OVERCOMER: **He that overcometh shall thus be arrayed in white garments; and
I will in no wise blot his name out of the book of life,
and I will confess his name before my Father and
before his angels.** These promises, of course, are all
to be taken literally. "Thus" as befits Christ's presence,—
"with *me* in white," they shall be *arrayed* and *walk!* Also,
"in no wise blot out" releases from anxiety. "The
Lord will deliver from every evil work, and *will* save
. . . unto his heavenly kingdom" (II Timothy 4:18). As
to "book of life," see Revelation 20:12. "Will confess
. . . before my Father and before his angels" (Revelation 3:5). What a day! As one very near to me said,
after a meeting in which some had been urged not to be
ashamed to confess Christ: "I am not ashamed to confess Christ, but my wonder is, how He can ever confess *me!*"

CALL TO HEAR: Again note that it is *after* the
remnant has been addressed: for real saints only will
truly give ear to the Lord by His Spirit,—*in any age,*
but with peculiar difficulty when *deadness* holds most professors. He that hath an ear, LET HIM HEAR!

VI. PHILADELPHIA

Awakened Saints of the Last Days

This name *Philadelphia* at once arouses our interest!
It is the seventh (and last) occurrence of this Greek
word in the New Testament. (The other passages are
Romans 12:10; I Thessalonians 4:9; Hebrews 13:1;
I Peter 1:22; II Peter 1:7, twice.) Hebrews 13:1 reads:
"Let brotherly love (Greek, *philadelphia*) continue."
Surely God speaks to us in this name, as we read the
character of the saints at Philadelphia, their devotion to
Christ,—His name and His word, and their consequent
love for one another,—in circumstances such as theirs so
precious and so necessary!

ADDRESS: **He that is holy, he that is true, he that
hath the key of David, he that openeth and none shall
shut, and that shutteth and none openeth.** *Christ* remains holy, even if the church has left her first love,
hearkened to Balaam, suffered Jezebel and her whoredoms, and has only a *name* to live, but is one with the
world in the *defilements* of *death. Christ* still is true:
though the church has listened to the enemy's lies through
the centuries! *Ah, if it were not for CHRIST!* The
church has a history that is worse than Israel's, which
was worse than the heathen! (II Chronicles 33:9). But
the Lord is unchanged; *He* is true. The more you read
church history the more you realize that *absolutely everything depends on CHRIST HIMSELF!*

And here we find Him opening this out to us. He said
to John in 1:18, "I have the keys of death and of Hades."
Now He has the "key of *David*." While those spoke of
His salvation-power as Victor over Death and the unseen
world—this announces His *royal* claims as Lord and
Head of David's House and looks toward the *kingdom*
to be established on earth. Even now, when men, in their
arrogance, and especially in *ecclesiastical position,* would
"shut out" Christ's servants (and do they not seek to do
it?) it is a blessed thing to "remember Jesus Christ, risen
from the dead, of *the seed of David,*" as Paul commanded

us (II Timothy 2:8). Although He has not yet come to take the *throne* of His father David, He yet has all royal authority in heaven *and on earth,* and He will open before His faithful servants, doors which *none* shall shut! All is in His hands, which exceedingly comforts saints in this world's "Vanity Fair"!

Also, mark, our Lord can *shut:* and then *none opens.* How He opened and shut for the apostles, in the early days! (Acts 16:6-10; 18:9,10; 19:8-20; I Corinthians 16:8,9). So, also, Christ may *shut* doors in lands where His gospel has been known and despised, and His saints slain,—as in Spain and France, and in those lands He gave over to the false prophet Mohammed.

So their Lord, whom they loved, had opened a door for these Philadelphians, which *none* could shut: no power of earth or hell! So they could go right on in the truth and in service, despite the devil, the world, and false professors!

CONDITION KNOWN: **I know thy works (behold, I have given before thee a door opened, which none can shut), that thou hast a little power, and didst keep my word, and didst not deny my name.** Here we have another spirit than that of Sardis,—yea, better even than Ephesus! Philadelphia lacked the *energy* of Ephesus of the early church days, but it had three precious things: first, a little *power;* second, obedience to Christ's *word;* third, not denying His *name.*

As to "little," see the same Greek word about Zacchaeus (Luke 19:3)—he was "little" of stature; and about the Lord's company in general—a "little" flock (Luke 12:32). The Philadelphian assembly was unimportant in the world's eyes, probably few in number, poor in property, and low in the social scale. Moreover, the spiritual power they had was feeble compared to Pentecost. But the Lord has nothing but commendation for them. They loved Christ. Jesus answered and said, "If a man love me, he will keep my word" (John 14:23). Mark again the contrast with the indifference of Sardis toward the

word they had received (as Protestantism in general);
and also, contrast with Thyatira (Romanism), where
Christ's word had been supplanted by Jezebel's. Here,
in Philadelphia, instead of ecclesiasticism or indifferent-
ism, we find *a living response to the known word* of the
blessed Lord.

Also in a world that says of Christ, "He was a good
man," "a great *teacher,*" etc.; and surrounded, as we are
today, by other assemblies with merely "a name to live,"
willing to have Christ's Deity doubted or denied, His virgin birth assailed, His atoning death rejected, His bodily
resurrection mocked at, His all-prevailing Highpriestly
work in heaven disdained, His headship over all things to
the Church despised, His second coming as Bridegroom
of the Church and King of kings over all the earth ignored or decried,—amid all this, Christ was *at home* in
Philadelphia, as in the household at Bethany! His person
worshipped, delighted in; and His coming expectantly
awaited!

Precious assembly! Our Lord's words of greeting
to them are *personal,* as their devotion to Him was
personal! No wonder that they have special promises—Behold, I give of the synagogue of Satan, of them
that say they are Jews, and they are not, but do lie;
behold, I will make them to come and worship before
thy feet, and to know that I have loved thee. Again
those truly awful words, "synagogue of Satan"! "Salvation," said Christ to the woman of Samaria, is "from
the Jews" (John 4:22). But their sun had set. Again,
(to Israel,) "I have loved you, saith Jehovah. Yet ye say,
Wherein hast thou loved us?" (Malachi 1:2). And again,
"When he drew nigh, he saw the city (Jerusalem) and
wept over it, saying, If thou hadst known the things which
belong unto peace!" (Luke 19:41, 42).

But now they had seen and hated both Christ and His
Father, and their house was left to them desolate! Nay,
they were *"the* synagogue of Satan." If they had been
like Nathanael, "Israelites *indeed,*" they would have believed on the Lord Jesus, and have proved themselves of

"the election of grace" of Romans 11:5, and have been *part* of that assembly which, as Jews by falsehood only, they reviled. Doubtless their predicted coming and worshipping before the feet of the Philadelphian church had a local, historical meaning. We also know that the day will come when the saints will judge not the world only, but also angels (I Corinthians 6:2), and this only because of Christ's special love for the Church! (So also the persecuting Gentiles will be compelled to treat the godly remnant of Israel in the coming day! [Isaiah 66:14.])

SPECIAL PROMISES: Now, most wonderful, cheering song to the hearts of the faithful today is the Lord's promise to deliver His true saints from The Great Tribulation! **Because thou didst keep the word of my patience, I also will keep thee from the hour of trial, that hour which is to come upon the whole world, to try them that dwell upon the earth.** As we saw in 1:9, "tribulation, kingdom, and *patience*," are connected in Jesus. Compare Acts 14:22. We who believe are *in* the kingdom,—by birth, by new creation, already. But both for our Lord, and for us, there is patient waiting for the kingdom's *setting up*. And as for Him when on earth, so now for us, there is tribulation from Satan and the world. *Patience* (connected with saints seven times in The Revelation), is a prime virtue. Listen: the good ground hearers "bring forth fruit with *patience*"; "with *patience* we wait for that which we see not"; "strengthened with all power unto all *patience* and longsuffering"; "who through faith and *patience* inherit the promises"; "let us run *with patience* the race," "let *patience* have its perfect work." This Philadelphia assembly steadily, unfalteringly, lovingly *endured,* and *waited for Christ;* as Christ waited and is yet waiting His Father's time to give Him *the throne* long promised to Him, of His father David.

This is a beautiful, reciprocal promise of their Lord to them: Ye kept my patience, I will keep you out of the coming hour of trial. This "hour," coming as it will, upon the whole earth, is seen in Revelation 13:7, 8, in the permitted frightful career of the Beast. Two things identify this hour: first, its extent; second, its object. It is to come upon all "the inhabited earth" (Greek, *oikoumenee*).* It is to *try* the "earth-dwellers," whether they will follow Satan's Christ or not—since they have chosen earth where Satan is the prince and the god, as their "good things" (Luke 16:25). Fearful trial! Read Revelation 14:9-12, where the issue is finally pressed home—an issue involving eternity!

Now, our Lord promises to *keep* Philadelphian believers *out of*† this coming hour.

Inasmuch as this verse (10) holds forth the great promise of being kept from The Great Tribulation, it behooves us to inquire most diligently about it.

1. What *is* the hour of *trial,* or *temptation,* of which our Lord speaks? There is no reasonable doubt that it *must* refer to The Great Tribulation of which Daniel wrote (12:1), and to which our Lord referred in Matthew 24: 15-21. This "hour" extends to the *whole* inhabited earth, —so does that. See Revelation 13:7, 8. And this is an hour of *trial*—the earth-dwellers, having rejected, or neglected, the Lord of heaven, and heavenly things, are now to be given Satan's Christ. A "strong delusion" will be sent by God; and all not God's elect will believe *"the lie"* (II Thessalonians 2:7-11).

2. What is meant by being *kept from* that terrible "hour"?

(a) It cannot mean merely, preserved *in* and *through* it: for the remnant of Israel, God's *earthly* people, will have *that* preservation (Jeremiah 30:7; Daniel 12:1), whereas this is a promise given by a *heavenly* Christ to His *heavenly* saints.

(b) It is from a peculiar *hour,* or *season,* not merely

---

*This word, *oikoumenee,* used fifteen times in the New Testament, seems to be set over against "the *wilderness*" . . . "where no man dwelleth." It is in the latter that God will miraculously preserve the remnant of Israel (see chapter 12).

†"The Greek preposition *ek,*" says Winer, "denotes procession out of the interior, the compass, the limits, of anything; and is the antithesis of *eis* (which means *into,* or into the midst of)."

from *trial*, but *from the hour and scene of the trial*, Christ's faithful are to be kept.

(c) It is as direct a reward to His saints for their "keeping the word of his patience," as was Christ's own exaltation because of His patiently doing His Father's will (Philippians 2:6-11). The word "keep" used in this promise is the same word our Lord applies to "keeping the word of his patience," which His faithful saints had done. It is, as we have said, beautifully reciprocal; but notice that Christ's "keeping" in His action toward them, was to protect them *from* something.

(d) He says, "I will keep thee out of" or *"away from"* that dread hour.*

This hour, we read, is *"about* to come." "While those ignorant of it are painting vain pictures of the happiness of earth, close at hand, to appear under the ordinary operation of the causes and agencies now at work, the student of prophecy knows *that this expectation will never be realized;* nay, that evil is about to expand itself to prodigious and overwhelming magnitude. The Lord, in vengeance for His truth rejected, is about to send on the earth an energy of delusion which seals all who receive it to utter damnation." (Govett)

LOVING COUNSEL: **I come quickly.** From Thyatira on, the eyes of the saints are directed to the Lord's return as the only hope, as it has really always been! To the faithful assembly at Philadelphia, the words were a thrill of cheer. One well says: "These words, 'I come quickly,' which in different senses and with varying references form the burden of this whole book (of Revelation) are here manifestly to be taken as an encouragement and comfort to the Philadelphian church, arising from the nearness of the Lord's coming to reward her."

---

*We would add still further that it cannot have the sense of *dia—through.* Note the Septuagint of Jeremiah 30:7 has *apo*—"out of it," in describing Jacob's preservation in *his* time of trouble. This seems to be in the sense of removed from it, as the remnant will have a "place in the wilderness" to flee unto! The preposition *ek* used in Revelation 3:10, describes those who are not in the trouble, but kept away from it.

It is well to note that Noah's family was preserved through *(dia)* water; whereas Enoch was translated that he should not *see* death!

Hold fast that which thou hast, that no one take* thy crown. "What thou hast" refers to spiritual possessions only,—to truth known, to progress in grace, to service to Christ already rendered. Intensely important this warning, that a crown may be won and lost through later watchlessness! "Take away from him the pound, and give it to him that hath ten pounds." I cannot agree with Alford that "it is not for himself that the robber would snatch away the crown, but merely to deprive the possessor." Service to the Lord *will be rewarded,* but the Lord may have to go *further back* to confer the reward,—perhaps to the person who brought to Him this worker who lost his reward. Doubtless also II John 8 teaches us that in order to "receive a full reward and lose not the things which we have wrought," we must be on our guard against wrong influences—we must *"look* to ourselves."

"Thy crown." All instructed believers know that the several crowns spoken of in the New Testament represent rewards for service, and not eternal life, which is a gift. Revelation 2:10; James 1:12; II Timothy 4:8; I Thessalonians 2:19; I Peter 5:4.

PROMISE TO OVERCOMER: **I will make him a pillar in the temple of my God, and he shall go out thence no more.** "A little strength" on earth, (but true love to Christ) and now made a *pillar!* This is, to be established in honor forever in the very presence of God, whose presence is the essence of bliss to a holy creature. All saints are being built therein as living stones, Peter tells us. Pillars (like Boaz and Jachin) in Solomon's temple, exhibited permanency, strength and beauty.

And I will write upon him the name of my God, and the name of the city of my God, the new Jerusalem.† We see this fulfilled in Revelation 22:4.

---

*The Greek word for *take* generally indicates receiving, not seizing, as in I Corinthians 3:8, 14; and 4:7, three times; and 9:24. Of the twenty-three times it is used in The Revelation, twenty-one describe *receiving.*

†Bengel says, "John in the gospel applies to the old city the *Greek* name *Hierosolyma,* but in the Apocalypse always to the holy city the *Hebrew* name, *Hierousalem.* The Hebrew name is the original and holier one; the Greek, the recent and more secular and political one."

And mine own new name. The meaning here, it seems to me, is opened out by the excellent note by Darby: "He who was hardly accounted to belong to the holy city (others had had the pretension to be the people of God, the city of God, by divine religious title on earth), has its heavenly name written on *him,* too, and Christ's new name—the name not known to prophets and Jews according to the flesh, but which He has taken as dead to this world. Associated in Christ's own patience, Christ confers upon him what fully associates him in *His own* blessing with God"!

Now who are the Philadelphians? We believe they are all Christ's faithful through the dispensation. If these promises were made to such saints *then,* they cover all saints *since.* Philadelphia was a local assembly at the same time with Ephesus and Smyrna. Let us not forget in viewing these seven messages, in their prophetic succession, that all *existed together.* Remember also that *all have existed through the dispensation,* so that not only is the hope of the *imminent coming* of the Lord preserved to all, but the promises to the overcomers are for *all* the saints. For example, *no* saint shall be "hurt of the second death,"—not Smyrna saints only! Those in Christ are already new creations, their history in Adam having ended at Calvary (Romans 6); and they, made alive together with Christ, raised up with Him, made to sit with Him in the heavenly places, in Christ Jesus: but it is "not yet made manifest what we shall be. We know that if he shall be manifested we shall be like him, for we shall see him even as he is." We have, *now,* "newness of life" in Christ. But what *His New Name* is, or will be, remains yet to be revealed!

CALL TO HEAR: **He that hath an ear, let him hear.** The Spirit keeps speaking to all opened ears and willing hearts in all these wondrous, solemn messages. Are we really *listening?*

VII. LAODICEA

The Last State—"Lukewarm"

The name comes from *laos,* people, and *dikao,* to rule:
the rule of the people: "democracy," in other words. (It
is the exact opposite of Nicolaitan!) We come now to
the sad and awful end of church testimony. That leaving
of first love in Ephesus, comes now to being left by the
Lord!

THE ADDRESS: **These things saith the Amen,
the faithful and true witness, the beginning of the creation of God.** Nothing of His appearance among the
churches in the vision of chapter 1 remains here.
The Church has failed; Christ remains. "The Amen."
It is the language of the faithful God who brings things
to pass as He has promised. See Isaiah 65:16; and II
Corinthians 1:20. There we read "How many soever be
the promises of God, in *him* (Christ), is the *yea;* (that is
the *possibility* of their being fulfilled) wherefore also
through him is the Amen, (the certainty and actuality, of
their *being* fulfilled) unto the glory of God through us."
This is a great announcement, for in ourselves we are
worse than failures, but in Christ all God's plans are
made good!

As the Faithful and True Witness, Christ is giving
now this seventh one of the searching messages to His
assemblies on earth: He will see all; He will withhold
nothing profitable; He will warn with perfect fidelity; He
will commend with absolute kindness. This is why we
can delight in The Revelation. It is not only *the word
of God,* but it is *the testimony of Jesus.* He speaks all
with unswerving faithfulness. He is also the Head, because the Beginner, of all God's creation. Here is a title
far above all dispensational responsibilities of creatures,
whether of Israel or of the Church—Christ speaks as
Creator. This puts us all in the dust. It likewise gives
our hearts hope. He who created all things can make
good the high calling of the Church as His Body and

Bride, despite the *corporate* failure of the Church's testimony on this earth.

CONDITION KNOWN: **Thou art neither cold nor hot: I would thou wert cold or hot. So, because thou art lukewarm, and neither hot nor cold, I am about to spew thee out of my mouth.** To Philadelphia our Lord had spoken in personal *fellowship*, "I am he that is *true*." To Laodicea, lukewarm, having no real heart for Him, He says, "I am the true *witness*": solemn difference!

Thou sayest, I am rich, and have gotten riches, and have need of nothing; and knowest not that thou art the wretched one and miserable and poor and blind and naked. Here we have, first, their spiritual state; second, their supreme self-confidence; third, their awful ignorance of their true condition; fourth, their imminent danger. The meaning of "hot" is seen in Romans 12:11, where the same Greek word is used—*fervent* (burning) in spirit. The word translated *cold* is used in Matthew 10:42, "a cup of cold water"; ("as cold waters to a thirsty soul," Proverbs 25:25). Either a hot drink on a cold day, or a cool one on a hot day, is acceptable and refreshing; *lukewarm* is *neither,* and *disgusts*. These Laodiceans were lukewarm: *chliaros*—a Greek word used only this one time in the Bible. It is the last stage of the Church's existence recognized by the Lord.

Note their proud, blind pretensions (although Christ is on the outside!): "I am *rich*"—become *wealthy*. Is not this a description of the professing church today? How they count up their numbers, the wealth and worldly importance of their "membership"; their great churches, cathedrals and universities; their worldly influence—even to the extent of having a lobby at the seat of government to "control legislation"! The Laodicean church would fain "reform" the world that crucified the Lord. It denounces as "pessimists" those who would show from Scripture that "evil men and seducers are waxing worse and worse," "the love of the many waxing cold," "the rulers of the age coming to nought," and Christ's personal return the only hope either for the Church or for the nations.

"Need of nothing": the loss of a sense of need, as the drowsiness that besets a freezing man, is *fatal*. People blindly go to hell in droves, in the Laodicean churches of these last days. With liars, blasphemers of the Lord, and teachers of pagan evolution in the pulpits, and the people "loving to have it so," we would cry, as of old, "What will ye do in the end thereof?"

"The wretched one"—of all the seven! That is, of all possible church states represented by these seven, Laodicea is the worst off! Worse than Thyatira, than Romanism, this last lukewarmness.

"And poor," alas! the *poverty*, in view of *their possible riches in Christ and His Word* and the *presence of the Holy Spirit!* The poverty of the Laodicean churches of this hour! Whole years, and no one born again! Whole denominations shrinking in numbers! "And miserable," literally, proper objects of *pity*. "Blind," looking at stones and towers and organs, and pews.

PREDICTED ACTION: **I am about to spew thee out of my mouth.** Darby says that "this threat is peremptory, not conditional: it brought irreconcilable rejection." The book of Revelation indeed plainly shows that the Church, having failed, will give way to the kingdom, to the Lord's personal appearing. But Christ does not say, "I *will*"; but, *(mello)* "I am *about to*." He says, "I am ready to: I have it in my mind, implying graciously the possibility of the threat not being executed if only they repent at once. His dealings towards them will depend on theirs toward Him." These words from Fausset more nearly express what the text sets forth.

LOVING COUNSEL: **I counsel thee to buy of me gold refined by fire, that thou mayest become rich.** Grace is ever free. We buy it "without money and without price," although it cost Christ the fire of God's judgment to get it for us. **And white garments, that thou mayest clothe thyself, and that the shame of thy nakedness be not made manifest.** White garments in the Bible, and especially in The Revelation, stand for manifested righteousness. If they would repent, and rely wholly upon Christ as the only righteousness of sinners, the world would see that instead of the shame of their nakedness. The world today sees the nakedness of the Laodicean church and has contempt for it, but the full *shame* of that nakedness will not be made manifest till the false church is rejected as Christ's witness on earth, and hated as a harlot by the Beast and his ten kings (Revelation 17:16).

And eyesalve to anoint thine eyes, that thou mayest see. "The Holy Spirit's unction, like the ancient's eyesalve, first smarts with the conviction of sin, then heals."

As many as I love, I reprove and chasten: be zealous, therefore, and repent. Astonishing love of the Savior! Loving even the lukewarm! Loving an assembly that has really no heart for Him! "I reprove"—Christ's wounding is the faithful wounding of a friend. "The ear that hearkeneth to the reproof of life shall abide among the wise" (Proverbs 15:31).

How many preachers love the saints enough to risk their resentment by obeying II Timothy 4:2: "reprove, rebuke"? I fear that we who preach are rarely as faithful in our love as our Lord!

"And chasten." As long as one's conscience *feels the reproof* of faithful preachers; as long as the Lord does not say, "He is joined to his idols, let him alone," there is hope. "Be zealous, therefore, and repent." I believe that "no word from God shall be void of power," and that some Laodiceans, through the church centuries, have, by divine grace, become zealous and repented. Only a godly sorrow, working the seven-fold result of II Corinthians 7:11, avails in such a case.

LAST YEARNING PLEA: **Behold, I stand at the door and knock: if any man hear my voice and open the door, I will come in to him, and will sup with him,***

---

*"The supper is the evening meal, it is the last taken before the morning breaks and the day dawns. It is long since the apostle said 'the night is far spent, the day is at hand': to sup with Christ before morning breaks is a foretaste of the coming glory—the antepast of heaven."—Ottman.

and he with me. Here we have *Christ in all His tenderness, His unfathomable devotion!* In these last words to the Church, *the love of the Bridegroom makes Him forget wholly the work of the Judge.* It is *The Beloved,* of the Song of Solomon (Song of Solomon 5:2).

This final plea of the Lord Jesus to the individual heart, where He has been shut out of the love and fellowship of the general company, *should win every heart that* UNDERSTANDS!

1. It is the plea of One who is meek and lowly of heart,—of a humility that is boundless and absolute. If we find ourselves shut out, where we have a right to be, we either rise to assert our rights, or leave in wrath. Not so Christ! After all the centuries, He still stands meekly knocking!

2. It is the plea of an active, *yearning love.* If the Lord Jesus did not *love* those who profess His name, even His lowliness would not keep Him at the door which is shut!

3. It is the plea of *deepest concern.* He knows what *losing Him* will mean,—what *a Christless future* will be. He was *troubled* over even Judas, who had already bargained to sell Him for the price of a common slave!

It is deeply instructive and touching to note the verb tenses here: it is literally, "Behold I have taken my stand at the door and am knocking": the first denoting an attitude deliberately taken, and the second, an action continually going on.

While the whole assembly in the person of its angel is addressed, we all instinctively feel and know that the words are personal to *us,*—yes, to the innermost heart of each of us, of you, of me. For the pleading voice goes on, "If any man hear my voice and open the door." Here we are face to face with three great facts: First, the awful fact that people can "belong" to an assembly of Christ's, and yet *not* hear, *never* hear, Christ's life-giving *Voice;* Second, the blessed fact that anyone may hearken who will; and, Third, the eternally solemn fact that the opening of the door is *from our side, not from Christ's.*

It is the action of unbelief to abuse the glorious truth of electing grace by making fatalism of it, thus seeking to lay the burden of an evil heart's unwillingness upon God. *"How often would I—but ye would not!"*

"I will sup *with him*": and what have we to give Him? What have we that He *could* wish, what that would give *Him* delight,—the Lord of glory? He *loves* thee! It is as the Bridegroom of the Church that He speaks,—"who loved the church, and gave himself for it." Of course His joy will be the *first,* and infinitely the greater! So He puts it first. Then, "he with Me." Those who open the door to Christ are the happy ones of the earth!

"I sat down under his shadow with great delight,
And his fruit was sweet to my taste.
He brought me to the banqueting-house,
And his banner over me was love."

Song of Solomon 2:3, 4.

Here, at the end of these seven church epistles, in this twentieth verse, we have the *second* of the two great truths of Paul's gospel: (1) ye *in Christ,* and (2) Christ *in you.* Paul begins to develop this second truth in Galatians: "It was the good pleasure of God . . . *to reveal his Son in me*" (1:16); "It is no longer I that live, but *Christ liveth in me*" (2:20); "My little children, of whom I am again in travail until Christ be formed in you" (4:19); then in Ephesians 3:14-19, "that Christ may make *his home down in your hearts,*"—a definite thing, as yet unaccomplished in the Ephesian believers to whom he wrote; and in Philippians 1:21, *"for me to live is Christ";* and in Colossians 1:27, *"Christ in you, the hope of glory"!* In a real definite sense Christ is in *every* true believer. See Romans 8:9, 10; where we read that all of Christ's own, because they have the indwelling Spirit, have Christ in them as their *life* (Colossians 3:3, 4). "Know ye not as to your own selves, that Jesus Christ is in you? unless indeed ye be reprobate" (II Corinthians 13:5). But in Revelation 3:20 there is a personal call,

like that of Ephesians 5:14: "Awake, thou that sleepest,
and arise from the dead, and Christ shall shine upon
thee."

How our poor selfish hearts turn to the next verse—
about the coming kingdom, and our *reigning* with Christ;
and forget His present, tender pleading for real, inward
fellowship with Him now!

PROMISE TO OVERCOMERS: **He that over-
cometh, I will give to him to sit down with me in my
throne, as I also overcame, and sat down with my
Father in his throne.** Christ's throne is the throne of
His father David at Jerusalem (II Samuel 7:12, 13, 16;
I Chronicles 29:3; Jeremiah 3:17; Luke 1:32; Acts 15:
14-18). But our Lord's royal inheritance by the Davidic
covenant extends to His heavenly Bride, the Church, as
Eve shared the dominion that God gave the first Adam.
In his first epistle (first in divine order), Paul writes,
"Concerning God's Son, who was born of the seed of
David according to the flesh" (Romans 1:3); and in
his last epistle, "Remember Jesus Christ, risen from the
dead, of the seed of David according to my gospel" (II
Timothy 2:8). We shall consider the millennial order in
Revelation 20. Here, in 3:21, at the close of the unfaithful corporate testimony of the Church, we are again
overwhelmed at this *infinite grace* of Christ. "The assembly whom Christ just before threatened to spew out
of His mouth, is now offered a seat with Him on His
throne."—Fausset. Trench truly says, "The highest
place is within the reach of the lowest; the faintest spark
of grace may be fanned into the mightiest flame of love."
Let not the most wretched, defeated believer despair,—if
only there be the least yearning for Christ. The most tender
plea of all the seven is made to a *lukewarm* assembly.
And the most distinct promise of actually sitting down
with Christ upon His throne is given at the very close
of the Church's testimony. Note that our Lord speaks
as one who Himself overcame, and is therefore now sit-

ting upon His Father's throne.* As a Victor He calls
to you and to me. It is only in *sharing by faith His victory* that any saint ever overcame! As Christ warned in
the upper room, "In the world ye shall have tribulation:
but *be of good cheer, I have overcome the world*" (John
16:33). He also triumphed over Satan and all his hosts
at Calvary, and *gives us the benefit* (Colossians 2:14, 15;
Hebrews 2:14, 15). "And *this is the victory* that overcometh—even *our faith*" (I John 5:4).

THE FINAL CALL TO HEAR: Saints of God
beloved, let the world go by and *give ear: "The time is
short!"* Your salvation is nearer than when you first
believed: "He that hath an ear, let him hear." The world
is full of voices today, calling you to hearken to what
man is, and has done, and will do, but be thou one of
whom some day your Lord will gladly say: "He had *an
ear*, and *heard My Voice!*"

---

*Our Lord is not now on His own throne, the throne of David. He is at the
Father's right hand, on the Father's throne, and is now the Great High Priest,
leading the worship of His saints; and also our Advocate against the enemy.
But He is there in an *expectant* attitude, as we read in Hebrews 10:12, 13:
"He, when he had offered one sacrifice for sins for ever, sat down at the right
hand of God; *henceforth expecting* till his enemies be made the footstool of
his feet."

THE LAST KNOCK

Art thou weary, sad, and lonely,
　　All thy summer past?
One remaineth, and One only—
　　Hear His Voice at last.

Voice that called thee all unheeded,
　　Love that knocked in vain;
Now, forsaken, dost thou need it?
　　Hear that Voice again.

"Open to Me, my beloved,
　　I have waited long,
Till the night fell on the glory,
　　Silence on the song;

"Till the brightness and the sweetness,
    And the smiles were fled,
Till thy heart was worn and broken—
    Till thy love was dead.

"Thou wouldst none of Me, beloved,
    Yet beloved wert thou;
Thou didst scorn Me in the sunshine,
    Wilt thou have Me now?

"Soul, for thee I left My glory,
    Bore the curse of God—
Wept for thee with bitterest weeping,
    Agony and blood.

"Soul, for thee I died dishonoured,
    As a felon dies;
For thou wert the pearl all priceless
    In thy Saviour's eyes.

"Soul, for thee I rose victorious,
    Glad that thou wert free;
Entered Heaven in triumph glorious—
    Heaven I won for thee.

"Soul, from Heaven I speak to woo thee—
    Thee, the lost, the lone;
Earth may fail thee, sin undo thee,
    All the more Mine own.

"Sorrow, sin, and desolation,
    These thy claim to Me;
Love that won thee full salvation,
    This My claim to thee.

"Soul, I knock, I stand beseeching,
    Turn me not away;
Heart that craves thee, love that needs thee—
    Wilt thou say Me nay?"

By V. M.

From *Hymns of Ter Steegen, Suso and Others* published by **Loizeaux** Brothers, New York. Used by permission.

THE THINGS AFTER CHURCH THINGS

The professing Church having failed, and been judged and rejected as God's house, must now be superseded by the *Coming and Kingdom of the Lord Himself*. So we enter upon what our Lord calls "the things that shall come to pass *after* the present (or Church) things." (See Chapter 1:19.)

We must, however, be *transferred to heaven* to view the great scene of our Lord's receiving the Kingdom at the hands of His Father and by the energy of the Spirit.

Daniel, the prophet, saw the same glorious sight (Daniel 7): the Ancient of Days enthroned, and "One like unto a son of man brought near before him" and given "dominion, and glory, and a kingdom, that all the peoples, and languages should serve him." Daniel was *not invited to heaven,* but saw all in "night-visions." There was no "Come up hither." Daniel was not of the Church, but of God's earthly people, Israel; and while he saw heavenly visions, was not taken to heaven to see them. John, when church things ended with Laodicea, hears (as will all the true Church), the Lord's words, "Come up hither, and I will show thee"—the *next* things, those that come *after these* (Church) things. Thus we come now to Revelation *4 and 5,* the Second Section of the book, and the first *directly prophetic* part.

CHAPTER III

THE THRONE OF ADJUDICATION IN HEAVEN
Revelation 4, 5

Revelation Four—The Throne Set in Heaven

Read this chapter over and over, and also chapter five; for they introduce the whole prophetic part of The Revelation.

After these things I saw, and behold, a door opened in heaven, and the first voice that I heard, a voice as of a trumpet speaking with me, one saying, Come up hither, and I will show thee the things which must come to pass after these things. Straightway I was in the Spirit: and behold, there was a throne set in heaven, and one sitting upon the throne; and he that sat was to look upon like a jasper stone and a sardius: and there was a rainbow round about the throne, like an emerald to look upon. And round about the throne were four and twenty thrones: and upon the thrones I saw four and twenty elders sitting, arrayed in white garments; and on their heads crowns of gold. And out of the throne proceed lightnings and voices and thunders. And there were seven lamps of fire burning before the throne, which are the seven Spirits of God; and before the throne, as it were a sea of glass like unto crystal; and in the midst of the throne, and round about the throne, four living creatures full of eyes before and behind. And the first creature was like a lion, and the second creature like a calf, and the third creature had a face as of a man, and the fourth creature was like a flying eagle. And the four living creatures, having each one of them six wings, are full of eyes round about and within: and they have no rest day and night, saying,

Holy, holy, holy, is the Lord God, the Al-

> mighty, who was and who is and who is
> to come.
>
> And when the living creatures shall give
> glory and honor and thanks to him that sitteth
> on the throne, to him that liveth for ever and
> ever, the four and twenty elders shall fall down
> before him that sitteth on the throne, and shall
> worship him that liveth for ever and ever, and
> shall cast their crowns before the throne,
> saying,
>
>> Worthy art thou, our Lord and our God,
>> to receive the glory and the honor and the
>> power: for thou didst create all things,
>> and because of thy will they were, and
>> were created.

To *adjudicate* is defined as "determining judicially conflicting claims"; and so we use the word here. Whether some creature, or whether Christ alone, shall take over the bringing back of judgment to righteousness is the question. When Christ stood before Pilate, *righteousness* was on His side, but *judgment* was in the hands of the Roman governor. Here the time has come to return judgment unto righteousness.

Consider that *the Throne of God,* which was not in sight in the first three chapters of The Revelation, now comes into view; and so prominently, and in such character, from chapter 4 onward, as to make The Revelation become, "the Book of The Throne."

The Throne was not seen when God walked with His first man Adam, in the garden. But later we read, "Jehovah sat *as king* at the Flood" (Psalm 29:10). Here it was for judgment, not worship.

The Throne is not seen in the history of Abraham or the patriarchs, for they were walking by simple faith, and were the depositaries of promises. They were not connected with a manifested Throne, but built *altars* for *worship*.

When God brought Israel out of Egypt, He had a nation for His name, and dwelt among them in glory (although Himself in thick darkness), sitting above the cherubim of the ark of the covenant, which was a type of the Throne on high.

Isaiah saw Him thus in the temple,—the *seraphim* above Him, crying, "Holy, holy, holy," and Ezekiel saw "the appearance of the likeness of the glory of Jehovah" enthroned upon the *cherubim.*

It is quite astonishing in view of such holiness and glory to find written in I Chronicles 29:23, "Then Solomon sat on the throne of Jehovah as king, instead of David his father." It will not be until our Lord returns to take that throne of David (as He *will*—Luke 1:32, 33) that it will again become "the throne of Jehovah." Christ will *inherit* it, as Son of David, but it was to David that it was promised (II Samuel 7:11-16). Our Lord will then reign as "a Priest upon his throne"—the full Melchizedek figure. This is "the tabernacle of David," a phrase quoted in Acts 15:16, 17, from Amos 9:11, 12. It is the millennial time.

That men like David and Solomon and their successors, should sit upon "the throne of Jehovah" is not as wonderful as that "unto us a child is born" and His Name shall be called, "The Mighty God"! Also, as in all other revelations of God's plan, men were to have the opportunity along all lines to undertake and to fail; and thus make room for *Christ,* in whom alone are all the real purposes and plans of God.

"Jehovah hath established his throne in the heavens;

And his kingdom ruleth over all." Psalm 103:19.

This is true from the beginning and through all dispensations. Generally speaking, His government has been hidden, in what is called "providence." If you desire to trace how fully God rules *behind the scenes,* study, for example, the book of Proverbs, noting that God declares how each course of life will *turn out:* the wicked, the righteous, the slothful, the diligent, etc. *Who makes things thus "turn out"?*

"Jehovah sitteth *as king* forever:
He hath *prepared* his throne for judgment;
And he will judge the world in righteousness,
He will minister judgment to the peoples in uprightness." Psalm 9:7, 8.

It is this *prepared Throne* that comes into view in Daniel 7:9: "I beheld till thrones were placed, and one that was ancient of days did sit"; as also in Revelation 4:2, "Behold, there was a throne set in heaven." It will be a *special arranging of the divine Throne of majesty,* for dealing in *manifested judgment,* although God is not now so dealing.

Today God is on the throne of GRACE: "God was in Christ, reconciling the world unto himself, not reckoning unto them their trespasses." The world's sin having been dealt with by God at Calvary, and thus all God's holy, righteous claims having been met, yea, and the world "reconciled" with His holy being, from God's side, the One sinned against, God sends forth His messengers to beseech men from *their* side to be *reconciled to God!* Furthermore, the believer is invited to come with boldness (literally, *freeness, freespokenness)* to this "Throne of *Grace"* (Hebrews 4:16).

"The throne of God and of the Lamb," the *eternal* manifestation of the divine Throne, as we shall note at the end of Revelation, is of unmeasured comfort: a *Throne,* certainly, necessarily, but—"they see *his face,* his *name* is on their foreheads"; and the *Lamb,* although Himself God, is forever Man,—"a Lamb as it had been slain," and He sits thus on the Throne! "The throne of God and of the Lamb"—*forever!*

In Revelation, chapters 4 and 5, we find God's Throne set in peculiar character before us. In fact, the scene of Revelation 4 precisely corresponds to that of Daniel 7:9: "I beheld till thrones were placed and one that was ancient of days did sit," John's words being, "And behold, there was a throne SET in heaven" (Revelation 4:2).

Let us note the particulars of this Throne, and the character of the worship:

1. The Throne of the Triune Eternal God "set" in heaven (as in Daniel 7) surrounded by a rainbow (Genesis 9).

2. The twenty-four elders* crowned and on thrones about the Throne of God.

3. The "lightnings"—"voices"—"t h u n d e r s ": these powers of nature made intelligent to man in judgment.

4. The "seven lamps of fire"—"the seven Spirits of God"; that is, complete active discernment of all matters and affairs in judgment,—the Holy Spirit: but in governmental administration, not as the "Comforter" of saints, and as Revealer of Christ to sinners, as now.

5. The glassy sea before the Throne: manifested eternal holiness and purity; (not, as now, the approach to the Throne of Grace!).

6. The "four living creatures"† (or, *living beings*). The cherubim who support the divine Throne (as in Ezekiel) intelligent fully of His ways in majesty.

7. God's *creatorship* declared by the living beings and the elders to be the basis of their worship (4:11).

We have seen in 1:19 the Lord's commission to John to write "the things which thou sawest"—the vision of the glorious Christ among the churches; "and the things which are" (now existing—that is the seven churches covering prophetically the whole church age) "and the things which shall come to pass after these."

It is very necessary that we grasp firmly this divine division of this great book of The Revelation, so we repeat it: Christ is speaking in Revelation 1:19, of the subjects of which John is to write. Literally, that verse

---

*See Appendix II on the twenty-four elders.

†The old rendering "beasts" is not a happy translation of this wonderful Greek expression *zoa*. Such a translation doubtless arose from a cumbersome attention to the described forms or appearances of these four living beings. God's designation of them gives only the number four and the fact that they are (as their four generic forms reveal) the very embodiment of created life. Their name *zoa* cannot be duplicated by any single word in our language. It indicates that they are real, literal beings, and that they are vibrant with life in every direction and degree. The fact that they are "full of eyes before and behind round about and within" and that they have "no rest day and night" (and need none) proves this. They celebrate constantly the being of the Lord God the Almighty, the Eternal, Thrice Holy One; seeming in this celebration and worship to join with the twenty-four elders constantly in adoration. This is their eternal occupation (4:9-11).

reads, "Write therefore what you saw, and what are being, and what is about to become after these." So, in
The Revelation, first *Christ* is seen in His personal risen
glory; then, we see the professing *Church,* which as His
witness upon earth finally proves as false as Israel, and
is "spewed out of his mouth"; and, third, we have the
earth's *governmental history* after the Church's rejection
by Christ, until His return to establish His kingdom.
During this third period, the true Church is, of course,
in heaven, though not in any sense manifested there until
the marriage supper of the Lamb in chapter 19.

There are several reasons why chapter 4 *succeeds
in time* chapters 2 and 3. Let us examine the opening verses:

1. **After these things** (Greek, *meta tauta*). This expression is most important, as we shall find throughout
the book. It may mean merely a new vision, or a new
phase of a vision, as in chapter 7:9. But in view of
chapter 1:19, the use of the phrase in 4:1 is quite indicative of *a change from the church matters* of chapters
2 and 3 *to an entirely different scene and subject.*

2. **A door was opened in heaven** as if for entrance or
egress (see 19:11). It is indeed for John's *entrance,* and
evidently, the whole Church is represented here! For
"churches" are mentioned not once after chapter 3, till
the apocalypse is *over!* 22:16.

3. **The first voice which I heard.** We know this is
the voice that John heard in chapter 1, the Lord's own
voice. He now speaks again to John, not as Himself upon
Patmos, but as from heaven.

4. **As of a trumpet.** Compare I Thessalonians 4:16,
"The Lord himself . . . with an assembling shout, with
the voice of the archangel, and with the *trump of God*";
and also I Corinthians 15:52—"The *trumpet* shall sound,
and the dead shall be raised incorruptible."

5. **Come up hither.** John had heretofore spoken of
those church things about which The Revelation concerned itself—namely, the state of the churches as wit-
ness-bearers *on earth.* He is now called up *to heaven,* as

if the course of things of which he had been speaking *was altogether over,* and he was henceforth to look at future things from the *heavenly* side.

6. The Lord's further words, **I will show thee the things which must come to pass. After these things,** surely indicate that the matters about to be revealed to the apostle succeed in time of occurrence those matters already considered in chapters 2 and 3.

7. Furthermore, upon examining the scenes following Revelation 4:1, we find as we say above, *no mention of the "churches,"* until The Revelation itself is over, and the Lord Jesus is setting His personal seal to it in chapter 22:16 ff. There, of course, The Revelation having been *sent* to the assemblies, our Lord speaks to them.

But it is of primary importance that the student of The Revelation leave the earth with John (in spirit) in Revelation 4:2 and not return until the Lord returns, *with* His saints, in Revelation 19:11.

There is evidently in these chapters 4 and 5 *a returning to the* Throne of God, and *a new beginning.* Church things are fully over (chapters 2 and 3).

The Throne, then, of Revelation 4, will have peculiar features displayed befitting the event. It is not merely a description of divine majesty, but that revelation of it that belongs to the matter in hand. It will not, for example, be like the "Great White Throne" of Revelation 20:11-15—the last judgment scene. There, of course, Deity is unveiled in absolute finality of judicial holiness and brightness. There, the heaven and earth have *fled away.* Final *eternal* issues, and *these only* are there involved. But here in chapters 4 and 5, the question is, Who shall execute the "judgments written" regarding *this earth,* and vindicate God's ways in its *government?*

But the Triune Eternal God—worshipped thus in 4:8, "Holy, Holy, Holy, *is* the Lord God, the Almighty, who was and who is and who is to come," is first revealed. In chapter 4 He is worshipped as the Creator, by the living creatures and the twenty-four elders. His appearance, indeed, according to 4:3 "like a jasper stone and sardius . . . clear as crystal" (21:11) sets forth His holiness in *essence* rather than in action, (as on the Great White Throne). There are, indeed, "lightnings," "voices" and "thunders" proceeding out of the Throne, indicating power and intelligence, acting in judgment.*

There was a rainbow round about the throne. This reminds us at once of God's covenant with Noah and every living creature of Genesis 9. The emerald is the fourth of the stones of the foundation of the City, as seen in Revelation 21:19. We might say that even this *number* 4 is indicative, as being the *earth* number; but, be that as it may, the fact of the rainbow round about the throne here described, must indicate God's calling the inhabitants of the earth to account for their "breaking of the everlasting covenant," as described in Isaiah 24:5. The "everlasting covenant" is the particular name by which God designates that agreement with Noah and all terrestrial creation recorded in Genesis 9:8-17. In this remarkable passage the word "covenant" is repeated seven times, and in verse 12 it is declared by God to be made "between me and you and every living creature that is with you for perpetual generations"; while in verse 16, "I will look upon it, that I may remember the everlasting covenant between God and all flesh that is upon the earth." The human conditions were: to be fruitful and multiply *(9:1);* to eat animal food as well as vegetable *(9:3);* to abstain from eating blood *(9:4);* and to shed the blood of murderers—that is, to continue capital punishment *(9:6)*—because to strike at man was to strike at the image of God in which he was made!

Now the Isaiah passage *(24:1-13)* which describes in a few verses the terrific visitations of judgment to come upon the earth prior to the coming of the Lord (for it

---

*How significant is the occurrence of the word *voices* between the *lightnings* and *thunders* which we now know in nature! Compare 8:5; 11:19; 16:18. Compare these verses with Exodus 19:16—God's appearance upon the top of Sinai. Also note that in Revelation 8:5: "There followed thunders, and voices, and lightnings" as if God had said, "You who rely on your knowledge of scientific facts, hearken while the thunders precede the lightnings and between the two are solemn voices showing the intelligent power that really produces all these things." How blind is human science which leaves out God!

is not the final burning up of the earth that is there pictured) gives as the reason for these terrible things: "The earth is polluted under the inhabitants thereof because they have transgressed the laws, violated the statutes, *broken the everlasting covenant.*"

Now the "laws" may well refer to the laws of man's own being, which we know from our Lord's words concerning the Sodom-like days which will precede His return, will be universally transgressed. The days before the flood were days of lust and violence, as the days of Lot were times of unnatural departing from the very laws of human being. "The statutes" may include such fundamental and universally recognized relations as those of the family—as to husband and wife, brother, sister and parental authority, and also obedience to the powers that be. These things we find written into the constitution and conscience of all people, even those that have had no contact with God's written Word. The "everlasting covenant" has been noted with its conditions, which every one knows are all openly ignored in our own days. Birth control in defiance of "be fruitful and multiply"; vegetarianism, despising God's distinct command to eat flesh as well as herbs and fruit (for flesh-eating protects the human body from demoniacal control), and finally the awful rejection of that fundamental ordinance of human government, the death penalty to murderers:—these things indicate the trend toward that condition which will be brought about in the preliminary judgments of Revelation 6 to 18.

"Few men (shall be) left," says Isaiah, "For thus shall it be in the midst of the earth among the peoples, as the shaking of an olive-tree, as the gleanings when the vintage is done."

People conceive of the "millennium" as the time of great peace and plenty on earth, whereas it will be introduced by the most awful day this world has ever known— the great Day of Wrath of God, the Almighty, and that Day of Wrath will be preceded by years of visitations so terrible as to decimate the population of the earth.

The Millennium, or thousand years' reign, will indeed
be a time of peace, but it will be peace by an iron-rod
rule in the hands of the Lord Himself and it will be
preceded by catastrophic judgments after which "there
shall be left therein gleanings, as the shaking of an olive-
tree, two or three berries in the top of the uppermost
bough, four or five in the outmost branches of a fruitful
tree, saith Jehovah, the God of Israel. In that day shall
men look unto their Maker, and their eyes shall have
respect to the Holy One of Israel."

We speak of these things merely to prepare our hearts
to believe what we shall see in the coming chapters of
Revelation. The voices of the prophets are one as to the
"day which the Lord shall make." Hear one more
prophet—Zephaniah. "The great day of Jehovah is near,
it is near and hasteth greatly, *even* the voice of the day
of Jehovah; the mighty man crieth there bitterly. That
day is a day of wrath, a day of trouble and distress, a
day of wasteness and desolation, a day of darkness and
gloominess, a day of clouds and thick darkness . . . And
I will bring distress upon men, that they shall walk like
blind men, because they have sinned against Jehovah; and
their blood shall be poured out as dust, and their flesh
as dung."

The Slain Lamb Takes the Book of Judgment

(Read Revelation, Chapters 4 and 5, over and over.
They are *one passage*. They contain the key to the rest
of Revelation.)

> And I saw in the right hand of him that sat
> on the throne a book written within and on
> the back, close sealed with seven seals. And
> I saw a strong angel proclaiming with a great
> voice, Who is worthy to open the book, and to
> loose the seals thereof? And no one in the
> heaven, or on the earth, or under the earth,
> was able to open the book, or to look thereon.
> And I wept much, because no one was found
> worthy to open the book, or to look thereon:

and one of the elders saith unto me, Weep not;
behold, the Lion that is of the tribe of Judah,
the Root of David, hath overcome to open the
book and the seven seals thereof. And I saw
in the midst of the throne and of the four living creatures, and in the midst of the elders,
a Lamb standing, as though it had been slain,
having seven horns, and seven eyes, which are
the seven Spirits of God, sent forth into all
the earth. And he came, and he hath taken it
out of the right hand of him that sat on the
throne. And when he had taken the book, the
four living creatures and the four and twenty
elders fell down before the Lamb, having each
one a harp, and golden bowls full of incense
which are the prayers of the saints. And they
sing a new song, saying,

> Worthy art thou to take the book, and to
> open the seals thereof: for thou wast slain,
> and didst purchase unto God with thy
> blood out of every tribe, and tongue, and
> people, and nation, and madest them to be
> unto our God a kingdom and priests; and
> they (shall) reign upon the earth.

And I saw, and I heard a voice of many
angels round about the throne and the living
creatures and the elders; and the number of
them was ten thousand times ten thousand,
and thousands of thousands; saying with a
great voice,

> Worthy is the Lamb that hath been slain
> to receive the power, and riches, and wis-
> dom, and might, and honor, and glory,
> and blessing.

And every created thing which is in the
heaven, and on the earth, and under the earth,
and on the sea, and all things that are in them,
heard I saying,

> Unto him that sitteth on the throne, and
> unto the Lamb, be the blessing, and the
> honor, and the glory, and the dominion,
> for ever and ever.
> And the four living creatures said, Amen.
> And the elders fell down and worshipped.

Note these seven facts in chapter five:

1. The seven-sealed book: fully written, ready to be opened, close-sealed, indicating finality and privacy.

2. All creation's utter inability even to look upon this book.

3. John's overwhelming sorrow at apparent delay of God's longed-for kingdom.

4. The Lion of Judah declared to have "overcome" and be ready to open the book.

5. The slain Lamb revealed in the midst of the throne, with seven horns of perfect power, and seven eyes, "the seven Spirits of God," sent forth into earth's affairs in utter discernment.

6. His formal coming and taking the book from the hand of God. This is that taking over of governmental power by the Mediator which is the burden of Old Testament prophecy, (and of all our hearts!) and all creation's celebration thereof! *(verses 7-14.)*

7. Worship now founded not merely upon creation, but upon *redemption*. "Worthy art thou . . . for thou wast *slain*" *(verses 9, 12)*.

The second character in which our Lord is seen in the book of Revelation is that of *the Slain Lamb,* now invested and exalted, opening the seven-sealed book written with the divine order of events, by which Christ is put in actual possession and active exercise of the kingdom denied Him when He was on earth before.

These two chapters (4 and 5) naturally become the most majestic and overwhelming of any portion of Scripture up to this point. They reveal that tremendous event toward which God the Father has been bending all events of the history of creation—*the investiture of Jesus* (who obeyed Him even unto death, yea, the death of the cross), with that inheritance of glory, honor, dominion and power which brings "every created thing which is in the heaven, and on the earth, and under the earth, and on the sea, and all things that are in them" to acknowledge aloud His place and majesty *(Revelation 5:13)*.

If we have followed the "spirit of prophecy" from the beginning of Scripture until this book of Revelation, and have found that *Jesus* is its constant testimony, we are prepared for the blessed scene of chapter 5. Because all creation has utterly failed to take over the business of carrying out the due judgment of God written in the sealed book, we hail with great delight this public (and that an absolutely universally public!) handing over of this book of judgment, to our Lord *as the Lamb that was slain.*

"A Lamb . . . as though it had been *slain.*" Do we wonder that the One who was so devoted to the will of God as to die in obedience to it,—so committed to holiness and righteousness as to be *slain* rather than submit to sin, should now be deemed worthy to take this book of judgment and open its seals? This thought of the *wounds* of Christ, blessed *comfort* to His own, (John 20:20) will strike stark *terror* to His enemies! For the *slain* Lamb *cannot* compromise with the iniquity they love!

Why are harps and bowls full of incense, which are the prayers of the saints (5:8), connected with the Lamb's taking the book of the inheritance? Did the prayers of the saints bring about this scene? Would our Lord have commanded His disciples to pray "Thy kingdom come, Thy will be done, as in heaven, so on earth," if (a) God had not meant to bring this to pass, and (b) if the prayers of the saints were not a vital factor in bringing about this glorious result? Follow through the book of Revelation whatever is said about the prayers of the saints. Some day it will be found that every soul that has been saved, every blessing any saint has received, every thwarting of Satan, every victory for God, as well as this final consummation of our Lord's taking over the book of the kingdom—all have been brought about through the saints' prayers, inspired of God, as essential elements in His great, all-comprehensive purpose.

How, in verse 9, is the worth of the Lamb brought out by His having been slain? We ask this again. Just why should our Lord's obeying the Father *even unto death* make Him the One to take over from the hand of His God and Father all judgment? Please study this. Do not pass it lightly.

John "wept much" when no one was found worthy even to *look* on this book.*

It was as if sin and Satan were to go on forever in the usurped control of affairs in this world. It was as if it must still be written:

> Right forever on the scaffold,
> Wrong forever on the throne.

The apostle was broken-hearted about this. The Greek indicates that he burst into tears of sorrow. The same word is used of our Lord in His weeping over Jerusalem. It would be well if we had the intense longing of the apostle John that the kingdom of God should come, that His will should be done on earth as it is in heaven; it would be well if even the thought of the continuation of evil should give us deepest anguish!

It is to be feared that oft our knowledge that our Lord is to return to earth to "straighten things out" has been the occasion of the temptation to a kind of spiritual patience with iniquity, that is hardening and deadening. We need to "vex our righteous souls" as Lot did, as we see their "lawless deeds." And we need to long and pray for the great denouement of Revelation 5!

It should be noted that the four living beings and the four and twenty elders have each a harp (verse 8) which indicates glad celebration of victory; and golden bowls

---

*Note that the preposition in the first verse is "upon" *(epi)* and not *in*, the right hand. The book was not grasped by God, but offered for any one to take who could.

full of incense, which are the prayers of the saints. That is, it is the prayers of the saints of all ages that have *brought about* this taking over of the kingdom at last by God. "Thy kingdom come" has been the heart cry of every believer since Abel the righteous. Our Lord taught the disciples to pray this prayer with the express desire that His Father's will should be done *on this earth* as it is in heaven. It is the prayers of the saints which in divine providence bring about this "returning of judgment to righteousness."

Another fact, in verse 9: they sing this new kingdom song to the Lamb: "For thou wast slain, and didst purchase unto God with thy blood of every tribe, and tongue, and people, and nation, and madest them unto our God a kingdom and priests; and they reign upon the earth." Notice that these beings are not in ecstasy over their own salvation (the word "us" in verse 9, in the old version, should not be there) but their rejoicing is that redeemed men have been made a kingdom and priests and are to reign *upon the earth*. It is not the escape to heaven by redemption that is being rejoiced over here, but the near-at-hand establishment *upon earth* of a reign of God by means of these redeemed ones, that gives joy before the throne of God. We should keep this in mind throughout The Revelation. God is at last setting His hand to interfere with the earthly sinful order of things to the extent of completely setting aside earthly authority, after overturning it by dire judgments: then causing certain saints to reign with Christ *on earth* with a divine absolutism for a thousand years (Revelation 20), and then bringing in final judgment and the disappearance from the scene of the present heavens and earth. The objective of God is the new heavens and new earth wherein righteousness will be *at home* (Greek of II Peter 3:13). This should be our objective in thought, hope and prayer.

At last the angels are admitted into the circle (where the Church has ever been) of worshippers and celebrators of the Lamb that had been slain! What were the angels hitherto? (Hebrews 1:14). In Revelation 5:11, 12 we find Hebrews 1:6 fulfilled: "When he again bringeth in the firstborn into the world he saith, let all the angels of God worship him." This glorious advancement should be rejoiced in by us, for the angels have evermore been giving glad service in *our* behalf; and they have ever "desired to look into" the blessed things of grace connected with the gospel (I Peter 1:12).

The number of the angels is stated as one hundred millions, to begin with, and then millions and millions! When they see the Lamb that they saw slain, (knowing that He was the Eternal Son of God) now take over the book of the kingdom, do you wonder that they say with a great voice,"Worthy is the Lamb that hath been slain"? Have *you* spoken thus about the Lamb of God? No other theme is really worth shouting over!

When every created thing in heaven and on the earth and under the earth and on the sea and all things that are in them say, "Unto him that sitteth on the throne, and unto the Lamb, *be* the blessing, and the honor, and the glory, and the dominion, unto the ages of the ages," all infidels will be included, and all "modernist" preacher-infidels, all rejectors of Christ, all your family—saved or unsaved, all your loved ones—saved or lost alike! *No creature will be left out.* This great universal confession will not be for salvation, but it will be the fulfilling of Philippians 2:9-11: "Wherefore also God highly exalted him, and gave unto him the name, which is above every name; that in the name of Jesus every knee should bow, of *things* in heaven and *things* on earth and *things* under the earth, and that every tongue should confess that Jesus Christ is Lord, to the glory of God the Father."*

Why was the book *sealed?* Why was it written *within* and on the *back?* Remember, it requires lawful *authority* to break a seal. You seal a private communication to your friend when you have written it and are ready to deliver it.

---

*Contrast this passage carefully with that glorious prospect of the new creation recorded in Colossians 1:20, where "the things under the earth" are significantly omitted!

Each seal as it is broken by the Lamb will have a revelation from God therein; a revelation of His divine purpose toward Christ and through Christ. It certainly will be a blessed day when one after another we see Him break the seals of the written book and bring to pass what is written under each seal.

CHAPTER IV
SIX SEALS OPENED
Revelation 6

Let us now consider the seals of chapter 6. They cover the whole book to the new creation; for the *seventh* seal contains the seven trumpets, and the seventh trumpet the seven bowls of wrath of chapter 16 (which chapter really ends the revelation of the judgments preceding the Lord's second coming; chapters 17 and 18 being a detailed description of the judgment of Babylon the Great of 16:19).

Let us remember, as we have already directed, that the Lamb opens all the seals *while still in heaven* in the midst of the throne.

It should be noticed also that the four living beings have directly to do with the first four seals. They are connected with the execution of divine judgment, being full of intelligence concerning the divine will.

The First Seal

I saw when the Lamb opened one of the seven seals, and I heard one of the four living creatures saying as with a voice of thunder, Come. (The words "and see," of A. V., should not be there.) **And I saw, and behold, a white horse, and he that sat thereon had a bow; and there was given unto him a crown: and he came forth conquering, and to conquer.**

This horse and rider are plainly connected with *the holy hosts and armies that are in heaven.* Heaven is no longer engaged in grace but in judgment. "White horse"—this is holiness in exhibition and in warfare, for thus do white horses appear in Scripture. The rider has a bow, the weapon of long distance conflict. The Lord and the heavenly host are not yet coming *(for the rider symbolizes not only Christ but the whole heavenly host now exhibited as antagonistic to earth).* "Thine arrows are sharp; . . . in the heart of the king's enemies" is written in Psalm 45:5 of our Lord's coming.

102

"And there was given unto him a crown" denotes the fact that the Lord and the powers of heaven are to take the kingdom away from men, and rule for God!

"He came forth conquering, and to conquer." Some have amazingly conceived this white horse to represent the Antichrist! Not only would this be absolutely out of time (for the career of the Antichrist constitutes a woe under the seventh trumpet of the seventh seal) but how impossible to conceive of the Antichrist as conquering and *to* conquer—that is, to get the *final* victory. This is what the phrase, "conquering and to conquer" means— to achieve final and decisive conquest. And only Christ will ever do that. This first seal then indicates the Lord and the hosts of heaven turned against the earth: a most solemn thought! It is a public change from the day of grace.

The Second Seal

And when he opened the second seal, I heard the second living creature saying, Come. And another horse came forth, a red horse: and to him that sat thereon it was given to take peace from the earth, and that they should slay one another: and there was given unto him a great sword.

If coming events cast their shadows before them, as goes the proverb, surely we have today, in the frantic and ceaseless efforts of the statesmen and economists of earth to secure even the stability that existed a few years ago, a suggestion of the awful time indicated by this "red horse."

We are sure that the peace of the earth has not yet judicially been taken away, for there is still quietness and order for the most part—despite increasing sin. But when the Lord opens this second seal, universal distrust, plotting, and carnage will follow.

It should be remembered that any ordered, peaceful life on earth is purely the result of God's gracious intervention. The "hinderer" of II Thessalonians 2 is holding back human passions. But there will come a day when all the murderous evil of the human heart will be unleashed, and "they will slay one another."

Also, I am inclined to think that the "giving" to this second rider of "a great sword" may indicate such participation in human battles by angelic intervention as is frequently noted in the Old Testament. The Lord set "liers-in-wait" from His angelic hosts more than once: for example, II Chronicles 20:22; 14:13; II Samuel 5:24; II Kings 7:6.

The Third Seal

A black horse; and he that sat thereon had a balance . . . a voice in the midst of the four living creatures saying, a quart of wheat for a day's wage, and three quarts of barley for a day's wage; and the oil and the wine hurt thou not.

The choenix measure was about a quart, and a denarius is shown in Matthew 20:2 to be a common day's wage. What its money value was as compared with our day, has nothing to do with the subject. The denarius was evidently, from the New Testament, a day's wage. The laborers "agreed" to work for a denarius a day. Therefore we read, "a quart of wheat for a day's wage" showing a desperate condition!

That the oil and wine are to be spared indicates, it seems, that the rich have their luxuries despite the terrible scarcity among the poor. This would agree with the description in James 5:1-5 of the self-indulgence of the rich in the last days, for we must read in the R. V. "Ye have laid up your treasure in the last days."

On the other hand, James warns the rich of "their miseries that are coming upon them," *in this world,* as it seems to mean. Before the tribulation is over, yea, even now, the rich cry out. For the whole movement of "government" is to appropriate private property. See Russia, Italy, Germany, and the "New Deal" in America. But the very rich are seen here as still having their luxuries, under this third seal, and the great mass ground to poverty.

We noticed not long ago in a Chicago newspaper a paragraph reading about as follows: "By modern methods of agriculture we have solved the question of famine. We can produce any amount of grain we decide to produce. Science has triumphed over the constant dread of less enlightened communities," etc., etc.

How baleful statements so contrary to the predictions of Scripture become when dealt out to people that are ignorant enough to believe them! The most fearful days of famine this world has ever seen lie, we believe, not very far ahead.

The Fourth Seal

Behold, a pale horse: and he that sat upon him, his name was Death; and Hades followed with him. And there was given unto them authority over the fourth part of the earth, to kill with sword, and with famine, and with death, and by the wild beasts of the earth.

Now death takes the body, and Hades the spirit, of lost men. Death is so spoken of in Scripture as often almost to compel us to regard it as a personality. Mark, I do not say it is such, nor can I fully believe it to be. Nevertheless Scripture, the narration of others, and personal experience have taught me profoundly to believe that death is more than simple dissolution. When death seizes upon the body of an unbeliever, something happens vastly beyond the departure of the spirit and the cessation of the breath of life. A *terrible* seizure (said by Paul to have been the result of Adam's sin—*Romans 5:12*) occurs to those dying. Of the death of our Lord, Peter said *(Acts 2:24)* "God . . . loosed the pangs of death: because it was not possible that he should be holden of it" (for He was not personally a sinner).

Death in connection with Hades is mentioned in three places in The Revelation. In 1:18, our Lord "has the keys of death and of Hades." In 20:13 death and Hades give up the dead which were in them, death holding the body and Hades the spirit. (Those given up by the *sea* are not, in my judgment, human dead.)

Finally, death and Hades are cast into the lake of fire. Now, we know that the lake of fire is literal. (Isaiah 30:33 describes it and its antiquity, as well as its kindling to receive the Beast, the last "king" of the Gentiles, Revelation 19:20.) Whatever that power is that holds the bodies of men, it will be cast finally into the lake of fire, and will lose forever its power of dissolution. For the bodies of the damned will be indestructible. Hades also, now located in the center of this earth (Matthew 12:40 with Acts 2:31 and Ephesians 4:9) will be cast into the lake of fire.

But under the fourth seal we see death and Hades given authority over the fourth part of the earth to kill; and that with God's four sore judgments of Ezekiel 14:21, "sword," "famine," "pestilence" and "wild beasts." People say, "Peace," but the sword is coming. People cry, "Prosperity and plenty," but famine is coming. People boast of conquering disease by medical science, but pestilence is coming. Hunters complain of the disappearance of beasts to hunt, of game to pursue; but wild beasts will (by and by) multiply again, even in America, to the slaying of thousands upon thousands! We must remember that a fourth of the population of the earth is given over to these four judgments alone. And let us also remember that the plagues hurled directly from heaven, as in chapter 16, have not yet begun, under the four seals, not even the locust plague of chapter 9, nor the career of the wild beast of chapter 13. These come later.. But the sword, famine, pestilence, and wild beasts, take a quarter of earth's population.

The Fifth Seal

And when he opened the fifth seal, I saw underneath the altar the souls of them that had been slain for the word of God, and for the testimony which they held: and they cried with a great voice, saying, How long, O Master, the holy and true, dost thou not judge and avenge our blood on them that dwell on the earth? And there was given them to each one a white robe;

and it was said unto them, that they should rest yet for a little time, until their fellow-servants also and their brethren, who should be killed even as they were, should have fulfilled their course.

To Moses was given a pattern of the things in the heavens *(Hebrews 9:23)*. Therefore, there was an altar in heaven, or rather there *is* an altar. It was possibly thither that our Lord was going in John 20:17 to present Himself, according to Hebrews 9:12, as the Great High Priest. Underneath this altar in heaven are seen the souls (yet disembodied) of God's martyrs, evidently from Abel on. Their martyrdom has cried to heaven, as did Abel's blood, for vengeance. These souls give expression now to the change of dispensation from grace to judgment: "How long, O Master, the holy and true, dost thou not judge and avenge our blood on them that dwell on the earth?" The answer is, that God is delaying judgment—not for salvation purposes, *but that the rest of the martyrs may join their fellows!*

"There was given them to each one a white robe (manifested righteousness) and it was said unto them, that they should rest (note this—they are at rest, personally) yet for a little time, until (1) their fellow-servants also and (2) their brethren, who should be killed even as they were, should have fulfilled their course"—(keep these two classes in mind).

This fifth seal exhibits especially three things: First, the patience of God—"He proceeds slowly and reluctantly from mercy to judgment." Second, the change of dispensation evidenced in the character of the prayers of these martyrs for vengeance. Third, the utter wickedness of the earth which is plainly expected to go on *martyring the full complement of God's saints.*

The Sixth Seal

And I saw when he opened the sixth seal, and there was a great earthquake; and the sun became black as sackcloth of hair, and the whole moon became as blood; and the stars of the heaven fell unto the earth, as a fig tree casteth her unripe figs when she is shaken of a great wind. And the heaven was removed as a scroll when it is rolled up; and every mountain and island were moved out of their places. And the kings of the earth, and the princes, and the chief captains, and the rich, and the strong, and every bondman and freeman, hid themselves in the caves and in the rocks of the mountains, and they say to the mountains and to the rocks, Fall on us, and hide us from the face of him that sitteth on the throne, and from the wrath of the Lamb: for the great day of their wrath is come; and who is able to stand?

Note: 1. The earthquake. These are on the increase to-day. This will be a *great* one, for God is arising to "shake terribly the earth," for man's sin. It shook thus when Christ bare our guilt; and at His resurrection (Matthew 27:51; 28:2).

2. The *first* darkening of the sun and moon, "before the great and terrible day of the Lord" (Acts 2:20 quoting Joel 2:31). The *second* will be "immediately after the tribulation" (Matthew 24:29). But men in terror believe the end has come! When it does not, they grow hardened like Pharaoh, and we see them in Revelation 19:19 boldly gather to war against the Lamb whom here they dread!

3. Such a "removing" of the stars and of material "heaven" as probably to render visible thereafter what cannot now be seen.

4. Unlimited *terror* upon *all the earth,* at the world-wide dreaded wrath of Him upon the throne and of the Lamb: for the Bible has gone *everywhere;* and the Throne seems at this moment to be seen by all the earth!

But the particulars remain to be filled in *(chapters 8 to 16)* of those preliminary visitations from heaven which we find only result in men's refusing repentance and becoming hardened (except in the one instance in Jerusalem when the two witnesses are killed—chapter 11).

Meanwhile, we shall find God giving, in chapter 7, a vision of His election and salvation; and in the following chapters particulars of judgment under the seventh seal.

38. Compare Genesis 49:10 and Psalm 108:8). Christ is "the Lion of the tribe of Judah."

Reuben, the first born after the flesh, is next recognized, when divine sovereignty has been shown. Gad and Asher come next. Leah's sons by her handmaid, Zilpah! Surely the *flesh* is not being honored.

Next comes Naphtali, Rachel's son by her handmaid, Bilhah. Dan, Bilhah's first son, is left out altogether here. He was ever a cherisher of idolatry. Yet Dan is mentioned *first,* when the land is divided in Ezekiel 48, for the 1,000 year kingdom: which shows God's *grace!* And that Dan should be *preserved through* The Tribulation, though not publicly *sealed,* is greater grace still!

Manasseh, younger son of Joseph, is next, with Ephraim, the proud tribe of Judges 8 and 12, left out. Ephraim also was a synonym of idolatry, as seen in the prophet Hosea. Yet Ephraim is in the *kingdom* (Ezekiel 48:5).

Simeon and Levi are next. Jacob their father called them cruel men (Genesis 49:5-7). Grace remembers them, however.

Issachar and Zebulun, Leah's fifth and sixth sons, come next. Zebulun and Naphtali—from these despised regions "light sprang up" (Matthew 4:12-17).

Then Joseph is next to the last, though the most beautiful in character of all. And finally his brother Benjamin, youngest of all the brethren, and smallest of all the tribes, and as to *sin,* fallen lowest,—almost destroyed (Judges 19-21). Yet it gave Israel its first king; and us *our apostle* (Romans 11:1).

There are various lists of these sons of Jacob in Scripture, and lessons to be learned from all.

Now if it be objected that 144,000 out of the nation of Israel is too small a number, recall God's words "If the number of the children of Israel be as the sand of the sea, it is the remnant that shall be saved." The most of the nation will perish under the awful blows of the last enemy of God *(Psalm 83; Zechariah 14; Isaiah 28:14-21).* The nation of Israel is being gathered back to Palestine just now for the coming time of trouble. All the wars of the nations have some bearing upon this elect nation.

It is refreshing to our hearts to remember that although the leaders of socialism, atheism and Godless commercialism are found among the Jews and are gathered back to their land in unbelief, trusting their money to purchase the favor of the Gentiles, yet God will have 144,000 whom He calls His *bond-servants,* who are sealed with the name of the Lamb and of His Father in their foreheads *(Revelation 14:1 compared with 7:3).**

*It should be noted that this 144,000 of Revelation 7:3, being God's *douloi,* or "bond-servants," will *understand the Book of The Revelation.* For God gave it unto Jesus Christ "to show unto his bond-servants" *douloi (Revelation 1:1).* Thus they all, however dark it be, *know where they are.* The Revelation involves a knowledge of all Scripture. It speaks of Israel, Moses, the Prophets, the Martyrs, the Bride of the Lamb, the Kingdom, and the New Creation,—as well as the present creation: and finds all blessing in the person and sacrifice of Christ!

THE SAVED MULTITUDE

Revelation 7:9-17

But not only the 144,000 elect remnant of Israelites are found in this chapter 7—given to cheer our hearts—but "a great multitude, which no man could number, out of every nation and of *all* tribes and peoples and tongues" will "wash their robes" and have a place "before the throne" in heaven. Here we have one of the most striking scenes in this great book.

After these things I saw, and behold, a great multitude, which no man could number, out of every nation, and of all tribes and peoples and tongues, standing before the throne and before the Lamb, arrayed in white robes, and palms in their hands; and they cry with a great voice, saying, Salvation unto our God which sitteth on the throne, and unto the Lamb. And all the angels were standing round about the throne, and about the elders and the four living creatures; and they fell before the throne on their faces, and worshipped God, saying, Amen:

Blessing, and glory, and wisdom, and thanks-
giving, and honour, and power, and might, be
unto our God for ever and ever. Amen. And
one of the elders answered, saying unto me,
These which are arrayed in the white robes,
who are they, and whence came they? And I
say unto him, My lord, thou knowest. And
he said to me, These are they which come out
of the great tribulation, and they washed their
robes, and made them white in the blood of the
Lamb. Therefore are they before the throne of
God; and they serve him day and night in his
temple: and he that sitteth on the throne shall
spread his tabernacle over them. They shall
hunger no more, neither thirst any more;
neither shall the sun strike upon them, nor any
heat: for the Lamb which is in the midst of the
throne shall be their shepherd, and shall guide
them unto fountains of waters of life: and God
shall wipe away every tear from their eyes.

John does not know who these are, as his answer to
the elder's question "Who are they and whence came
they?" plainly shows. We feel he would have known
them if Old Testament saints, as he and Peter and James
knew Elijah and Moses on the Transfiguration Mount.
Also, he would have known them if Church saints. He
is told that they "come out of the great tribulation." Also
that they "washed their robes, and made them white in
the blood of the Lamb." That means salvation, and salvation by faith in God's Word regarding the blood of
Christ. These are not of the Church, which is Christ's
Body, yet they are in heaven.

It is necessary for us to have a largeness of heart concerning heaven and its hosts—even of its saved hosts.
The Lord Jesus said, "In my Father's house are many
abiding-places. I go to prepare *a place* for you." But
let us not forget that other companies from earth, besides
saints of the Church, are to be there—according to Revelation 7:9.

For it is the result of unbelief to seek to bring back to earth, to a lesser calling, this mighty company seen *before the throne*. The throne of God here in chapter 7 is necessarily that revealed in chapter 5. It is on that *heavenly* throne that the Lamb is seen "in the midst of the throne and of the four living creatures and . . . the elders" (Revelation 5:6). It is not that throne of *"his* father David" *(Luke 1:32, 33),* not the "throne of his glory" upon which the King shall sit when He returns to earth *(Matthew 25).* There is no account of the living creatures at the throne of David! And it is directly stated that the angels will not have to do with the millennial order *(Hebrews 2:5).* The angels of 7:11 would have absolutely no place if the scene were earthly.

I would rather credit the general spirit of reverent commentators of all the Christian centuries (which regards this company as a heavenly one) than the opinions of some, whose awakened sense of the literalness and glory of the millennial kingdom led them, in commenting on both chapter 7 and 21:9, to ascribe to earthly millennial times what the passages themselves necessarily make heavenly and eternal.

The Millennium is a reign on earth "with Christ" of 1,000 years. Its form of worship is fully set forth in Ezekiel, Zechariah and other Old Testament prophets.

But the language used of this company in Revelation 7:9-14 is *not* one of reigning; nor of any scene on earth; but "they are before the throne of *God"* (the throne of Revelation 4) "and they serve him day and night in his temple." "Day and night" is used of eternity in 20:10. It sets forth ceaselessness. Moreover, the complete resemblance of those divine comforts given to those of Revelation 7:15-17 and to those of 21:3, 4, 6, is convincing. It is heavenly service—not that of a reign on earth that is described.

Moreover, (and please note this matter well) if you make 7:9-17 millennial, what disposition do you make of this great company after the brief 1,000 years? Answer this, beloved. Go to the Scriptures. Call no man on

earth "Master." You cannot regard these Brethren—
especially beloved Darby, more than I do. But the strong-
est argument against accepting a system handed to him
from men whom he confessed he reverenced for their
godliness, is made by Mr. Darby himself in his essays
against Presbyterianism as "legality" and Anglicanism as
"authority."

Now it should be evident, we feel, that this great company is not the Church, the Bride. For the Church is
the Body of Christ, the fulness of Christ (*Ephesians
1:22,23*). Her relation to Christ in The Revelation is
as the Bride, the Lamb's wife. But this company is
before the throne—not the place of the Church (which is
hidden until chapter 19).

There arises also the difficult question as to what means
were used, what message, to save this great company?

We are told that they "came out of the great tribulation (literally, *the tribulation, the great*), and we know
from Daniel 12; Matthew 24; Mark 13; Jeremiah 30-33;
and Revelation 3:10; that this must be the last half of
the 70th week of Daniel 9. This tribulation (1) is future; (2) is overwhelmingly terrible; (3) will be a particular "time of trouble" for Jacob—that is, Israel, and
(4) will come on "all them that dwell on the earth."

But in the last named passage (Revelation 3:10) we
find that its object is "to try them that dwell on the
earth." The true saints of this age, the Church (even
Loadicean overcomers), are to "sit with Christ in his
throne" and will be "kept from" this hour of trial.

But what of those left after the rapture of the Church?
It is upon these that the hour of trial comes.

Now, we are not told it is the hour of universal damnation, but of *trial*. Doubtless those who "received not the
love of the truth" will be given over to believe "the lie"
(*Revelation 13*)—devil worship. But does not the use
of the word "trial" indicate that some may *endure* it?

Even the enemies of God knew about God—the throne
and the Lamb—under the sixth seal (*chapter 6*). Bibles

have been scattered all over this earth. In every nation men not yet saved know about the Lamb of God and His sacrifice for sin. When the awful world-wide "hour of trial" sets in, it seems that thousands will wash their robes and make them white in the blood of the Lamb, at all cost.

We must confess that this is a difficult question to determine, as to the exact relation of this great multitude to The Great Tribulation, in view of the fact that the same preposition *(ek)* is used here as in Revelation 3:10, where the saints are kept *out of (ek)* "the hour of trial."

CHAPTER VI

THE SEVEN TRUMPET ANGELS AND THE OTHER ANGEL

Revelation 8:1-5

When the Lamb opens the seventh one of the seals of the book of judgment of 8:1, we read,

There followed a silence in heaven about the space of half an hour.

On the one hand, all vocal worship and praise wholly cease; on the other, there is not seen any creature activity, even in the prosecution of those terrible visitations from heaven so soon to be sent on earth. All is silent.

The meaning, it seems to me, is two-fold: "The steps of God from mercy to judgment are always slow, reluctant, and measured." It is God's "strange work," this of actually proceeding to visit from a long forbearing heaven direct strokes upon men. In the seals of chapter 6 men slay *one another*. Even the fourth seal sets forth death by sword, famine, pestilence and wild beasts—God's four sore judgments, but not such as we shall see under the trumpets. So there is "silence in heaven." All the heavenly hosts will soon be engaging in actual warfare against earth. But it is God's "strange act" *(Isaiah 28: 21)*. He "hath no pleasure in the death of him that dieth." God is love.

Again, on the other hand, this is an *ominous* silence! It is the calm before the storm. God, the Lamb, the four living ones, the twenty-four elders, the seraphim of Isaiah 6, the hundred million and millions of angels, the Church, the martyrs beneath the altar—all *silent*. Meditate on this scene: it greatly grows upon your soul!

And I saw the seven angels that stand before God *(8:2)*. These are mentioned as if we knew of them before. But, so far as I am aware, there is no previous instruction regarding them in Scripture. Over and over again in The Revelation such unexpected words are used—especially regarding the arrangements in heaven. For this book, as its name signifies, is a *revelation*. If John says

"I saw," we, by the Spirit and by faith, also see. Perhaps Gabriel is one of these seven, though probably filling a yet special place. "I am Gabriel, that stand in the presence of God" *(Luke 1:19, R. V.)*.

God is "the great king"; and He is surrounded as is described in Daniel 7:10, "Thousands of thousands ministered unto him." We know little of that scene of ineffable majesty: let us treasure what is told us!

And there were given unto them seven trumpets *18:2).* The trumpets were appointed in Israel by God for calling of the princes, and the congregation, and for the journeying of the camps, as an alarm, or public notification *(Numbers 10:1-6).**

The trumpets were to be blown also in the days of Israel's "gladness," "set feasts," and over their sacrifice in the beginnings of their months—"for a memorial before your God." Jehovah also loved them *(Numbers 10:10).*

But we find an especial use of the trumpet, in arousing to war the hosts of Jehovah against their enemies *(Numbers 10:9).* Compare Ezekiel 33:1-7, where the watchman's trumpet blown faithfully could deliver all who would "take warning." But it was too late in Jeremiah 4:19 (for the Israel of that day). "Thou hast heard, O my soul, the sound of the trumpet, the alarm of war. Destruction upon destruction is cried; for the whole land is laid waste . . . How long shall I see the standard, and hear the sound of the trumpet? For my people are foolish . . . no understanding . . . wise to do evil . . . to do good—no knowledge!" What a state! And the prophet *heard* the trumpet of judgment.

So with these seven angels. They blow the very trumpets of heaven against an earth become "as it was in the days of Noah . . . as the days of Sodom," as Joshua and Israel blew the trumpets against Jericho.

Remembering the angelic governmental control that obtains over earth's affairs, until Christ and the Church

---

*Numbers 10:7 is interesting indeed to one who knows the real hope of the Church: "When the assembly is to be gathered together, ye shall blow, but ye shall not sound an alarm!"

possess the kingdom *(Hebrews 2:5,6)*, we are not interpreting but perverting Scripture, unless we believe these seven angels to be angels indeed, and their trumpets, trumpets indeed, and the results, results indeed, as described. God had priests blow ram's-horn trumpets a week around Jericho's walls: and they "fell down flat." Of course it was God's power that caused it. But God thus proclaimed Himself the God of Israel, working wonders, as Israel blew and shouted.

So will He do, on an earth-wide scale, as these angels blow their trumpets in heaven. It is idle to call all these literally described scenes by the favorite word, "symbolic." Symbolic of *what,* pray tell us! Do you have a plainer account of definite things anywhere in the Bible than we here have in The Revelation?

It is true that we must needs know the rest of Scripture to understand The Revelation fully; for it takes for granted such knowledge. But when God declares that definite things follow—"by reason of the . . . voices, of the angels" (8:7, 13, R. V.), who dares say that some fact of history, or some imagination of the human mind, other than the plainly described event, is to be understood?

Let us beware of finding ourselves finally aligned with the Sadducees who denied both angel and spirit (Acts 23:8). There are figures and "signs" *(semeia)* in The Revelation; but we learn from Scripture, not from history, or reason, what such things mean.

And another angel came and stood over the altar, having a golden censer; and there was given unto him much incense, that he should add it unto the prayers of all the saints upon the golden altar which was before the throne. And the smoke of the incense, with the prayers of the saints, went up before God out of the angel's hand. And the angel taketh the censer; and he filled it with the fire of the altar, and cast it upon the earth: and there followed thunders, and voices, and lightnings, and an earthquake.

This angel is not Christ, who is the Lamb opening the seals, and directing these processes of judgment. The fact that this angel is at the altar, and has incense, has led many, in their very jealousy for the Great High Priest, to forget the vision of the Lord in chapter 1 as Judge, clad in the robe of the Judge, not of the Priest. The vision of chapter 1 must control all the book—"Write the things which thou sawest (the glorious Lord); and the things which are (that are on—Church things); and the things which shall come to pass after these things." (Revelation 1:19). It is not a book of salvation, nor of intercession, but of processed judgment.

This angel of 8:3 is publicly to bring before all heaven three things:

1. That the prayers of *all the saints* are ever had in memory before God: a most blessed and solemn truth! No saint's prayer is forgotten, but has its effect in due season, in bringing in the Kingdom, that is, our Lord's return!

2. That the incense (ever in Scripture setting forth the power of Christ's atonment *acting upon God)* the incense, I say, representing our Lord's person and work at Calvary, added in due time to the prayers of all the saints, makes them *instantly effectual before God.*

3. That the prayers of all the saints, in the power of Christ's atonement, *is that which really brings about judgment.* It is the answer at last to "Thy Kingdom come" which the saints of all ages have prayed. No other answer could be given, inasmuch as earth has rejected the rightful King!

It is of the utmost importance that we understand Revelation 8:3-5. This incense is "given" to this angel. *(Christ would have needed none!)* And it is God's hour to begin *from* heaven that direct heavenly intervention which will be the answer to the saints' prayers. Enoch prophesied of it *(Jude 14, 15).* Jacob waited for it *(Gen. 49:18).* All the prophets spake of it. Now, in Revelation 8:3-5,—inasmuch as its hour has begun to be, what caused it must be openly brought in and shown upon "the golden altar which was before the throne" (of God).

Now this angel takes his censer, and, filling it with the fire of the altar, he "cast it into the earth." The altar of old was the place of substitutionary atonement, and the fire represented the judgment of a holy God upon sin visited upon a sacrifice rather than the sinner. Here it is reversed. When the censer is cast into the earth, there follow thunders, and voices, and lightnings, and an earth-quake" *(8:5, R.V.).*

Notice first, that the "scientific" explanation of the "processes of nature" utterly fail—thunders precede light-nings!

Again, *voices,* intelligent, significant, warning, come *be-tween* the thunders and the lightnings.

And finally *all* these are physical disturbances. The *earthquake* is a real *earthquake:* one of God's constant ways of arousing men.

When we proceed to what follows each trumpet, things will be simple, *if we but believe what is written.*

Four of the Seven Trumpets 8:6-13

And the seven angels that had the seven trumpets prepared themselves to sound.

These seven presence-angels, having waited until the incense (the power of Christ's sacrificial work) and the prayers of all the saints should be formally presented be-fore God *(8:3-5)* as the means of direct judgment from heaven upon men (as before these were the means of salvation) are now ready to act. Until this time the judg-ments have been preliminary and indirect: now we shall see direct visitations from heaven upon men.*

And the first sounded, and there followed hail and fire, mingled with blood, and they

---

*It is probable that these trumpet-blasts will be *heard on earth;* and that all the world will know whence these troubles come. In 16:9 we read "they blas-phemed the name of God who hath the power over these plagues" (the bowls of wrath). Men will know what is going on. The heaven, under the sixth seal (6:14) "was removed as a scroll when it is rolled up." We cannot avoid the conclusion that there will be at that time manifest knowledge that *God* is the direct Author of earth's calamities. He will make men feel it.

> were cast into the earth, and the third part
> of the earth was burnt up, and the third part
> of the trees was burnt up, and all green grass
> was burnt up.

Now this is a book of *revelation* we are reading. And it is *not sealed (22:10)*. Therefore we have just read an exact description of *what will take place!* If you should read to someone an account of the seventh plague in Egypt, from Exodus 9:18-26, he would hear such words as these:

"I will cause it to rain a very grievous hail, such as hath not been in Egypt since the day it was founded even until now . . . Jehovah sent thunder and hail, and fire ran down into the earth . . . so there was hail, and fire mingled with the hail, very grievous, such as had not been in all the land of Egypt since it became a nation . . . Only in the land of Goshen, where the children of Israel were, was there no hail."

Now if your hearer should say, "I believe that literally happened, just as related," you would reply: "Certainly. God does not speak in a riddle; all this happened in Egypt." But if you then read him what God says *will* happen when the first angel blows his trumpet in Revelation 8:7: "hail and fire, mingled with blood . . . cast upon the earth," and he declares, "That is not literal hail or fire or blood," your only proper course would be to call him a doubter, a caviller at God's plain statements. He might reply, "The book of Revelation is full of 'symbols'—you cannot take it literally as you do Exodus."

Your true course then would be to show him, in all meekness, but with all firmness, that if God does not mean what He says here, *no one on earth* can tell what He means! When God uses emblems, or "signs," as, for example, the two evil women, Jezebel in Thyatira, and the harlot on the Beast in chapter 17, God *tells* what He means. But when God says that such and such *events* will take place, *they will take place!* It is folly to pretend that the trumpet-judgments have already been "fulfilled in Church history." God says John here was beholding

the things that should come to pass *after* Church things
(4:1).

Tell me, when was exactly one third of this earth *burnt,*
so that the grass and the trees were destroyed? History
has no record of such an event!

But it will occur, literally! And the very inventions
that help geographers to chart this earth (and there are
many), will enable the men living in the days of the
Seventh Angel quickly to compute that *one third* of the
earth has been affected by this great judgment.

One third! Three is the *divine* number (as all Bible
students know) and *four* is the earth-number.

Now under the first four trumpets, we read the words
"a third" twelve times! And twelve is God's governmental number concerning this earth.

> And the second angel sounded, and as it
> were a great mountain burning with fire was
> cast into the sea; and the third part of the
> sea became blood; and there died the third
> part of the creatures which were in the sea,
> even they that had life; and the third part
> of the ships was destroyed.

Manifestly, to understand this, we have only to believe
it. UNBELIEF is the greatest enemy of prophecy.

Also, it is idle to talk about this "third part" as "the
Roman earth." What but your imagination ever told you
such a thing? These judgments are world-wide (as is
plainly seen from verse 12, where the *sun* is smitten).
Is there a "Roman" sun?

God says a third part of the sea will become *blood.*
God will do this: and will let all the earth know three
things: (1) That it is a heavenly judgment, by the loud
blast of the angel's trumpet; (2) that a great body like
a burning mountain has been cast into the sea; (3) that
just one third—God's number—of the sea becomes, like
the river Nile under Moses' rod, *blood.* And the lines
of it will be absolutely defined in the ocean, that men
may know it is God's hand that is at work.

For example, now the Gulf Stream flows, a great sea-river, many miles in width, with a color so marked that a ship's bow enters it with the stern plainly back in the common ocean. Also, it keeps on its distinct way clear across the Atlantic.

And it will not be difficult for the nations to ascertain that one third of their ships have been "destroyed." Louder and louder are the divine voices which should awake men. "When thy judgments are in the earth, the inhabitants of the world learn righteousness" (Isaiah 26:9). But many perish *under the judgments!*

And the third angel sounded, and there fell from heaven a great star, burning as a torch, and it fell upon the third part of the rivers, and upon the fountains of the waters; and the name of the star is called Wormwood: and the third part of the waters became wormwood; and many men died of the waters, because they were made bitter.

Wormwood is the bitterest shrub known. Several varieties are found in the East, and in Syria and Palestine. It would be easy for any one to understand what the Seer meant. "The star is called Wormwood." Men are reaping the bitter fruits of sin; and they know that heaven is sending these troubles upon them.

It should be carefully noted, that the order of these first four trumpet-judgments is the same as that of the bowls of wrath in chapter 16. (1) Earth; (2) Sea; (3) Rivers and fountains of waters; (4) The Sun.

Men get their water supply from the rivers of earth, and from the "fountains of waters"—which sometimes flow from the snows and glaciers of the mountains, and sometimes become the underground sources of springs and wells. To cut off their "water supply" is to render men desperate and helpless. The greater part of earth's inhabitants (Matthew 7:13—"wide is the gate") is evermore hastening on to "the pit wherein is no water" *(Zechariah 9:11)*. What wonder, then, that God now lets them have a hint of what is coming! The day was, that "all the Egyptians digged around about the river for water to drink; for they could not drink of the water of the river." Then God let them find water—though at great labor. And here in The Revelation He smites only a *third* of the sources of their drinking water.

As we before quoted: "The steps of God from mercy to judgment are always slow, reluctant, and measured."

But now comes a stroke that even the lowest and least of men can, and must, recognize and interpret:

> The fourth angel sounded, and the third part of the sun was smitten, and the third part of the moon, and the third part of the stars; that the third part of them should be darkened, and the day should not shine for the third part of it, and the night in like manner.

On the fourth day of creation God said, "Let there be light bearers (Hebrew—*maorim*) in the firmament of heaven to divide the day from the night; and let them be for signs, and for seasons, and for days and years." Men's almanacs deal with *seasons, days* and *years:* but God said these heavenly bodies were *primarily* for SIGNS!

"And there shall be *signs* in the sun and moon and stars," Christ, the Creator of them, said *(Luke 21:25)* speaking in connection with His own second coming.

Revelation 8:12 will surely set the "star-gazers" on their heads! There is the loud blast of a heavenly trumpet, and lo! out goes the sun! And the daylight turns into *night*. And *such* night! No stars, no moon, just black, impenetrable darkness. Then lo! again the sun shines. And when men compute the duration of it, they find again that *third*—ominous indeed to those who know not, and who desire not to know God.

Our Lord tells us plainly that "the powers of the heavens shall be shaken"—evidently referring to such physical powers as the so-called laws of gravitation, and celestial attraction: for the "distress of nations" referred to in Luke 21:25, 26, is terror arising from "the roaring of the sea and the billows." They will be "in perplexity" (R. V.), for no science will be able to explain these things.

All their confidence has been in "all things continuing as they were"—in the "fixity of nature's laws," etc., etc. Now all is overset. And, the Lord continued, "men will be fainting (or expiring) for fear, and for expectation of the things which are coming on the world."*

Then, indeed, to Israel's sealed remnant, such Psalms as 46 will be a source of confidence that will be unknown except to God's own: "God is our refuge and strength, A very present help in trouble. Therefore will we not fear, though the earth do change, And though the mountains be shaken into the heart of the seas; Though the waters thereof roar and be troubled, Though the mountains tremble with the swelling thereof."

But now in Revelation 8:13 comes the great eagle's announcement of the three woes that trumpets five, six and seven, will usher in in chapter 9.

> **And I saw, and I heard one eagle, flying in mid heaven, saying with a great voice, Woe, woe, woe, for them that dwell on the earth, by reason of the other voices of the trumpet of the three angels, who are yet to sound.**

The warning is that trumpets five, six and seven will bring a new quality and degree of divine displeasure and consequent disaster. We shall see the first woe in the locusts (9:1-11); the second, in the Euphratean horsemen and hosts (9:13-21) and the plagues wherewith the two witnesses (11:5, 6) smite the earth. The third we see in the handing over of the earth to the Beast-worship of chapter 13—worst by far, of all!

---

*We see from Matthew 24:29, that the greatest physical convulsions are to take place "immediately after the tribulation." But the Lord's own are, in Luke 21:28, told to be encouraged "when these things begin to come to pass." The Church escapes from earth at the end of Church-things, in Revelation 4:1. But God has others of His saints, who will behold, and "lift up their heads," in the dark days before The Tribulation, as well as after it.

CHAPTER VII
LOCUSTS AND HELLISH HORSEMEN
Revelation 9

We have now the sounding of trumpets of the fifth and sixth angels in Revelation 9, with their fearsome following effects upon men.

The fifth angel sounded, and I saw a star from heaven fallen unto the earth: and there was given to him the key of the shaft (Greek, phrear, as in John 4:11, "The well is deep") **of the abyss.**

That there is a passage from the earth to its heart not only is indicated by Scripture, but was believed by the ancient Greeks, and is today known to the followers of Satan. In Revelation 20:1-3 we find Satan himself cast down there, and the passage sealed for 1000 years. In this latter passage, "an angel coming down out of heaven" has the *key* of the abyss. In Revelation 9:1 it is a "fallen" one of those beings so often called stars (e.g., Daniel 8:10, 24; Isaiah 14:12) to whom is given the key of the shaft of the abyss. We know from our Lord's words in Revelation 1:18 that He has Himself "the keys of death and of Hades." Inasmuch as the word "abyss" describes the region, and Hades (literally "the unseen") describes the state or class of beings—spirits who go there—we judge both words refer to "the heart of the earth" (Matthew 12:40). For our Lord, we know, during that three days was in the Old Testament Sheol, which is the New Testament Hades. (Compare Psalm 16:10 with Acts 2:25-31—both R. V., for the King James version is quite confusing in its varied translations of Sheol and Hades.) In Romans 10:7 also, Paul shows that to bring our Lord up from the dead, was to "descend into the abyss."

And he opened the shaft of the abyss; and there went up smoke out of the shaft, as the smoke of a great furnace; and the sun and the air were darkened by reason of the smoke of the shaft.

Now if we should read of the eruption of a great volcano darkening the sky for thousands of miles, we would believe it to be physical smoke and literal darkness. Such phenomena have actually occurred, as may be found upon consulting any physical geography.

So we shall proceed to believe that God's Word is as true as are man's records, and we shall have no trouble in considering this smoke and consequent darkening just as literal as the words express them to be.

When we remember that The Revelation is *not a sealed book,* we shall have no difficulty in regarding the *locusts* that God says will proceed from this smoke, as actual locusts. In Exodus 10 we are told concerning the plague of locusts in Egypt that they were such "as neither thy fathers nor thy fathers' fathers have seen, since the day that they were upon the earth unto this day." "Before them there were no such locusts as they, neither after them shall be such."

Now no one who believes the Bible has any trouble believing the record of that past plague. Nor has any one any *right* to have any difficulty about the terrible locust plague of Revelation 9. It is because of *the fog of unbelief,* and *the super-fog of "historical interpretation,"* that this passage has been considered "hard to understand." If we do not *believe* that God means what He so plainly and explicitly says in Revelation 9, let us *say* we do not believe it, and be honest. But let us not dare to bring in vain imaginations and call them interpretations of Scripture. (As, for example, the grotesque and absurd notion that the "hair as the hair of women" [9:8] was fulfilled in the horse-tails tied by the Saracens to their spears!) Remember that we are reading from Revelation 4 onward "the things that must come to pass" *after* the present Church period. See Revelation 1:19, where the Lord Himself makes the division; and compare it with 4:1 where He carries it forward. It preens our pride to point as wise ones to this or that in Church history, and say, "There was the fulfilment of, for example, this locust army." But the trouble is, that denies what Christ said about this part of the book, namely, that it was to be fulfilled *after* Church times and Church history are closed.

Out of the smoke came forth locusts upon the earth; and power was given them, as the scorpions of the earth have power.

Then follows the command of the Creator of these creatures, reversing utterly their habits as to manner of food! They are directed not to hurt the grass, nor green things, nor trees (the natural food of locusts until then) "but only such men as have not the seal of God on their foreheads"!

Five months (the natural life-period of locusts) is assigned them to "torment men." Down in Egypt (the plagues of which throw great light on the earth-plagues of Revelation), God "put a difference" (Hebrew—*set redemption)* between His people Israel, and the Egyptians (See Exodus 8:22; 9:4, 6, 26; 10:23). God will do likewise when these terrible visitations are again in the earth. Whatever persecutions the saints of those days may endure from men, they will have constant miraculous evidence that *their God* is not against them!

Their torment was as the torment of a scorpion, when it striketh a man.

The writer was once struck on the heel by a small scorpion, and the unrelievable, indescribable anguish extended clear to the head. Of course we are simply to *believe* Revelation 9:5. To seek to twist it from its natural sense is wickedness: for unbelief is wickedness!

In those days men shall seek death, and shall in no wise find it.

We remember one who was dragged years ago from the Chicago river, after attempted suicide, crying, "Oh, let me drown! I cannot face another day!" Now God does not tell us by what means men shall in this terrible time be kept back from the longed-for oblivion of physical death: but He *does* reveal that they shall seek it and not find it. This giddy, pleasure-mad age little realizes to what extremities of trouble it is fast hastening. And if, dear reader, you should die without Christ, before these judgments from God set in, it would be only to enter the dark gates of Hades (in the center of this earth), to be kept there till the judgment of the Great White Throne of Revelation 20:11-15; for the Word of God must be fulfilled.

Now, further regarding these locusts, a detailed description is given in verses 7-10. Their aspect will be truly terrible. I have seen an onslaught of white hornets, whose nest has been disturbed, drive men frantic before them. How much more these fearsome creatures! "Shapes . . . like unto horses prepared for war." Faces like humans—horrible! Crowns on their heads—as God's avengers. Teeth like lions', breastplates like iron, wings like a thousand rushing war-chariots. Stinging tails like those of scorpions—is not this a horrid host! God once promised to send the hornet to drive out His people's foes *(Exodus 23:28; Deuteronomy 7:20)*. Probably there were "wise ones" also in those days who said, "The Lord does not mean *literal hornets;* but some terrifying *thoughts* sent into the Canaanites." But Jehovah tells us in Joshua 24:12: *"I sent the hornet before you,* which drove them out from before you." It is utterly amazing to confront, even in commentaries by excellent men, complete disbelief that these will be literal locusts, though God takes such pains to say explicitly that *they will be just that!* So we will believe Him, and be thankful that the Church will not be here at that time; and that the other sealed ones, God's own, will be secure from their terrifying attacks.

They have over them as king the angel of the abyss: his name in Hebrew is Abaddon, and in the Greek tongue he hath the name Apollyon.

Of ordinary locusts, the Word of God says, "the locusts have no king" *(Proverbs 30:27)*. But of this devastating judgment a grim leader is seen—revealed but this once

in Scripture. This is evidently not Satan; as he is nowhere connected with "the abyss" till he is cast therein
in Revelation 20:1-3. He walks up and down in *the earth*
and accuses the saints before *God, in heaven (Job 1, I
Peter 5, Revelation 12)*.

Abaddon means *destruction,* in the Hebrew; but the
Greek, *Apollyon,* is *destroyer.*

Perhaps, just as Satan has "the power of death"
(Hebrews 2), so this angel of the abyss has the doleful
power and authority to execute on creatures the effects
of death that give him his name! So he heads this army
of judgment-bearing, tormenting, locusts, which, we read
in Revelation 9:12, constitutes the first WOE.

> The first Woe is past: behold, there come
> yet two Woes after these things.
> And the sixth angel sounded.
> I heard a voice from the horns of the golden
> altar which is before God.*
> One saying to the sixth angel that had the
> trumpet, Loose the four angels that are bound
> at the great river Euphrates. And the four
> angels were loosed, that had been prepared
> for the hour and day and month and year,
> that they should kill the third part of men.
> And the number of the armies of the horse-
> men was twice ten thousand times ten thou-
> sand: I heard the number of them.

How little the nations that are seeking just now to
restore Mesopotamia to its ancient fertility (foremost
among these being England) realize that they are working in the immediate region of four of Satan's most powerful princes, which are bound there for a special purpose! (See II Peter 2:4, where we read of certain angels,
probably those of Genesis 6, as cast down to *Tartarus,*—

---

*This is not the brazen altar, as under the fifth seal, but the altar where
prayer was offered up in 8:3.   Its pattern is seen in Exodus 30.   In the tabernacle the prayers of the Israelites who had been atoned for at the brazen altar
were offered up before the golden altar, but now, just as we saw in 8:3, 5, the
voice from the golden altar which was meant to speak for mercy, now calls for
judgment; and it is from the "horns" that the voice comes in Revelation 9:13.
The horns symbolize the power of that which was done at that altar.   Therefore
it is an answer to the prayers of God's saints based upon Christ's atonement
that this terrible judgment now comes!

perhaps the lowest part of the abyss, and committed to pits or chains of darkness.) Most of Satan's angels are yet free—being the principalities against which we *wrestle* (Ephesians 6), but some terrible offenders of high rank have been *bound*. These four angels have this ominous destiny: they "had been prepared for the hour and day and month and year, that they should kill the third part of men." Some think that this designation of time is intended to set forth thirteen months; a year plus a month, plus a day and an hour. But this seems to be straining the meaning of the passage, and not to be in accord with the spirit of it: for it is the *object* of the chaining of these angels, not the duration of their infliction upon men, that is in view. They have been prepared for this particular moment—chained there until this command from the golden altar.

Attention has been abundantly called by commentators to the region of the Euphrates as that place where human sin began and also Satan's empire over man; where the first murder was committed; where the first war confederacy was made (Genesis 14); and back of this it is where Nimrod began to be "a mighty one in the earth," and where the vast system of Babylonian idolatry, with its trinity of evil—"father, mother and son" originated, to deceive the whole world by the Satanic fable of "the queen of heaven." Here, moreover, as we saw in Zechariah 5, iniquity is to have its last stage on earth (see Revelation 18 also).

The two hundred million horsemen whose number John heard are not human beings at all. It is so belittling to Scripture to treat it as if its words were not definite. It blinds the mind to the whole force of the *coming chapters* of Revelation, to accept such foolish notions as those of the historicists (that is, those who apply these chapters to what has already taken place during Church history) bring forth here. John plainly declares,

> I saw the horses in the vision, and them
> that sat on them, having breastplates as of
> fire and of hyacinth and of brimstone: and

> the heads of the horses are as the heads of
> lions; and out of their mouths proceedeth
> fire and smoke and brimstone. By these three
> plagues was the third part of men killed, by
> the fire and the smoke and the brimstone,
> which proceedeth out of their mouths.

Here God goes into descriptive detail. *Believe*, and
you scarcely need any comment. Every one knows what
fire and smoke and brimstone are. The only trouble is
to believe that God would (of course He *could*) turn
loose such horrific agents against men on earth.

To doubt that this is fire and smoke and brimstone in chapter 9, is to proceed to doubt whether the
lake of fire is literal fire burning with brimstone.
Doubt as to this has already spread through Christendom.
Yet it *must* be literal—there is no possible escape *if we
believe the Bible true at all!*

In Genesis 19, we read in verse 24, "Then Jehovah
rained upon Sodom and upon Gomorrah brimstone and
fire from Jehovah out of heaven; and he overthrew those
cities and all the Plain, and all the inhabitants of the
cities, and that which grew upon the ground. And Abraham gat up early in the morning to the place where he
had stood before Jehovah: (do you believe Abraham was
a literal man?) and he looked toward Sodom and Gomorrah (they were literal cities), and toward all the land
of the Plain (it lies there yet, covered by the Dead Sea),
and beheld, and, lo, the smoke of the land went up as the
smoke of a furnace.

Do you believe this record to be an inspired statement
of what Abraham actually saw? Why then do you seek
to reject in Revelation what you accept in Genesis?

In Revelation 14:10 and 11, we read that certain men
will be "tormented with fire and brimstone in the presence
of the holy angels, and in the presence of the Lamb: (If
you do not believe in the actual existence of *angels* you
are a Sadducee and an infidel. You might as well confess you do not believe in the risen Lamb of God.) "And
the smoke of their torment goeth up unto ages of ages."

Again, you find in Revelation 20:10, that the first Beast and the false prophet have been in "the lake of fire and brimstone" for 1000 years, and are not annihilated, and then that the Devil is cast therein. Do you realize that to claim that you do not believe in literal fire and literal brimstone, but believe in something more awful than this, is *just silly nonsense?*

It becomes necessary to contemplate deeply and with absolute *faith* the visitations that destroy *the third part of the earth's remaining population* (a fourth having been slain under the fourth seal of 6:8). One-half of the population of the earth has been removed. Thus, at the low estimate of 1,600,000,000, 400,000,000 were slain in chapter 6, and a third of the rest, or 400,000,000 more in chapter 9.

The prophecies concerning the decimation of earth's population prior to the bringing in of the kingdom (that is, the Millennium), we shall see thus gradually fulfilled in these preliminary judgments,—of the seals, the trumpets, and the bowls of wrath,—*before* "the great and terrible day of the Lord" of Revelation 19:11-16; when the Lord as King of kings will tread "the winepress of the fierceness of the wrath of God, the Almighty": with the results seen in 19:17, 18.

Now in Revelation 9 these hellish horsemen, which are literal and which are certainly coming, belch forth on this earth fire and smoke and brimstone; "which proceeded out of their mouths." It is idle to talk about this being "a figure of false doctrine"! When God desires to tell of certain "spirits of demons going forth to deceive the earth" for Armageddon, He is able to describe them perfectly in Revelation 16:13, 14. And when God speaks of fire and smoke and brimstone, He means what He says.*

---

*The final, unescapable demonstration of this is in Matthew 13 in our Lord's interpretation of the parable of the tares (verses 36-43). In this interpretation He gives the meaning of the figures of the parable, The good seed—sons of the kingdom; tares—sons of the evil one; the enemy—the Devil; the harvest—the end of the age; the reapers—angels. Now read verse 41: "The Son of man shall send forth his angels, and they shall gather out of his kingdom all things that cause stumbling, and them that do iniquity, and shall cast them into the furnace of fire; there shall be the weeping and the gnashing of

We are compelled therefore to envisage untold future horrors to come upon this earth, even *before* that Great Day of Wrath when our Lord personally comes in chapter 19:11-15. A third part of the humanity remaining (after one-fourth of the whole had been destroyed under the fourth seal) are now killed. This is physical death. They are removed in judgment from the earth. What awful days they will be when one third of earth's remaining population will be slain by this foretaste of the pit, the fire and smoke and the brimstone, proceeding from the mouths of these dread horsemen! Also those not killed, according to verse 19, may be smitten into torment with the *tails* of these horses, which are "like unto serpents, and have heads; and with them they hurt."

This is a taste of hell on earth that is coming. One of every three humans left on earth succumbs to its fury.

Yet, when we come to Revelation 13, to the strong delusion of the worship of the Beast, and through him of the Devil, the destruction will be greater yet!

Now read Revelation 9:20, 21—the *end* of our chapter.

We must remember that the inhabitants of the earth are already in our day far gone in utter rebellion and impenitence: what wonder then that such terrible infliction as these horsemen of hell, which we shall now consider, come upon the condition of hardened iniquity described in the closing verses of chapter 9.

> **And the rest of mankind who were not killed with these plagues repented not of the works of their hands that they should not worship demons, and the idols of gold, and of silver, and of brass, and of stone, and of**

teeth." You can't say the furnace of fire is a figure here, without falsifying our Lord's words, for He is telling what the figures of the parable mean. And you must also traduce your own intellectual processes, for you imagine an imagination (because you are terrified at the truth) but you have no basis for your imagination. You cannot reach it by logic, for logic leads you to the truth—of eternal literal fire in Matthew 13. Therefore when you claim you do not believe in literal fire but in something "more awful," you are giving heed to your deceitful heart, to those subtle lies fostered there by the Devil. Whoever really heard of or described anything more awful than God's visiting men with fire and brimstone?

Spiritistic mediums all talk about the "spirit world" as being lovely and pleasant, etc. Every false doctrine denies literal eternal fire. Keep out of that class!

wood; which can neither see, nor hear, nor walk: and they repented not of their murders, nor of their sorceries, nor of their fornication, nor of their thefts.

We see here the two tables of God's holy law set at naught by the impenitent. First, in *demon-worship*—and who knows how far this has progressed in our day! Take Chicago: Arriving in this city at the close of 1893, (the former World's Fair) I found nearly two pages of the Saturday issue of the newspaper were taken up with announcement of services at the various churches, and the sermons were generally on solemn subjects by godly men. In 1935, four or five announcements, at most a half a dozen, invited to places where one's soul would be safe to attend; while the announcements of Spiritualists, Theosophists, Christian Scientists, Unity followers, etc.— those cults that have direct traffic with Satan—ran into the scores. (Six orthodox, against 75 Satanic, in the *Chicago Daily News* of November 14, 1931.)

Next *idolatry*—literal idols that are coming fast into Christendom again, and that not only in Romish (Jezebel) circles, but among "Protestants," both in England and in this country. Moreover, as toward God, that will be the characterizing condition at the time of the visitation of which we are about to read. (See especially the "image of the Beast" of chapter 13—worshipped by the *world!*)

Next, their attitude toward one another (verse 21)— *murders*. The daily press already fairly screams of "killings," and that not only by gangsters, but by fathers and mothers of families, by college students, young people and even children! Violence is indeed filling the earth, "as it was in the days of Noah."

Then come *sorceries*. The Greek word *pharmakeis* is used three times in the New Testament: here, and in Revelation 18:23 and Galatians 5:20. The corresponding noun is used in Revelation 21:8 and 22:15. It fundamentally indicates the charming of others by means of drugs or magic, which is, of course, commonly practiced in the pagan world; and more secretly in so-called

"Christendom." Its connection seems to denote an *evil*
intent upon others by means of enchantments. Its place
next to "murders" here, and to "enmities" in Galatians
5:20, would show this. Generally speaking, it is calling
the energies of the evil spirit-world, by whatever means,
into human affairs. It forms a horrible and increasing
maelstrom from which few escape who once enter it.
The literal meaning of *pharmakeia* "enchanting by
drugs," can also include the fearful and increasing prevalence of the "dope" habit in all lands. Gangsters rely
on drugs to stupefy their fears when they assassinate.
All this is in accord with the prophecy of Isaiah 28 regarding "the drunkards of Ephraim." It seems to portray
clearly the future use of the vineyards now being planted
by the returning Jews in Palestine.*

Let the dreamers of dreams who do not read God's
Word reflect on this. I fully believe these last days
will prove the most drunken and drugged age the world
ever saw! Unregenerate man's refuge from intolerable
conditions is suicide or drugged oblivion.†

The next prevailing sin *(Revelation 9:21)* is *fornication*.
One has only to glance about at the pictures in newspapers, at magazine covers, at the advertisments of thea-
tres and moving pictures, to see what a wave of lust has
begun to sweep the earth. God's Spirit seems to be with-
drawing and letting the sinful heart of man have its fill
of uncleanness. Gradually we become accustomed to

*This prophecy is plainly one for the last days—yea, the last seven-year
treaty of the "majority" (Daniel 9:27) of Israel with the last Roman emperor.
Isaiah 28:15, 18, compared with Revelation 17:8 proves that. As to the prevalence of drunkenness in Palestine at that time, read Isaiah 28:7, 8: "These
reel with wine, and stagger with strong drink; the priest and the prophet reel
with strong drink, they are swallowed up of wine, they stagger with strong
drink; they err in vision, they stumble in judgment. . . . All tables . . . full of
vomit *and* filthiness . . . no place clean."

†We have only to think of the use of alcoholic stimulants, of opium, of
tobacco, of the rage of cosmetics and medicaments to increase love attractions,
of resorts to the pharmacopoeia in connection with sensuality—of the magical
agents and treatments alleged to come from the spirit-world for the benefit of
people in this—of the thousand impositions in the way of medicines and remedial
agents, encouraging mankind to recklessness in transgression with the hope of
easily repairing the damages of nature's penalties—of the growing prevalence
of crime induced by these things, setting loose and stimulating to activity the
vilest passions, which are eating out the moral sense of society—for the beginnings of that moral degeneracy to which the seer here alludes as characteristic
of the period when the sixth trumpet is sounded.—*Seiss.*

reading or hearing of these things until we scarcely realize how far in a few years we have drifted toward the morals of Sodom. Nor will man repent of his dear sin in this respect. We remember that although Jezebel was given space to repent in Revelation 2:20, 21, it was of her fornication she *willed not* to repent. In a certain real sense, just as a Christian father lives watchfully to care for his wife and family, so the unregenerate world, uncontrolled as it is by the fear of God or the Holy Spirit, really lives for the essence of self-indulgence in the abuse of the sexual relation. One has only to recall the conversation he may have heard from worldlings off their guard to understand this!

Finally, the sin that brings about the terrific judgment of the horsemen of hell is theft. *Get money,* by whatever means, is the slogan of these last days. Dishonesty, trickery, irresponsibility in business circles, have become proverbial. A prominent man in a great commercial house some time ago said to me, "We never count as we used to on contracts being lived up to. Cancellation without notice is so common as to cause no surprise." And what enormous trickery has the covetousness that has brought about the wrecking of hundreds, probably thousands, of banks, often revealed. Nor will there be any permanent change except for the worse. "Lying and false swearing," according to Zechariah 5 (two remarkable visions!) are the special forms of iniquity in the last days, as revealed in Palestine but finally centered in "the land of Shinar" (Zechariah 5:11).

CHAPTER VIII
NO LONGER DELAY!
Revelation 10

And I saw another strong angel coming down out of heaven, arrayed with a cloud; and the rainbow was upon his head, and his face was as the sun, and his feet as pillars of fire; and he had in his hand a little book open: and he set his right foot upon the sea, and his left upon the earth; and he cried with a great voice, as a lion roareth.

We may call this angel the *herald* angel of the great things that belong under the seventh trumpet, as seen in chapter 11:15-19. The great burden of this angel's message is that "there shall be delay* no longer" (10:6, R.V.). The angel of chapter 10 is not Christ, but His messenger sent to announce a most solemn crisis.

This angel in chapter 10 really introduces chapter 11, with God's two witnesses prophesying *at Jerusalem;* the great view of God's plans concerning *Israel,* and Satan's opposition, of chapters 12 and 13—in fact all these great events described in chapter 11:18. (Read this verse most carefully, for its importance is great.)

Let us return now to the beginning of chapter 10. "Another strong angel . . . a little book." This is in plain reference to the strong angel of chapter 5:2 who also speaks of a book.

Note at once that John's position in chapter 10 seems to be on earth (as it undoubtedly is in chapter 11), for he sees the angel *coming* down out of heaven.

That this angel is merely such, and not Christ Himself, as some maintain, seems to me fully evident. Over sixty times angels are mentioned in The Revelation apart from the "angels" of the churches; and they are always

---
*The translation of *chronos* by the word "time" is impossible, as well as unreasonable, in view of the context. We know that after our Lord's coming back to earth in chapter 19 there will be one thousand years of His reign with His saints on earth (20:4-6) and after that "a little season," before the earth and the heaven flee away at the Great White Throne judgment.

seen in service to Him who is opening the seals of the book of judgment. For the Master of the house to take the place of one of the servants at a time such as we are now considering is wholly incongruous. The more we study the book of The Revelation the more we become impressed and over-awed at the dignity and authority conferred on these beings called angels (Greek—*messengers*).

We need not, therefore, be surprised at the description of this angel in Revelation 10:1—"arrayed with a cloud; and the rainbow was upon his head, and his face was as the sun, and his feet as pillars of fire." He is not sitting upon the cloud as the "one sitting like unto a son of man" of chapter 14. "Jehovah maketh the clouds his chariot." But this angel was "arrayed with a cloud; and the rainbow was upon his head." Here we are again taken back to Genesis 9 as in Revelation 4:3. God is about to call earth to account for breaking the everlasting covenant, of which the rainbow was the token (Isaiah 24). This angel's face "as the sun" and his feet "pillars of fire" declare the supreme, searching, fixed character of his message. Of the angel who announces the final doom of Babylon it is written in chapter 18:1, "the earth was lightened with his glory,"—yet no one supposes *him* to be the Lord!

His right foot upon the sea, and his left upon the earth.

The sea often seems in Scripture a distinct province, with a responsibility and judgment distinct from that of the earth. In the issue of the seventh angel's message introduced by this present angel, we find at the time the dead are judged, that the sea will give up the dead which are in it, before the human dead held by death and Hades are given up (Revelation 20:13). What the sea covers, no man knows, though it has been surmised, and that from certain Scriptures, that other than human remains are covered by its depths. We know that Satan was a murderer "from the beginning" (John 8:44), and that

demons seem to be disembodied spirits ever seeking
abodes, as Satan's angels do not. At all events, the sea
is *covered* by judgment, as this angel's position shows.
He cried "as a lion roareth." Compare Isaiah 21:8 where
the watchman "cried as a lion." He represents Him who
will shortly "roar from Zion" (Amos 1:2).

> **And when he cried, the seven thunders ut-
> tered their voices. And when the seven
> thunders uttered, I was about to write: and
> I heard a voice from heaven saying, Seal up
> the things which the seven thunders uttered,
> and write them not.**

We remember "the God of glory thundereth" (Psalm
29) and Job 26:14, "How small a whisper do we hear
of him! But the thunder of his power who can understand?"; and Job 37:5, "God thundereth marvellously
with his voice; Great things doeth he, which we cannot
comprehend." Indeed, in Psalm 29 is a striking commentary on the seven thunders of The Revelation. Beginning with verse 3 "The voice of Jehovah is upon the
waters: The God of glory thundereth," we have "the
voice of Jehovah" repeated exactly seven times!

It is characteristic of that presumption which belongs
to error that Seventh Day Adventism professes to tell
us (and that through a woman!) the very things which
the seven thunders uttered: although God commanded
John to seal them up and write them not.

It is well to observe that what the seven thunders
uttered is the *only part* of the whole book of Revelation
which is *sealed* (see 22:10). There is a perfect, mighty,
secret operation of God's power in judgment, as well
as in salvation (read Deuteronomy 29:29). Probably
some day we will understand this sealed message. John
did: he was about to write!

> **And the angel that I saw standing upon
> the sea and upon the earth lifted up his right
> hand to heaven, and sware by him that liveth
> forever and ever, who created the heaven and**

the things that are therein, and the earth and the things that are therein, and the sea and the things that are therein.*

With the little book open *(verse 2)* in one hand he lifts up his right hand to heaven, and announces a solemn oath by Jehovah the Creator. It is plain here again that this angel is not the Lord Himself; for when God took oath, "since he could swear by none greater, he sware by himself" (Hebrews 6:13). Now Christ is Himself the Creator, but this angel takes oath by other than himself.

There shall be delay no longer! We are entering upon a new phase of divine judgments. In chapter 5 John wept much because no one appeared able to take at all the book of judgment, or even to look upon it. The Lamb then took the sealed book. Upon the opening of the first six seals, dire results followed among men: and again, after the seventh seal, six of the seven trumpets brought direct visitations from heaven upon impenitent men. Now, however, solemn oath is taken that **in the days of the voice of the seventh angel, when he is about to sound, then is finished the mystery of God, according to the good tidings which he declared to his servants the prophets.**

This expression, "the *mystery* of God," in this connection seems to indicate all those counsels and dealings of God made known by Him to and through the Old Testament prophets, concerning His governmental proceedings with men on earth looking always toward the establishment of the kingdom in the hands of Christ.

When Christ comes to take the kingdom, there will be no mystery, but, on the contrary, manifestation. "The earth shall be full of the knowledge of Jehovah, as the waters cover the sea"—that is, universally and compulsorily (Isaiah 11:9). It is important for us to remember that we are ourselves still in the days of "mystery." If a man would walk godly, there is "the mystery of godliness" by which he walks, unknown to the world (I

---

*This phrase is repeated three times, once in connection with each sphere of creation, as emphasizing the Creator's rights as Creator, to proceed in judgment as He pleases.

Timothy 3:16); those who would walk "lawless," must at present walk in "the mystery of lawlessness," for God is not yet allowing "the lawless one" to be revealed, but *restrains* (thanks be to Him!) (II Thessalonians 2).

But when the seventh angel sounds, all this will be finished, and there will be open manifestation of all. So we shall expect Antichrist to be brought forth; Israel to be hated and persecuted by all nations, and Satan universally worshipped, for he is the *god* of this age! And we shall expect God to *manifest* His anger. He will do so, and fully—"in the days of the voice of the seventh angel." *"Delay no longer,"* then, is the word that governs things—let us hold this fact in mind, from this seventh angel onward.

> **And the voice which I heard from heaven, I heard it again speaking with me, and saying, Go, take the book which is open in the hand of the angel that standeth upon the sea and upon the earth.**

John is evidently, in spirit, upon the earth here. Also, that the voice should come *from heaven* to him, anew emphasizes the fact that the holder of the book is not Christ, but, as is said, simply an "angel." It is again brought to our attention that this little book is "open," not sealed; so that when the Seer has taken, eaten, and digested it, the revelations will all be such as can be understood from "the prophets" of the Old Testament, whose writings already have lain before men, "open," for a long time.

> **And I went unto the angel, saying unto him that he should give me the little book. And he saith unto me, Take it, and eat it up; and it shall make thy belly bitter, but in thy mouth it shall be sweet as honey. And I took the little book out of the angel's hand, and ate it up; and it was in my mouth sweet as honey: and when I had eaten it, my belly was made bitter.**

God's words, to one who loves them, are always sweet, as David says, "sweeter also than honey and the . . . honey-comb." Jeremiah said, "Thy words were found, and I did eat them." But, while to Jeremiah, God's words became "a joy and the rejoicing of my heart," to John, upon digesting this little book, they became bitter.

Its contents were such as, when pondered and understood, were of anguish to the prophet. It evidently contained the revelation found in chapter 11 concerning the future awful "Sodom and Egypt" spiritual state of Israel (11:8) and the Remnant's experiences under the rage of Satan and his vassals, in chapters 12 and 13.

They say unto me, Thou must prophesy again over many peoples and nations and tongues and kings.

Now this is exactly what John goes on to do, ending up with the *ten kings* allied with the Beast: their career and doom, in chapters 13, 17, and 19.

"They," who told John he must thus prophesy, we may surmise were heavenly "watchers" *(as in Daniel 4:13, 17):* for the mind of God as to earthly judgments and prophetic programs is well known by those dwelling in the light of heaven *(compare Revelation 7:13,14; 11: 15; 21:1; 22:9).*

And now, let us reflect upon the fact that blessing to earth's nations waits upon the condition of Israel, the *elect* nation. Christ will come, and "will turn away ungodliness from *Jacob*" and the receiving into favor of national Israel, will be as "life from the dead" for *"the world":* as Paul so clearly sets forth in Romans 11:26, 15; and James, in Acts 15:16, 17; as also all the prophets.

But these same prophets with one voice witness that before Israel can become a joy in the whole earth, they must first taste the full bitterness of rejecting their true Messiah. The "false shepherd" must come. Apostate Israel will make a "covenant with death" and a treaty with God's great enemy. The last state of "Israel after the flesh" will become "worse than the first."

But the *counsels of God* are ever settled and His word faithful. So that we shall see the Lord in Revelation 11 commanding John to measure "the Temple of God," with its altar and worshippers—even when the nation is apostate and the city "as Sodom"!

And the heavenly mind regarding Israel sees her as in Revelation 12:1; though her future experience on earth will be terrible *(12:13-16)*. And a remnant will stand upon Mount Zion to sing heavenly praise! *(14:1-5)*

The two great prophets or "witnesses" whose testimony preserves Israel from doom, and lays the foundation of *the fear of the Lord* in the remnant, will now be considered.

CHAPTER IX

GOD'S LAST PROPHETS: THE TWO WIT-
NESSES: THEIR TREMENDOUS TASK

Revelation 11

**And there was given me a reed like unto
a rod; and one said, Rise, and measure the
temple of God, and the altar, and them that
worship therein. And the court which is without the temple leave without, and measure it
not; for it hath been given unto the nations:
and the holy city shall they tread under foot
forty and two months.**

The moment the words "the temple of God" are used,
we know ourselves to be on Jewish ground. During the
present dispensation Stephen definitely testifies that "the
Most High dwelleth not in temples made with hands";
while Paul tells us in I Corinthians 3 and Ephesians 2,
and Peter likewise *(I Peter 2:5)*, that *The Church* is at
present the temple or sanctuary of God; none other being
recognized on earth.

We are reminded also in the opening of Revelation 11
that the only temple of Israel recognized by God is in
their own land, in their appointed city Jerusalem. We
must go thither for the interpretation of the remarkable
passage which is now before us.

In accordance with this, let us conceive the Jews back
in their land, and having built a temple unto their God,
and that there are "worshippers" discerned by God,
though not yet publicly recognized by Him. The "altar"
is that for sacrifice, not for prayer.

This whole eleventh chapter of The Revelation is
anticipative in character. Matters are set before us that
must later on in Revelation find their delineation in detail.
Other Scriptures, especially in the Old Testament, have
abundantly prophesied a restoration or returning of the
Jews to their land in unbelief, with not only a racial, but
a national consciousness; and the construction of a temple

such as John is told to measure here. The interpretation
of The Revelation reasonably demands familiarity with
God's prior words. Such passages as Zephaniah 2:1,2;
Isaiah 66:1-4; Isaiah 28:14-22 indicate what will be the
moral and spiritual character of those who "gather themselves together" as a nation in the last days.*

In accordance with Israel's "temple of God" being again
recognized, the Gentiles immediately take their place
without: so we read in Revelation 11:2,

> **And the court, which is without the temple
> leave without, and measure it not; for it hath
> been given to the nations: and the holy
> city shall they tread under foot forty and two
> months.**

Now some may ask, "Are not the Gentiles at present
treading down Jerusalem?" Certainly, according to Luke
21:24, Jerusalem shall be trodden down of the Gentiles
until the times of the Gentiles be fulfilled. But take care!
Jerusalem is not here in Luke called "the holy city."
On the contrary, our Lord left the temple in Matthew
23:38, with the words, "Your house is left unto you
desolate." Today, no one spot on earth is recognized
as holy above another: "there is no distinction between
Jew and Greek."

---

*There are several distinct goings into the land of Canaan by Israel: *first,*
under Joshua; *second,* under Zerubbabel and Joshua the High priest (see Ezra);
third, under permission of the Gentiles, "before the decree bring forth . . .
the day of Jehovah's anger come upon you" (Zephaniah 2:2). This returning
we see before our eyes today, especially since the Balfour declaration of 1917.
This movement will proceed until Jerusalem becomes, as we find it in Revelation 11, a "great city," and Palestine, through human methods of irrigation
and development has become prominent, especially financially so, among the
nations.   This will be the situation when the majority of Israel make their
"covenant with death," the treaty with the "Prince" of Daniel 9:27, and Isaiah
28:14, 15.   Having rejected Christ, the Jews will accept Antichrist (John
5:43).   This situation will end, as we know, in Jerusalem being compassed
by all nations to cut them off (Zechariah 14, Psalms 83, etc). It will be
then that "the overflowing scourge shall pass through and tread them down"
(Isaiah 28).   The most of the Jewish nation will be slain. *Fourth,* that returning to Palestine described by the Lord when He says He will "set His
hand again the second time to recover the remnant of His people, that shall
remain, from Assyria, and from Egypt, and from Pathros, and from Cush,
and from Elam, and from Shinar, and from Hamath, and from the islands
of the sea" (Isaiah 11:11). It is prophesied in other passages that Israel and
Judah shall be one nation at last, without enmity as to God's sovereign election
of Judah as the royal tribe, and David's seed as the royal house.
Christians, "Pray for the peace of Jerusalem"!
But that does not involve the Jews' participation in the present movement
(number three above). For Jews to gather back to Palestine now is to go
back to a fearful program!

But the Church age having ended (Revelation 4:1), and God having sent certain preliminary judgments (Revelation 6, 8, 9), with the result that men simply harden themselves against Him (Revelation 9:20, 21), He now proceeds to final things. And in order to bring on "Jacob's trouble," He must recognize that nation upon whose blessing the whole world waits, namely, Israel (Romans 11:15; Deuteronomy 32:8); but whose terrible chastening must come before they become "a praise in the earth."

We see, therefore, that the Gentiles in Revelation 11:2 have the "without" place, being subordinate to the national acceptance and restoration of Israel.

Next we notice the Gentile's blindness, maliginity and Satanic inspiration in the words, "shall they tread under foot." When Jewish times come on with God, a Gentile has no business in Jerusalem whatever, unless he comes as a humble worshipper of the God of Israel and in His prescribed way! Jerusalem is the city of the great King, and while it is at present unrecognized by God, yet the very expression, "Jerusalem shall be trodden down," shows the abhorrence of God for the gross, hideous uncleanness, godlessness and blindness of the Gentile. Read the account in Ezekiel's last nine chapters of the millennial Jerusalem, or Zechariah's closing verses, "In that day shall there be upon the bells of the horses, HOLY UNTO JEHOVAH; and the pots in Jehovah's house shall be like the bowls before the altar. Yea, every pot in Jerusalem and in Judah shall be holy unto Jehovah of hosts: . . . and in that day there shall be no more a Canaanite* in the house of Jehovah of hosts!"

We must now notice the expression "forty-two months." This we see is exactly equivalent to three years and a half, as it also is to 1260 days. This exact expression "forty-two months" is also used concerning the duration of the blasphemy and power of the wild beast of Revelation 13:5.

---

*The word "Canaanite" means "trafficker." Thank God, the day will shortly come when one land will be entirely free from commercialism and "business"!

We should be familiar with the great prophecy (which is indeed the secret of God's arrangements with Israel) in the ninth of Daniel, the *seventy sevens*. We know that one "seven" of years remains yet in the future, to pass upon Israel in their land and in their city, before the great six-fold eternal blessing of Daniel 9:24 comes to that nation. This time is spoken of in Daniel 12:7 as a "time, times (dual) and a half"—or three and one-half. This will be the time according to this Scripture when the Gentiles will conclude their "breaking in pieces the power of the holy people."

It becomes important to consider carefully these two time-measures in Revelation 11, the forty-two months of verse 2 and the 1260 days of verse 3. Of course, these two periods are equal in duration, but the question is whether they cover the same span or are successive. However, before we can consider this question intelligently, we should read further on in our chapter.

> **And I will give unto my two witnesses, and they shall prophesy a thousand two, hundred and threescore days, clothed in sackcloth. These are the two olive trees and the two candlesticks, standing before the Lord of the earth. And if any man desireth to hurt them, fire proceedeth out of their mouth and devoureth their enemies; and if any man shall desire to hurt them, in this manner must he be killed. These have the power to shut the heaven, that it rain not during the days of their prophecy; and they have power over the waters to turn them into blood, and to smite the earth with every plague, as often as they shall desire.**

Here we have the most astonishing task ever committed to men—God's last two great prophets, His "witnesses," before the earth is given over to Satan and to Antichrist.

Let it be at once observed, though it may not be pleasing, that the question is *not* who these witnesses are. If that had been important here, God would plainly have told us. Some would make them Enoch and Elijah; some Moses and Elijah. We know indeed that Elijah is coming before the great and terrible day of the Lord, from Malachi 4, and from our Lord's words to the disciples descending from the transfiguration mount; but this at present should not occupy our vision, but on the contrary, the fearful realities before our eyes! Let us be concerned here with *God's words*, not with our surmises.

Suddenly, in the "great city," Jerusalem, now called according to verse 8, "spiritually . . . Sodom and Egypt," two divinely sent messengers appear. Iniquity, pleasure-seeking, godlessness is rampant—what could the words "Sodom and Egypt" stand for, otherwise? The Jews, with untold millions of money will have built up a city where, according to verse 9, "peoples and tribes and tongues and nations" like very Babylon, are present. Yet those Jews will have built a temple in the name of Jehovah their God, although not really *knowing* Him,— and the majority of the nation will be ready to make a covenant with Antichrist!

The fact that today, in the midst of utter godlessness, Jewish synagogues as well as "Christian" cathedrals keep springing up, surely signifies that the building of a temple of God in a city that is spiritually called "Sodom and Egypt" is a possibility. The Lord Jesus even acknowledges the temple that old reprobate Herod, the Edomite, the Esau-man, had built (or so enlarged as practically to build), as His "Father's house," at the beginning of His ministry, and "My house" at the end; only finally He leaves it "desolate" in Matthew 23 when they had rejected Him officially.

In the midst of the gross darkness that is covering the earth and the peoples, before Jehovah has risen upon Israel (Isaiah 60:2), there is this temple; and doubtless to it will these two witnesses be sent, just as the Lord Jesus preached in the temple, and the apostles after Him, even Paul, did likewise,—though it was "desolate," as regards God's presence in it.

The newspapers and radios will one day be crowded full of this news: "Two prophets appear in Jerusalem clothed like Elijah of old in sackcloth and crying out that judgment is at hand!"

Day after day the excitement will increase as these witnesses give their testimony. And what will that testimony be?

1. They will say that the Lord Jesus Christ, who has been rejected, is the "Lord of all the earth." They will say (as said Elijah of old, in sudden apparition, at the court of Ahab), "As Jehovah, the God of Israel, liveth, before whom I stand, there shall not be dew nor rain these years, but according to my word." We see from the last phrase of Revelation 11:18, that they are addressing those that "destroy the earth."*

2. They testify unsparingly of human wickedness to men's very faces. You have probably never heard a preacher that told you to your face just how bad you were. I hope you have, but I doubt it. These witnesses will tell to the teeth of a horrid godlessness which is ready to worship the Devil, just what they are *before God!*

3. They will testify of the character of the judgments just past (chapters 6, 8 and 9) as having been directly from God, and warn of coming judgments infinitely more terrible. So did every prophet, and so will they.

4. They will decry the blasphemous claims the wild beast will shortly be making *(chapter 13),* that *man* is to be deified! They will denounce all the goodness of man as *a lie!*

---

*"God is resuming again His place as *Lord over the earth.* The two witnesses render testimony to this Lordship—to *the Lord over the earth;* not to the Father, nor to the heavenly glory, nor to the Lord of Heaven" *(Darby).* It should be remembered that God had committed rule upon earth to Israel; they having wholly failed. He gave it to Nebuchadnezzar and the Gentiles until the times of the Gentiles should be fulfilled. We are reading in Revelation 11 of the ending of Gentile times and the transferring again of the kingdom to Israel *(Acts 1:6).* Israel must pass through the time of Jacob's trouble, through The Great Tribulation; and the Son of David, who is now waiting at God's right hand, must come to make Israel's title and tenure good. It is a dreadful crisis which we are studying.

Man, under Satan, has in every sphere of his being denied, and will to every possible limit, deny, God's lordship of this earth. As concerning Christ, man has said, "This is the heir, come, let us kill him, and take his inheritance." Men say in their hearts, "There is no God"; for they desire none. The absolute antipathy of this world for God—oh, it is wholly *awful!*

5. They will testify that Jerusalem, although the holy city in God's purposes, is spiritually "Sodom and Egypt," and will announce *coming* judgments upon the city and people. They will tell the Jews that they "killed the Lord Jesus" *(I Thessalonians 2:15, 16),* and that He will yet be the King over all the earth.

Now such witnessing as this *brings out men's wickedness.* People fairly *rave* to destroy these witnesses! Many evidently attempt it, just as two presumptuous bands approached Elijah in II Kings 1 to their destruction.

Divine authority of such character and world-wide extent as was never committed to men, is given these witnesses. Elijah indeed shut heaven to the whole earth for three years and six months so that it rained not. But now if any even *desire* to hurt these witnesses—"fire proceedeth out of their mouth and devoureth their enemies." Not only do they also shut heaven that it rain not during the days of their prophecy, but, like Moses, they turn the water into blood! They smite the earth *with every plague* as often as they shall *desire.*

We emphasize the view that not the identity of these witnesses, but the character and history of their testimony is what the Spirit of God brings out here.*

Let us reflect upon the *awful gap* between this world and God, despite the "religious" forms we see about us. There is utter hatred of all that is really of God, and it is daily increasing. Hath not Judaism slain its thousands, and Romanism its tens of thousands, of God's witnesses? Finally will be sent these two—*the last prophets earth shall have from God!*

> And when they shall have finished their testimony, the beast that cometh up out of the abyss shall make war with them, and overcome them, and kill them. And their dead bodies lie in the street of the great city, which spiritually is called Sodom and Egypt,

*It would be well to reflect, for example, regarding Enoch, that he trusted God's Word that he would not see death. So he will not, we are sure, see that Word fail!

> where also their Lord was crucified. And
> from among the peoples and tribes and
> tongues and nations do men look upon their
> dead bodies three days and a half, and suffer
> not their dead bodies to be laid in a tomb.
> And they that dwell on the earth rejoice over
> them, and make merry; and they shall send
> gifts one to another; because these two
> prophets tormented them that dwell on the
> earth.

Let us note first of all that these witnesses will *finish*
their testimony. Every one of God's witnesses, every
believer, is "immortal until his work is done." No servants
of God ever encountered such fearful opposition and utter
odds as they, yet they finish their testimony. Satan can
do nothing without divine permission.

Next we read words that transport us over into chapter
13 and into 17—of the Wild-beast* that cometh out of
the abyss.

This awful being, the last head of the Roman Empire
revived, and Satan's very counterpart of the risen Christ,
will be given power at last over these mighty witnesses
of God, to "make war with them, and overcome them,
and kill them."

Thus, before the eyes of deluded humanity, who have
chosen falsehood, will be enacted a scene of apparent,
complete victory of Satan's Christ over God's holy
prophets.

As our Lord said, "It cannot be that a prophet perish
out of *Jerusalem.*" It will be in the very city where, as
we read in verse 8, "their Lord was crucified," that these
two mightiest of all God's messengers among the sons
of men will be ignominiously slain. (Their Lord also
seemed in this same city to pass under utter eclipse—

*Greek, *therion*. This word is first used in Mark 1:13, when our Lord was
with the "wild beasts" in the wilderness. Its meaning in Revelation may be
seen from chapter 6:8. The word indicates a beast of prey, of rapacity, of
cunning, of unreasoning violence, acting according to its own cruel nature. It
is God's word for the last two great enemies of mankind as seen in chapter
13, and mentioned in 11:7 in anticipation.

yea, and did so—when He died at the hands of sinful men.)

Now comes the real revelation of the heart of man: glee, horrid, insane, inhuman, hellish, ghoulish *glee!* There is actual delight at the death of God's witnesses— utter unbounded *delight!* Newspapers have whole front pages of jubilation. Excursions are run into Jerusalem to see the unburied corpses of these prophets of God: peoples, tribes, tongues and nations look upon their bodies three days and a half, and suffer not their corpses* to be laid in a tomb.

These two witnesses, for 1260 days, in utter self-denial, clothed in the sackcloth of humiliation, lamentation, prayer, mourning and warning, had cried out on God's behalf. Now the tables are turned, and "they that dwell on the earth rejoice over them, and make merry"! A regular Christmastime-of-Hell ensues: "They shall send gifts one to another." (Do not believe for a moment, that the gift-giving of the world at the present "Christmas-tide" has the least thing to do with divine *grace!*)

Notice now the rush to Satan's banner (the Beast), the moment he is allowed to kill God's witnesses. There is no moral or spiritual restraint left—no qualm of conscience! *You must learn to believe the worst about humanity, or join the Devil's theology finally!*

Now comes a change:

> And after the three days and a half the breath of life from God entered into them, and they stood upon their feet; and great fear fell upon them that beheld them. And they heard a great voice from heaven saying unto them, Come up hither. And they went up into heaven in the cloud; and their enemies beheld them.

---

*The singular number of *ptoma* is used first, to emphasize their condition "their wreck," as a German commentator puts it; but the plural afterwards when their individual bodies are distinguished.

Like their Lord in suffering and shame, they are now
made like Him in resurrection and exaltation. They go
up to heaven in the cloud and (what was not true of
Christ), their enemies behold them! Great fear has
already fallen upon them that beheld them, with the breath
of life from God in them, and standing upon their feet.
Now that utter denial of heaven, which has even now
begun to spread over the earth, and will increase to awful
proportions in those days, is itself denied by the mount-
ing up to heaven, in the sight of men, of these two witnesses! Christ's resurrection comforted those who "saw
him after he was risen"; the resurrection and ascension
to heaven of these witnesses will verily terrify their foes!

> And in that hour there was a great earth-
> quake, and the tenth part of the city fell; and
> there were killed in the earthquake seven
> thousand names of men; and the rest were
> affrighted, and gave glory to the God of
> heaven.

Four things follow in that very hour:

1. A great earthquake: God "shakes like a hut" this
whole guilty earth, as He did at the time our Lord Jesus
was slain by men, in the same city, Jerusalem.

2. One-tenth of this "great" rebuilt Jerusalem falls.
There is yet to come, under the seventh bowl of wrath
(chapter 16:18-20), the greatest earthquake that has ever
been. Be it noted here, however, that earthquakes are one
of God's judgments *(Matthew 24:7; Luke 21:11)*. Five
distinct ones are mentioned in The Revelation. Men have
forgotten to fear the God who declares in Isaiah 2:20, 21,
"Men shall cast away their idols . . . go into the cav-
erns of the rocks, and into the clefts of the ragged rocks,
from before the terror of Jehovah, and from the glory
of his majesty, when he ariseth to shake mightily the
earth." What does the modern scientist know about earthquakes, after all his "investigation"? In the last great
earthquake of Revelation 16, the cities of the Gentiles will
fall. But do they believe it as they build their skyscrapers
today?

3. Seven thousand are killed. When Elijah thought himself alone, God spoke of a remnant of seven thousand whom He had preserved. Here, however, matters are reversed. There is judgment—seven thousand are killed. We cannot avoid the belief that the number is significant. When Moses avenged the holiness of God upon the worshippers of the golden calf and the breaking of the law—three thousand were killed. When Peter preached the first sermon under grace—three thousand were saved. The form of expression in Revelation 11 is peculiar in the Greek: "names of men seven thousand." Many have believed that this indicates prominent men. Seiss remarks, "They would not allow burial of the slain witnesses, and now they themselves are buried alive in the ruins of their own houses, and in hell forever."

4. There is a general fright and a giving glory to the God of heaven. Let us notice at once that this is the only *record* of any public, human regard of God on earth, between the Church days in chapters 2 and 3, and the coming of Christ in the Day of Wrath and the setting up of the Millennium in 19. This is awfully significant! Notice further, that here in chapter 11, there is no ground to believe that it was a general, gracious operation. "There was the general effect of unrepentant religion—but the *testimony* not received—for that would have broken their wills. Fear acted on them externally to honor God formally, but only as One in *heaven*." Again another writer calls attention to the demons confessing Christ's deity, standing aghast at His approaching judgments, but showing not an element of change in their character: "When men have sinned their day of gracious visitation away; fighting, killing and glorying in the destruction of God's prophets, they are not likely to be suddenly transformed into saints by the constraints and terrors of the day of doom, although obliged to confess that it is the invincible God of heaven that is dealing with them."

The second Woe is past; behold the third
Woe cometh quickly.

Thus ends the second Woe, an awful time indeed!
Men smitten by every plague at the hands of two of their
fellow men, whom they could not help but know were
God's own, direct *witnesses*. So we read, "the third Woe
cometh quickly."

This will be the handing over of all men to Satan, according to II Thessalonians 2—"because they received
not . . . the truth." It will be the awful story of Revelation 13—which we must duly and solemnly study.

Meanwhile it may be well to resume the question of
whether the forty-two months and 1260 days of this
chapter run concurrently or are consecutive.

Let us observe that if the Beast kills the two witnesses
at the *end* of the forty-two months of his career, it
would be just at the time of our Lord's second coming;
for we read in Matthew 24:29, 30:

"Immediately after the tribulation of those days the
sun shall be darkened, and the moon shall not give her
light, and the stars shall fall from heaven, and the powers
of the heavens shall be shaken: and then shall appear the
sign of the Son of man in heaven: and then shall all the
tribes of the earth mourn, and they shall see the Son
of man coming on the clouds of heaven with power and
great glory."

But here in Revelation 11 instead of the awful advent
of the Lord from heaven "immediately" after the killing of these witnesses, we read of a hideous celebration
of their death by the nations and tribes of earth. True,
after three and one-half days, these witnesses are raised
and taken back to heaven, but there is no hint that the
advent of the Lord takes place "immediately" as Matthew
24 calls for, if this 1260 days be the *last* half of Daniel's
seventieth week.

We do not find either, in the account of the fearful
history of the Beast in Revelation 13, which continues for
"forty-two months," any account of, or any place for, the
prophesying of these two witnesses. For forty-two

months "a mouth speaking great things and blasphemies" is given to the Beast to blaspheme God, His name, His tabernacle and them that dwell in heaven. Also "to make war with the saints, and to overcome them"; and to have "authority over every tribe and people and tongue and nation. And all that dwell on the earth shall worship him"—save the elect ('Revelation 13:5, 6, 7, 8). Furthermore, the godly Israelites of those days were distinctly warned by the Lord to flee "the abomination that maketh desolate" (the person and image of the Beast in the temple of God).

The impression I feel very strongly from Revelation 11:7 is that it is at the *beginning* of the Beast's successful blasphemous career, *that he kills these two witnesses.*

From the object of the prophesying of these two witnesses, we see also that there must be a preparatory work done in the heart of the Israelite of those days. The extent of Israel's present blindness and alienation from Jehovah, and of her utter worldliness and commercialistic idolatry, is too vast and awful to be measured by us.

That these two witnesses have a ministry of judgment on the whole earth and to apostate Israel, *as apostate,* we see at once, but we must remember also two things: *First,* that they are the "two olive trees" which supply the oil of the Spirit by God's grace and providence to that wretched, but true Israel, which really is the remnant. See Zechariah 4:2, 3, 6, 11-14 (R. V.)—a wonderful passage! *Second,* that these two witnesses are "candle-sticks" as well as "olive trees" *(Revelation 11:4).* The Church will have gone to heaven. No one on earth yet has *faith,* although many have been sealed as the Lord's. Luke 18:8 puts a question which must be answered in the negative: "When the Son of man cometh, shall he find faith on the earth?" After the Church is gone, the earth waits Israel's conversion. We read in Isaiah 60:2:

"For, behold, darkness shall cover the earth, and gross darkness the peoples; but Jehovah will arise upon thee, and his glory shall be seen upon thee. And nations shall come to thy light, and kings to the brightness of thy rising."

Now Israel will not themselves be converted until they *see* the "sign of the Son of man (that is, Himself) in heaven" according to Zechariah 12:10 and 13:1.

"And I will pour upon the house of David, and upon the inhabitants of Jerusalem, the spirit of grace and of supplication; and they shall look unto me whom they have pierced. . . . In that day there shall be a fountain opened to the house of David and to the inhabitants of Jerusalem, for sin and for uncleanness."

So that, all things considered, I am compelled to believe that the two witnesses will prophesy during the *first* half of Daniel's seventieth week. Their witnessing will lay the foundation of the fear of Jehovah in the remnant (although Jehovah will not be known, nor reveal Himself, until the *end* of the week, as the One "whom they have pierced").

The Days of the Voice of the Seventh Angel

And the seventh angel sounded; and there followed great voices in heaven, and they said, The kingdom of the world is become the kingdom of our Lord, and of his Christ; and he shall reign for ever and ever.

And the four and twenty elders, who sit before God on their thrones, fell upon their faces and worshipped God, saying, We give thee thanks, O Lord God, the Almighty, who art and who wast; because thou hast taken thy great power, and didst reign.

And the nations were wroth, and thy wrath came, and the time of the dead to be judged, and the time to give their reward to thy servants the prophets, and to the saints, and to them that fear thy name, the small and the great: and to destroy them that destroy the earth.

Although this passage seems so simple and plain, yet for three reasons we should mark it closely.

1. It marks a crisis in God's dealings which must be fully understood and remembered as we proceed in this great book.

2. It gives God's own outline of the events that follow, so that we know the things He Himself emphasizes.

3. Preliminary meditation upon these themes (especially divine wrath, the rage of the nations and the "taking" by God of His own great power), will clear our minds in these days of Satanic fog, to understand the delineation in the succeeding chapters of the matters given in outline in our passage.

Our lesson extends to "the destroying of them that are destroying the earth," therefore it includes the overthrow of the Beast and his armies at the end of chapter 19 and the destruction of Gog and Magog at the end of the Millennium in chapter 20; and, inasmuch as it covers the time of the dead to be judged, spans the great white throne judgment itself. The seventh angel's trumpet therefore, brings us to the portals of the New Creation— to chapter 21.

We need to notice at once that the voices in heaven, and the twenty-four elders, celebrate the great events both in realization and in anticipation: in realization, because, at the seventh angel's sounding, God's whole administrative attitude changes, from *hidden,* to openly *exercised,* authority; in anticipation, because the actual subjugation of the enemies is yet to be accomplished.

The "great voices in heaven" said, "The kingdom of the world is become *the kingdom* of our Lord, and of his Christ."

Note the word *kingdom* here, not "kingdoms," as in the King James version.

The verse means that the whole dominion of the world has, at the sounding of the seventh angel, become God's in actuality; that is, in the *exercise* of the power He always has had. Hitherto, in the divine program, it has

not been fitting to pull the lever releasing the resistless
flood of kingly energy. The sealed book was given to
Christ in chapter 5 with the acclamation of the universe.
The succeeding chapters (6-9), showed certain visitations
of divine displeasure, but God's Christ remained in
heaven, the souls under the altar are commanded to *wait*.
Men, meanwhile, repented not. Then the angel of chapter 10 most solemnly announces that ""in the days of the
voice of the seventh angel" God will finish His mystery
and will reveal all His authority, according to all that
the prophets foretold.

When for example, Israel compassed the walls of Jericho, blowing warning ram's horns each day, there was
a moment on the seventh day, when they had compassed
the city the seventh time, that there came a long blast
from the ram's horn, and God said "shout," and the walls
fell flat. This may serve as an illustration of God's ways,
both in judgment and in training His people.

Until the sounding of the seventh trumpet (Revelation
11:15), what all heaven with holy eagerness had long
looked forward to, had not been done—the *taking* of His
great power by the blessed and only Potentate.

And now hear in exultant acclamation: "The kingdom
of the world is become *the kingdom* of our Lord and of
his Christ: and he shall reign unto the ages of the ages"!

We all have seen the celebration of a successful political party after an election. The "campaign" is over; the
stress and struggle, the, at times apparently, doubtful
issue; the intense devotion to the candidate for office;
and now the battle is won, jubilation fills the air! Relief
in victory and hope of the future, fill men's very hearts!

So, when at last "delay" is over, and the long, long
ages of conflict between light and darkness are about to
end, heaven with *great voices* of *utter delight* bursts
forth into celebration!

We do not well, unless we also enter into the very
spirit of this rejoicing. Our Lord taught us to pray,
"Thy kingdom come, Thy will be done, as in heaven, so
on earth." All the hosts of heaven are waiting today

the sounding of this seventh trumpet, with an eagerness of desire and a holy consuming longing we can hardly imagine. In utter, absolute devotedness to their God and to His blessed government and purposes, they have served through these ages since rebellion began in heaven, with jealous hope, every day, every hour, every moment, looking for the coming of the day when God will take over the government of this rebellious earth—take it over in power; TAKE HIS GREAT POWER AND REIGN. The prophetic account of that glad day is given us, that we may join by faith in the scene that shall "soon come to pass," and may rejoice with those that shall rejoice, in that blessed consummation!

Notice, first, that the elders, themselves already crowned, cannot therewith be content till God takes His great power, and exercises it. Rapture and worship then thrill them!

Again, they address God in His full revealed name as "Adonai-Elohim-Shaddai, who art and who wast," no longer adding, "who is to come"! This act of *taking* His great power and *reigning,* has ended the long night of mystery, where, amid great trials, *faith* held fast to "who art to come." Now it is in *manifestation,* heaven has stepped into a new stage of blessing! Our God, who is and who was, *is reigning* at last! He has taken His great power.

Once again, note that the words "didst reign," show how definite, in the view of these elders, is that act of God by which He lays aside all obscure providential government to assume His royal prerogatives. The construction is remarkable: "Thou hast taken thy great power, and didst reign."

Let us now study humbly the five-fold results of God's "taking" His power.

1. "The nations were wroth." The anger of earth at heaven's beginning royal interruption, is unbounded. It is a great subject of prophecy—"why do the nations rage?" (Psalm 2; Psalm 83; Joel 3:9-13; Zechariah 14:2-4).

The hatred of fallen man against divine control began with Cain, in Genesis 4. Though a murderer, he utterly resented Jehovah's interference. Saul pursues David, God's elect king, like a partridge in the mountains. Absalom will be a patricide, ere he will submit. Ahab and Jezebel hunt Elijah in every kingdom on earth, once the prophet takes control of the elements! Why did Israel slay the prophets of the Lord? Only because they asserted Jehovah's authority! Nebuchadnezzar is full of fury against Shadrach, Meshach and Abed-nego, if they dare disobey his blasphemous decree. Haman would have not only Mordecai, but all the Jews, killed, to appease his wounded vanity: for Mordecai "bowed not down."

The Jews spit in the face of the Lord Jesus saying, "We will not have this man to reign over us." When it reaches Nero's ears that Paul preaches "another king, one Jesus," he must have him back to a second imprisonment at Rome and cut off his head. Look at the blood-stained path over which the martyr-saints have come, who dared claim *rights* for God and His Son in this world! Today men will tolerate a preacher *if he lets them alone.* They can even patronize a preacher who does not touch their *wills.* Religion is decent, but *surrender to God* is *intolerable* to the nations of this world.

Now, in our lesson, when God ends all this time of long-suffering, and steps out, *claiming in power* that obedience to Him upon earth that is due Him from all His creatures, humanity will be found a hotbed of *rebellion.* It will be like striking a vast hornet's nest!

Do you know that it is a public scandal in this universe —the history of this world? Men have so long been let alone, or visited by only occasional displays of divine power, that there is "no fear of God before their eyes." Look today at Russia, the anti-God nation. But the denial of God in Russia is but a hint of what all nations will shortly display, as we shall find in Revelation 13. When man's long carnival and carousal of selfishness is confronted by a *will* that is *resistless,* so that nations must bow to it or be stricken off the earth—then shall we see

the events that lead to "the war of the great day of God,
the Almighty"; and to the thousand years of *iron-rod*
rule so lightly called "the Millennium," even by uncon-
verted people today. It will be a time when this earth
will *obey the will of another* than *themselves!*

2. "And thy wrath came."

God's wrath has been postponed so long that men deny
altogether a God capable of anger and vengeance. Paul
disposes of this in one searching question: "Is God unrighteous who visiteth with wrath? Be it not! for then
how shall God judge the world?" (Romans 3:5, 6). God
is Love; but God also is Light; and He hates sin with
all the infinite eternal abhorrence of His infinitely holy
being and nature! And He has already "appointed a day
in which he will judge the world in righteousness by the
man whom he hath ordained; whereof he hath given
assurance unto all men, in that he hath raised him from
the dead" (Acts 17:31). "Unto them that are factious,
and obey not the truth, but obey unrighteousness, *shall be*
wrath and indignation, tribulation and anguish."*

Perhaps the truest test of a doctrine, next to the reason
why Christ shed His blood (and directly connected therewith), is, does it set forth a God capable of hatred of sin
as *sin* (not merely for its disastrous effects upon creatures), and capable of visiting personal and eternal wrath
upon those who choose sin as their way, who "loved the
darkness rather than the light; for their works were evil"?

We speak of this, because we must get ready, now, if
we are to go on with The Revelation, to hear and believe
the *facts* regarding the wrath of God. The "God" of
Modernism, Universalism, Russellism, Spiritism, Christian Science, in short, the "God" the world dreams of,
does not exist. The "god of this age" is Satan. He has
blinded the minds of them that believe not. Men are in
a fool's paradise who prate of the God of the Bible not
being such a one as will punish sin! Wrath is indeed

---

*Note the fearful *progress* in these words: *wrath*—stored up but possibly
appeasable; *indignation*—more personal, at sin persisted in; *tribulation*—the
attack, finally, upon the impenitent, of poured-forth fury; *anguish*—the eternal,
terrible *effect!*

waiting, in this day of grace, but "Thy wrath *came*" will shortly be fulfilled.

3. "And the time of the dead to be judged."

The "coming" of divine wrath involves that measuring out to each (unsaved) creature, that recompense due, in view of light had, and attitude and deeds. This is called *judgment.* Only the unbelieving will be *judged,* as we see in John 5:24, R. V., and John 3:18. Thus only the lost are in view in the words, "the time of the dead to be judged." For the *sin* question, for believers, was brought up at the cross of Calvary; and a judgment day was held there, with all the infinite demands of God's justice against sin fully allowed, and fully and forever met! He "shall appear a second time, apart from sin, to them that wait for him, unto salvation."

> "Payment God will not *twice* demand—
> First, at my bleeding Surety's hand,
> And then again at mine!"

4. "And the time to give their reward."

This seventh trumpet ushers in the glad day of *rewards!*

"To thy servants the prophets." *The prophets* are first; and do we wonder? The prophets of God were first in time, and peculiar in duty and suffering.

The word "prophet" means, one *who speaks for another (Exodus 4:15, 16* illustrates it). These Old Testament men of God gave out God's message to their fellows at all and any cost! Only read such experiences as fell to the lot of Elijah, Isaiah, Micah, Jeremiah, Daniel, Hosea and Amos.* Shall they not be *rewarded?* They shall, and *first.*

"And to the saints." Probably all the saints of God are here included. The rapture of the Church (I Thes-

---

*Read, if you would walk with a *prophet,* Jeremiah 1:4-10—his commission; his sorrow over sinning Israel in 4:19-22; 8:18—9:1, 2 and 10; and the whole book of Lamentations; his terrible loneliness, Jeremiah 15:10; 20:7, 8; his burden to speak his God's message despite all, 20:9; 10:19-22; his persecution and suffering, 38:1-13. Hath not God all these things in His heart marvelously to repay? The prophets are peculiarly dear—all of them, to their God. All heaven values and remembers them, though earth hated and killed them. Blessed coming day—wait for it!

salonians 4) occurs, we believe, at chapter 4:1. We know
that Paul, Moses, David and Abraham are all looking
to a "day" of rewards. That day has not come yet,
though they have been eagerly awaiting it for centuries.
Rewards are connected with the *kingdom,* as Paul shows
in II Timothy 4:18. We know "the day of *Christ*" is
connected with the rapture; "the day of the *Lord,*" with
The Revelation. But let us reflect that the seventh angel
sounds at least three and one-half years before the revelation of Christ with His saints, as in Revelation 19:11-16.
The seventh angel sounds *before* The Great Tribulation,
into which the Church does not go. But we feel that
God, dealing as He does *according to works* in the matter
of *rewards* and only by *grace* in the matter of salvation,
justly postpones *giving* these rewards unto this time—
giving the prophets precedence, then all those called
"saints" (as having separating light and privilege); and
then,

"And to them that fear thy name, the small and the
great." Here are those (like the "righteous" ones of
Matthew 25:37-39), who did not have much light, but
yet "feared the Lord."

It is a comfort to the heart, here, also, to find the
"small" named before the "great": (contrast the judgment of Revelation 20:12, where the order is natural, not
gracious).

5. "And to destroy them that destroy the earth."

The seventh angel's trumpet does not say that all these
things have been brought to pass; nor (as do the prophets) merely that they shall come to pass; but, as Alford
says, "the hour *is come* for it all to take place."

Man, since the Fall, has been a *destroyer* of God's
earth. "Destruction and misery are in their ways." It
is said there were *nine* Troys; Homer's Troy is the
second, built on the ruins of the first!

Also, man has appropriated all those inventions of
"science" which he can to selfishness, and especially to
war. The time will strike to stop all this. The destroyers
shall be destroyed. "They shall not hurt nor destroy in

all my holy mountain; for the earth shall be full of the knowledge of Jehovah, as the waters cover the sea"—that is, resistlessly!

The Heavenly Temple and Ark: The Faithful God.

And there was opened the temple of God that is in heaven; and there was seen in his temple the ark of his covenant; and there followed lightnings, and voices, and thunders, and an earthquake, and great hail.

This passage, if simply *believed,* becomes a key to seven chapters,—Revelation 10-16.

1. There *is a literal temple* in heaven. The one on earth was a *pattern* of the *things* in heaven (Hebrews 8:5; 9:22).*

2. The real *"ark of his covenant,"* which declares His purposes and His faithfulness, is there.

3. This ark's *pattern* was given to *Israel,* not to the Church: the Church does not have to do with earthly temple-worship, nor with those governmental affairs of earth with which God has connected Israel.

4. The ark of Israel's temple disappeared (for it was all typical of things to come); but when God begins again to deal with Israel and those governmental affairs with which Israel is bound up, the real ark appears in the opened temple on high.

5. The ark of old was the place of God's dwelling in the Holy of Holies, *with* His people. But here we see the ark connected with the putting forth of *judgment,*—

---

*Moses made a *pattern* of *the things* in the heavens—"the heavenly things" *(Hebrews 8:5; 9:24).* If there were no sanctuary, no ark, literally, in heaven, of what did Moses make a pattern? And what mean such words as Revelation 11:19: "There was opened *the temple of God that is in heaven"?* That there will be no temple in the heavenly Jerusalem *(21:22)* is just as much to be expected as that there will be a temple, or formal worship, for others than the Bride, (the wife of the Lamb). "And there was seen in his temple *the ark of his covenant."* If these are "symbolical," symbolical of *what?*

I have sometimes been asked "What became of the ark of the covenant when the temple was destroyed by Nebuchadnezzar? It surely must be preserved somewhere." Human thoughts are surely not God's thoughts, for He distinctly tells us (Jeremiah 3:16) that in the future kingdom the ark shall not be remembered nor come into mind. Of course, the Apocrypha must have Jeremiah running and hiding that ark! (II Maccabees 2:1, 8). Why is it that the very folks who thus inquire beyond what is written, concerning the temple of old, are filled with doubt concerning what plainly *is* written of the temple in heaven?

lightnings, thunders, an *earthquake.* For God had said to Moses, when He renewed His covenant with Israel, after the great breach, of the calf-worship, that He would do thus: "Behold, I make a covenant: before all thy people (Israel) I will do marvels, such as have not been wrought in all the earth, nor in any nation . . . for it is a terrible thing that I do with thee." "In the day when I visit, I will visit their sin upon them" (Exodus 34:10; 32:34). God is here in this part of The Revelation, showing that He *will do as He has said:* therefore is His temple in heaven opened, and the ark—symbol of His covenant-keeping, seen.

6. This judgment-action of God will involve all the earth: for Israel are to be established as God's elect royal nation,—*but punished first.* And *all nations* will be brought up against Jerusalem to battle, at Armageddon.

7. Therefore, Revelation 11:19 and 15:5-8 become luminous: God is acting *in judgment, from His temple in heaven,* and *according to His covenanted arrangements,* to restore the Kingdom to Israel, albeit by means so severe as to be *bitter,* indeed, for the Seer, who loved his nation, to know.

CHAPTER X

THE WOMAN, THE DRAGON, THE MAN-CHILD

Revelation 12

And a great sign* was seen in heaven: a woman arrayed with the sun, and the moon under her feet, and upon her head a crown of twelve stars; and she was with child; and she crieth out, travailing in birth, and in pain to be delivered.

That this woman represents Israel is evident, for:

1. The *place in the prophecy* is Israelitish: The two witnesses have been stationed at Jerusalem, where temple-worship is again going on.

2. The words, "sun," "moon," and "stars" immediately remind us of Joseph's dream, Genesis 37:9—"Behold, the sun and the moon and eleven stars made obeisance to me,"—a forecast of *Israel,* in the last days.

3. The Church cannot be spoken of in this language, for she was chosen "before the foundation of the world" and her glory is not at all describable in terms of this present creation. She has union with Him who has gone "far above all the heavens"; whereas this woman's connection is plainly with what we call the "solar system,"—that is, as viewed from *earth.*

4. That she is clothed with the sun, with the moon under her feet, and on her head a twelve-star crown, indicates the subjection of earth to her governmental glory: "The splendor and fulness of governmental authority on earth," belong, by God's sovereign appointment, to Israel: and the restoring of the Kingdom to

---

*The Greek word *semeion,* translated "sign" is used 77 times in the New Testament, and generally means an object set forth, or action done to *accredit* a person, or an utterance. Our Lord's miracles are thus often named (John 20:30); and those of the enemy also (Matthew 24:24 and Revelation 13:13, 14). But the sense of the word here in Revelation 12:1, 3, is to set forth in picture, the facts and counsels *as they are before God.* The woman thus shows God's counsels and plans concerning Israel and Christ, as regards *rule on earth;* and the dragon in the character he bears before God; and his hate of, and opposition to, God's plan to have Christ rule the earth. For the whole question, from chapter 10 to chapter 16, is, Who shall rule, Satan or God? God's Christ, or Satan's?

Israel, under Christ, is the subject before us in this part of The Revelation.

5. Israel is described in the prophets as travailing in birth; the Church never is (Micah 5:2, 3; Israel 9:6; 7:14).

6. Israel, not the Church, gave birth to Christ (Roman 9; Micah 5; Isaiah 9:6; Hebrew 7:14). In no possible sense did the Church do so. Seiss, generally very helpful, most strenuously asserts the Woman to be "the Church Universal"—whom he calls "the Mother of us all," etc. But this is a Romish relict, nothing else. The "church of all ages" is a pleasant theological dream, wholly unscriptural. No wonder Mr. Seiss proceeds to call the Child "the whole regenerated purchase of the Savior's blood," though how the Mother and the Child can be thus *the same company,* even the author's utmost vehemence fails to convince you! (Seiss: Lectures 26 and 28.)

7. It is very evident, and is most important to recognize, that this woman's real *history* is on earth, persecuted by the enemy. (See verses 13-16.) It is the *sign* that is seen in heaven, while her *experience* proceeds on earth. When seen as a "sign," we see God's glorious purposes regarding her,—heavenly purposes, but to enter upon them, she is seen in a process of earthly persecution.

8. The subsequent earthly history (Revelation 12) of the woman, corresponds exactly with what other prophets tell us concerning the trouble of Israel in the last days.

9. The period of that trouble, as we see in Revelation 12:6, coincides also with the last of Daniel's seventieth week—The Great Tribulation of three and one-half years.

> And there was seen another sign in heaven: and behold, a great red dragon, having seven heads and ten horns, and upon his heads seven diadems. And his tail draweth the third part of the stars of heaven, and did cast them to the earth: and the dragon standeth before the woman that is about to be delivered, that

> when she is delivered he may devour her
> child. And she was delivered of a son, a
> manchild, who is to rule all the nations with
> a rod of iron: and her child was caught up
> unto God and unto his throne.
>
> And the woman fled into the wilderness,
> where she hath a place prepared of God, that
> there they may nourish her a thousand two
> hundred and threescore days.

In this second "sign," or symbolic vision, of this great
passage we have: (1) The dragon, his greatness and
murderousness; his regal form; perfect wisdom (seven
heads) and almost perfect governmental power (ten
horns) soon to be developed in the revived Roman Empire
as the Beast of chapter 13; next, his fatal influence in
drawing to their ruin a third of the angels; then his
devouring enmity toward the child of the woman. (2)
The birth of the Male-child destined to rule with iron-
rod the nations, and the taking up to God and to His
throne (for the then present) of the Child. (3) The
flight for 1260 days of the woman to a divinely prepared
protection, and her "nourishment" there.

Although, be it noted, he is here called "great" and
"red" and a "dragon," in Ezekiel 28 he seems to be the
highest creature ever made, the anointed one of the
cherubim, "full of wisdom, and perfect in beauty," probably leading the worship of the universe. Even Michael,
the archangel, "durst not bring against him a railing judgment," because he was of a higher order of being than
angels—a "dignity" *(Jude 8, 9)*.

Moreover, he is seen as *red*. This is the color of murder and of blood. Our Lord says of him in John 8:44,
"he was a murderer from the beginning"—awful history!
Pride caused his apostasy; and utter hatred, deceit and
violence continue his story, even after the Millennium
(Revelation 20:7, 8).*

---

*Let us remember, however, that although the Devil was a murderer from
the beginning, yet God commands Ezekiel to take up a *lamentation* over him
(Ezekiel 28:11, 12). God "delighteth not in the death of any," although
He will fulfill Revelation 20:10).

Also, he is called a *dragon*. In this is a picture or the hideousness and horror that sin brings. Contrast the beauty in Ezekiel 28 with this shuddering word "dragon." This word is used only in The Revelation, and occurs thirteen times, twelve of these concerning Satan.*

If we compare him with the Beast of 13:1, we read: "A beast coming up out of the sea, having ten horns and seven heads, and on his horns ten diadems." We find readily, the likeness to, and the distinction between, Satan and his final world-power developed by Satan and headed up by the fearful man of Revelation 13:18. In the dragon the seven heads (complete wisdom, Satanic sagacity, and "the concentration of earthly power and wisdom in cruel despotic exercise") wear the diadems, while the ten horns, (since the head controls the horn which springs from it) set forth what will be the utmost form of his diabolical *exercise* of power. Now in 13:1, while the seven heads are there, it is the ten *horns* that wear the diadems. Satan, who is pictured in the dragon, has projected his plan of universal earth-rule by ten kings, who are to wear the crowns! He sees to that! It is the final form of the fourth world-power of Daniel 7. And how fearful the thought that the earth will, at that time, be so wholly *given over* to Satan (whom it chose instead of Christ) that the very *dragon-form* of seven heads and ten horns will appear in God's description of that revived Fourth Empire which is coming! Compare Revelation 12:3 and 13:1.

Again we read concerning the dragon, that "his tail draweth the third part of the stars of heaven, and did

---

*"The dragon figured prominently in ancient and medieval mythologies as an embodiment of evil principle. It has been superstitiously dreaded and even worshipped, as in China, where it is the imperial emblem. It is commonly represented as a large winged serpent, with a crested head and powerful claws. In classical mythology, a dangerous, often a supernatural serpent" (*Standard Dictionary*). "The Hebrew word *tannin* or *tannim* is rendered by Greek, *Drakon* in the Septuagint. It seems to refer to any great monster, either of land or sea, as in Genesis 1:21; Job 7:12; Lamentations 4:3" (*Bib. Cycl. McClintock and Strong*). It is striking that just as inner Buddhism names its deity *Sheitan*, although not allowing the name to be pronounced because of dread; so the *dragon* was worshipped under that form and name in Babylon and many other lands. This shows how God *compels* this world to acknowledge whom they serve! Doubtless Satan hates to be portrayed as a monster with great jaws and claws and serrated tail. But the dragon legends of the nations simply support the Word of God!

cast them to the earth." This seems a direct indication of that proportion of the angels of God who are perverted by him into utter ruin. As we read in Daniel 8:10, 24, of Satan's Christ, "It waxed great, even to the host of heaven; and some of the host and some of the stars it cast down to the ground, and trampled upon them"; and "he shall destroy the mighty ones (angelic beings) and the holy people" (Israel).

When we remember the hundred million angels, and millions upon millions after that, of Revelation 5:11, who remained true to God, we get some conception of the host, who by Satan's "traffic" *(Ezekiel 28:16)* were drawn away from the adoration of God to idolatry of this highest creature of His. The actual casting down of Satan's angels with him is recorded a little later in our chapter *(12:7-9)*.

The dragon's desire is to devour the *child,* evidently knowing His destiny, that He is to shepherd all the nations with an iron rod. (Of course, this is Christ, and none other.) Satan has always known from Genesis 3:15 God's plan—that the Seed of the woman should bruise the serpent's head. All Satanic activities are carried on under the double motive of *ambition to rule and be worshipped,* and, *hatred toward the One whom God has chosen* to take the kingdom Satan has usurped.

The dragon, then, is Satan (verse 9). We have here the beginning of the end of the great warfare between God and His adversary begun in Eden. There the Serpent beguiled the woman, and God declared He would put enmity between the Serpent and the Woman, and between her Seed, and his seed. Now her Seed is *Christ,* and none other, as Paul shows in Galatians 3:16. "Unto us a child is born" cries Isaiah (9:6, 7) "of the increase of whose *government* and of peace there should be no end," which is the exact subject before us in Revelation 12. Satan's enmity and jealousy was against Christ, who was to "rule all the nations": for had not Satan himself been their prince and god?

This scene in Revelation 12 (like Zechariah 9:9, 10), looks only at Christ as coming *Ruler,* and disregards all other history. Just as Zechariah saw Him ride into Jerusalem, *lowly and meek,* yet *Zion's King,* and speaking peace to the nations, with dominion unto the ends of the earth, so with this passage (Revelation 12:5). Zechariah looked *forward* to His First Advent, John looks *back* to it: and both look on to His *ruling*—to the *Second* Advent. With Isaiah, Christ is the virgin-born Immanuel, the Child born who will have the *government* on His shoulder; Zechariah sees Him ride into Jerusalem upon the lowly ass—yet has Him *ruling* (making no mark of His rejection by Israel); John sees Him born unto Israel, despite the dragon's efforts through Herod, the chief priests, and Rome; and then caught up to God and to His throne, as One that *shall rule all the nations* with an iron rod (without considering how long He shall have to wait in heaven before He "receives the Kingdom").

It is necessary to remember that God emphasizes the fact in Revelation 12, that He is speaking in *sign-language.* Prophecy often speaks thus, noting desired facts, irrespective of chronological arrangement. So we have only to view those other Scriptures that concern the great end before us in Revelation 12, the setting forth of God's King in triumph (though having to wait upon God's throne) despite all Satan's malice, to see who this Man-child *must be.*

The Church is to be caught up "in the clouds" *(I Thessalonians 4);* but it is nowhere said of her that she is "caught up *unto God,* and unto *his throne."* This place belongs alone to our Lord Jesus, according to Revelation 3:21. The Church will indeed share Christ's future throne, but *He only* sits on His Father's throne, "on the right hand of God."

To claim that the child is a victorious company of the Church, while the rest are pursued by the Devil through the great tribulation days, has, we are persuaded as its root, self-righteousness; as its fruit, division of the Body: and as its character, terrible blindness as to what God's sovereign *grace* is. "I labored more abundantly than they all; yet not I, but the grace of God which was with me," said Paul.

"The things which are (the Church period), and the things which shall come to pass after these" *(Revelation 1:19)* is our Lord's division of this book; and we must not depart from it. Therefore, we are not looking for Church things in Revelation 12, but on the contrary, we have from chapter 11 in the testimony of the two witnesses, as well as in the measuring of the temple, and the designation of the city as that city where "their Lord was crucified," an indication that we are on Israelitish ground.

Now there are three scenes in Revelation 12: First, Christ born to Israel, and ascended, despite the dragon, to await His destined rule of the nations; second, the casting out of Satan and his angels from all place in heaven, and the joy of the heavenly throng over this; third, the wrathful persecution of the Woman (Israel) and her Seed, and her divine protection for 1260 days—The great tribulation.

The woman flees to "the wilderness." If we do not understand prophecy, we make Israel's fleeing immediately consequent upon our Lord's ascension. But instead of this, we find the Jews in the Book of Acts long and steadfastly resisting and persecuting those who are really the godly remnant of Israel—those who had believed on Jesus of Nazareth as the Messiah.

Therefore, we must see between verses 5 and 6 of Revelation 12, the whole stretch of history from our Lord's ascension to the yet future Great Tribulation; for the woman is nourished under divine protection 1,260 days: the latter half of Daniel's seventieth week.*

And there was war in heaven: Michael and his angels going forth to war with the dra-

---

*Historical interpretations of this 1,260 days, which seek to apply it to church history, simply reveal neglect or ignorance of, the great principle of prophetical interpretation to which we have referred. It is my profound and increasing conviction that "the historical interpretation" of The Revelation is not only wholly astray, *but is a great stumbling block to the understanding of the book.* It ignores our Lord's plain outline in Revelation 1:19 (See Greek or Revised Version, and follow the phrase *"meta tauta"* through the book).

gon; and the dragon warred and his angels; and they prevailed not, neither was their place found any more in heaven. And the great dragon was cast down, the old serpent, he that is called the Devil and Satan, the deceiver of the whole world; he was cast down to the earth, and his angels were cast down with him. And I heard a great voice in heaven, saying, Now is come the salvation, and the power, and the kingdom of our God, and the authority of his Christ: for the accuser of our brethren is cast down, who accuseth them before our God day and night. And they overcame him because of the blood of the Lamb, and because of the word of their testimony; and they loved not their life even unto death. Therefore, rejoice, O heavens, and ye that dwell in them. Woe for the earth and for the sea: because the devil is gone down unto you, having great wrath, knowing that he hath but a short time.

Michael, as we know from Jude 9, is *the* archangel; (although other "chief princes" are there, *Daniel 10:13*). We also find from the last verse of Daniel 10, and the first verse of Daniel 12, that Michael has been assigned by God to care for the destiny of the Jewish nation, and that his special activity on their behalf will come at the time of "the great tribulation." He will "stand up" at the very time which we are now considering *(Daniel 12: 1, 2)*.

We should be moved deeply at the former humility of the mighty archangel, in the Jude account, in his actions toward the very being he is now at last sent to war against, and to overthrow! Many of us are kept from preferment by our arrogant or critical attitudes toward those foes whom God has not yet cast down; to say nothing of our too ready tongues toward other saints and servants of our Lord. There is a great lesson for all of us in the example of Michael! "Before honor goeth humility."

Now, at last, the longsuffering of God permits the Devil and his fallen host to be cast out of any access to heaven whatever! The record states they are cast down *to the earth,* and of course, it means what it says. Satan's sphere will be "the earth and the sea." He will, evidently, be allowed his freedom on earth: and it will be "woe," both to the earth and to the sea.*

Upon the occasion of his casting down to earth, all his Scripture names are announced: "The great dragon . . . the old serpent" (his hideous character and malignant, poisonous deceit as God sees it) "he that is called the Devil (slanderer) and Satan (God's absolute adversary and ours), the deceiver of the whole world"—what a list! If, in the back yard of your home, were a den of rattlesnakes, headed by a king cobra, and they had been there *all your life,* hissing and threatening, and you should come home some evening to find that they had been at last utterly driven out, to return no more at all, would you not rejoice? So will heaven when the enemy and his host are cast out forever!

It is well to remember constantly that we who have believed in the Lord Jesus Christ have an Advocate with the Father; and that it is, "if any man *sin,* we have an Advocate." Also, as in Peter's case *(Luke 22)* our Lord prays for us before Satan is even allowed to sift us! Also, that we have already been forgiven *all* our trespasses once and for all *(Ephesians 1:7; Colossians 2:13)*

---

*It will be well to remember the successive steps in Satan's judgment: 1. He is cast, as the "covering cherub" as "profane" from the midst of "the stones of fire," that is, from his first place as leader, evidently, of the worship of God in heaven (Ezekiel 28:14-16). This, I have always felt, is what our Lord meant in Luke 10, "I beheld Satan fallen as lightning from heaven." The *brightness* of this being would make his fall as "lightning." Also, the distance from his former glories, even to that "place in heaven" he now holds as the accuser, would be great and absolute. 2. He is cast down, here in Revelation 12, from whatever position he is allowed at present (as in Job 1:12; I Kings 22:21; Zechariah 3:1), to the earth. 3. He is cast into the abyss, in the center of the earth, at Christ's coming, and there spends 1,000 years (Revelation 20:1-3). 4. Upon being released at the Millennium's end "for a little season," and leading men again in desperate rebellion against God and His people, he is cast into the lake of fire and brimstone forever (Revelation 20:10).

so far as the pardon of the Judge is concerned. There is now "no condemnation." It is the forgiveness of *fellowship* of which God speaks in I John 1:9, forgiveness by the Father of His *child,* not to be confused with the once-for-all act of the Judge.

It is very significant that Satan accuses the saints before *God,* as if by our sins or failures as saints we are brought up again into God's court (as all *were,* indeed in Romans 3). But it is *with the Father* that we have an *Advocate,* and He Himself, *Jesus Christ, the Righteous, is* the propitiation for our sins! No real believer's sins come up in *judgment,* to endanger his eternal *safety* (John 5:24 R.V.). They do not come in before God as Judge: they did so come at Calvary, and were all put away forever!

The accusation of the saints by the enemy may be a mystery to you, but God suffers it at present, so be patient. And reflect that Satan's accusations have never availed against one saint; that they drive the saints to dependence upon God; that they get rid of his self-confidence (as with Job and Peter); that they make to shine his choice of holiness and God and heaven as against all difficulties, and that faith through all, highly honors God and brings about the eventual utter overthrow of the enemy. "Know ye not that we shall judge angels? *(I Corinthians 6:3).*

The "great voice" heard in verse 10 is that of the redeemed—it seems to me, all of them. They are those whose "brethren" have been the object of Satan's enmity and accusation. (It is, of course, only saints on earth that Satan accuses; those in heaven are entirely beyond it.)

The word "they" of verse 11 seems to indicate that this verse has to do with such saints as are still upon earth; although the verb is in the past tense—"overcame."*

---

*Alford calls the present tense of *accuseth* "the present participle of the *usual habit,*" and many excellent students believe that the word "overcame" has reference to those already in heaven. This may be true. Yet those saints still on earth also get the victory over the dragon, as we shall see, and their only path is to "love not their lives."

The three elements of victory over Satan in any event are shown in verse 11: (1) The ground of it—the blood of the Lamb; (2) the outward course of the victors—the word of their testimony; (3) the inward settled attitude of the victors—they loved not their life—unto death.

Now let us look at the opening words of this celebration in verse 10: "Now is come the salvation, and the power, and the kingdom of our God, and the authority of his Christ." How utterly idle is the discoursing of modernists and religious educationalists and social reformers about "the kingdom." Their talk is full of "the *kingdom* this" and "the *kingdom* that"; whereas our Lord Jesus has not yet taken His kingdom. It has not yet been given Him of the Father. We are not living in kingdom days, but in days when Satan is the prince of this world and the god of this age, also, when he is accusing the saints before God. Only those born again ever *see* the kingdom of God; and "righteousness, peace, and joy in the Holy Ghost"—wholly a separate thing from human arrangements and reforms! is the only form of the kingdom of God now.

Woe is announced to the earth and sea upon the Devil's going down; for he has "great wrath, knowing that he hath but a short time."

Our Lord Jesus told us that there is no truth in the Devil; that is, he receives none, holds none, loves none; yet he knows that Scripture will be fulfilled and he will shortly be in prison in the abyss; though the knowledge is not a belief in the sense of controlling his life, bringing about any repentance.

> And when the dragon saw that he was cast down to the earth, he persecuted the woman that brought forth the man child. And there were given to the woman the two wings of the great eagle, that she might fly into the wilderness unto her place, where she is nourished for a time, and times, and half a time, from the face of the serpent. And the serpent

cast out of his mouth after the woman water
as a river, that he might cause her to be carried away by the stream. And the earth helped
the woman, and the earth opened her mouth
and swallowed up the river which the dragon
cast out of his mouth. And the dragon waxed
wroth with the woman, and went away to
make war with the rest of her seed, that keep
the commandments of God and hold the testimony of Jesus.

The persecution, desperate and deadly, by the enemy
of the nation of Israel is now before us—"the time of
Jacob's trouble." Satan *hates Israel:* first, because they
are God's elect royal people; next, because of that nation
is Christ *(Romans 9:5)* who is to have the kingdom
upon Satan's over-throw; and finally, because Israel is
the perpetual proof before the eyes of men of the truth
of the Scriptures and of the fact of Jehovah God.

But we find God rendering peculiar miraculous assist-
ance in those terrible days to the real Israel, not those
merely "of Israel" *(9:6).* That is, the remnant of those
last days, in the "time, times, and half a time"—the three
and a half years of The Great Tribulation.

Armies are sent out "as a river" by the serpent to
destroy Israel. These forces are swallowed up by miraculous cataclysms:—as an ancient army was completely ob-
literated by a sand storm. God will protect Israel. He
will make the earth help His nation when Satan and
man seek to overwhelm them. Forty years, once before,
in a great and terrible wilderness, Jehovah sustained
them!

Finally, unable utterly to destroy Israel, the dragon
goes to make war with any other godly left on earth:
"the rest of her seed, that keep the commandments of
God, and hold the testimony of Jesus."

Now this is not the description of the Church of
God, as we know. The Church is not under law, but
grace; whereas these keep "the commandments of God"
(that is, the Old Testament). They also keep and hold

the testimony of Jesus" (that is, especially, the four Gospels). This is not "holding fast the Head" in heaven, as the Church does. It is, rather, a holding the truth that Jesus was the true Jewish Messiah and that He will come and have a kingdom shortly.

Dark, dark days, these! Let us thank God for the Gospel of grace and publish it everywhere while it is called today. The night cometh.

CHAPTER XI

THE BEAST AND HIS PROPHET

Revelation 13

The Lord Jesus said, "I came not to judge the world, but to save the world." We now come to consider those who come not to save the world, but to damn the world, and whose fearful work, except for God's elect being preserved by His infinite power, would destroy all men!

And he stood upon the sand of the sea. And I saw a beast coming up out of the sea, having ten horns and seven heads, and on his horns ten diadems, and upon his heads names of blasphemy. And the beast which I saw was like unto a leopard, and his feet were as the feet of a bear, and his mouth as the mouth of a lion: and the dragon gave him his power, and his throne, and great authority.

Now, however we may regard these words as descriptive of the revival of the Fourth Empire in its last form (and we know it is so) yet it seems to me far better to take the last verse of the chapter as the key to its understanding. "The number of the beast . . . is the number of *a man!*" Just as it is *the judgment* of the great harlot of chapter 17 that is in view, rather than her history, so here in chapter 13 it is the man who heads up and becomes the exponent of this last phase of the fourth world power that is before the mind of the Spirit. That there are difficulties is freely acknowledged; nor is the claim made that all these difficulties are here dissolved or disappear as we study this great chapter—great in the depiction of the quintessence of evil!

We see at once, upon looking on the verses above, that this awesome being called the *wild-beast (therion)** is *the utmost* production of him who is called "the great

---

*This word is used 46 times in the New Testament—38 of them in Revelation; and its first use, in 6:8, reveals its meaning, a beast of prey. Contrast *ktenos* (as Luke 10:34).

dragon, . . . The Devil . . . Satan, the deceiver of the whole world," *in his fury* upon being cast from the heavenly regions down to this earth.

Not until now has God permitted His great adversary to bring forth this "man of sin." There has been hitherto "one that restraineth" *(II Thessalonians 2:7 R. V.)* who we believe to be the Holy Spirit, by His presence on earth in the Church—a *direct action* of God *(Psalm 76:10).**

Now from Daniel 2:42 and 44, we know that the ten toes were to be ten kings, in whose days "shall the God of heaven set up a kingdom." The ten horns of Revelation 13:1 correspond to those of 17:3, interpreted in 17:12, "The ten horns . . . are ten kings . . . receive authority with the Beast for one hour. These have one mind, and they give their power and authority unto the Beast."

The Beast, therefore, of Revelation 13 is a man who controls absolutely the royal authority of the ten kings at the time of the end, and this by their own united will. Thus we see on these horns in Revelation 13:1, ten *diadems (R. V.)*. They are ten distinct powers; perhaps (according to the two feet of the image) five in the east and five in the west, although, knowing that "all that dwell on the earth" shall worship this last World emperor, we do not need to insist upon this. Moreover, the ten horns are *kings,* not *kingdoms;* and kings that do not become such *till the Beast arises.* Revelation 17:12.

The fact that the leopard of Greece, the bear of Medo-Persia, and the lion of old Babylon *(Daniel 7)* are all seen in this Beast, shows how all-inclusive of human things will be his character; he sums up all the brilliancy (Greece), all of the massive ponderousness of power (Persia), all of the absolute autocratic royal dominion (Babylon), that the Gentiles have ever known.

---

*Remember that while II Thessalonians 2:6 reads, "That which (*to,* neuter) restraineth," the seventh verse, in detailing more particularly the fact, uses the masculine, "he who *(ho)* restraineth." The words, "ye know" of verse 6 *(oidate)* rather indicate, it seems to me, a knowledge arising from *consciousness,* as well as instruction on the apostle's part. The Greek word originally means "to see," "to know for one's self." Christians are all aware that their protection from the inrush of the enemy is the indwelling Spirit. "Greater is he that is in you than he that is in the world."

Satan, being the prince of this world and the god of this age, and being desperately set on *ruling* men and being *worshipped* by them, is now given his chance. Because men by trifling with the truth, and by utter impenitence have opened the way, God will now send them a strong delusion that they may believe the devil's lie (*"the* lie"—*II Thessalonians 2:11, Greek*).

The Beast, therefore, set before us in Revelation 13, is the dragon's masterpiece of delusion, leading to worship of *himself (Revelation 13:4)*.

But, men being what they are, it will require a "Christ," or specially prepared man, to lead them to adore as their god, Satan, who sends forth his "Christ." In this, of course, Satan copies God's plan of salvation by the Lord Jesus. "No man hath seen God at any time," "He that hath seen me hath seen the Father," our Lord told us. To God it was infinite condescension and love that "God (should be) manifest in the flesh." Christ humbled Himself by becoming "in the likeness of men" *(Philippians 2)*. It was also in Christ as man that the eternal counsels of God lay. The climax for the redeemed is, "They shall see His (God's) face." "Blessed are the pure in heart, for they shall *see God*."

Now Satan *imitates* all this. Instead of revealing himself directly to the mass of humanity, he selects two men, one to be worshipped, and the other to be his "prophet," to *secure* such worship; for men are gross and crass generally, unable to perceive or appreciate the intellectual and spiritual marvels of the being who is called "the dragon." And so it would be contrary to the *pride* of Satan openly to reveal himself to them. But it is in direct conformation to man's nature to place before his eyes this Beast, a being who is the exponent and expression of the Satanic power behind him. Thus the superstitious awe and wonder of man would be drawn out; and the human imagination (which marvelous faculty man almost lives in, and which is fairly *creative* in its power) would be appealed to more powerfully than in any other way.

Even the Beast himself will retreat one step from man,

in the same way, when an "image" is made of him by the *second* beast!

Thus will lie in the deluded world's inner consciousness "the likeness of an image" of *man,* a wonderful man, who has returned in a manner beyond their knowledge from the unseen realm of the dead. And all the while the *worship* of all men will really be retained by Satan himself; for it will be known by all that it is the *dragon himself* that has *given* "his authority unto the Beast."

We have, then, Satan worshipped through his chosen vessel, or "Christ," a worship carried on through a fearful, speaking, breathing *image,* that can kill non-conformists or cause their death!

This is "the lie," the inescapable damning lie, that the world in its dreamed of "progress" is about to enter into!

And I saw one of his heads as though it had been slain unto death; and his death-stroke was healed: and the whole earth wondered after the beast.

Here then is Satan's permitted imitation of the death and resurrection of Christ! The Greek word for "slain" is the same as that of chapter 5:6: "a Lamb . . . as though it had been *slain.*" It is because of His victory over death, after being publicly killed, that God's saints hold fast to Christ; and all the world has been put in awe of Him.

Death is the unconquerable tyrant, the universal terror, through fear of which men are "all their lifetime subject to bondage" (Hebrews 2:15). But now, they are able to cast off their fears at last! One who has been slain with the death-stroke of a sword is "healed"; a killed body stands up! One who has been in the "abyss" re-possesses this slain body. It is not *resurrection* like unto Christ's, who left the realm of the dead forever, in "newness of life." But neither is it mere resuscitation of a body in which life has not become extinct; for this "beast" will have gone down into "the abyss,"—will have left the body entirely. There will be, therefore, first, the killing by a sword-stroke of the body of one of these "heads"; and, second, the entrance into that body of that one of the seven kings whom God will suffer to be brought up from "the abyss" to be the "beast" to deceive men and to "war against the Lamb" (19:19).

It is not merely the fourth world power (Rome) that is here (as in Daniel 2), but chiefly the history of the "little horn" of Daniel 7, which springs out of that empire. This must be kept in mind. It is *a man* that is before our eyes in Revelation 13, all through. God *says* he is a *Man* in 13:18.

Now as to the "heads," we must go to God's own interpretation of them in Revelation 17, where we find, as regards the woman, "the seven heads are seven mountains, on which the woman sitteth"; but we note that this sentence reads right on, "and they are seven kings; the five are fallen, the one is, the other is not yet come; and when he cometh, he must continue a little while. And the beast that was, and is not, is himself also *an* eighth, and is *of the seven;* and he goeth into perdition." Returning to Revelation 13, as to the empire, it is in verse 3 "one of his heads . . . slain unto death." But we see from Revelation 17, that this head was one of the seven Roman emperors, of which five had *fallen* when John wrote The Revelation. One, Domitian, was reigning, "the other" the seventh, not yet come. It might be such a man as Napoleon, for the Fourth Empire is still on until the stone strikes it; but it is more probably one who will rule after the more formal restoration of the Roman Empire.*

Now from these seven, the Beast of Revelation 13 comes. He is *an* eighth (not *the,* as A. V.) but is, withal, one "of the seven." We remember that he was said in Revelation 11:7 to "come up out of the abyss." Now the abyss *(Greek abussos)* is a word used ten times in Scripture, seven of these in The Revelation. We found in Revelation 9:1 that there was a *shaft* leading down to it;

---

*Mussolini, with his ambitions for the restoration of old Rome, his Caesar-ideals, his inflexible will, his undiminishing energy, is a portent of what one of these emperors will be; and also proof how quickly such an one may rise into power! Of course Mussolini does not begin to fill the vast picture of the Beast of Revelation 13.

that it was in the heart of the earth according to Romans
10:7, compared with Matthew 12:40; that it is, so far as
the human race is concerned, the realm of departed
spirits—those who have died (not of the saved, of course,
for these are now "with Christ").

We are forced, therefore, to the conclusion that the
Beast of Revelation 13 has been brought back by permitted Satanic agency from the realm of the dead, and
that this fact is known to those on earth; to whom the
fact that the Beast had had the death-stroke of the sword,
and then afterwards lived *(Revelation 13:14)* was a well-
known event of his history. Consequently the whole
earth *wonders* after the Beast! How quickly now is
swallowed up all the "wisdom of man" which God had
long ago declared to be foolishness, as concerning *divine*
things. Now it is shown to be futility itself also against
the *delusions* God permits to come upon those who "received not the love of the truth, that they might be
saved."*

How frightful then the scene! Men have rejected the
wounded, slain but risen Lamb of God. And now they
are given over to bow in absolute helpless "wonder" before *another* wounded one "slain unto death," but who *lives,*
—a fearsome lost creature from "the abyss," re-entered,
for Satan's fell purposes, into a body that by its very death-
scar compels the world's worship as the *victor over death!*
(All, thank God, but those written in the book of life of

---

*Seiss well comments: "Did not men (at the French Revolution) sing
halleluias to the busts of Marat and Lepelletier, and conveyed a woman in
grand procession to the Cathedral of Notre Dame, unveiled and kissed her before
the high altar as the Goddess of Reason? Nay, at this very hour, there resides
a man in the city of Rome, whom one-half of christendom itself hails, honors
and adores as the vicar of Jesus Christ, the vicegerent of God upon earth, in-
fallible, the sole possessor of the keys of heaven,—a man whom the greater
festivals exhibit as a divinity, borne along in solemn procession on the shoul-
ders of consecrated priests, while sacred incense fumes before him. Let there
come, then a man from among the distinguished dead! Let him prove by signs
evident that he is verily a great emperor returned to life again; let him show
the intelligence, the energy, the invincible power, and whatever else has made
and marked the glory of the mighty, and let there come with him a great prophet
to exercise all this power in the one direction of a new universal religion, advis-
ing and urging with eloquence and miracles, in the name of absolute Wisdom,
the worship and adoration of that man, as the only right worship in the universe; and what is there in humanity to withstand the appeal! As surely as
man is man, the same that he has hitherto been, it will and must be a grand
success. The Saviour so anticipated, and says that if it were possible to break
down Jehovah's promises the very elect would be deceived!"

the Lamb; and these are kept not by their *own* power, let us well remember!)

And they worshipped the dragon, because he gave his authority unto the beast; and they worshipped the beast, saying, Who is like unto the beast? and who is able to war with him?

Here we have the utter helplessness of the Christ-forsaking world falling into the very jaws of the Devil, most fearfully set forth! On the one hand their *worshipping* the dragon and his awful Christ; and on the other their shrinking *impotence* to resist him. The whole earth will have suddenly become a thousand-fold worse off than Russia today! For in Russia they are denying God; but the whole nation has not yet been given up *consciously to worship the Devil himself,* as verse 8 of Revelation 13 declares all on earth, but God's elect of that day, will do.

Of course, no one is "like unto the beast."* They have back on their hands a "son of perdition" *(II Thessalonians 2),* one they knew to have *died,* one whose *history* was universally known. Rome once was in anguish over the irresponsible hideousness of Nero. What if an individual of these seven emperors (of which Nero was one), should return to be "the man on horseback," the "superman," the great "world hero" that they have so long desired? *And one will come!*

And there was given to him a mouth speaking great things and blasphemies; and there was given to him authority to continue (literally to do, or go ahead) forty and two months. And he opened his mouth for blasphemies against God, to blaspheme his name, and his tabernacle, even them that dwell (are tabernacling) in the heaven. And it was given unto him to make war with the saints, and to overcome them: and there was given

---

*As to this solemn, divine characterization of this man, it is well to recall that one of Napoleon's marshals shouted in horror when he heard of the emperor's escape from Elba to rush back to his power in France: "What! is the *wild beast* loose again?"

to him authority over every tribe and people
and tongue and nation. And all that dwell on
the earth shall worship him, every one whose
name hath not been written from the foundation of the world in the book of life of the
Lamb that hath been slain.*

"There was given to him"—six times (the number of
manifested evil) this phrase is used *(verses 5 twice, 7 twice,
14, 15),* in connection with this dreadful man called
the Beast (literally, *Wildbeast).* It indicates judicial un-
leasing of powers of incipient evil of which this world
does not yet dream.

"A mouth speaking great things"—that is what the universities, the scientists, the wise ones of the earth throng,
even *rush,* to listen to; and God will let them hear from
the mouth of this man of sin, marvels beyond their utmost
imaginings. Even today Theosophists, Christian Scientists, Spiritists, and "psychical" folks of all sorts, prate
about the undiscovered, unused "powers" that lie in
human nature; while science glories in its discoveries of
the physical secrets of this universe. With such knowledge today human educationalism is captivated. What
will happen when God permits Satan's super-man to tell
them utterly unexpected marvels!

But connected with these marvels will be *blasphemies.*
Such derision of God, of His Son, of His salvation, as
has never been heard or permitted on this planet will then

---

*Alford here remarks, "These last words are ambiguously placed. They may
belong either to *gegraptai* (was written) or to *sesphagmenou* (was slain)."
He connects them with the latter, adducing I Peter 1:19, 20: "That death of
Christ which was fore-ordained from the foundation of the world, is said to
have taken place in the counsels of Him with whom the end and the beginning
are one."

But the habit of Scripture is to connect election with the writing rather than
with the ground, of that election, the death of Christ. The passage from Peter
is rather against, than for, Alford's contention: Christ was "foreknown indeed
before the foundation of the world, but was manifested at the end of the
times for your sake," etc. In Daniel 12:1, referring to the exact "time of
trouble" with which Revelation 13 is concerned, we read of those being delivered who "shall be found written in the book; as also in Isaiah 4:3, the spared
remnant are described as "every one that is written unto life in Jerusalem."

Hengstenberg says, "The expression 'from the foundation of the world' (in
Revelation 13:8 and 17:8) must not be referred to the slaying of the Lamb";
and quotes Bengel: "The Apocalypse often speaks of the Lamb slain; it never
adds *from the foundation of the world* (Hebrews 9:26). They who hold Him
to have been slain in the divine decree from the foundation of the world, may
with equal justice speak of Him as having been also born, raised from the
dead, ascended to heaven."

come forth. Especially those "tabernacling in the heaven" —probably referring to Christ and His Church lately caught up and known (despite all earth's hatred) to be above the earth, will come in for blasphemous execration. Satan, filled with disappointed hatred, will pour through this creature such words as will make Russian blasphemies seem trifling! He will deny that Jesus is, or ever was, *the Christ* of the *Jews* (I John 2:22); and also deny the Father and the Son, as all *Christians* hold.

Forty-two months (three and one-half years, or 1260 days) the Beast is thus to continue on his way. The Lord Jesus said to the rabble who came to arrest him, "This is your *hour,* and the power (Greek *exousia)* of darkness." What a scene followed in the next few hours! But God will give up the whole earth, except His elect, for three and one-half years to this direful scene of Revelation 13.

The saints (for there will be saints then, although not the Church) will be "overcome," that is, over-powered, by this monster. Right will be trampled. Testimony will be stilled by the quick hand of martyrdom. "Behold, darkness shall cover the earth, and gross darkness the peoples."

If any man hath an ear, let him hear. If any man is for captivity, into captivity he goeth: if any man shall kill with the sword, with the sword must he be killed. Here is the patience and the faith of the saints.

This thrice-repeated word, *"if any man"* is addressed to any gracious ears then upon earth. First, let them *hear God's words,* for there is no other possible way of deliverance at any time for God's saints but through *faith,* and faith cometh by *hearing.*

Moreover, let them be warned against opposing this awful Satanic power by *force.* If any one undertakes to take captive this monster or his minions—into captivity such a one will go. If any one shall undertake to oppose him with the sword, by the sword he will fall; for God has *given things over* for the "hour" to Satan, whom the world has *chosen.*

We are emphasizing lastly words that we always need
to lay to heart, "the patience and the faith of the saints."
Patience means suffering on in steadfastness, through
trial, and it takes *faith* thus to do. But God's grace of
patience and the faith of His saints will triumph even in
the darkest hour the earth has ever known or ever will
know! The saints of those days (though not the Church)
will find true "As thy days, so shall thy strength be."

Satan's Steel Trap: "Worship My Christ, or Starve!"

And I saw another beast coming up out of
the earth; and he had two horns like unto a
lamb, and he spake as a dragon. And he exerciseth all the authority of the first beast in
his sight. And he maketh the earth and them
that dwell therein to worship the first beast,
whose deathstroke was healed. And he doeth
great signs, that he should even make fire
to come down out of heaven upon the earth
in the sight of men. And he deceiveth them
that dwell on the earth by reason of the signs
which it was given him to do in the sight of
the beast; saying to them that dwell on the
earth, that they should make an image to the
beast who hath the stroke of the sword and
lived. And it was given unto him to give
breath to it, even to the image of the beast,
that the image of the beast should both speak,
and cause that as many as should not worship the image of the beast should be killed.
And he causeth all, the small and the great,
and the rich and the poor, and the free and
the bond, that there be given them a mark
on their right hand, or upon their forehead;
and that no man should be able to buy or to
sell, save he that hath the mark, even the
name of the beast or the number of his name.
Here is wisdom. He that hath understanding,
let him count the number of the beast; for it

**is the number of a man: and his number is
Six hundred and sixty and six.**

Let us now look briefly at the rise of this second Beast,
the third of the Satanic trinity. The first Beast was from
"the sea," this one from "the earth." Of course John, in
chapters 12 and 13, is speaking in *sign* language *(12:1-3);*
yet it must be remembered that both these "beasts" are
human beings. The first is definitely called a *man (Revelation 13:18)*. But the doom of both the first and second,
as described in Revelation 19 and 20, prove both to be
human beings. Systems, forms of empires, etc., are dealt
with by God on earth; but only *persons* are cast into
the lake of fire.

It is generally taken that "the sea" from which the first
Beast arises, denotes (as in Revelation 17:15) "peoples,
and multitudes, and nations, and tongues." Inasmuch as
in Daniel 7, the rise of the four great world-powers, which
are all expressed in the Beast of Revelation 13 is described (compare Daniel 7:1-8 with Revelation 13:1),
this interpretation of Revelation 13 seems necessary. We
may add, that while in Daniel it is "the great sea," the
Mediterranean, around whose shores all four great earth-empires had their existence, it is "the sea" in Revelation
13. For here the Beast secures *universal* dominion, hence,
perhaps, the more general expression.*

---

*To use the term *ecclesiastical* to describe the character and career of the
second Beast of Revelation 13, seems to me both an inaccurate and a misleading thing. The Beast and his ten kings have destroyed from off the earth the
harlot of Revelation 17, and in so doing, have annihilated all things "ecclesiastical" whether of apostate Christendom or of paganism. "All that is called
God," or that is *"an object of worship"* (II Thessalonians 2:4, Greek), has
been *banished*. Therefore, to call the second Beast an "ecclesiastical power"
is delusive. Just as well, might Jannes and Jambres with their God-opposing
miracles in Egypt, or a Simon Magus with his "magic," or a Hermann the
Great, be called "ecclesiastical."

The whole business of the second Beast is to support him "whose coming
(parousia) is according to the working of Satan with all power and signs and
lying wonders" (II Thessalonians 2:9). The mere fact that he "doeth the
great signs" of Revelation 13:13-15, gives him no claim to be called "ecclesiastical" in any sense, for that term carries with it the idea of human religion:
whereas, this second Beast is wholly, directly, and openly Satanic.

To employ, therefore, the term "ecclesiastical" regarding him, as over against
"the civil power" is to imagine the present religious constitution of society to
have, at least in some measure subsisted, and consequently to destroy or render
impossible a conception of the real situation in those dire days. The second
Beast is merely the *prophet,* the willing but absolute *tool,* of the first Beast.

That he has "two horns like unto a lamb" does not necessarily imply that

But it must be remembered, from Revelation 11:7, that it is the *first* Beast who is operating *at Jerusalem* at the close of the first half of Daniel's seventieth week (when he kills God's "two witnesses"); also, from Revelation 11:9, that Jerusalem is at that time crowded with peoples, tribes, tongues, and nations. Hardly a "settled state"!

Again, the second Beast is always close to the first— his Prophet, Premier, exponent, and *nothing else but that,* according to Scripture.

And it is the first Beast that he lauds and acclaims as the object of worship, and that chiefly on the ground that the first Beast had had a "death stroke," and has been "slain unto death" (13:3—Greek) and now lives!

We now quote the Endor witch's description of Samuel's appearance (and he did appear!); "I see gods coming up out of the earth." Many draw from that the inference that the second Beast is likewise a spirit from Hades. It may be so—(see Seiss). But it is the *first* Beast that the Scripture *declares* comes up from the abyss—and whom the whole world recognizes as having had a previous earth-history. Let us remember this carefully. Prophecy is full of this *one man's* career, both in type and direct prediction.

If Judas Iscariot (as some predict) were permitted to return and direct the Israelitish nation's apostasy to Satan-worship, as he once helped them to crucify their true Messiah, he would scarcely let himself be known as Judas! For he is despised as a traitor, even by godless Jews—*was* despised in his own day *(Matthew 27:3, 4).* Judas went from apostleship to "his own place" for future judgment; the phrase "his own place" merely contrasting with that place of honor from which he "fell away."

---

he is imitating the Lamb of God, for men will have then rejected the very thought of that meek and lowly One. What the world is looking for even today, is not a meek One, but "a man on horseback," one who will *lord* it over them. The "horns like unto a lamb" merely indicate that the second Beast instead of being "a king of fierce countenance" like the first, will have the relatively plausible and persuasive ways of a great deceiver of men. The "civil power" has *become* the "ecclesiastical,"—if by the latter term you mean that which engages the worshipping faculties of man; for it is the first Beast who is a god to men: and that *before* the second is on the scene!

IS THE FIRST BEAST "ANTICHRIST"?

That the first Beast is the Antichrist of Scripture, may appear from the following considerations:

1. In John 5:43, our Lord says, "I am come in my Father's name and ye receive me not: if another shall come *in his own name,* him ye will receive." (The Greek is "en to onomati to idio," which we almost might read, "in name peculiar to himself".) But the second beast of Revelation 13, comes to establish the name of the first. He (the second beast) "causeth all, . . . that there be given them a mark . . . that no man should be able to buy or to sell, save he that hath the mark, *even* the name of the Beast (the first beast) or the number of his name" *(Revelation 13:16, 17).*

2. In Revelation 16:13, the *trinity of hell* is named "the Dragon . . . the Beast . . . and the false Prophet"; as also in 19:20, "the beast was taken, and with him the false prophet that wrought the signs in his sight." A prophet is one who speaks for another, coming in the name of another, as all know. How could this second beast of Revelation 13 fulfil John 5:43, if he comes in the name of the first Beast, and not in his own name?

Mr. Darby says (Coll. Writings, Prophetic Vol. 1, p. 306) "When the question as to power comes on, and *Antichrist* rises up *in his full form* against the Lamb, *he* is finally cast down, and put, *with the false prophet,* in the lake of fire, and *his* followers killed" (italics mine). Whatever question Mr. Darby ever had regarding the identity of Antichrist, his words here reveal that when he wrote them he counted Antichrist as the *first* Beast, and the second merely as his "prophet."

Proper interpretation must regard these two Beasts of Revelation 13 as two *men.* They are on the scene at the same time; both have fearful energies of evil; but the second does nothing independently of the first. We read, "he exerciseth all the authority of the first beast in his sight" (or presence). He also works wonderful "signs" which are done "in the sight" (presence) of the first Beast. The word means just what the same word *(enopion)* means in John 20:30, where our Lord's miracles are said to have been wrought "in the presence" of His disciples,—emphasizing that fact!

3. Practically common consent regards "the man of sin" of II Thessalonians 2 as the Antichrist. But of him it is said, "he . . . opposeth and exalteth himself against all that is called God or that is worshipped; so that he sitteth in the temple of God, setting himself forth as God." But this is the exact contrary of the actings of the second beast in Revelation 13:12, 14, who "maketh the earth and them that dwell therein to worship the first beast, whose death-stroke was healed . . . saying to them that dwell on the earth, that they should make an image to the beast who hath the stroke of the sword and lived." The second beast is nothing but the "prophet" of the first Beast. Once admit (which we shall find we must do) that the first Beast is a man, and not any kind of a system, not even the Fourth Empire as such *(Revelation 13:18)* and we are driven to conclude that the first Beast of Revelation 13 is "the man of sin" of II Thessalonians 2—the "lawless one": for he owns no one but *himself*. He could not be described as leading the earth to worship *another,*—as does the false prophet, the second beast of Revelation 13. And exactly the same is true of "the king" of Daniel 11:36.

4. Some assert that the character of the second beast as the "false prophet" to the first Beast, is a later form of his evil energy; the first stage having been as an independent or at least distinct "king" rising in Palestine and fulfilling in that country such passages as Daniel 11:36—the wilful king; or II Thessalonians 2, "the man of sin"; and later bringing by deceit the Jewish nation who have received him as Christ to subjection to and worship of the civil power, of the first Beast, etc. But such an interpretation cannot fill the picture drawn in Revelation 13, even if we could conceive of the second beast ever doing anything in his own name. For the first Beast is immediately set before us in Revelation 13 as himself the great and direct religious blasphemer of those days.

"And he opened his mouth for blasphemies against God, to blaspheme his name, and his tabernacle, them that dwell (tabernacle) in the heaven" (that is, especially, the Church which has at that time been raptured and is "tabernacling," after the first stage of Christ's coming, in the regions out of which Satan has been cast).

He makes also immediate and successful "war with the saints." Again, there is given him authority over every tribe and people and tongue and nation (including Palestine!); and still again, "all that dwell on the earth shall worship him"—except the elect of those days (Revelation 13:6, 7, 8).

Moreover, there is given him "authority to continue forty and two months," *i.e.,* the whole duration of the tribulation, the last half of Daniel's seventieth week.

Now where is there room in this scene for more than one being to "set himself forth as God," in "the temple of God" or anywhere else on earth? All prophecy crowds down stupendous issues into this brief and terrible period!

5. We know from Daniel 9:26, 27, that the last prince of the Roman Empire will make "a firm covenant" or treaty with the Jews in their land for seven years, and that "in the midst of the week," *i.e.,* after half the seven years are passed, he (this Roman prince) will "cause the sacrifice and the oblation to cease." If there is at that time in Palestine an "Antichrist" setting himself forth as God, where does the fancied alliance between this king and this false Christ in Palestine come in, so that Revelation 13 can be fulfilled? There is *no hint* that the second beast of Revelation 13 ever has been anything other than subservient to, or "prophet" of, the first Beast! It is without question the first Beast, the last Roman emperor, who will fulfil Daniel 9:27, causing Jewish worship to cease, and becoming "the abomination that maketh desolate" by "standing where he ought not" *(Mark 13:14),* "in the holy place" *(Matthew 24:15) i.e.,* in the rebuilt Jewish temple at Jerusalem as seen in Revelation 13, where, (although not yet owned of God) with respect to the Gentiles the place will be "holy."

It is reliably reported that Dr. Theodore Herzl, the great organizer of Zionism, in his zeal to secure a national home in Palestine for Israel, not only appealed to the Pope for help, but to the Sultan Abdul Hamid of Turkey ("Abdul the Damned"), even telling the latter that if he would let the Jews have Palestine, they would adopt him as their promised Messiah.

If we compare the history of the first Beast as seen in Revelation 13 with the career of the wilful king of Daniel 11:36 and "the man of sin" of II Thessalonians 2, we find complete simplicity and accord, the second beast of Revelation 13 coming in merely as what he is called— a *prophet* of the first. But if we undertake to name the second beast a mere Jewish Antichrist, deceiving that nation finally into worship of the "civil power," the Roman ruler, we cannot claim either II Thessalonians 2 or Daniel 11 as referring to him, because these passages set forth one operating "in his own name," in *resistless power,* and in self-deification.

6. The condition of the Jewish nation in the last days must be considered. First, they will say, "we (will be) like all the nations" (I Samuel 8:20). Second, they will be possessed of tremendous treasure in which they are trusting to "redeem them,"—to buy them independent political status. Third, they will have established their own worship in their own temple, with daily sacrifices, offerings, etc. Fourth, there will be a godly remnant living in Jerusalem and Palestine—though the mass of the nation will be apostate—who will sustain the fear of Jehovah, and His worship. Fifth, this worship will be interrupted by intrusion from without (according to Daniel 9:27), by a power in which the majority of the nation have a frightful confidence, according to Isaiah 28:15: "We have made a covenant with death, and with Sheol are we at agreement . . . We have made lies our refuge, and under falsehood have we hid ourselves." This can be nothing else than a conscious and intelligent recognition of the source and nature of the first Beast; for he is "the beast that cometh up out of the abyss." He

will be a spirit from the lost world who will be allowed to come back on earth for Satan's purposes. Indeed, he will be one of the seven former emperors of Rome, according to Revelation 17:8, 10, 11. Here, then, is Jewish worship suddenly interrupted, not by a Christ who has arisen among them, but by the last prince of the Roman Empire (Daniel 9:27) who, as we shall find in studying Revelation 13 and 17, is Satan's counterpart and counterfeit of the risen Christ, having been "slain (margin Greek) unto death" and his "death-stroke was healed" (Revelation 13:3) to the amazement of the world. It will not do to call this "death-stroke" the fall of the Roman Empire.

7. We should remember also that Satan offered Christ "all the kingdoms of the world, and the glory of them" (Matthew 4:8), if He would worship him. Our Lord refused, but another will accept, and receive these kingdoms (Revelation 13:7, 8).

But this is the first Beast and not the second! Our Lord Jesus Christ, we know, will finally take over the kingdoms of this world. "All kings shall fall down before him; all nations shall serve him" (Psalm 72:11). What else but a king was Christ to be? "Pilate therefore said unto him, Art thou a king, then? Jesus answered, Thou sayest it, because I am a king (margin Greek). To this end have I been born."

Consequently, we see in Revelation 19:19, "the beast and the kings of the earth, and their armies, gathered together to make war against him that sat upon the horse, and against his army." What is this but Antichrist? It is the awful climax of intelligent opposition to the Lamb: "These (the ten kings and the beast) shall war against the Lamb, and the Lamb shall overcome them, for he is Lord of lords, and King of kings" (Revelation 17:14).

So that Mr. Darby's words quoted under point 2, express the exact truth!

To call the Antichrist merely an ecclesiastical deceiver of the Jewish nation, is not to fill the scripture account of this monstrous being, who sets himself above all that is called God,—to whom the second beast is merely the "false prophet that wrought the signs in his sight" ('Revelation 19:20). This "prophet" is always at the Beast's side,—working in his presence.

8. The voice of history and tradition calls to us that the Antichrist and the last Roman emperor are to be identical. Victorinus, voicing an impression that was very common in early Christian centuries, says, "Nero will be raised from the dead, appear again at Rome and persecute the Church once more, and finally be destroyed by the Messiah." Augustine first mentioned this idea concerning Nero. Even Tacitus, the Roman historian, spoke of many believing rumors about Nero's possible return (Hist. II. 8; 1, 2). Sulpicius Severus said, "It is current opinion of many that he (Nero) is yet to come as Antichrist." Note carefully, we are not insisting at all that Nero will be the Antichrist, but that the early Christians believed that a Roman imperial persecutor, possibly Nero, would be the Antichrist.

9. We are distinctly told in II Thessalonians 2 that "the man of sin" will be brought to nought by "the forth-shining of our Lord's arrival" (*Rotherham's Translation, II Thessalonians 2:8*). The Greek words are, *"te epiphaneia tes parousias autou."* Our Lord's coming (parousia) opens with the rapture of the Church.*

Note the exact meaning of the word in Philippians 2:12, "As ye have always obeyed, not as in my presence *(parousia)* only, but now much more in my absence *(apousia)."* Now, we know from Revelation 19:20, 21, that it will be at our Lord's manifestation as described in Revelation 19:11-16, that this last World emperor will be brought to nought. Indeed, the lake of fire, long prepared, is at that time, according to Isaiah 30:33, to be "made ready" for him!

We are compelled, therefore, to view the future as filled with *one* great figure; although, as we shall see, the

---

*We believe this occurs in *time* at Revelation 4:1, where Church testimony ends. It is *Christ*, in connection with His *ruling the nations*, who is the man child of Revelation 12:5 and His ascension is viewed there *only in connection with His rulership*, and not as to its date in history.

second beast will be "exercising all the authority of the
first beast in his sight"; he is the active agent by means
of Satanic signs and wonders, (done where the first Beast
is,) in turning the worship of the earth to the man whose
name is set forth by those numerals that express all that
man in himself can be, or do, energized by Satan—"Six
hundred and sixty and six." We feel that the first Beast
must be called the Antichrist.*

In brief review, we find Revelation 13 to reveal:

1. As to Satan:

(a) His hatred toward God and toward His saints.

(b) His peculiar rage at being cast from heaven to
earth.

(c) His deadly ambition to be worshipped as God.

(d) His copying God's plan: of a "Christ," or one
fully empowered, under his control, through whom to
work; and then of an agent or "prophet" of that false
Christ, who will carry directly into effect the Satanic program; and of astonishing miraculous energy to accredit
before the world his system and himself. (All this God
calls "the lie" in II Thessalonians 2:11—Greek.)

2. As to Man:

(a) Man's willingness to lose his own soul to gain
the whole world (as do these "beasts," who are human
beings).

(b) Man's desire, from the fall onward, to "be as
gods."

(c) The finale of man's refusing to "have God in his
knowledge," and his turning to the "likeness of an image
of corruptible man" (Romans 1).

(d) The development by man to the full of that final
form of economic life, godless international commercialism, by which man falls into Satan's steel-trap: they can
"neither buy nor sell," except they have the beast's (that
is, Satan's) mark.

---

*We desire to commend the three lectures of Joseph Seiss on Revelation 13,
as found in the second volume of his, "Lectures on the Apocalypse."
On Revelation 12 we cannot agree with Seiss that the Woman is "the Church
of all the ages"; but his chapters on the Antichrist, Revelation 13, are spiritual,
masterly, and very edifying indeed.

3. As to God:

(a) The inexorable, unescapable, righteous operation of God that "gives up" such to believe an eternal damning falsehood (II Thessalonians 2).

(b) The bringing upon the earth of the "third woe," "The Great Tribulation"; because of which, except, for His elect's sake, God had "shortened the days," no flesh would be saved! (Mark 13:19, 20).

(c) God's infinite unconquerable grace, which preserves His saints, with "patience and faith" even in those frightful days (Revelation 13:8-10).

We must read and ponder these scenes of Revelation 13; as we hope to be protected from the last-day errors; as we hope to understand the prophetic Scriptures of both Old and New Testaments; as we desire to "escape all these things that shall come to pass, and to stand before the Son of man" (Luke 21:36).

For all the forces of hell that head up in Revelation 13 are marshalling in public or in secret today!

While it is most interesting to seek to identify this second beast, it will perhaps be better, to discover the general plan of Satan, in turning the world from the worship of God to the worship of himself—for this is what he seeks.

Satan's creed concerning man, and the way to manage man, is plainly seen in the first two chapters of Job, and may be summed up in Job 2:4: "Satan answered Jehovah, and said, Skin for skin, yea, all that a man hath will he give for his life." And we all know this to be true, except concerning God's elect, in whom are the operations of the infinite power of divine grace. "They loved not their life even unto death" *(Revelation 12:11)*.

Satan will take advantage of this "self-preservation law"; and, while on the one hand exhibiting vast miracles, and uttering unheard of blasphemy against God, through his great final agent (the first Beast), he will also, by the second, drive men into the desperate alternative of accepting his Christ, or being refused sustenance on the earth; no man shall be able to buy or sell without the mark of the Beast stamped upon him, upon his body.

We read from chapter 14:9-11, this means eternal damnation! So that what takes place in Russia, of blasphemy, coercion, persecution and death, is but a small whisper, is but a feeble portent, of what will be worldwide under the fearful trinity of evil, Satan, the Beast, and the False Prophet.*

Satan's own Prophet now springs the double jaws of the Great Dragon's awful steel-trap on the souls of men. Between the jaw of damning miracle-backed soul-delusion, and the jaw of bodily self-preservation, man is caught! He cannot escape if he would, for he must eat to live on this earth; and he would not escape if he could, for, like the flame-dazzled moth, he has fallen in blinded worship at the feet of his destroyer! No pen of any language can describe a doom so awful, a fate so fearful!

Human science and philosophy are in the dust: for here is a being returned from past history, from the unseen realm of the dead—and how can man's puny wisdom cope with this? And here is a breathing image—speaking, no one knows how! Men fall in worship. And to crown the terror, this fearsome image is able relentlessly to slay those who refuse it homage. Where, then, are man's boasted powers, his vaunted progress? Vanished, gone forever! The whole world has fallen below the level of the African fetish-worshipper. The whole world has fallen flat before mysteries it cannot even dare to seek to solve! Men will know they are worshipping the Devil; and, being given up to believe THE LIE, they will actually be content and confident to abandon their intelligence and all their natural God-given judgment, and

---

*It is ever the plan of the great ones of earth to retire from direct gaze, and operate through representatives. This enhances the mystery and power of their names. It is hard to obtain readily an interview with the "big bosses" either of business or of politics! When the Dragon sets forth the Beast, men worship the Dragon all the more fatuously. When the Beast retires behind his Prophet working miracles in his name, and most especially when that Prophet causes an *image* of the first Beast to be made and to speak, to exercise even murderous powers for those refusing adoration—then Satan's steel-trap on mankind has been sprung indeed!

have their consciences murdered. Nay, they will delight to do all this. There never will have been a day so certain of itself as the day that receives Satan's Christ! Reason confronted by Satanic miracle, will abdicate her throne to credulity. "All power and signs and lying wonders" said Paul in II Thessalonians 2. They "shall show great signs and wonders; so as to lead astray, if possible, even the very elect," says the Lord in Matthew 24.

And then "the *mark* of the beast" or "the number of his name," branded in the flesh of men, on forehead or right hand—what fearful tyranny!

Yet men dream they are free! While God says of them in I John 5:19, "The whole world lieth in the evil one." Men hate preachers who tell them this today, but they will shortly find whose slaves they are—all they who are not born of God, God's elect.

And then *eternal* doom follows! God will graciously and most solemnly and strikingly warn of this, by sending a loud-crying angel over all the lands *(Revelation 14: 9-11)*, announcing in every tongue that those who worship the Beast and receive this fatal mark of hell on the forehead or hand, shall be tormented with fire and brimstone in the presence of the holy angels, and in the presence of the Lamb; and that "the smoke of their torment goeth up for ever and ever."

The fearful guilt of this apostasy to Satan and his Christ, is seen in its punishment. No unwitting sin is this; but wilful revolt to hell from all the love of heaven. It will be a world that has heard and rejected the Gospel that will fall into Satan's steel-trap. "A savor from death unto death; to the other a savor from life unto life," the Gospel of grace ever is. "Let us break their (God's and Christ's) bonds asunder, and cast away their cords from us"—this is the cry of the raging nations of those terrible days. It is "against Jehovah, and against his anointed" that they thus "set themselves" and "take counsel."

"Cease ye from man." His pride is folly; his wisdom is foolishness; his freedom is bondage; his "program"

is rebellion; his "progress," delusion. All his thoughts
are, "There is no God"!

As to the man whom the number "Six hundred and
sixty and six" represents, God will give full "understanding" when it is needed, in those three and half years of
horror and danger. He has never failed His saints. The
Church saints will not be there (as we have seen), but
many there will be who "worshipped not the beast . . .
and received not the mark" (Revelation 20:4). And they
will know and understand this man. His number will
be plain then, for it is the number of a man. Those
who "keep the commandments of God and hold the testimony of Jesus" will all have divinely given wisdom in
this matter.

Probably the marking out of this terrible Satan-Christ
has been hinted at all through the Christian centuries;
even as John says, "As ye heard that antichrist cometh,
even now have there arisen many antichrists" *(I John
2:18)*. Irenaeus reminds us that the word *Latin,* spelled
with Greek letters *Lateinos* (which Alford shows "would
be the usual way of writing the long 'i' by the Greeks
of the time") makes Six hundred and sixty-six in their
numerical value. Others have called attention to the
same fact concerning Nero Caesar, spelled in Hebrew.
Many other remarkable tracings have been made through
the years, as if Satan were ever seeking to bring forth
his "man of destiny"; but (as is actually true) ever being
hindered by God's restraining action, as we read in II
Thessalonians 2. It is startling in our own days to see
the number, Six hundred sixty-six used boldly for advertising commercial products! Godless commercialism
will be the final flood which rushes down the Devil's sluice-
way, to be dammed and governed by the Beast and his
Prophet to control all men. The mathematical probability,
that the number, Six hundred sixty-six should be selected
by *chance* in such advertising, is too remote to consider.

Now, concerning the present state of preparation for
that "universal monopoly" by which Satan, through his
two terrible agents, will control the bodies and souls of

men, much may be seen in our own day! Modern invention and industrialism has brought into being vast properties and holdings such as railroads, automobile companies, radio corporations, utilities of all sorts; which, finding competition unprofitable, have formed and are reforming combinations of ever greater extent. This enables private men of outstanding ability to manage and control more real power than many of the smaller governments! *Plutocracy* has come into its own! A world-bank and world-coinage are at hand.

We also see in our times the rapid and resistless accumulation of capital prophesied in James 5 (R. V.), "Ye (rich) have laid up your treasure in the last days." Communism will not succeed in crushing capital utterly, as it so fondly hopes. For Daniel told Nebuchadnezzar as to the final form of Gentile government, "There shall be in it of the strength of the iron," though "mixed" with "earthenware."*

"Internationalism" (Satan's own darling plan) is supposed even by many preachers, ignorant of God's Word, to be human large-mindedness. But God formed nations, and set "the bounds of their habitation," as well as "their appointed seasons" (Acts 17:26). And it was as a judgment upon earth-unification that nations came to be at Babel: "Jehovah said, Behold, they are one people, and they have all one language; and this (their self-idolatrous tower) is what they begin to do: and now nothing (in the way of rebellious pride and sin) will be withholden from them, which they purpose to do. Come, let us go down, and there confound their language, that they may not understand one another's speech" (Genesis 11:6, 7). Yet a "world-language" has been what men have been seeking to invent ever since! The idea is inspired of hell. Since Babel it is unnatural sin for a man to forget patriotism, and talk about world-stuff! Leave that to the

*It is striking to note that the democratic principle (as over against the imperial iron) is first called in Daniel 2 merely "clay" (the masses of men), verse 33; then "potters' clay" (men moulded by orators and agitators), verse 41; and finally "earthenware" verse 41 (R. V. margin), and "brittle," verse 42 —after the fires of revolution have hardened them for action into solid *blocs.*

atheists, the Communists. (The Christian rises above all earthly things, indeed, in Christ risen: but yet Paul said, "I am a Roman," and, "I am a citizen of Tarsus—no mean city." The loveliest Christians we have known were glad to reveal their God-given love for their own land!)

In Russia the tyranny of monopoly is in flower. One can hardly buy or sell, except he abjure God with the atheistic Soviets. In America, that capitalism (which the Soviets profess to hate) is none the less stealing the liberty of the poor man, or the small-business-man, quietly away. And no one but Christ (at His second coming) will ever deliver the oppressed *(Isaiah 11; Psalms 72:14)*.

It is the story of history that man never, except by *revolution,* recovers lost freedom. And then it is only by selling something more precious than what is gained!

CHAPTER XII

THE 144,000 ON MT. ZION

Revelation 14:1-5

There are seven distinct sections in Revelation 14:

1. The Vision of the One Hundred and Forty-four Thousand (verses 1-5).

2. The Angel Proclaiming the Eternal Gospel (verses 6, 7).

3. The Prophetic Announcement of Great Babylon's Fall (verse 8).

4. The Angelic Warning of the Eternal Doom of the Beast-worshippers (verses 9-12).

5. The Proclamation of the Especial Blessedness of those who should "die in the Lord" from that time (verse 13).

6. The Vision of the Harvest of the Earth (verses 14-16).

7. The Vision of the Vine of the Earth and the Wine-press of Blood (verses 17-20).

To outline the chapter in brief:

1. The Lamb's 144,000 seen in contrast to the nations and Antichrist.

2. The six "other" angels and their messages.

3. The two "sharp sickles" and what they reap.

The Vision of the One Hundred and Forty-four Thousand

And I saw, and behold, the Lamb standing on the mount Zion, and with him a hundred and forty and four thousand, having his name, and the name of his Father, written on their foreheads. And I heard a voice from heaven, as the voice of many waters, and as the voice of a great thunder: and the voice which I heard was as the voice of harpers harping with their harps: and they sing as it were a new song before the throne, and before the four living creatures and the elders: and no

man could learn the song save the hundred
and forty and four thousand, even they that
had been purchased out of the earth. These
are they that were not defiled with women;
for they are virgins. These are they that follow the Lamb whithersoever he goeth. These
were purchased from among men, to be the
firstfruits unto God and unto the Lamb. And
in their mouth was found no lie: they are
without blemish.

This is one of the most remarkable scenes, in every
way, of The Revelation thus far.

The "servants of our God" whom the angel sealed *on
their foreheads* in chapter 7:2-8, *before* any "hurt" should
come, are here seen with the Lamb, having, like those
three in the fiery furnace, passed *through* the fearful
divine judgments unharmed *(see 9:4)*, and then through
the horrors of the forty-two months of Antichrist *(chapter
13)*. They are seen on Mount Zion, the selected seat
of the glorious earthly reign of one thousand years, of
Christ and His saints.

THE 144,000 OF CHAPTER FOURTEEN— WHO ARE THEY?

I. Are they the sealed company of Israelites of chapter 7?

(1) The number 144,000 agrees. (2) They and these
in chapter 14 are sealed on their foreheads. (3) They
stand on Mount Zion in Jerusalem. (4) They pass
through the time of trouble, are victorious, etc.

II. Are they specially devoted saints from all the ages?

(1) The repetition of the number 144,000, one of
governmental completeness and fulness, is not necessarily
conclusive proof that the two companies are one and
the same. (2) Those in chapter 14 are indeed sealed on
their foreheads, but the form of the seal is the Lamb's
name and the name of His Father; whereas those of
chapter 7 were sealed as "the bondservants of our God."
(3) Those in chapter 14 were "purchased out of the

earth": they are not said to be of Israel's tribes. (4) They are all men (14:4): note the double statement "not defiled with women," and "virgins." (5) They are therefore Nazarites unto God, having forsworn even lawful things for a separate walk. (6) They "were purchased from among men, the firstfruits unto God and unto the Lamb"(14:4). (7) They were absolutely truthful: consequently, "without blemish." (8) They "follow the Lamb whithersoever he goeth."

We will give certain further comments concerning this company, not seeking dogmatically to assert, however, that they are the Israelites of chapter 7, though they seem to be these.

For, although we have thus spoken of them, we cannot but leave the question open for further light. Because, in all other Scripture we can recall, Israel's victors are always named as belonging to that elect nation, and the favor of God is seen as arising from that national election. Whereas, these of Revelation 14 do not have that mark, but rather seem to be from a larger circle than Israel— even "from among men"; and their peculiar distinction appears to be a reward for their utter self-abnegation. As Dean Alford says, "We are perhaps more like that which the Lord intended us to be; but they are more like the Lord Himself." Only let it be remembered, a "greater" place is given, in sovereign grace, to the Body of Christ: as our Lord spoke regarding John, in Matthew 11:11.

They are the "firstfruits" of the millennial reign. They connect the dispensations—somewhat as Noah did, who passed through the judgment of the flood into a new order of things. Therefore, the Lamb is seen standing on Mount Zion (before He actually comes there, as in Revelation 19 and Psalm 2), that with Him may be seen this overcoming host, who will very shortly share His actual reign there.*

*That the number 144,000 is literal you cannot doubt, without sitting down beside some Sadducee. It is well, when people claim that the Scripture does not mean what it says, to ask, "Who, then, shall say *what* it means?"

Seven things are told us of this amazing company.

1. They had written on their foreheads *the Name* of the Lamb, and *the Name* of His Father! In marvellous manner they were thus blessedly blazoned out, that all might see! It proclaimed their *ownership*—they were the Lamb's and His Father's. It exhibited their character—they were Nazarites to God, and His holy ones forever. It announced their destiny—they were to be associated wholly with the Lamb whom they had wholly chosen! Beautiful badge of blessedness!

Now, no one who thoughtfully reads chapters 13 and 14, together, can avoid the profound conviction that these, with the Lamb's and His Father's Name in their foreheads, are set before us *in direct contrast* with those who took in their foreheads the name or number of Satan's awful Christ.*

This earth will at last learn what the words mean, "Choose you this day whom ye will serve!" Of course the Church is not in this scene—cannot be. But how instructive all is for us in a day when darkness is put for light, and light for darkness! And how it thrills our hearts to know that GOD can triumph as easily in such days as Revelation 14 portrays, as in our own days. *Grace* enabled Enoch to walk with God while the earth was ripening for judgment; *and grace* enabled Noah to pass safely through the judgment!

2. This 144,000 (and no others) could learn and sing the "new song" that burst forth "as the voice of many waters, and as the voice of a great thunder: . . . of harpers harping with their harps."

A "new song" was begun in Revelation 5:9, 10, upon the Lamb's taking the seven-sealed book of judgment, and in celebration of His worthiness to do so, and in view of the earthly "kingdom of priests" He thus made

---

*Indeed, it has occurred to us that the presence of the heavenly seal in the foreheads of the remnant from chapter 7 on, is so evident to men that Satan is forced to undertake to break its influence by demanding the opposite seal in the foreheads of his devotees. And especially may this be true, when we reflect that God preserves (as in 9:4) those who have His seal, from woes to which others are subject.

possible. The angels, and then all creation, celebrated thus Him that sat upon the throne and the Lamb.

Here in Revelation 14, we are not told the words of the "new song." But we know it was of rapturous, thunderous exultation. All heaven has been looking forward eagerly to it. It is connected directly with the setting up of the glorious reign on earth: for the prophetic appearance of the Lamb on Mount Zion with the 144,000 is the signal for it. Only one other event outdoes it in the rapture it gives to heaven, and that is the marriage of the Lamb, in chapter 19. Therefore we ought to wait here; to let our hearts be *filled full*, as it were, with the spirit of this song and its occasion. If we are in tune with heaven, what gives heaven such ecstasy, must move us deeply!

To those who have followed, in the prophets, the story of "the remnant," noting all God's love, His earthly purposes of blessing, His sympathy through their sorrows, *in* their sorrows (for, "in all their affliction he was afflicted"), His promises to them for the hideous days of the end—to such, the scene that opens Revelation 14, is a delight indescribable!

Into the heavenly song that now breaks, and swells on with its many "harpers harping with their harps" no one of earth could enter in spirit. Why? These 144,000 souls have passed through *fire*, have dwelt among lions— to be faithful! So, in their measure, have all those saints who have "suffered with Christ." After the troubles are over, and the Lord is come, and the kingdom set up in glory and majesty and power, on Mount Zion, and the Lord is "King over all the earth," and the thousand years of peace are come, it will no longer be possible to learn the song that these will learn—the song of absolute *fellowship* with the Lamb *in suffering*.

Ah, how much we miss! "All that would *(will)* live godly in Christ Jesus shall suffer persecution" *(II Timothy 3:12)*. There is a *will* here. Do we *choose* to suffer with Christ, that we may also reign with Him?

The Millennium, the peaceful days—how lovely they

séem to us! But ah, how much more will this 144,000 know (though they are earthly saints) than others whether of Israel, or of the Gentile nations! Christ Himself, "though he was a Son, yet learned obedience by the things which he *suffered.*" God is *infinite;* and there are things of God, and in God, that only suffering gives the *capacity* to know! And the days are coming, when suffering for and with Christ will be forever over. Oh, let us listen when God tells us that this suffering remnant, while remaining earthly saints (and not having *died,* though being *at the gates of* death constantly, under Antichrist) *learn* that new song that will be sung "before the throne, and before the four living creatures and the elders." No one else on earth will know it, or can know it!*

3. "They had been purchased out of the earth." That is, though being men on earth, they are not, properly, *in* the earth. Neither do they belong to heaven—though they learn, and can sing, the song that is being sung there. They have been "purchased." They belong only to the Lamb and to His Father. They will be connected with the Lamb's earthly rule and reign. They will therefore have their sphere on earth; but it will be manifest publicly that they have been purchased *out* of the earth. This, in reality, is true of *Christians, now!* Yet we are to remain among men, for Christ, as *witnesses,* and are bound up in many proper earthly relationships and responsibilities. But not these 144,000! They will have manifestly been *bought away* from earth entirely. We look for a body like to Christ's heavenly body—a higher state than these. But these will be men in human flesh with the

---

*We should constantly remember that the Church, the Body of Christ, as ministered by Paul, as indwelt by the Holy Spirit, has a calling immeasurably above and beyond this 144,000; or, for that matter, far beyond anything yet revealed in the book of Revelation! Even in Hebrews, Christ and His own are seen as *"all of one,"* and they, His "brethren." Where, so far, in Revelation, is such a relation set forth? Even in the seven churches of chapters 2 and 3, Christ is (and must be) *Judge.* The glorious, overwhelming truth of *oneness with Christ, His "fulness," members* of Him, is not set forth. Oh, alas, we do not *see it;* or we *forget* it; or we *neglect* it; or we *grieve* the indwelling Comforter. And then, we are *blind.* We can no longer interpret Scripture. We part company with Paul's epistles, and we desire Moses and Elijah along with Jesus—Moses to give a "rule of life," and Elijah to call down fire if we fail to keep the "rule."

open seal of the Lamb and of His Father upon their foreheads!

Their history looks three ways:

a. It is the elect remnant of the old nation of Israel.

b. It looks forward to that "receiving" of Israel in the 1000 years that shall be "as life from the dead" (Romans 11:15).

c. It is in touch with heaven—it knows the song sung there!

Most wonderful counsels are those of God! And what a day it will be, when the Lamb of God returns to reign gloriously! What a day—with the Church in the heavenlies (instead of the angels—*Hebrews 2:5-8)*, with the twelve apostles (Matthias in Judas' place) on thrones judging (as those with heavenly wisdom) the twelve tribes of Israel; with the Lord, the Lamb, as their returned Messiah, delighted in as the King in His beauty, the King of Israel; with the mountain of the Lord's House (Zion) raised above all hills of earth, the wondrous temple of Ezekiel 40-48 upon it, and all the nations coming up to worship the King, Jehovah of Hosts! And Christ, the Bridegroom saying to *us,* "Behold, thou art all fair My love, there is no spot in thee!" And all about us, at that time, these personal attendants of the Lamb, who follow Him "whithersoever He goeth"!

4. The fourth particular revealed regarding this company of 144,000 is, "These are they that were not defiled with women; for they are virgins."

Now there is one way only to take these words, and that is, in their literal sense. To do this aright, we must compare Scripture with Scripture: for the opinions or prejudices of men must not be allowed here.

And first, let us remember again, that we are not dealing with Church things or with Church days. "Marriage is honorable in all, and the bed undefiled," we read in Hebrews 13:4. And again, Paul directs Timothy, "I desire therefore (in view of the tendencies described in *I Timothy 5:14)* that the younger (women) marry, bear children, rule the household, give no occasion to the

adversary for reviling." And concerning himself (I Corinthians 9:5), "Have we no right to lead about a wife
that is a believer, even as the rest of the apostles, and
the brethren of the Lord, and Cephas?" And even in I
Corinthians 7:1, 7, 8 where Paul declares, "It is good for
a man not to touch a woman. . . . I would that all men
were even as I myself. . . . It is good for them if they
abide even as I," he proceeds with the plainest directions
for life in the marriage relation; which, even for those
saints who are so desirous of *prayer* as to separate themselves "by consent for a season," is yet the normal and
safe relation in which to continue.

Yet we must, as the days grow darker, weigh well the
apostle's words in I Corinthians 7:25-31. These days are
evil. "Distress" is upon us. The apostle uses the fact
here to counsel the saints to ponder well the steps they
take. "The time is shortened, that henceforth both those
that have wives be as though they had none; and those
that weep (especially in bereavement, evidently), as
though they wept not; and those that rejoice (especially
in domestic bliss), as though they rejoiced not; and those
that buy, as though they possessed not; and those that
use the world, as not using it to the full: *for the stage
scenery of this world is passing away!"*

It is not to be with us (since our Lord and Head and
Bridegroom is absent, rejected) as it was with Israel
when they were told by Jehovah to enter Canaan and sit
peacefully under their vines and fig trees. This world
hates us as it hated Christ. Nor is it with us as it will
be when our Lord returns, and the meek shall at last
inherit the earth. All is really *present distress!* Christ
is off His throne. The Church is away from her Bridegroom. Israel is out of her land. The servants have not
yet their rewards. Satan is yet in the heavenlies. Creation yet groans. Christ has not yet seen of the travail of
His soul, and been *satisfied*.

But if "distress" is upon us, so that we are to use earth-
things "as though we used them not," what will be the
condition of those shortly to pass into The Great Tribu-

lation—the elect remnant of Israel, the 144,000? If, even *now,* the apostle can say, "Art thou loosed from a wife? seek not a wife" *(I Corinthians 7:27),* what would he say to those of the days of which the Lord said: "Woe unto them that are with child and to them that give suck in those days! . . . For then shall be great tribulation such as hath not been from the beginning of the world until now, no, nor ever shall be" *(Matthew 24:19, 21).*

But not merely in the wisdom of avoiding the complexities of days of distress, do these 144,000 appear. They are complete *Nazarites unto God,* as touching their relation to women. They are as was their Lord. The explanation given us is explicit: "They are *virgins."* Because of the awful doctrine of Rome (really of *demons, I Timothy 4:2, 3),* which forbids to marry, earnest students of Scripture have feared, or at least failed, to let the plain words of the Lord and His apostles have their simplest meaning—that it may be "given" of God to some men to abstain from the marriage relation, not from tradition or bondage, but to be the more peculiarly separated, in some service, unto *Him.* Only those thus divinely led and gifted, our Lord plainly says, in Matthew 19:11, 12, can "receive this saying." Also, the connection with the kingdom is quite striking here in Matthew, though Paul speaks of the same "gift" in I Corinthians 7:7, 17.

But in the fearful days of abandonment "as in the days of Noah"—when lust and violence will again fill the whole earth (as we see beginning *now!*) how wonderful to behold this company of 144,000 who have chosen to be entirely separated unto the Lamb and unto His Father, and who *are* thus, despite the days!

5. "These are they that follow the Lamb whithersoever he goeth." Let us again remember that they are not the Church, which, as the *wife* of the Lamb, has a wholly different and closer relationship than any others *can* have. But these are the personal attendants—the bodyguard, so to speak, of the Lamb. Their movements with Him "whithersoever he goeth" remind us of that absolute one-

ness of mind and movement of the cherubim (with Jehovah enthroned) of Ezekiel 1. Remember also the devotedness of David's mighty men, who may well typify these: for both are connected with the *throne of David*— on Mount Zion.

6. The next word about this 144,000 is that they were "purchased from among men, the firstfruits unto God and unto the Lamb."

Now James tells us that the Church saints *now* are "a kind of firstfruits" of God's *"creatures."* Paul definitely says, "If any man be in Christ, he is a new *creature"* (or *creation*) ; and this is the great *fact* to be held by us in our walk, by the rule of *a new creation (Galatians 6:15, 16 R. V.).*

We must discriminate here in Revelation 14:4. "Firstfruits unto God and unto the Lamb" are *kingdom* words; and not mere salvation words. The "Church of the firstborn" *(Hebrews 12)* has already gone up on high; the millennial things are not yet come, the kingdom is not yet set up. But this 144,000 belong to that kingdom (as is seen at once by their being *with the Lamb on Mount Zion*). Marvelous wonder of God's grace and keeping power: they come *alive* through the fire of Antichrist's days, to walk as "firstfruits" into the 1000 years—an *earnest*-purchase from among men for the reign of heaven on earth! And *"firstfruits"* mean that *harvest* is on! The sight of this 144,000 should remind us that "life from the dead" for the world is made doubly sure by this *preserved* remnant, just as its promise is connected with the national *receiving* of Israel. Read Romans 11:15.

7. And finally we read: "In their mouth was found no lie: they are without blemish."

The days of Antichrist were *days of falsehood.* His miracles are called in II Thessalonians 2:9, "signs and lying wonders" (Greek, *pseudos*). And it is there said that because they received not the love of the truth God sent them "a working of error that they should believe *the lie"* (Greek, *to pseudei*). "The Lie" is that Satan is God, and that the Beast is his Christ and to be worshipped. The *gulfs* of deceit of damnation are opened wide! All is *pseudos*, PSEUDOS, on every side.

But in the mouth of this 144,000, we read, was found "no lie." And the Greek word is, no *pseudos!*

Now when we turn to Zephaniah 3:13, and read the description of the remnant of Israel after the Millennium has begun, we find: "The remnant of Israel shall not do iniquity, nor speak lies; neither shall a deceitful tongue be found in their mouth; for they shall feed and lie down, and none shall make them afraid"—we are at once reminded of those great passages in Jeremiah 31 and Ezekiel 36, which describe in detail the manner of God's salvation which He will visit upon the saved of Israel in millennial times. "I will put my law in their inward parts, and in their heart will I write it" (Jeremiah). "A new heart also will I give you, and a new spirit will I put within you; and I will take away the stony heart out of your flesh, and I will give you a heart of flesh. And I will put my Spirit within you, and cause you to walk in my statutes, and ye shall keep mine ordinances and do them" (Ezekiel 36:26).

Now all this must be literally fulfilled for Israel. This is no description of *our* salvation—which is that ye are in Christ; Christ is in you; and the indwelling Spirit would *"form* Christ" within you. But this prophetic utterance describes the fulfilment by restored Israel of "every jot and tittle of the law" before the "heaven and earth pass away"—as they must do at the close of the 1000 years *(Revelation 20)*.

These firstfruits, therefore, of Israel, this 144,000, are "without blemish" *(Revelation 14:5)*. They are a public example and pledge of what the "all-righteous" nation of Israel will be in the Millennium! What will happen to Israel has *already* happened to *them!* "Without blemish" —men on earth in the flesh!

Brethren, we have no excuses to make for dwelling thus upon this 144,000. To understand prophecy is to become absorbed (amidst other wonders) with what God has said He will do to, and through, the remnant of Israel!

And we would the more magnify Jehovah's promises concerning Israel and the coming thousand years' reign of Christ "before his ancients gloriously" (A. V.), because some who claim loudly to be "fundamentalists" either deny Israel's future glory wholly or resort to some poor word like "*a*-millennialism,"—that is, *no* Millennium.

In the rest of Revelation 14, God witnesses publicly by six angels against the awful state of things brought about by Antichrist in chapter 13, and prophetically pictures the fast coming judgment in the two sickles.

CHAPTER XIII
THE SIX "OTHER" ANGELS
Revelation 14:6-20

And I saw another angel flying in mid heaven, having eternal good tidings to proclaim unto them that dwell on the earth, and unto every nation and tribe and tongue and people; and he saith with a great voice, Fear God, and give him glory; for the hour of his judgment is come: and worship him that made the heaven and the earth and sea and fountains of waters.

This is a *gospel,* not an announcement of doom, as is verse 8; although there is no record that it is believed or heeded. It may not be. Noah was a "preacher of righteousness," in view of the coming flood; but no one believed him except his own family. This gospel is called (and here alone in the whole Bible) an *eternal* gospel; one adapted for all ages (the adjective is *aionion,* that is, "constantly befitting," "everlastingly applicable"). But it is peculiarly so at the hour when the whole earth, except God's elect, are madly and blindly worshipping the Beast and his image *(Revelation 13:8).* And it must be constantly remembered that the days of the Antichrist are on, from chapter 13 through 18—despite *prophetic* visions of both the coming victory and kingdom of Christ, and of the Great Day of Wrath which shall bring that kingdom in. Universal idolatry, hideous, unreasonable, absurd, God-provoking, as it is, will fill the earth during the time of our present chapter. Slavish, abject prostration before an image of the most wicked man of the human race, with its consequent obliteration of the glory of the Creator, will prevail, even among the majority of Israel *(Daniel 9:27; Isaiah 28:15).*

God created man in "his own image"; but six times in Revelation the worship of the Beast is described as directed to *"his* image."

Now this hateful thing *idolatry* is called in Romans

220

1:23, changing "the glory of the incorruptible God for the likeness of an image of corruptible man." And the fact is that this departure was wilful, as seen in Romans 1:20, "The invisible things of him since the creation of the world, are clearly seen, being perceived through the things that are made, *even* his everlasting power and divinity."

We see then at once a most cogent reason for calling this message an *eternal gospel;* for it is the recalling of men to the fear of the living God as Creator, and giving Him worship; inasmuch as He is the One who hath "made the heaven and the earth and sea and fountains of waters."

In the midst of the multitude of utterances by the Old Testament prophets as to God's anger at idolatry, *one* stands out like a flash of lightning in a blackening sky. It is the single Aramaic verse in the great Hebrew prophecy of Jeremiah—(Aramaic or Syrian being the language of the nations, over and against God's language, the Hebrew)—Jeremiah 10:11, "Thus shall ye say unto them, The gods that have not made the heavens and the earth, these shall perish from the earth, and from under the heavens."

Now we find an *angel* flying in mid heaven proclaiming this eternal gospel. This should not astonish us. It is then no longer the Church age, when the gospel of reconciliation through the blood of the Cross is being proclaimed for simple faith. (How astonishing that any Christian should *dream* that the true *Church* is on earth at the time we are considering!) Angels warned Lot in Sodom and rescued him there from doom. The Law on Sinai was ministered by angels *(Acts 7:53; Galatians 3:19)* and especially by one—possibly Michael *(Exodus 23:20-23; 33:2).* Jehovah distinctly declares of this angel "my *name* is in him," although Moses was not permitted to know him *(Exodus 33:12).*

The very name "angel," both in Hebrew and Greek, means "messenger," and an angel from God is one with a message or commission from Him. Therefore we do not wonder that when universal idolatry prevails, man having refused to harken to the preachers of the gospel of grace, and God having withdrawn them by the rapture of the Church, he will declare this *eternal gospel* by the mouth of a mighty angel, who, flying "in mid heaven" all over the earth, will proclaim to every creature, in words understandable, and unmistakable, that *the hour of God's* JUDGMENT *has come;* bidding men *turn quickly to the Creator of them, and of all things!*

The Prophetic Announcement of Great Babylon's Fall

And another, a second angel, followed, saying, Fallen, fallen is Babylon the great, that hath made all the nations to drink of the wine of the wrath of her fornication.

Babylon occupies much notice in Scripture but chapters 17 and 18 are devoted to it. Here, however, let us note:

1. Babylon has been the center of Satan's operations from the flood onward; idolatry as far as we have any knowledge began there; and the Babylonian system was extended to all the nations, being Satan's plan to destroy the knowledge and worship of Jehovah; substituting therefor *himself.*

2. We find here the pregnant expression concerning Babylon the great, "The *wine* of the *wrath* of her *fornication.*" These are three distinct subjects. First, in Jeremiah 51:7 we read, "Babylon hath been a golden cup in Jehovah's hand that made all the earth drunken: the nations have drunk of her wine; therefore the nations are mad." It is the madness of Babylon's idolatry that is described in Jeremiah 50:38: "It is a land of graven images, and they are mad over idols." This was Babylon's wine. Next, we have in Jeremiah 25:15, the wine of wrath, "Take this cup of the wine of wrath at my hand, and cause all the nations to whom I send thee, to drink it." Loving the creature rather than the Creator, and idolatry rather than God, God gave them over to the system of Babylonian Satanism that brought God's wrath upon them.*

---

*Jeremiah 25:15-26 is an astounding passage, revealing as it does the judicial operations of Jehovah through His prophets outlined in God's commission to

Thirdly, the last subject is "fornication." Remember this, when we study Revelation 17:1-5 and 18:3.

3. "Fallen, fallen" indicates coming *double* destruction, as Revelation 17 and 18 will show: of a *system,* then of a *city.*

The idolatry which originated at Babylon will yet bring wrath on all the nations, and lastly cast Babylon down to the doom of Sodom. See Jeremiah 50:40—*yet future,* we believe.

The Angelic Warning of the Eternal Doom of the Beast-worshippers

And another angel, a third, followed them, saying with a great voice, If any man worshippeth the beast and his image, and receiveth a mark on his forehead, or upon his hand, he also shall drink of the wine of the wrath of God, which is prepared unmixed in the cup of his anger; and he shall be tormented with fire and brimstone in the presence of the holy angels, and in the presence of the Lamb: and the smoke of their torment goeth up for ever and ever; and they have no rest day and night, they that worship the beast and his image, and whoso receiveth the mark of his name. Here is the patience of the saints, they that keep the commandments of God, and the faith of Jesus.

God's faithful warning comes again by the mouth of an angel, and that "with a great voice." Not only that the Beast's rebuilt capital city Babylon is to "fall"—*is* fallen, in God's vision, but that unending torment awaits the Beast's worshippers.

Jeremiah in Jeremiah 1:10: "I have this day set thee over the nations and over the kingdoms, to pluck up and to break down and to destroy and to overthrow, to build and to plant." Next is recorded the awful power for evil committed to Babylon, destroying with its idolatrous influence one nation after another,— Judah, Egypt, Uz, Philistia, and so on, 21 or 22 peoples being enumerated in the series, ending with the king of Sheshach—"he shall drink *after* them!" That is, the city of Babylon, the source of destruction, was to be the *last destroyed,* which we find fulfilled in The Revelation—Sheshach is the ancient name of Babylon (Revelation 16:19).

What a fearful "hour of trial" is coming on the earth! *(Revelation 3:10)*. Note that to involve the torment of verses 10 and 11, one will not only have "worshipped" the Beast or his image, but have deliberately taken his *mark* —shut out all God's warnings, and *chosen Satan's Christ.*

Now see what God at last justly does:

1. He *withdraws all mercy forever*—the wine of His wrath that these shall drink will be "unmixed," unmingled with any compassion whatsoever.

2. It will be in *"the cup of his anger"* that His wrath will be served out to them. The impenitent daily and hourly "treasure up for themselves wrath in the day of wrath": but God withholds His anger. He waits. He suffers long and is kind. But—"who may stand in Thy sight when once thou art *angry?" (Psalm 76:7)*. Consider an Infinite Being "willing" (at last) "to *show* His wrath and make His power *known."* Consider His words, "Vengeance is mine: I will repay." The same verse that says "love is strong as death" declares "jealousy is cruel as Sheol." The creature of this human race for whom His Son died who turns his back on the God whose name is Love, and chooses His enemy, the old serpent and murderer—God plainly tells us what He will do with him! He shall have "indignation forever"!

3. Consider the carefully described *means of visitation* upon such: "tormented with fire and brimstone." Brimstone is the most terrible substance known in its action upon human flesh—in its torment when it touches the body. Combined with fire it is absolute agony, unutterable anguish! And it is meant to be so: for it will be the infliction of *divine vengeance unlimited.*

4. Consider the *onlookers:* "In the presence of the holy angels, and in the presence of the Lamb"! Vast, "innumerable hosts," of those holy servants of God who watched the fearful choice of these now doomed humans, for whom, to the angelic astonishment, the Son of God once *tasted death,*—men that hated love and despised holiness: all the countless millions of angels are there, in deep, awful and holy approval of the divine sentence,—

for their God hath done this! And in the presence *of the Lamb!* Oh, where in the universe is such a sight? Mercy is gone forever if the Lamb stands there: and He will!*

5. Consider the *duration:* "The smoke of their torment *(compare Genesis 19:24, 28)* goeth up for ever and ever."† And its *unceasingness:* "They have no rest day and night." Let God speak. Let us be still, and believe, and fear. The wickedness of those who even *think* rebellion against the eternal retribution described thus plainly by God, will become so great as to ruin all faith in God's Word. It is *not your right* to question. "Woe unto him that striveth with his Maker! a potsherd among the potsherds of the earth!" *(Isaiah 45:9).*

6. Finally, behold *the marks of God's patient elect,* "the saints," in contrast with these self-doomed and damned rebels. God will have His witnesses, in every scene of man's sin. These, of course, are not the Church. They are God's "elect" of Luke 18:1-8, who will cry for avenging from the *adversary,* in that awful time of trouble,— the remnant of Israel and those who help them. They are marked by "keeping the commandments of God," for they are on Old Testament ground yet, as to law. And they have also "the faith of Jesus," which is the earthly, Jewish confession of Him, according to Matthew's gospel. What they show, preeminently, is "patience." They must wait, and suffer, and still wait; as the Lord saith in Luke 21:19: "In your patience ye shall win your souls."

Saints' Death Best!

And I heard a voice from heaven saying, Write, Blessed are the dead who die in the Lord from henceforth: yea, saith the Spirit, that they may rest from their labors; for their works follow with them.

---

*Let the daringly foolish that deny eternal punishment, and who profess to believe in a God incapable of wrath stay away from this spot!

†The definite article is not used here. It is *eis aionas aionon;* for the *abstract* thought of "age-abidingness" is before us. In Revelation 20:10 the definite article is used, referring to this passage, and emphasizing the fact that the torment (which the wicked share with the Devil—*Matthew 25:41)* will endure through all the endless ages.

Never before could such a word be spoken! Always it had been better, heretofore, to live out the full time of a saint's pilgrimage on earth: both for the sake of others, and for the learning of obedience by daily divine discipline. Now, however, the fearful days of Antichrist are on! Death is better than life, and for two reasons here announced by the Spirit:

1. Rest will be entered upon from their labors. The word here is *hina*—*in order that* they may rest. Rest is at last obtainable in no other way but by death. When our Lord said to the mob led by Judas in Gethsemane, "This is your hour, and the authority of darkness" (Luke 22:53—Greek), He contrasted that hour with "when I was daily with you in the temple, ye stretched not forth your hands against me." No wonder the next words are, "And they seized him." There was no path then open to Him but death, if He would come home to His Father. And there is a like hour coming on the whole world (Revelation 3:10). He (the Beast) shall "wear out the saints of the Most High" (Daniel 7:25). "And it was given unto him to make war with the saints, and to overcome them" (Revelation 13:7). Not a life of discipline under God's hand (as now) but death, (and doubtless with tortures such as only ages of Satanic malignity make possible), will be the lot of the faithful of those days— those "in the Lord." Rest, therefore, will come only through dying!

Neither will it be, as now with us, that they can expect the Lord *at any moment*. Prophetic *times* will be known *then,* and just how much of the 42 months is left!

2. The second reason that those will be "blessed" who die "in the Lord" at that time, is—that their works *accompany* them. Four times in this very chapter the Greek work translated "follow" *(akoloutheo)* is used: in verse 4, *"follow* the Lamb whithersoever he goeth"; in verse 8, " a second angel *followed*"; in verse 9, "a third, *followed* them." It is the word used of the disciples and multitudes "following," in accompanying our Lord *(Matthew 4:25; 8:1, etc.).* So that we see that these are

the *last* martyrs, in Revelation 14:13. They are seen as the third company of the reigners *with Christ,* in Revelation 20:6.* They get a higher place than those, even of Israel, who merely "inherit the kingdom" as in Matthew 25:31-46.

Notice that John is called to *write,* here. It is of especial importance, therefore,—to be laid to heart in particular. And while verse 13 of our chapter has always a precious *application* to the death of any saint, it is only these last martyrs to whom the Word is directly *addressed.* "From henceforth" is a definite time-mark. (It is *aparti,* as in Matthew 23:39, and 26:29, 64.) It denotes a *change* of circumstances and conditions; and literally is: "from now."

The Vision of the Harvest of the Earth

And I saw, and behold, a white cloud; and on the cloud one sitting like unto a son of man, having on his head a golden crown, and in his hand a sharp sickle.

And another angel came out from the temple, crying with a great voice to him that sat on the cloud, Send forth thy sickle, and reap: for the hour to reap is come; for the harvest of the earth is ripe.

And he that sat on the cloud cast his sickle upon the earth; and the earth was reaped.

It is, we have no doubt, the Lord Jesus who is set forth here; but we must attend, in interpreting a passage, to what *that passage* sets forth. Then we compare it with other Scriptures. And thus we see here:

1. The *"white cloud."* This is the first object brought before the Seer's eyes.

2. One is *sitting upon* the cloud. Although He "mak-

---

*The first are those who are already seen sitting on the thrones, to whom "judgment" was given—the Church, according to I Corinthians 6:2; the second company are, we believe, those martyrs seen under the fifth seal, in Revelation 6 —now at last raised *(they lived)* and those also up to the days of the Beast; and the third—the martyrs under the Beast, as in Revelation 14:13. They are the last; when their company is made up, the Lord arrives to avenge them all. See Revelation 6:11.

eth the clouds his chariot" and will come thereon, it is His *position*, not His *movement*, here noticed.

3. This Sitter appears as a *son of man*. There is no note here of the marvellous display of glory which our Lord always emphasized as attending His return as Son of man (Matthew 24:30; Mark 8:38, etc.). The fact that this One who is to reap the earth *is* a son of man, is alone set forth. But compare the words of our Lord in John 5:22, 27: the Father "hath given all judgment unto the Son; that all may honor the Son, even as they honor the Father: . . . and he gave him authority to execute judgment, because he is a son of man." (Do not read *"the* son of man," here, or you will miss the meaning.)

4. On the head of Him sitting on the cloud is a *golden crown*. The mere fact that He is sitting as a God-appointed *King,* is indicated—His royal right, for He will come as Son of man, and inherit all dominion *as such*. Psalm 8:6 will be *fulfilled*.

5. "In his hand *a sharp sickle.*" Not the *glory* of His person, or the *process* of His coming, but the fact that He is ready with a *reaping* instrument, is here emphasized. Rights over the harvest, (whatever the harvest is to be) are manifest. "Thou shalt not move a sickle unto thy neighbor's standing grain," said the law. Therefore, He is to reap a field over which He has authority. Now, it is striking to discover that the "sickle" is mentioned just twelve times in the Bible, and *seven* of these are in our verses here! Also that the Greek word translated "sharp" *(oxus)* occurs seven times in The Revelation: four times describing the sickle here, and three times, that two-edged sword which proceeds from the Lord's mouth for searching *judgment*. Inasmuch, therefore, as all after Revelation 4:1, as regards Church matters is *meta tauta,* or *"after* these things"; and inasmuch as the *preserved* remnant of 144,000 is seen before this (in 7 and 14:1-5); and inasmuch as the martyrs under the Beast are addressed in verse 13, as the blessed who shall

die : are there any left for this sharp sickle, but the *wicked* of the earth?

6. "Another angel . . . from the temple"; this is evidently the temple in *heaven,* as in verse 17. From the presence of the Father, who hath set within *His own* authority—time and seasons *(Acts 1:7; Matthew 24:36)* the message is sent by this angelic mouth to *the Lord* to "send forth his sickle." We need not wonder at this. Angels have the present world in their administration; they know and report to God continually as to its matters; especially, as in Sodom's case *(Genesis 18 and 19);* and that of Ahab *(I Kings 22),* concerning times when iniquity is *full,* and *judgment* is *due.* So the "crying with a great voice" is really God's message to Christ, who has been, all along "expecting" such a message *(Hebrew 10: 12, 13; Psalm 2:7-9).*

7. "Send forth thy sickle, and reap." Many say this reaping is of both saints and sinners. But we feel that this 'Revelation scene is purely one of *judgment.*

From the parable of the tares (Matthew 13) we learn that "the harvest is the consummation of the age." But, while in the parable, the householder says : "In the time of harvest I will say to the reapers, Gather up first the tares, and bind them in bundles to burn them; but gather the wheat into my barn"; in the interpretation of the parable, the Lord says : "The harvest is the end of the age; and the reapers are angels. As therefore the tares are gathered up and burned with fire; so shall it be in the end of the age. The Son of man shall send forth his angels, and they shall gather out of his kingdom all things that cause stumbling, and them that do iniquity and shall cast them into the furnace of fire : there shall be the weeping and the gnashing of teeth. Then shall the righteous shine forth as the sun in the kingdom of their Father." Now note most carefully here, that while the angels gather out the wicked for the fire, they leave the righteous where they are, on earth, where the kingdom is set up. "My barn," then, of the parable, becomes, necessarily, this earth as ruled by the Lord, when

His Father's kingdom has at last come. Therefore the "sickle" of Revelation 14 is seen to be one primarily of judgment on the wicked.*

8. "The hour to reap is come."

This is an ominous announcement! Through the Old Testament prophets again and again we have the warning of a harvest time for the wicked, at this very end-time. We shall note this especially in the next vision—of the vintage. But both harvest and vintage are set forth in Joel 3:13: "Put ye in the sickle; for the harvest is ripe: Come, tread ye; for the winepress is full, the vats overflow; for their wickedness is great." This verse in itself is a complete answer to those who claim that the harvest in Revelation 14 means the saved, and the winepress the wicked. Both passages in Joel refer to the wicked; and that both refer to the wicked in Revelation 14, is shown by the place in The Revelation where it is found and by its conformity to all other Scripture. Note also the sickle, in Joel 3! It is there used, as here, for cutting down the over-ripe workers of iniquity!

9. "For the harvest of the earth is dry." The Greek word here is the same as is used of the fig-tree in Mark 11:20; and in Luke 23:31 the adjective form is used: "What shall be done in *the dry?*"—meaning the dreadful "last state" of Israel in the last days! And at this reaping time of *all* the earth!

Next we have the Actor, the act, and the result—all that God desires us to see: all in one brief sentence! It involves, of course, the second coming of the King of kings, of chapter 19, with all the heavenly hosts in the Great Day of Wrath. But God wants us to behold, in the majestic simplicity of Deity, *what* will be done, ere the *details* come before us. Ah, and alas! how little men *dream* of the end of all their pride and their ambitions! "The earth was *reaped*": that is the end of all things of which *man* boasts!

---

*That the angels will also "gather together" the earthly elect at the Son of man's coming is seen in Matthew 24:31. But that these are not "reaped" as are the others, is seen from the preceding verse, where "all the tribes of the earth *mourn*" at His appearing.

The Vine of the Earth and the Winepress of Blood

And another angel came out from the temple which is in heaven, he also having a sharp sickle. And another angel came out from the altar, he that hath power over fire; and he called with a great voice to him that had the sharp sickle, saying, Send forth thy sharp sickle, and gather the clusters of the vine of the earth; for her grapes are fully ripe.

And the angel cast his sickle into the earth, and gathered the vine of the earth, and cast it into the winepress, the great winepress of the wrath of God.

And the winepress was trodden without the city, and there came out blood from the winepress, even unto the bridles of the horses, as far as a thousand and six hundred furlongs.

Here is before us—not the *harvest*, but *the vine* of the earth. *Christ* is the *true* Vine. But we now have before us those in *active living league with Antichrist!* The true Church is gone; false Christianity swallowed up by the Beast and his ten kings *(Revelation 17:16, 17, 18)*, and all the earth (but "the elect" of those days) of "one mind, to give their kingdom unto the beast"—Satan's Christ.

Thus comes "the vine of the earth." Moses spake long ago of this day, in his great song in Deuteronomy 32: 31-35:

"For their rock is not as our Rock,
Even our enemies themselves being judges.
For their vine is of the vine of Sodom,
And of the fields of Gomorrah:
Their grapes are grapes of gall,
Their clusters are bitter:
Their wine is the poison of serpents,
And the cruel venom of asps.
Is not this laid up in store with me,

Sealed up among my treasures?
Vengeance is mine, and recompense,
At the time when their foot shall slide:
For the day of their calamity is at hand,
And the things that are to come upon them shall
    make haste."

When we come to the gathering of the nations, in Revelation 16, to Armageddon, we can look more fully at the great movement under Antichrist to "cut off Israel from being a nation." But we must quote Joel's words here:

"Proclaim ye this among the nations: Prepare war; stir up the mighty men; let all the men of war draw near, let them come up. Beat your plowshares into swords, and your pruning-hooks into spears." (Just the *reverse* of what Christ the Prince of Peace will do when He comes!—*Isaiah 2:4.*) "Let the nations bestir themselves, and come up to the valley of Jehoshaphat (just east of Jerusalem); for there will I sit to judge all the nations round about. Put ye in the sickle; for the harvest is ripe: come, tread ye; for the winepress is full, the vats overflow; for their wickedness is great. Multitudes, multitudes in the valley of decision! *for the day of Jehovah is near in the valley of decision"* (Joel 3:12-14).

It needs to be known and remembered by us all that this earth is *at war with God Almighty!* And, although today is a time of salvation, and of restraining grace, when that salvation *ceases,* and restraint is *removed,* the whole earth will rush to cut off the name of Israel from the earth *(Psalm 83).*

Then God will *meet* them! "He that sitteth in the heavens shall laugh." The Lamb of God will come forth. As the Deliverer of Israel He will fulfill Isaiah 63. He will trample the embattled nations of this whole earth, millions upon millions of them, from Bozrah, in Edom, (where He will begin—*Isaiah 63:1)* to Megiddo at the foot of Mt. Carmel—the Har-magedon, or Armageddon of Scripture.

What movements of God's "mighty ones" are in verse 19. For now we quote the verse in Joel 3 which we omitted above: "Haste ye, and come, all ye nations round about, and gather yourselves together: thither cause thy mighty ones to come down O Jehovah." We know, from Revelation 16:13, 14, that the movement of the nations to Armageddon will be of Satanic energy (though commanded, prophetically, of God) but the *disposition* of those forces of all the earth into such a place and order that they may be *trampled as one mass by the Son of Man Himself (Isaiah 63; Revelation 19:15)* will be by *angelic* power.

Ah, such a fearful sight! Rivers of human blood "unto the bridles of the horses"! Yet it will be. If Josephus could say that when Jerusalem was taken by Titus, the Roman soldiers "obstructed the very lanes with dead bodies; and made the whole city run down with blood, to such a degree indeed that the fires of many of the houses was quenched with these men's blood" (Wars: 6, 8)—what folly to doubt this word of God that a *river* of blood will run when the Son of God tramples the nations of *all the earth* in the Almighty's anger! Yea, a river from Edom to Carmel, 1600 furlongs! We dare not read the verse that tells this, except as God's literal foreview of fact!

Here in verse 20 is the Great Day of Wrath of *all* the prophets. Isaiah 34 tells us that Edom (where the slaughter begins) shall be "made drunken with blood," and its very dust "fat with fatness" at that slaughter. "Without the city" means Jerusalem. Blood to "the bridles of the horses"—four feet of human blood for two hundred miles!

It is a literal trampling of the enemies of the Lord, in His fury: for He so declares, in Isaiah 63.

Reader, no honest soul can read Revelation 14, and ever hear again Satan's preachers of "a world growing better and better."

"O earth, earth, earth, hear the word of Jehovah."

CHAPTER XIV
THE SEVEN LAST PLAGUES
Revelation 15, 16

The Day of Wrath is begun by the appearing on earth of the Lord Jesus as Son of Man, in Palestine, trampling the allied armies of all the earth (Revelation 14:20; 19: 19-21). This day inaugurates the thousand-year reign.

Therefore, all judgments seen under the seals, trumpets and vials are prior to this Great Day. They are preliminary visitations of wrath *before* the Great Day of Wrath at Christ's coming to earth. This fact should be constantly kept in mind. We shall repeat it again and again.

The Four Gospels furnish us with an excellent example of that method of God's Word which we find in the book of Revelation. Matthew sets forth Christ as Israel's Messiah; Mark, as Jehovah's Servant; Luke, as Son of Man; John, as Son of God; each book goes over the same period, each bringing out certain peculiar phases of the Lord's life on earth.

In The Revelation we saw that the sixth seal revealed in a panoramic, prophetic way the Great Day itself, though several years before it. Then, under the seventh seal, we went back to various *particulars,* leading up to that Great Day. Again, the seventh trumpet *(11:15-18)* revealed the anger of the nations, the coming of *God's* wrath, and the accompanying tremendous matters: yet we went back, in chapters 12 and 13, to consider in vision God's plan about Israel,—the woman's warfare with Satan, the development of the Antichrist, etc.

Then again, at the close of chapter 14, we had a vision of the Son of Man reaping the harvest of earth, and treading the winepress of Armageddon, destroying the rebel nations, who had gathered to destroy Israel.

But now, in chapters 15 and 16 we return to consider certain particulars preceding the Great Day of Wrath and Armageddon: visitations of God's preliminary judgments, just as the ten plagues in Egypt were preliminary to the complete overthrow of Pharaoh and his host in the Red Sea.

We must keep this in mind, lest we try to make the book of Revelation a mere chronological narrative.

We may call attention further to this method in the case of "Babylon the great."

In chapter 14:8, Babylon is announced as fallen, but it is only so in anticipation. In our present chapter (16:19) we observe her visitation in the earthquake of the seventh vial. Then, in chapters 17 and 18 we go back to consider what Babylon is; her history; her relation to the world-power and to the Antichrist; and her final earthly destruction.

Chapters 15 and 16 are a complete section so we will give the outline of their contents here:

1. "Another sign in heaven"—the Seven last Wrath-Angels, 15:1.

2. The Vision of the Victors Over the Beast, 15:2-4. (As always preceding judgment, the triumph of Grace is shown: compare 7:1, 3, 9.)

3. The Connection of the Seven Vials of Wrath with the Heavenly Temple, and the Reason Therefor, 15:5-8; compare 11:19.

4. The Seven Terrible Vials of Wrath. (Literal plagues, of course, like those upon Egypt) 16:2-21.

The Seven Last Wrath-Angels

And I saw another sign in heaven, great and marvelous, seven angels having seven plagues, which are the last, for in them is finished the wrath of God.

The first "sign,"* in 12:1, revealed God's heavenly coun-

---

*We find the word *seemeion* (translated "wonder" in the King James Version, and "sign" in the Revised Version) occurs seventy-seven times in the New Testament, beginning with Matthew 12:38, 39. It is sometimes rendered "miracle" in the King James Version (where rhetoric rather than accuracy so often governs). It is not to be confused with "mystery" (*musteerion*); for in the very first verse of Revelation the word is used in verb-form: "The revelation of Jesus Christ, which God gave him to show unto his servants, the things about to come to pass . . . and he *signified* it, by his angel," etc. The whole book of The Revelation thus is governed by this word, which sets forth the manner in general of its presentation to John. Our Lord's use of this verb in John 12:33; 18:32 and 21:19, *signifying* by what . . . death he should

sels concerning Israel; the second in 12:3, the great
opposer of those counsels, the Dragon, in his opposition
to God's plan of governing this earth by His Son through
redeemed Israel. Satan opposes God's Christ with his
false Christ in chapter 13. All the nations of the earth
are by this devilish scheme led into Satan-worship. This
brings the flood of evil to its height and calls forth the
divine judgments of the seven vials of wrath, chapters
15 and 16.

Consequently, when those judgments are about to take
place, it is announced that it is a "great and marvellous"
thing that is signified.

When Israel had the terrible breach with Jehovah at
Sinai, and God had finally agreed to pardon them, He
said in Exodus 34:10: "Behold, I make a covenant: before all thy people I will do marvels, such as have not
been wrought in all the earth, nor in any nation."

These seven angels, pouring out the seven bowls of
wrath, are indeed a "great" sign, for "in them is finished
the wrath of God." We shall see them proceed from *the
temple of God in heaven*—all patience having been now
exhausted. (The temple stood for mercy and worship.)

The sign is also "marvellous," for the more we study
these chapters the more the weight of these final terrible
visitations grows upon us. It is the last expression of
God's indignation before Christ comes *'in person* in the
Great Day of Wrath.*

---

die," plainly shows that instead of the word setting forth something
mysterious or hidden, on the contrary the plainest announcement of *the facts*
that would occur was given.

It is necessary to rid our minds of that unbelieving conception of The Revelation that fills it with constant *secrets,* making it amount to an hallucination.
The Lord commanded John *not* to seal it up *(22:10)*; and it is therefore *not
sealed,* but *open* to Christ's own *(1:1).*

The use therefore of the word "sign" in 15:1 is not intended to convey in
the least the thought that this chapter and the following one contain unreal
things, or those not literal facts; but the exact opposite. The word "great,"
moreover, indicates that something of outstanding importance is to be set forth.

---

*Remember constantly that Christ must come Himself, at the last, and tread
the winepress alone, in His anger (Isaiah 63:3-5). The wrath of God is general, world-wide, and in view of man's iniquity and idolatry. The wrath of
the Lamb is particular—against Antichrist and his king and armies gathered
for the double purpose of cutting off Israel from being a nation (Psalms 83:4),
and of "making war" against the Lamb (whose presence, with His army, seems
to be evident to those on earth—Revelation 19:19; Zechariah 12:10) to prevent
His rescue of beleaguered Israel.

The Victors Over the Beast

Before the out-pouring of these terrible vials, however, God gives us a vision of those who triumphed over the indescribable awfulness of the days of the Beast *(15:2-4)*.

> And I saw as it were a sea of glass mingled with fire; and them that come off victorious from the beast, and from his image, and from the number of his name, standing by the sea of glass, having harps of God. And they sing the song of Moses the servant of God, and the song of the Lamb, saying,
>
> Great and marvellous are thy works, O Lord God, the Almighty; righteous and true are thy ways, thou King of the ages. Who shall not fear, O Lord, and glorify thy name? for thou only art holy; for all the nations shall come and worship before thee; for thy righteous acts have been made manifest.

Again the "sea of glass" comes into view. It was "like unto crystal" in chapter 4:6 when first seen. From that passage also we are shown its position "before the throne." This description is of vastness—a sea: like unto glass—settled, unruffled, peace; like unto crystal—the purity of God's own Throne. See "the terrible crystal" of the firmament above the cherubim in Ezekiel 1:22, which appears to be the same as in Exodus 24:10.

Now, in our lesson, this sea of glass is "mingled with fire." And this has, we believe, a two-fold significance. First, these saints "that come off victorious" have been called to pass through the very worst furnace of trial ever known. It has been well said that while we are called on to oppose the world, the flesh, and the Devil, these have had a fourth foe, even Satan's Christ, a being brought back from the abyss, and known to be such, to whom all the earth has been given over, and whose delusions were so strong as to deceive if it were possible, the very elect. Second, God Himself is "a consuming fire." Moses saw the bush, that it was not burnt, although the fire was there! We are here beholding the last martyrs before Christ's coming, and it should thrill our hearts to read that this glassy sea before God is now "mingled with fire." It celebrates on the one hand what they will have passed through and on the other hand their nearness to and association with God!

We have then, "those that come off victorious (literally *'those conquering away from'*) from the beast and from the image of him, and from the number of the name of him," standing upon this sea. We also find that they have "harps of God," *i.e.*, as Alford so well says: "part of the instruments of heaven, used solely for the praise of God"; and (Govett) *"real instruments,* of *God's* making."

Now, although the Church of God (which these are not) has an unspeakably higher vocation than they, being *members of Christ Himself,* yet we must not fail to give God the glory for the victory of these through the greatest possible temptation and trial God's great enemy could bring upon them. We must not fail to enter in spirit into the glorious reward given them. Earth has bowed beneath the hideous blandishments of Satan's Christ; these resisted him *unto death.* They then passed through fire, yea, all the fires and agonies possible, and now they stand on that glorious crystal sea, mingled with heavenly fire, which celebrates their victory.

And what do they sing to the accompaniment of those heavenly harps? "The song of Moses the servant of God, and the song of the Lamb."*

Note then, in the song they sing, the celebration first of the *works,* and then of the *ways* of "the Lord God,

*It is deeply suggestive that Moses is here called "the bondservant *(doulos)* of God" and the Lord is called, as is usual in this book, the diminutive *arnion,* which means "the *little* lamb"! (Compare *amnos* in John 1:29-36; I Peter 1:19; Acts 8:32). DeWette surely rightly believes that the change to the diminutive *arnion,* a word used only in the Apocalypse, is meant to put forward permanently the idea of His meekness and innocence. It is the exaltation noted as the result of perfect obedient patience in Philippians 2:6-11; and it is of the utmost importance that we grasp firmly and hold fast constantly the fact that it is God the Father who exalts Christ as the result of His patience; that it is God the Father who insists upon Christ's judging and executing judgment because of His infinite patience and humiliation (He being the Creator) in becoming a Son of Man, and dying the death of the cross. In our Lord's lovely life He left absolutely everything to the Father, who will in due season absolutely exalt Him, and that in the scene of His former rejection and shame.

the Almighty," the "King of the ages." No gracious heart can read verses 3 and 4 repeatedly without being profoundly moved.

The song of Moses celebrated the overthrow of Pharaoh and his hosts at the Red Sea—the mighty work of God. Jehovah is "fearful in praises, doing wonders." The song of the Lamb brings out God's ways as righteous and true. Christ prayed, "If it be possible, let this cup pass away from me: nevertheless, not as I will, but as thou wilt." The ways of God with the Lamb involved for him all meekness and suffering, as the path to kingdom and power.

Moses stands for the *power* of Jehovah who "caused his glorious arm to go at the right hand of Moses," who brought Israel up out of the land of Egypt, out of the house of bondage, by the stretched-out arm of might.

The expression, *"the Lamb,"* reminds us of those ways of unutterable *grace,* though in righteousness and truth, in which our Lord walked on earth. These witnesses, upon the glassy sea, celebrate this double song before God.

How beautiful are their words as they address them directly to the God for whom they suffered all things rather than yield to Satan! "Who shall not fear, O Lord, and glorify thy name?" Again, "Thou only art holy." These witnesses chose holiness in the face of a world gone over to sin; and they have come where holiness alone is! There is exquisite beauty here.

And again, their faith in the victory of their God is declared: "All the nations shall come and worship before thee." Not yet has this come to pass, yet they are celebrating it in God's very presence!

Finally they cry, "Thy righteous acts have been made manifest." Coming from those who passed through the horrors of the persecution, torment and fire of the Beast, through all the rage of Satan, these are most beautiful words!*

*"The fiery persecution under the Beast was a trial far exceeding in its combination of suffering anything hitherto experienced (Mark 13:19). The pagan persecutions of early times, and the still more exquisite and refined torments under Papal Rome, come short of the horrors of the Great Tribulation" (Scott).

They find not a word of fault with their God. All His acts they call *"righteous* acts"! Mediate upon this, ye who feel yourselves tempted and tried and suffering over-much. Some day you will declare His ways to be good and His acts to be righteous!

The Connection of the Seven Vials of Wrath With the Heavenly Temple

And after these things I saw, and the temple of the tabernacle of the testimony in heaven was opened: And there came out from the temple the seven angels that had the seven plagues, arrayed with precious stone, pure and bright, and girt about their breasts with golden girdles. And one of the four living creatures gave unto the seven angels seven golden bowls full of the wrath of God, who liveth for ever and ever. And the temple was filled with smoke from the glory of God, and from his power; and none was able to enter into the temple, till the seven plagues of the seven angels should be finished.

1. There is a literal temple of God in heaven.

Unless this is clearly seen and believed, much will be obscure. Was not Moses commanded when he was to make the tabernacle, "see that thou make them after their pattern, which hath been showed thee in the mount" (Exodus 25:40)? Now these tabernacle things are distinctly called, in Hebrews 9:23, "copies of the things in the heavens."

We saw in Revelation 11:19, that "there was opened the temple of God that is in heaven; and there was seen in his temple the ark of his covenant." Also, in chapter 8:3, we find a golden altar before the throne of heaven.

2. It is true that in the New Jerusalem John beholds no temple; and the reason is given that our Lord God, the Almighty, and the Lamb, *are* the temple thereof. In that city they will *see His face* directly. All formal mat-

ters are past—especially governmental matters such as
are connected with the temple of which we read in The
Revelation.

3. With the heavenly temple in The Revelation, only
judgment matters are connected. Even in 8:3-5, where
the prayers of God's saints come up, it is with the effect
upon earth of thunders, and voices, and lightnings, and
an earthquake! Again in 11:19, upon the opening of the
temple of God in heaven, and the vision of the ark of
His covenant, there follow "lightnings, and voices, and
thunders, and an earthquake, and great hail." And now,
upon the opening of the temple in our present chapter
there came forth the seven angels with the *seven last
plagues*.

4. We find in the temple, in 11:19, the ark of God's
covenant; and again, in 15:5, the remarkable expression
"the temple of the tabernacle of the testimony in heaven."

This indicates that God is about to fulfill His covenanted promises toward Israel, for to Israel belong the
covenanted things *(Romans 9:4)*.

We are back on Old Testament ground, prophetically.
Consequently, we saw in 12:1, immediately after the mention of the ark of God's covenant, the great sign which
sets forth in heaven God's counsels concerning the
Woman, who represents Israel. They will involve the
full accomplishment of God's word in Psalm 2—that He
will set His king upon His holy hill of Zion,—despite
the opposition of all the earth!

In connection with the opening of the temple in chapter 11, we had not only the vision of the Woman and
the Dragon, but the war in heaven, the casting out of
Satan into earth, the bringing forth of the Antichrist and
his False Prophet, and the ghastly reign of *iniquity* on
earth, with the fearful persecutions of God's saints.

5. Now we are to behold the *last* plagues, *i.e.*, those
final visitations of God upon the nations, and the vexing
of them in His sore displeasure, before He sends His
Christ, the Lamb of God, to execute the fierceness of
His wrath *in person*. For the earth is now worshipping

the Beast: and the jealousy of the Living God burns like fire!

6. One of the four living creatures, those beings "full of eyes," deep in the intelligence of the purposes of the Almighty, now gives to these seven angels "seven golden bowls full of the wrath of God." There is a *finality* about this scene that brings the utmost awe into our hearts. The temple from which these angels come; their holy glittering aspect; the bowls of wrath ready to be bestowed for pouring; the solemn formal presentation of a bowl to each angel; the material of these bowls —*gold,* setting forth *the very glory of God;* the fact that these bowls are *full;* and that they are full, not of grace, as when David said, "I will take the cup of *salvation";* nor of *mixed* mercy and wrath, as when Habakkuk cried, "In wrath remember mercy"—no longer this: but *"full of the wrath of God."* The name of God here is connected definitely with these solemn words, "the wrath of God, who liveth unto the ages of the ages." Let us speak in low, slow, measured words here. Let us *fear;* and observe earth's wickedness with its attendant punishment, with deep humility and awe!

7. What follows should be contrasted with like scenes, when mercy was present:

> "The temple was filled with smoke from the glory of God, and from his power."

We read in Exodus 40:34, 35 words of great blessedness. Moses had constructed the tabernacle which God said He desired that "He might dwell among them," and had finished it, according to the divine directions:

> "Then the cloud covered the tent of meeting, and the glory of Jehovah filled the tabernacle. And Moses was not able to enter into the tent of meeting because the cloud abode thereon, and the glory of Jehovah filled the tabernacle."

This was blessing indeed! Again, when Solomon had built the temple according to the directions given David, his father, by the Spirit of God, and had made his great prayer of dedication, we read in II Chronicles 7:1-4:

> "Now when Solomon had made an end of praying, the fire came down from heaven, and consumed the burnt-offering and the sacrifices; and the glory of Jehovah filled the house. And the priests could not enter into the house of Jehovah, because the glory of Jehovah filled Jehovah's house. And all the children of Israel looked on, when the fire came down, and the glory of Jehovah was upon the house; and they bowed themselves with their faces to the ground upon the pavement, and worshipped, and gave thanks unto Jehovah, *saying* for he is good; for his loving kindness *endureth* for ever."

Here again was unlimited blessing. The very priests are unable to enter the temple or to minister; for all was full of the glory of the blessed presence of Jehovah.

But what a fearful contrast here in Revelation! Sin had caused God to *leave* His earthly house in Jerusalem: first the glory left *(Ezekiel 8-11)*; then the Lord of the house Himself· came and saw, and left it *desolate (Matthew 23:37, 38)*.

Now, in Revelation 14, the majority of Israel are in covenant with Antichrist himself *(Daniel 9:27; John 5: 43)*; the nations are in hellish league with Satan to refuse God's Son His throne. So we read these awful words:

> "None was able to enter into the temple, till the seven plagues of the seven angels should be finished."

No words of ours are needed here. Only calm reflection upon the *fact*. God will so turn to *anger,* at last, that all else ceases, even in heaven! Wrath will be the only business. "Who may stand in thy sight when once thou art angry?" (Psalm 76:7).

Ah, Russia, could you but read and mark and turn and repent!

Ah, America, could you but know the end of your godless ways!

The world seeks today the cause of the "great depression"; but she does not seek *that God who caused it,* and who alone can relieve it!

That we may understand these seven last plagues, three things must be held firmly in mind:

First, that the whole earth (except God's elect) has gone mad after the Beast *(Revelation 13:8),* and God's "hot displeasure" must be manifested, according to Revelation 15:8. "God will listen to naught now but to the demands of His righteous indignation. The sin of earth is beyond endurance; the unpardonable sin is abroad." "Ah," cries the Lord, Jehovah of hosts, "I will ease me of mine adversaries!" There must be this divine relief for Him who declares, "Vengeance is mine." Centuries of long-suffering mocked, despised, by a devil-worshipping earth, arouse at last divine fury. So these bowls of wrath are poured out on the whole world of rebels.

Second, that the all-nation invasion of Palestine by the Beast and his armies, while it is prepared for, under the sixth bowl *(Revelation 16:12-16),* and though the earth-armies are gathered to Armageddon, yet they will be given over to Christ Himself, to be trodden down at His personal coming in the Great Day of Wrath, according to Revelation 19:11-15. That great day will come as "destruction from Shaddai" *(Isaiah 13:6).* Rebellion will be crushed then: for the rebels will be taken off the earth *(Matthew 13:40-43).* On the contrary, these seven bowls are seven visitations from God in anger on men, while the Lord Jesus is yet absent from earth; and while men are still suffered to rebel and blaspheme. They are hardening judgments, like those upon Pharaoh; indeed, men grow steadily and rapidly more hateful toward God, from the opening of the first seal of judgment in Revelation 6.

Third, that these seven bowl-judgments are *literal!* There is no other reasonable interpretation possible. Shall we believe that the ten plagues upon Egypt were actually as described in Exodus, and dare to turn away these "seven last plagues" of The Revelation from their evident open significance? Four of the ten Egyptian plagues are here repeated: boils, blood, darkness, and hail. What kind of interpretation is it that believes the one and denies the other! There the visitation was in a single land: here, in all the earth. Is it the extent of the horror that appalls the heart? Have we not read, through all the prophecies, of the day when God will "return judgment to righteousness" amidst earth-wide visitations? "Knowest thou not yet that Egypt is destroyed?" said Pharaoh's servants to him. Nay, he knew it not nor did he believe it, but rushed madly on into the overwhelming sea! So will earth, under Satan (Pharaoh's antitype), rush madly to its end.*

For we need to consider, that God hates what men call "civilization," and "human progress"! All man's system: his philosophy (which has self-wisdom as its postulate); his science (which discovers "Nature" and denies its Creator); his art (which demands the beautiful in form, but abhors holiness in fact); his inventions (designed,

*Because these seven judgments, like the other judgments we have considered, are as definitely hardening judgments as were the plagues upon Pharaoh, it will be profitable to the real students of The Revelation to read the account of the plagues in Egypt (Exodus 7-12). Read the different expressions concerning Pharaoh: when he "saw that there was respite, he made strong his heart and hearkened not unto them"; "the heart of Pharaoh was stubborn (Hebrew—heavy), and he did not let the people go." "Jehovah hardened (Hebrew—made strong) the heart of Pharaoh, and he hearkened not unto them." "When Pharaoh saw that the rain and the hail and the thunders were ceased, he sinned yet more, and made heavy his heart, he and his servants. And the heart of Pharaoh was strong, and he did not let the children of Israel go." "Moses and Aaron did these wonders before Pharaoh: and Jehovah made strong Pharaoh's heart, and he did not let the children of Israel go out of his land."

Remember, in Exodus 5:2, Pharaoh's first word to Moses: "Who is Jehovah, that I should hearken unto his voice to let Israel go? I know not Jehovah, and moreover I will not let Israel go." But remember chiefly God's word to him by Moses, in Exodus 9:14-16: "For I will this time send all my plagues upon thy heart, and upon thy servants, and upon thy people; that thou mayest know that there is none like me in all the earth. For now I had put forth my hand, and smitten thee and thy people with pestilence, and thou hadst been cut off from the earth: but in very deed for this cause have I made thee to stand, to show thee my power, and that my name may be declared throughout all the earth."

Remember that Romans 9:14-18 is just as much inspired by the Holy Spirit as John 3:16. The whole history of this present world is meant to show forth, through God's gift of His Son at Calvary, not only His own infinite love, but also the absolutely deadly nature, character and power of sin; together with its proud insanity, as rebellion of the mere creature against the Infinite Creator: together with the sure and just end of all such rebellion; in order that all eternity may be able to look back, and contemplate, and fear, and reverence forever, and serve the Holy One!

from Cain's city onward, to make earth livable without
God) ; his religion (which denies God's righteousness and
hates God's Christ and His shed blood) ; his government
(which has no place whatever for the King who patiently
awaits, upon His Father's throne, the moment when He
shall receive the throne to which He only has the right)
and, finally, those pleasures which man delights in—all of
which consists in the indulgence of that "mind of the
flesh" which is "enmity against God."

The Lord will shortly strike, crush, destroy, wipe out,
efface and remove even from memory* this hateful,
abhorrent, abominable thing—man's "independence"!
"Thy will be done, as in heaven, so on earth," will be
carried out to the letter! And that involves crushing the
present earth system as one would stamp out a nest of
wasps.

> And I heard a great voice out of the tem-
> ple, saying to the seven angels, Go ye, and
> pour out the seven bowls of the wrath of God
> into the earth.

Out of the heavenly sanctuary—where the redeemed
multitude *(Chapter 7:15)* serve their God day and night
—comes this awful command! God's house, meant to
be "a house of prayer for all nations" now becomes the
court of judgment upon God's enemies: for it is evidently God's voice which we hear in this verse.

> And the first went,† and poured out his
> bowl into the earth; and it became a noisome
> and grievous sore upon the men that had the
> mark of the beast, and that worshipped his
> image.

Compare Exodus 9:9, where Moses and Aaron sprinkled ashes of the furnace upward in the sight of Pharaoh,

---

*"The memory of the righteous is blessed; but the name of the wicked shall
rot." There goes the whole history of Adam the First, and all his selfish line!
"The former things shall not be remembered, nor come into mind."

†"The first departed *(apelthen)*: each angel, as his turn comes, leaves the
heavenly scene, and, from the space between heaven and earth, empties his
vial upon the appointed object" *(Alford)*. It is astonishing to mark, in The
Revelation, the direct control God gives His angels over the powers of "nature,"
and the power to execute "the judgment written."

"and it became small dust over all the land of Egypt, and became a boil breaking forth with blains (or blisters) upon man and upon beast." Since we believe Exodus, we believe Revelation. God creates evil as well as good, as He says: "I make peace, and create evil; I am Jehovah that doeth all these things" *(Isaiah 45:7)*. We will do well to arm ourselves with this thought. God is constantly creating judgments, as well as saving the lost. Right in this world, new diseases which baffle boasted science spring forth, and men take no thought of God in the matter! The judgment of the influenza killed more people than the great war. But even in Christian circles, where is there a solemn asking of God as to the cause of either the war or of the influenza? Just as truly as the Egyptians in Pharaoh's day turned to their magicians, so does Christendom turn to "science" to solve all its troubles. We thank God for every alleviation of misery that it pleases Him to grant. But we must not forget that He has declared in countless places in His Word that His government involves the infliction of calamity upon persistent evil doing.

Note that it is the time of the Beast, the Antichrist, all through these seven bowl-judgments. Also note that they are crowded into a relatively brief space: for the sores of the first bowl are still upon men in the darkness of the fifth bowl. The sixth bowl, involving the gathering of the hosts to Armageddon will not need more than a few months to bring to pass. It will be as in Egypt, one plague crowding upon another.

Now when this first angel pours out his bowl, sores, or ulcers, break out upon those who have the mark of the Beast, and those who worship his image. It is this infinitely hateful thing that makes God's jealousy burn like fire. Not upon the animals also, as in Egypt under the sixth plague, but upon men *only*—men who have allied themselves with Satan, does this universal and horrid thing come. "A noisome and grievous sore": "Evil—in itself; painful to the sufferers" *(Alford)*. One feels that the words involve hideousness, and incurability *(Deuteronomy 28:27,35)*. These Beast worshippers are final rebels; they are shortly to be with the damned. Now they taste of hell on earth. Read Revelation 15:8 again: this will not be a time of mercy. And on their part, as we shall see, they hate God more and more, and are "still stricken."

> And the second poured out his bowl into the sea; and it became blood as of a dead man; and every living soul died, even the things that were in the sea.

Blood is the vivid, terrible mark of death—the wages of sin. This was the first plague in Egypt—the Nile turned to blood.

Now the sea covers far the greater portion of this globe. God, who made it, now turns it to blood—"as of a corpse lying in its own gore." So the billions, trillions, shoals, of sea-creatures die; and come floating to the surface in horrible, rotting witness of the wickedness of men! There is no escaping these words of God: "every living soul died." What a frightful stench! What fearful possibilities of disease! Yet remember that this is exactly what God is doing. "Behold, Jehovah maketh the earth empty, and maketh it waste, . . . and scattereth abroad the inhabitants thereof. . . . Therefore . . . few men left . . . For thus shall it be in the midst of the earth among the peoples, as the shaking of an olive-tree, as the gleanings when the vintage is done" *(Isaiah 24:1-13)*. "I will make a man more rare than fine gold, even a man than the pure gold of Ophir. . . . As the shaking of an olive-tree, two or three berries in the top of the uppermost bough, four or five in the outmost branches of a fruitful tree, saith Jehovah, the God of Israel" *(Isaiah 13:12; 17:6)*. When God cleared off this race in the days of Noah, He left eight persons. It will be "as it was in the days of Noah" again, shortly: and, although God will yet suffer the human race to have another thousand years on earth *(Revelation 20:4-6)*; nevertheless, He will so reduce earth's population, that "few men will be left" to start that thousand years. And this will be so whether you believe it or not: for God cannot lie!

And the third poured out his bowl into the rivers and the fountains of the waters: and it became blood.

I stood some time ago at De Leon Springs in Florida, where a great volume of wondrous water poured like a crystal river from—whence no one knows: but it will be a fountain of blood in that day, and all the rivers of earth and all the fountains of water! (You need not be worried over God's own elect in that time: for He called water out of the flinty rock through forty years for His people, and He will not let His elect suffer from His hand!)

And I heard the angel of the waters saying, Righteous art thou, who art and who wast, thou Holy One, because thou didst thus judge: for they poured out the blood of saints and prophets, and blood hast thou given them to drink; they are worthy. And I heard the altar saying, Yea, O Lord God, the Almighty, true and righteous are thy judgments.

Here we see that angelic being in charge of the waters that supply the earth,—a beneficent being certainly; and also the altar itself, which should have spoken for men's forgiveness: both bowing to God's judgments as just and true! For men had poured out the blood of those messengers of God who warned and pleaded with them: and underneath the altar were thousands upon thousands of martyrs, whose prayers for divine vengeance must now be fully answered. So the angel bows, as the beautiful rivers and fountains he had administered are now turned to blood! All sympathy of heaven is with God: note that, sinner, or world-bordering Christian! Let this speaking altar make you tremble! Flee to Christ and be safe: for the breakers of judgment show just ahead for this whole world! Oh may we be among those that "only with our eyes shall behold, and see the reward of the wicked"!

I cannot leave this third awful visitation of avenging the blood of God's saints and prophets, without a word of earnest warning to all Christians to beware of the false security of these days! "Blood, it polluteth the land; and no expiation can be made for the land for the blood that is shed therein, but by the blood of him that shed it" (Numbers 35:33). Very many known man-killers are abroad in America today. God will yet remember it. And especially will He remember and avenge the blood of His martyrs.

I shall quote here from a really great man of God, already almost forgotten, but who will shine in Christ's swift-coming day! In prison over and over for the Word of God in England, hear one of the experiences narrated in his "Journal". (This occurred in 1651):

> "Being at liberty (from prison) I went on, as before, in the work of the Lord, passing through the country into Leicestershire, having meetings as I went; and the Lord's Spirit and power accompanied me. As I was walking with several friends, I lifted up my head, and saw three steeple-house spires, and they struck at my life. I asked them what place that was. They said, Lichfield. Immediately the Word of the Lord came to me, that I must go thither. Being come to the house we were going to, I wished friends to walk into the house, saying nothing to them whither I was to go. As soon as they were gone I stept away, and went by my eye over hedge and ditch, till I came within a mile of Lichfield; where, in a great field, shepherds were keeping their sheep. Then was I commanded by the Lord to pull off my shoes. I stood still, for it was winter; and the Word of the Lord was like a fire in me. So I put off my shoes, and left them with the shepherds; and the poor shepherds

trembled, and were astonished. Then I walked on about a mile, and as soon as I was got within the city, the Word of the Lord came to me again, saying: 'Cry, Wo to the bloody city of Lichfield!' So I went up and down the streets, crying with a loud voice, *'Wo to the bloody city of Lichfield!'* It being market-day, I went into the market-place, and to and fro in the several parts of it, crying as before, *'Wo to the bloody city of Lichfield!'* And no one laid hands on me. As I went thus crying through the streets, there seemed to me to be *a channel of blood running down the streets,* and the market-place appeared *like a pool of blood.* When I had declared what was upon me, and felt myself clear, I went out of the town in peace; and returning to the shepherds, gave them money, and took my shoes of them again. But the fire of the Lord was so in my feet, and all over me, that I did not matter to put on my shoes again, and was at a stand whether I should or no, till I felt freedom from the Lord so to do: then, after I had washed my feet, I put on my shoes again.

"After this deep consideration came upon me, for what reason I should be sent to cry against that city, and call it, THE BLOODY CITY! . . . But afterwards I came to understand, that in the Emperor Diocletian's time, a thousand Christians were martyred in Lichfield. So I was to go, without my shoes, through the channel of their blood, and into the pool of their blood in the market-place, that I might raise up the memorial of the blood of those martyrs which had been shed above a thousand years before, and lay cold in their streets. So the sense of this blood was upon me, and I obeyed the word of the Lord. Ancient records testify how many of the Christian Britons suffered there. Much I could write of the sense I had

of the blood of the martyrs, that hath been shed
in this nation for the name of Christ, both under
the ten persecutions and since; but I leave it to
the Lord, and to His book, out of which all
shall be judged; for His book is a most certain
record, and His Spirit a true recorder" (*Geo.
Fox's Journal, page 98*).

Alas, how many faithful preachers of this our own
day have died of broken hearts and starvation wages,
at the hands of self-righteous professors, wicked spirit-
resisting church officials, and purse-proud "influential"
people: who do not dream that they, too, have shed the
blood of the martyrs!

**And the fourth poured out his bowl upon
the sun; and it was given unto it to scorch
men with fire. And men were scorched with
great heat: and they blasphemed the name of
God who hath the power over these plagues;
and they repented not to give him glory.**

First, note the absolute power of God over His creation. The Beast, whom the earth has chosen, has no
power at all to direct creation, or to deliver his votaries
from these troubles.

Second, our Lord said there would be signs in sun and
moon and stars: and here they are!

Third, "science" says the sun is "cooling off" which
proves afresh God's words, that "the wisdom of men is
foolishness with God." And the reason is, they leave
God out!

Fourth, since "there is nothing hid from the heat of
the sun" (*Psalm 19*), there will be no refuge from this
plague: nor does God intend there shall be (except for
His own, for whose sake He even "shortens" these fearful times).

Fifth, men know well—ineradicably, that the true God
(whom they have abandoned and hate) has "power over
these plagues." Even Russia today cries she will drag

down God from His heaven: thus advertising that she knows He is there!

Sixth, they "repented not to give him glory." These are true God-haters. And we see anew the folly of those who claim that the fires of hell will "purify" any one! Every one who goes into judgment goes in sin's awful hatred and resentment against God. It is the goodness of God that leads to repentance *(Romans 2)*. *Men not won by grace will never be won.*

Seventh, they blaspheme. Settle this, that men will increase in this fearful sin till the Lord comes. Do not look for human nature to mend: it never will! Only the restraining power of God keeps under the flaming out of "the wrath of man" from the most hideous blasphemies, this hour. And God's restraint will by and by be fully "taken out of the way" *(II Thessalonians 2).* Ah, the wickedness that will then be loosed!

> ⸜ And the fifth poured out his bowl upon the throne of the beast; and his kingdom was darkened; and they gnawed their tongues for pain, and they blasphemed the God of heaven because of their pains and their sores; and they repented not of their works.

First, the Beast is a man *(13:18);* therefore his throne is in a definite place: rebuilt Babylon on the Euphrates, we believe,—Satan's ancient capital, in the "land of Shinar," where "wickedness" is to be set on its base in the end-time *(Zechariah 5:5-10).*

Second, darkness, like that of Egypt in the ninth plague in Exodus, suddenly falls upon the throne and capital and kingdom of the Beast. Satan cannot relieve it. How long it lasts, we know not. "Thick darkness," that could be felt was on Egypt three days; while God's people had "light in their dwellings" *(Exodus 10: 21-23).*

Third, men are shut in with their horrid sores and pains: there is no alleviation. What must the "outer darkness for ever" be, and that with the Almighty's wrath following them on!

Fourth, still the consciousness that "the God of heaven" is doing this, is upon them! The dragon cannot efface that consciousness, even when he is worshipped!

Fifth, these lost wretches are set in their evil ways and works: "they repented not." If there is no repentance under God's hand here, when men still breathe the breath of earth, how infinitely less in hell! Yet fools hope for "repentance beyond the grave."

Sixth, it should be carefully noticed that this darkness is not that darkening of the sun and moon just before our Lord's arrival in the Great Day of Wrath, of Revelation 19:11-15. This is merely one of the "signs" connected with The Great Tribulation, as spoken of in Luke 21 and Mark 13. For the sixth bowl, which follows this, must cover time for the nations to gather to Armageddon, whereas, immediately after the sun's final darkening, the Lord, as "Son of man" comes as lightning upon a black heaven.

> **And the sixth poured out his bowl upon the great river, the river Euphrates; and the water thereof was dried up, that the way might be made ready for the kings that come from the sunrising.**

This is the literal Euphrates. There can be no other real interpretation of this passage.* Imagination has very often substituted for exposition, even in such a plain passage as this.

Let us note regarding the Euphrates and its "drying up":

1. It is mentioned twenty-one times in Scripture; and called "the great river" five times, as the Mediterranean

---

*"This is the only understanding of these words which will suit the context, or the requirements of this series of prophecies" *(Alford)*. "This must mean the literal river" *(Seiss)*. "This means the literal river Euphrates" *(Larkin)*. Darby *(Synopsis)* and Kelly *(Lectures)* both so state. Govett *(Apocalypse Expounded)* 1813-1901, who wrote, as Spurgeon quaintly says, "a hundred years before his time," and whom Seiss largely follows, says with his usual common sense: "Against anyone traveling from the East to the West, the Euphrates interposes its broad barrier, difficult to be surmounted even by individuals; and much more by kings and their armies."

was called "the great sea": for the Euphrates was the eastern, as the Mediterranean was the western boundary of God's own people's inheritance.

2. It was a protection to Israel, both because of the difficulty of its passage, and because of the fact that God had placed a wilderness west of it, between it and Canaan. Only at the upper or northern part was it practically passable (so that Babylon is called by the prophets, the enemy "from the north country"). Even the Roman Empire had its eastern bound here.

3. It is nearly two thousand miles long (1,780). It rises in the Armenian Mountains, flowing at first toward Palestine, to within less than 100 miles of the Mediterranean, then turning away southeast to the Persian Gulf, winding upon itself constantly. It is navigable for 1200 miles. It flowed through old Babylon, which was (and may yet be) the commercial center of the whole world *(Revelation 18)*.

4. It was first seen just outside Eden in Genesis 2, where human sin begins, and is last seen here in Revelation 16:12, where sin reaches its height. Twice in The Revelation does it appear: in chapter 9:13-15, where "at the great river Euphrates" we saw four angels bound, the loosing of which issued in killing the third of the earth's population. Here in 16:12, its drying up permits countless thousands to rush forward to their doom at Armageddon.

5. The solemnity of the crossing of the Euphrates to invade God's land, by these eastern hosts, is very awful indeed. That the western nations, under the Beast, the last Emperor of the fourth world-power, should invade Palestine does not startle us so much: (the Roman Empire often persecuted the Jews, and ruled them many centuries). But that these recently pagan hosts from the East, who have now heard the gospel of Christ from thousands of faithful missionaries and *rejected it,* choose the Antichrist and march to Armageddon to help destroy the Jews (since the Church has been taken up out of their reach) is appalling! That dry bed of Euphrates will be

an eastern Rubicon: for all will know whither they are bound, and why, as the sequel shows.

6. Now it is well to reflect that the greater part of mankind is east, not west, of the Euphrates: witness in millions, China's 440; India's 330; Japan's 80; then Siam, Indo-China; the wild hordes of Afghanistan, of Turkestan, of Tibet; not to mention old Persia. I omit purposely Siberia and Asiatic Russia, which prophecy assigns to an entirely different invasion of Palestine than that of Revelation 16—see Ezekiel 38 and 39. These vast peoples of the East have ever marched overland, in hordes like those of Genghis Khan (who conquered the earth, from China to Poland). They are not accustomed to travel as Westerners do. They come on foot and horseback. So that the drying up of the great military barrier, the Euphrates, will "open their way" to Palestine. (Otherwise, through Russia—impossible! or a long ocean voyage—likewise.)

But they must be stirred up by a mighty movement, if they are to leave their homes and their lands, and go on a vast "crusade" to a far off goal; and that with Westerners! For there is an almost unaccountable, but terribly real, enmity of jealousy, between Orientals and Occidentals. As Kipling sang,

"Oh East is East and West is West, and never the twain shall meet,

Till earth and sky stand presently at God's great judgment Seat."

But Kipling perhaps did not know what the word of prophecy plainly tells us, that East and West, like Herod and Pilate, will come together in a great meeting to oppose God and His Christ, over a thousand years before the last Judgment! All the earth will be friends in a common cause, when the hour for Armageddon strikes.*

*Prophecy after prophecy tells of the united rush of the nations into Palestine, just before the Great Day of Wrath of Revelation 19:11-15 *(See Joel 3:9-14; Zephaniah 3:8; Zechariah 12:3, 9; Isaiah 24:1, 2, 8; Obadiah 15, etc.)*. Tens of millions, probably hundreds of millions will gather to that slaughter! The weak, those too old or feeble to go to war, will cry, "I am strong," says the word of the Lord in Joel 3. The blood will be "to the bridles," remember. That word will be fulfilled!

> **And I saw coming out of the mouth of the dragon, and out of the mouth of the beast, and out of the mouth of the false prophet, three unclean spirits, as it were frogs: for they are spirits of demons, working signs; which go forth unto** (literally upon) **the kings of the whole inhabited earth, to gather them together unto the war of the great day of God, the Almighty.**

Now comes the gathering unto the most fell war, fallen man, under Satan, has ever yet rushed into.

1. Note, that it is a war for which they gather: the battle is never joined: for the Lamb has but to come forth, and the Beast is taken, and the False Prophet, and hurled into the lake of fire; and the Devil cast into the abyss. But the gathering unto this war *becomes the business of this world* for weeks, months: what a scene!

2. Note the source of this earth-wide movement:— three special evil spirits, doubtless leading millions of others who help them, from hell's trinity, the Dragon, the Beast, the False Prophet.

3. Note the means of persuasion: miracle-working, before the rulers of all the earth. Jannes and Jambres, Egypt's magicians, thus blinded Pharaoh. They also brought up frogs! *(Exodus 8:7)*. Scripture's constant testimony is that "great signs and wonders" will be performed in that time by Satan's agency.

Seiss well says: "These demon-spirits are the elect agents to awaken the world to attempt to abolish God from the earth; and they are frog-like in that they come forth out of the pestiferous quagmires of the universe, do their work amid the world's evening shadows, and creep, and croak, and defile the ears of the nations with noisy demonstrations, till they set all the kings and armies of the whole earth in enthusiastic commotion for the final crushing out of the Lamb and all His powers." Alford's phrase is, "The uncleanness and the pertinacious noise of the frog." Go by a marsh some Spring evening, when the slimy filthy unseen frogs are fully squawking. You can hear nothing else!

And now comes a solemn, direct word of warning from the Lord's own mouth, to such saints as may be here in those days. We read in verse 15:

> (Behold, I come as a thief. Blessed is he that watcheth, and keepeth his garments, lest he walk naked, and they see his shame.)

1. Note the aspect of His coming here emphasized by the Lord: it is as a thief—to surprise and to despoil. This is His coming to the world. It is "the day of the Lord so cometh as a thief in the night" *(I Thessalonians 5:2)*. But *we* are not looking for that day but for the day of Christ; as the Spirit tells us in II Thessalonians 2: 1-3: "We beseech you brethren in behalf of *(huper)* the arrival of our Lord Jesus Christ, and our gathering together unto him"—that is, the rapture—"be not quickly shaken from your mind," (into which I brought you) by feelings, or false preaching, or pretended epistle from me—into believing that the day of the Lord is just at hand: for the apostasy must come before that, etc. In I Thessalonians 5:4, Paul contrasts absolutely the state of the Church with that darkened state of carnal security, in which the Lord's coming catches the world as a snare. Paul says, "But ye, brethren, are not in darkness, that that day should overtake you as a thief: for ye are all sons of light," etc.

2. Note again, that the Lord faithfully keeps His saints posted as to where they are, in His dealings, (if only they will hear!).

3. Note that watchfulness (the hardest of all tasks) is necessary at all times, by all saints, since the Lord ascended.

4. Note that blessedness is connected with watching; shame, with carelessness.

5. And lastly, that there is here no promise of rapture to be waited for; but a danger of having to walk (here on earth) exposed to the gaze of angels and a godless

world—naked, that is, publicly bereft of evident divine direction and protection. I know this passage is difficult, in view of the warning to Sardis *(3:3)*, and the counsel to Laodicea *(3:18)*. But both watchless Sardians, and naked Laodiceans share (as it seems to us) the doom of the world; with the added shame of having had a place and a name and through carelessness, lost all.

And now proceeds the vision of the great gathering of the nations by the foul spirits from hell's trinity.

And they gathered them together into the place which is called in Hebrew Har-Mage-don.

We cannot emphasize too strongly that in the three series of divine judgments—first the seals, second the trumpets, third the vials (or bowls) of wrath—we have those preliminary hardening actions of God upon an impenitent world, by which He prepares that world for the Great Day of Wrath—at Christ's coming as King of kings, as seen in Revelation 19:11-15. From the advent of the Antichrist in chapter 13 there is no mingling of mercy with wrath. Read again 14:9-11. The purpose of God in bringing the ten plagues upon Egypt was "to show in Pharaoh his power, that his name might be published to all the earth." Pharaoh had said, "My river is mine own and I have made it for myself" *(Ezekiel 29:3)*. This is the exact spirit of the world today and it is intensifying hourly.

Now the effect of the judgments of the plagues was so to harden, by mighty miracle after miracle, the hearts of Pharaoh and his host, that they rushed madly upon "the thick bosses of his (the Almighty's) buckler" into the most stupendous scene human eyes had ever witnessed: the waves of the sea piled like a wall on each side: and ahead, the hosts of Israel, marvellously lighted in their march by a vast pillar of fire.

Such a scene comes before us under the sixth seal. Then the overwhelming was of the armies of one nation, Egypt. Now, we behold the hosts of all the nations of earth gather for an indescribably vast overthrow at Armageddon.

We have seen the first bowl become a horrid sore upon the Beast-worshippers: the second turn the waters of the sea into blood; the third, the rivers and the fountains of the waters, so that all the earth had blood to drink; while the fourth bowl is the signal for power, such as has never been known, to be given to the sun (which the scientists had told them was "cooling off"!)   The result of all being blasphemy against the God whom they knew had power over all these plagues. Now, under the fifth bowl, utter darkness enthralls the throne of the Beast and his kingdom—that is, all the earth, except, doubtless, the dwelling places of God's people then on earth *(Exodus 10:23)*.

Now out of this darkness, instead of repentance, comes only increased blasphemy and utter impenitence *(Revelation 16:11)*. At the darkness under the sixth seal *(Revelation 6:12-17)* there was exhibited great terror: "they say to the mountains and to the rocks, Fall on us, and hide us from the face of him that sitteth on the throne, and from the wrath of the Lamb: for the great day of their wrath is come; and who is able to stand?"   That men under these divine judgments will be increasingly hardened is doubtless the truth: but when the most hardened of all come to the Great Day of Wrath itself, there will be no blaspheming, but sheer blasting terror *(Isaiah 2:12-22)*. Remember the text of the Book of Revelation *(1:7)*: "Behold, he cometh with the clouds; and every eye shall see him, and they that pierced him; and all the tribes of the earth shall mourn over him."

Armageddon

Here, then, by divine appointment, but by Satanic agency, are gathered the hosts of earth; as Ahab, by God's counsel and command, was deceived by an evil, lying spirit, to go to battle to his death *(I Kings 22)*.

1. What is Armageddon, or, more accurately, Har-Magedon? Its name means, "Mountain of Megiddo."

(See Stanley's *Sinai and Palestine,* chapter 9; or Thomson's *Land and the Book* on "Megiddo.") It was here the Lord so marvellously helped Barak overthrow the Canaanites *(Judges 5:19).* The region is named from Megiddo, a royal Canaanite city *(Joshua 12:21).* To the northwest is Mount Carmel where, at the mouth of the Kishon River, Elijah killed the hundreds of Baal's prophets. Mount Gilboa, where King Saul, the persecutor of God's king—David—fell, is southeast. And on the north or northwest, overlooking all, is Mount Tabor, where Barak assembled the hosts of the Lord against the enemy. From Judges 4:6, 12, 14, and Jeremiah 46:18, I feel that the "mountain" *(Hebrew Har)* in Har-Magedon is Tabor. "Megiddo" is named twelve times, the governmental number, in Scripture; and the last time in almost the form we have it here: Megiddon, in Zechariah 12:11—a reference to the mourning for poor Josiah who fell in the same region, trying to defend Babylon against Egypt *(II Chronicles 35:22-25).* (Oh that he had been the only saint to fall meddling in world-quarrels!)

2. Why does God bring this host here? *For destruction.* God will yet deal with this earth according to His offended majesty, until a man shall be "more rare than fine gold," until the land is "drunken with blood."

God has no apologies for slaying the Canaanites; or giving Jerusalem over to Babylonian captivity, and then to Roman slaughter; or letting famine waste millions; or the plague, ten millions. We desire to offend this adulterous generation's apologists for God.

3. Christians should arm their minds with this outlook as to "the rulers of this age, who are coming to nought" *(I Corinthians 2:6);* so that when they "hear of wars and rumors of wars," they may obey their Lord, and "see that they be not troubled"; knowing that whatever marchings to and fro, in this war or that, may occur, they can be only some preliminary to the earthwide crusade against God and His Christ that will gather in that great plain of Esdraelon, in Palestine—not many miles from the very town where the Christ they hate grew up before the

Father as a tender plant, and of that dry ground, Israel.

Yea, they will rush as Egypt after Israel, over the Euphrates' bed and over the "tongue of the Egyptian sea" (also dried up) in pursuit of the remnant of God's chosen nation, to "the mountain of destruction"—Armageddon *(Isaiah 11:15, 16)*.

So in the sixth and seventh bowls of wrath we have these two most awful things: the gathering of all earth's nations to Palestine into actual warfare against Almighty God—this is the sixth bowl; and that fearful shaking of this earth in divine retributive anger so long prophesied, which divides Jerusalem into three, reduces all Gentile cities to ruins, engulfs in the earth restored Babylon, the last great world capital, banishes all islands and mountains, and casts those terrible hailstones over this earth, which had been reserved "against the day of battle and war" in Jehovah's "treasuries of the hail" *(Job 38:22, 23)*.

"It is done!" is the great voice from the throne, when this seventh bowl is poured out. Men would not have the Saviour's "It is finished!" on Calvary; so they must have the awful "It is done!" from the Judge! Alas! Alas! Oh, that men today would hear and be warned to flee from the coming storm!

> And the seventh poured out his bowl upon the air; and there came forth a great voice out of the temple, from the throne, saying, It is done: and there were lightnings, and voices, and thunders; and there was a great earthquake, such as was not since there were men upon the earth, so great an earthquake, so mighty. And the great city was divided into three parts, and the cities of the nations fell: and Babylon the great was remembered in the sight of God, to give unto her the cup of the wine of the fierceness of His wrath. And every island fled away, and mountains were not found. And great hail, every stone about the weight of a talent, cometh down out of heaven upon men: and men blasphemed God because of the plague of the hail; for the plague thereof is exceeding great.

CHAPTER XV

THE JUDGMENT OF BABYLON
Revelation 17, 18

Introductory

We are not able to resist the conclusion that there is a *double* destruction before our eyes in these two chapters.

1. The overthrow of the woman in chapter 17 is accomplished by the Beast and his ten kings.

2. The Beast and his ten kings are being at the time adulated by the earth, the Beast himself universally worshipped (except by God's elect). All the kings and powers of the earth are subject to him, as we saw in chapter 13.

3. The Beast, his kings, and of course the whole earth with them, join in the destruction of the harlot, whom we see at the beginning of chapter 17 riding the revived Roman Beast.

4. Evidently Romanism, with its situation on the seven hills of Rome, is indicated by this woman, "drunken with the blood of the saints, and with the blood of the martyrs of Jesus." The whole earth, with its kings, is delighted at the removal of the last vestige of this hateful harlot, who really has been a *burden,* spiritual, mental, political, and financial, to all the nations over which she has held sway; although they committed spiritual "fornication" with her: that is, she pronounced them "Christian," and they gave her money and "reverence."

5. But in chapter 18 everything is reversed. While the destroying of the drunken harlot, "mystery Babylon," was a delight and a relief to all the earth, the overthrow of the great *city* Babylon in chapter 18 is *exactly the opposite*. The kings of the earth wail and lament over the smoke of her burning!

6. Instead of being an external directress of the last empire, the Babylon of chapter 18 is the beloved capital of the whole earth's activities, and for this cause men mourn her overthrow.

7. The Beast and his ten kings could not have destroyed the harlot in "one hour"; but such is declared to be the suddenness of the doom of the great city of chapter 18. "One day," and "one hour," God says.

8. That which characterized the iniquity of the harlot was the martyrdom of God's saints, and especially of the witnesses of Jesus; but the character of the iniquity of the city overthrown in chapter 18 is that of a godless, luxurious commercialism, making "merchant princes" of those dealing with her. Roman Catholicism, as a system, has never enriched the nations of the earth, but rather the contrary. Witness the late rebellions against Rome's arrogating to herself, free from taxes, vast parts of the territories of such lands as Mexico and Spain. At the height of her power over the European nations, in the days of Hildebrand, Gregory VII, in the eleventh century, we see the spirit of the harlot who rides the Beast in chapter 17. The Emperor Henry IV of Germany and his whole people are excommunicated, for disregard of a papal decree; and the Emperor must stand in the cold three days in Italy, waiting on the proud Pope's arrogance, before he is "forgiven." No wonder that when the world gets loose by divine permission from the restraints of conscience toward the name of the Father and the Son under Antichrist's blasphemies (which holy names the "harlot" has *had* to use) they rush in hate to destroy this hideous religious tyranny from the face of the earth! But, on the exact contrary, the kings of the earth and their subjects weep and wail in bitter mourning over the destruction of the great city of Babylon of chapter 18.

9. The manner of the final overthrow of Babylon, as described in Revelation 18 and in the Old Testament prophets, forbids us to conclude that the destruction of the papacy is there contemplated, and proves that it is rather a sudden, direct visitation of God. In Jeremiah 51:25, 26, Jehovah speaks: "I . . . will make thee a burnt mountain. And they shall not take of thee a stone for a corner, nor a stone for foundations; but thou shalt be

desolate for ever, saith Jehovah." Again in Jeremiah 51:8 "Babylon is suddenly fallen and destroyed."

Now Cyrus captured Babylon (about B. C. 540) on the night of Belshazzar's great feast of Daniel 5, but it was not at that time "destroyed." In fact, many in the city did not know for two or three days that the city had been taken! Babylon became a provincial capital in the Persian Empire. In the third empire, that of Alexander the Great, we find that it was a place much loved and delighted in by the great conqueror, who indeed drank himself to death there.

Peter wrote his first epistle from Babylon—*(I Peter 5:13)*. At the end of the fifth century, the "Babylonian Talmud" was issued by the Jews of Babylon, who had several universities there. It seems to have been a center of activity of this exiled race. In the tenth century Babylon is again mentioned as still in existence; and 200 years later it has grown considerably. It was afterwards further increased, and was called Hillah, as at present. Over 10,000 people were there thirty years ago. The town is constructed of the bricks of ancient Babylon.

Therefore, it appears impossible that the great prophecies concerning Babylon's final overthrow, whether in the Old Testament or in Revelation 18 have been finally fulfilled. For instance, "And Babylon, the glory of kingdoms, the beauty of the Chaldeans' pride, shall be as when God overthrew Sodom and Gomorrah. It shall never be inhabited, neither shall it be dwelt in from generation to generation: neither shall the Arabian pitch tent there; neither shall shepherds make their flocks to lie down there" *(Isaiah 13:19, 20)*.

Again, "It shall be no more inhabited for ever; neither shall it be dwelt in from generation to generation. As when God overthrew Sodom and Gomorrah and the neighbor cities thereof, saith Jehovah, so shall no man dwell there, neither shall any son of man sojourn therein" *(Jeremiah 50:39, 40)*. And in Revelation 18:21-23, "Babylon, the great city, (shall) be cast down, and shall be found no more at all. And the voice of harpers and minstrels and flute-players and trumpeters . . . no more at all in thee; and no craftsman, of whatsoever craft, . . . any more at all in thee; and the voice of a mill . . . no more at all in thee; and the light of a lamp . . . no more at all in thee; and the voice of the bridegroom and of the bride . . . no more at all."

Here is utter desolation, and it is accomplished according to 18:19, *in one hour*. "In one hour is she made desolate." Verse 17, *"In one hour* so great riches is made desolate." *"In one hour* is thy judgment come," we read in verse 10. The horror of her overthrow is "as when God overthrew Sodom and Gomorrah"—it is so fearful! In verse 9, "The kings of the earth . . . when they look upon the smoke of her burning" stood *"afar off* for the fear of her torment"; and in verse 15, the merchants of all luxuries (29 being specified) "stand *afar off* for the fear of her torment." Again, in verse 17, "every ship-master, and everyone that saileth any whither, and mariners, and as many as gain their living by sea, stood *afar off,* and cried out as they looked upon the smoke of her burning."

We are reminded of Abraham's gazing upon Sodom's destruction (which Babylon's final overthrow will equal): "And Abraham gat up early in the morning to the place where he had stood before Jehovah: and he looked toward Sodom and Gomorrah, and toward all the land of the Plain, and beheld, and, lo, the smoke of the land went up as the smoke of a furnace" (Genesis 19:27, 28). (Abraham, thank God, was already "afar off" from that burning, for he lived twenty miles away, up in the Hebron mountain with God!)

10. There remains this solemn fact: that there is a great commercial metropolis overthrown by God in Revelation 18, and that in connection with the seventh bowl of wrath, immediately preceding our Lord's second coming (Revelation 16:19; 19:11, ff.). (Now the harlot was destroyed at least three years before, when the Beast and his ten kings began their power!) We read in connection with Babylon's overthrow as described in Isaiah 13:

"Wail ye; for the day of Jehovah is at hand; as destruction from the Almighty shall it come . . . For the stars of heaven and the constellations thereof shall not give their light; the sun shall be darkened in its going forth, and the moon shall not cause its light to shine . . . And Babylon, the glory of kingdoms, the beauty of the Chaldeans' pride, shall be as when God overthrew Sodom and Gomorrah" (verses 6, 10, 19).

Now, it matters not that in verse 17 of this chapter, God mentions the invasion by the Medes, for it is the common method of prophecy to look upon some event for a moment, and then see through it, as in a dissolving view, the *greater* event of which it was merely a *type*. For instance, in Zechariah 9:9 our Lord is seen riding into Jerusalem upon a lowly ass and its foal, but verse 10 goes on, without explanation of *what intervenes,* to say, "And he shall speak peace unto the nations: and his dominion shall be from sea to sea, and from the River to the ends of the earth"—which is at His *second* coming!

11. When the final destruction of Babylon, the literal city, was prophesied by Jeremiah, we find God's solemn warning to His people to *flee from it:* "Flee out of the midst of Babylon, and save every man his life; be not cut off in her inquity: for it is the time of Jehovah's vengeance . . . My people, go ye out of the midst of her, and save yourselves every man from the fierce anger of Jehovah" *(51:6, 45).*

Now note that Jeremiah could not have been prophesying of the mystical or papal Babylon; for "the mystery of iniquity" did not then exist; but Babylon the city was the avowed enemy of Jehovah's nation Israel. Again, mark carefully that when Cyrus took Babylon, neither Daniel, who that night prophesied to Belshazzar the end of his kingdom, nor the other Jews, fled from Babylon! As a matter of fact, Daniel was immediately elevated to the triumvirate of presidents under Darius the Median, who received the kingdom at the hand of the conqueror, Cyrus. But these prophecies of Jeremiah accord perfectly with the voice from heaven of Revelation 18: 4, "Come forth, my people, out of her, that ye have no fellowship with her sins, and that ye receive not of her plagues." If the city of Babylon is restored as Antichrist's capital, at the end of this age, godly Jews will be warned fully to flee, as in Jeremiah 51: 45, 46, 50.

12. We are forced then, to the conclusion, that the overthrow of Babylon, as the revealed center of iniquitous luxury and Satan-worship, the culmination of man's glory, lies yet in the future, in the land of Shinar, where Babylon's history began! The vision of the ephah of Zechariah 5 corroborates overwhelmingly the thought of the revival of commercial Babylon. A woman, called *Wickedness,* is seen sitting in an *ephah* measure, covered with a round piece of lead. (An ephah would be, to a Jew, a perfect symbol of commerce.) Two women with "wings of a stork" (an unclean bird to Israel—*Leviticus 11:19)* bear this ephah away "between earth and heaven." The prophet asks the revealing angel, "Whither do these bear the ephah?" And the significant answer is, "To build her a house *in the land of Shinar:* and when it is prepared, she shall be set there in her own place." What *could* such a vision portray, if not the final concentrating of wickedness in a great center which should reach the whole earth? *Direct* rebellion against God, in a new, and astounding, and organized way, began in that very land of Shinar, and it will complete its cycle and come back for judgment to that same place!

Whatever dark, persecuting history the harlot woman sitting on the Beast has been guilty of; and even if, as is very probable, she represents all false worship since the Flood: doctrines which, pretending to teach worship of God, have led men into the depths of uncleanness of idolatry; this much is certain: the harlot represents the *mystery* of iniquity, and the Beast, *manifest* iniquity. The harlot does not "deny all that is called God or that is worshipped"; the Beast does this very thing.

Furthermore, the harlot does not partake of the fearful bowls of wrath poured by God upon the Beast worshippers *(Revelation 16)*. The two principles of iniquity are distinct and diverse, and must be kept so in our minds. All false religions tell the consciences of their devotees that they are serving a *god,* or *gods.* This iniquity, of course, is headed up by Romanism. But the fearful character of the Beast's career is that he directs the worship of the whole world to himself, in order to make them *conscious Devil-worshippers (Revelation 13).* They are no longer deceived, as to whom they worship: they are enlightened with darkness! Even the majority of the Jewish nation, having made their seven-year contract with Antichrist, cry confidently: "We have made a covenant with death, and with Sheol are we at agreement; when the overflowing scourge shall pass through, it shall not come unto us; for we have made lies our refuge, and under falsehood have we hid ourselves" *(Isaiah 28:15).*

In order for this fearful program of Satan-worship to prevail without hindrance, there must be removed from the earth three things: *first,* the true Church, the Bride of Christ; *second,* apostate Christendom, represented by the harlot, which, however much she lacks the spirit, keeps the names of Christian things; and, *third,* the nation of Israel. God removes the first; the Beast and his ten kings destroy the second; while Armageddon is the final, supreme Satanic effort to obliterate the third —Israel—from the earth.

The Judgment of Mystic Babylon
Revelation 17

OUTLINE:

I. The vision of the woman on the scarlet beast *(verses 1-6).*

1. It is the *judgment* of the harlot which is to be revealed in this chapter.

2. Her dealings with:

a. The kings of the earth—"fornication."

b. The earth-dwellers—making them "drunken."

3. Her position on the Roman beast, now become fully blasphemous.

4. Her luxurious attire and her abominable cup.

5. Her mystic name: "Mystery, Babylon the Great, Mother of the harlots and of the abominations."

6. Her blood—drunken state.

II. The unfolding, or interpretation of the vision as to the woman and the Beast *(verses 7, 8)*.

1. The Beast.

a. The Beast is a man *(Revelation 13:18)*. (Though the Beast is the Roman Empire, that Empire with its iniquity full, is seen in its *head,* the Beast.)

b. He had had a former history on earth: "He *was.*"

c. He was not then on earth: "And *is* not."

d. He is to have a future history: "to come up out of the abyss" (where he was in John's day—the jail of lost human beings in the center of the earth).

e. He will go thence directly into the lake of fire: "into perdition" *(Revelation 19:20)*.

f. He will cause astonishment among the non-elect of those days, because of their knowledge that he was once on earth and disappeared and shall return: "he was, and is not, and shall come."

2. The Woman.

a. The woman is a city.

b. She is Rome (see below).

c. She will be "hated" by the Beast and his ten kings.

d. She will be utterly destroyed by them.

III. The great *double interpretation* (for "the mind that hath wisdom").

1. The seven heads of the Beast represent *seven mountains.*

a. These are the "seven hills" of literal Rome: (for prophecy at the end-time deals with the fourth world-power, Rome; and every reader knows that both pagan and Christian writers call Rome the seven-hilled city).

b. In this application, the woman "sits" on those mountains: she is the Babylonian system, transferred to

Rome by Attalus III of Pergamos—itself a colony from Babylonia—in B. C. 133.

c. The Woman "is the great city, which hath a kingdom over the kings of the earth" *(verse 18)*. (The present tense "hath a kingdom" *must* indicate Rome: for Rome alone was ruling the earth in John's day: "many waters" where she sits are said to be "peoples, and multitudes, and nations, and tongues.")

2. The seven heads also represent *seven Roman emperors*.

a. That these are Roman emperors is shown by the words "the one is"—that is, in John's day.

b. Five had "fallen": (*fallen* probably indicating a violent death—*see Govett, Apocalypse, p. 445, 446*).*

c. "The other" the seventh, was not yet come in John's day: he was to come and to "continue a little while." (The spirit of the passage indicates that this seventh will be as really *Roman* as any of the others: either reviving the Roman Empire or its spirit—as Mussolini is attempting to do!)

d. The Beast himself will be *an* eighth but will be also "of the seven." (This involves his release from the abyss in the center of the earth, the present prison of the lost spirits; and such release is affirmed of him in Revelation 17 and 13:3 and 14. Which of "the seven" he will be, God does not tell.)

IV. The ten kings (not *kingdoms*) represented by the ten horns.

1. They had not received "kingdom" in John's day.

2. They are to receive authority (*exousia*) along with the Beast (not till then) for "one hour" (the word *hour* here denotes a time of special character, or activity: as in Luke 22:53).

3. The committal to the Beast of their power and authority — by divine ruling. (Like Alexander's and

---

*Thus the seven "heads," or kings would have a double mark: (1) They would blasphemously *arrogate deity* to themselves *(see 13:1)*; and (2) they would *"fall" by violent means.* The five before John's day thus would be Julius Caesar, Tiberius, Caligula, Claudius and Nero. The sixth, who reigned when John wrote was Domitian—most blasphemous—who was assassinated.

Napoleon's generals, they come, with their leader, into sudden power, and their transfer of all to the Beast seems as speedy as it is unanimous.)

4. Their union with the Beast, the Antichrist, in the utter desolation (because of their absolute hatred) of the harlot. (This will be the end absolutely, finally, of Babylon in *mystery*. It is the complete *destruction* of the *papal harlot,* and of all earthly forms of worship except adoration of the Beast, and through him of *Satan, openly* —13:8.)

5. Their final, fearful presumption: Armageddon— "war *against the Lamb.*" (See Revelation 19:19-21 for the outcome!)

WHAT BABYLON IS

1. Babylon is *a literal city on the Euphrates River, with a form of idolatrous worship* which began almost immediately after the Flood, in the days of Nimrod, and extended throughout the whole earth. We find this *first form of Babylon opposed to God's people Israel.* Babylon is Satan's capital, just as Jerusalem is God's capital, and we find this first Babylon was permitted under Nebuchadnezzar to destroy Jerusalem and its temple.

2. Babylon, next, is the *same system* in another city— Rome, and *opposing the same idolatrous system to God's saints of the Church age:*—a monstrous system of evil doctrine that unites the church with the world.

3. The final *form of Babylon is the literal city on the Euphrates, rebuilt* as Antichrist's capital of the last days, *opposing Israel as God's earthly people* who will have gathered back to their land (the Church of course, having been raptured), and *opposing Jehovah's worship with the most powerful and enslaving form of idolatry that the world has ever known*—the worship of the Beast and his image!

Let us get well fixed in our minds these three phases of Babylon the Great.

And there came one of the seven angels that had the seven bowls, and spake with me, say-

ing, Come hither, I will show thee the judgment of the great harlot that sitteth upon many waters; with whom the kings of the earth committed fornication, and they that dwell in the earth were made drunken with the wine of her fornication.

Let us first remark that the meaning of this vision, whether important or not to us, is terribly distinct in the mind of the Spirit—this great harlot! She is called "the great harlot" in verse 1; "the harlot" in verses 15 and 16; "the mother of the harlots and of the abominations of the earth" in verse 5; and "the woman" six times, in this chapter. We do not well if our perception be dim of an existence so supremely hateful to God. Forty times the pronouns "she," "her," "thy," and "thee," are crowded into this divinely indignant record of the judgment of the great harlot.*

Now it is one of the seven angels that had the bowls of wrath of chapter 16 who comes to show John this judgment; as also in striking contrast, one of these seven in 21:9 leads the Seer to the vision of the Bride, the Lamb's wife.

Constantly remember that Revelation 17 and 18 is not a history of Babylon, but the record of its *judgment*. We see this harlot "sitteth upon many waters," which in verse 15, is said to represent "peoples, and multitudes, and nations, and tongues"—terrible mass-words of the hordes of idolatry of the last days, ending with *tongues*, which reminds us at once of Babel!

With this monstrous harlot, the "kings of the earth" are said to have "committed fornication," and the inhabitants of the earth were drunk with the wine of her fornication. Here then is a world-wide influence from the rulers down to the lowest subject which can only be spoken of by God by this awful word "fornication."

We must, as is usual in The Revelation, go to the Old

---

*Babylon is named over 260 times in Scripture; 37 times in one prophecy, Jeremiah 50 and 51! It is more frequently mentioned than any other city except Jerusalem.

Testament to find the roots of the meanings of the terms used. God arraigns Israel in the prophets over and over for "playing the harlot," "committing adultery," and "whoredom." In Jeremiah 3:2, 3, 9:

"Thou hast polluted the land with thy whoredoms and with thy wickedness . . . thou hadst a harlot's forehead, thou refusest to be ashamed. . . . Through the lightness of her whoredom that the land was polluted and she committed adultery with stones and with stocks."

No one who will take the trouble to read Ezekiel 16 and 23 can fail to understand God's plain language. In these two chapters of Ezekiel alone, whoredom is mentioned over twenty times, as describing the sin before God of those who turn His worship into shameless fellowship with demons and commerce with the world! It must be remembered that God is love; that He has always been as He is now, and is *jealous* toward those who, having a revelation from Him, turn from Him to that world which is controlled by His deadly enemy Satan; for "the things which the Gentiles sacrifice, they sacrifice to demons, and not to God."

Religious sin, therefore, is especially in view in this great harlot of Revelation 17. It is Satan's religious system controlling men by such doctrines as will salve and quiet their consciences, while suffering them to walk in their natural lusts. This "wine" the whole world has greedily drunk, and is by it *drunken!* Men love their lusts, but their consciences must be appeased that they may follow their lusts unrestrainedly. This, "mystery Babylon," by her insidious and finally shameless teachings, supplies; so that Satan's system, promulgated originally at Babylon, finally controls the whole world !*

---

*As regards idolatry being a post-diluvian development, consider:

1. There is no scriptural record of idolatry before the Flood.
2. The presence of the cherubim "at the east of the Garden of Eden" and "the flame of a sword which turned every way, to keep the way of the tree of life" would beyond doubt indicate a dispensation that allowed no such hideous caricature of Jehovah as idolatry sets up.
3. Joshua, in tracing Israel's origin, says, "Your fathers dwelt of old time beyond the River, even Terah, the father of Abraham, and the father of Nahor: and they served other gods. And I took your father Abraham from beyond the River" (*Joshua 24:2, 3*).
4. Shortly after the Flood and probably in connection with the daring scheme of the Babel tower of Genesis 2, appears the earliest historical record

If we make "mystery Babylon" mean *only* Roman Catholicism, we have to explain:

First: Why the same manner of language is used in the Old Testament prophets against Babylon as is used in The Revelation (compare, for example, Isaiah 21:9 and the great prophecies of Jeremiah 50 and 51 with Revelation 14:8 and the rejoicing over her destruction as seen in Revelation 19).

Second: How the blood of all that were slain upon earth was found in her finally (Revelation 18:24). We know from our Lord's words concerning Jerusalem (which stood for self-righteousness) that upon her came *cumulatively* "all the righteous blood" shed upon earth from the blood of Abel: but upon final Babylon, the blood of *all* that had been slain.

Third: We must explain how "the blood of the prophets" (evidently referring to Old Testament prophets) as well as of other saints, was found in her. This was not so as to Rome. Even if we limit the last verse of Reve-

---

we have of idolatry. "The discoveries of Nineveh and Babylon reveal that a secret organization of unbelievers was formed soon after the death of Nimrod *(Genesis 10)*, at a time when open apostasy was dangerous, and that its members established their headquarters at Babylon. From this center they labored with ceaseless activity to confuse and destroy the knowledge of Jehovah in the world and to bring men under the yoke of demon gods. They soon became a powerful and influential body continuing to be a secret society, not wishing to share their power and privileges with any but those willing to pass through the *ordeal of initiation*, which included a baptism, after which the initiate was termed 'twice-born' or regenerate (Greek *diphyees*), and worship was originally offered to a trinity consisting of father, mother and son. But the first person was very commonly confused with the third, and at last almost entirely forgotten; so that the prominent deities were the mother and son. Of these the former was by far the most popular and has been known according to time and place as Queen of Heaven, Mother of the Gods, Mylitta, Astarte, Diana of Ephesus, Aphrodite, Venus, Isis and the Blessed Virgin" *(Pember—*"Great Prophecies"). Mr. Darby remarks: "There appear to me to have been four sources of idolatry: *first*, an ineffaceable consciousness of God; *second*, deification of ancestors; *third*, the stars; *fourth*, the principle of generation. These were interwoven, at last giving rise to corruption inconceivable, the consecration of degrading lusts."

5. The Scripture gives Babylon as the origin of idolatry which spread to "all the nations." As Jeremiah cried, Babylon "is a land of graven images, and they are *mad over idols*. The nations have drunk of her wine; therefore, the nations are mad . . . all the earth is drunken" *(Jeremiah 50:38; 51:7)*. I have found no other final source of idolatry in Scripture than Babylon.

How fitting to Rome, the present form of Babylon, is the double statement that the kings of the earth committed "fornication." "Rome's influence over kings is a sort of *personal* influence, such as that of a harlot: her power over the nations is more distant, like that of wine. Her doctrine is 'wine of fornication.' Christianity is too holy, strict, self-denying, humbling for men by nature. Rome discovers to the nations a way of enjoying the world to the full, yet with the flattering belief that they are the servants of Christ" *(Govett)*.

lation 18 to the blood of God's people, this difficulty remains.

Fourth: It is in the nature of things impossible, or at least most improbable, that a name which marked the enemy of God's work in the world since the days of the Flood, right through the Old Testament, that of the city which destroyed Jerusalem and vaunted itself and its gods above all, should now in the New Testament be limited to a false church, which, although headed up in Rome upon the Tiber (that is, in the Papacy) never as such reached the world-wide sphere of the damning influence the Spirit of God declares Babylon to have had: "Babylon hath been a golden cup in Jehovah's hand, that hath made all the earth drunken" *(Jeremiah 51:7).*

Fifth: We expect in the book of Revelation the heading up of all the principles both of good and evil, which have appeared in human history. If we allow Babylon to express Satan's system of evil, as especially developed from Babel onwards after the Flood, and including all those various systems of idolatry and false worship which have had their spring, or root, or direct teaching in Babylon, we find in the picture presented to us in Revelation 17 and 18 an adequate portrayal; otherwise, we must leave out vast populations that Romanism as such has never touched, but which has indeed drunk of the intoxicating idolatrous cup of Babylon.

Sixth: If we thus consider Babylon as an expression of the whole Satanic system from the earliest times since the Flood onward, we are quite prepared to understand the position of the *harlot,* "mystery Babylon," in Revelation 17. For no one can deny that the nations which have influenced the history of mankind since the days of the apostles when the Church began until the present, have been those nations that have come under the influence of the harlot as represented in the papacy. Thus we can fully consent to the "seven hills" on which she sits, being the well-known hills of Rome, the fourth world-power, as so constantly described by Latin writers. But that this great harlot called "mystery Babylon" in Revelation 17, had her *beginning* with the papacy, we feel to be contrary to the Scripture taken as a whole and to the known historical facts.

Seventh: Of course, as illustrated in France under Clemenceau, Mexico under Calles, and Russia under Lenin and Stalin, we see the chief obstacle of the secular power, and the one chiefly hated by them, to be established Christianity as represented (or sadly misrepresented) in these countries. Every one senses, for instance, the two *directly opposing powers in Rome itself,* in Mussolini and the Pope. At present the papacy "rides" the Roman beast, although, as we know, to a most fearful fall, and that we believe not far distant.

Even when the Church maintained its early holy separateness from the world and the State, it was the object of the supreme hatred of the secular power, the fourth world-power. Magisterial authority is committed by God to man, but he immediately abuses it by arrogating independence of God who "ordained" him. See Nebuchadnezzar of Babylon in Daniel 3, and Darius of Persia in Daniel 6.

> And he carried me away in the Spirit into a wilderness: and I saw a woman sitting upon a scarlet-colored beast, full of names of blasphemy, having seven heads and ten horns. And the woman was arrayed in purple and scarlet, and decked (literally, gilded) with gold and precious stone and pearls, having in her hand a golden cup full of abominations, even the unclean things of her fornication, and upon her forehead a name written, MYSTERY, BABYLON THE GREAT, THE MOTHER OF THE HARLOTS AND OF THE ABOMINATIONS OF THE EARTH. And I saw the woman drunken with the blood of the saints, and with the blood of the martyrs of Jesus. And when I saw her, I wondered with a great wonder.

Note here, first the setting, then the vision, and last the effect upon the apostle.

First, we behold a *wilderness*. This is a literal description of the region surrounding both Babylon on the Euphrates and Rome on the Tiber: the former, marshes and swamps; the latter, the Campagna—"a marble wilderness"; in John's day rich and inhabited, but "desolated about the time the popes began to flourish."

But it is the *spiritual* wilderness which we need to observe. Babylon, in whatever form, has been a desolator of God's people and His truth.

We next notice that it is a *woman* that is first presented to us in this vision. Remember that we are here reading mystic terms *(verses 1-6);* and that the angel in verse 7 proceeds to *unfold* the "mystery." Who the woman is, or what she is, is revealed in the last verse of the chapter: "The woman whom thou sawest is the great city which *hath a kingdom over* the kings of the earth" *(R. V. margin).*

> And the angel said unto me, Wherefore didst thou wonder? I will tell thee the mystery of the woman, and of the beast that carrieth her, which hath the seven heads and the ten horns. The beast that thou sawest was, and is not; and is about to come up out of the abyss, and to go into perdition. And they that dwell on the earth shall wonder, they whose name hath not been written in the book of life from the foundation of the world, when they behold the beast, how that he was, and is not, and shall come. Here is the mind that hath wisdom. The seven heads are seven mountains, on which the woman sitteth: and they are seven kings; the five are fallen, the one is, the other is not yet come; and when he cometh, he must continue a little while. And the beast that was, and is not, is himself also an eighth, and is of the seven; and

he goeth into perdition. And the ten horns
that thou sawest are ten kings, who have received no kingdom as yet; but they receive authority as kings, with the beast, for one hour.
These have one mind, and they give their
power and authority unto the beast. These
shall war against the Lamb, and the Lamb
shall overcome them, for he is Lord of lords,
and King of kings; and they also shall overcome that are with him, called and chosen and
faithful. And he saith unto me, The waters
which thou sawest, where the harlot sitteth,
are peoples, and multitudes, and nations, and
tongues. And the ten horns which thou
sawest, and the beast, these shall hate the
harlot, and shall make her desolate and naked,
and shall eat her flesh and shall burn her utterly with fire. For God did put in their hearts
to do his mind, and to come to one mind, and
to give their kingdom unto the beast, until
the words of God should be accomplished.
And the woman whom thou sawest is the
great city, which hath a kingdom over the
kings of the earth.

Now the "great wonder," with which John was struck
at the vision of her, shows, it seems to me, that there was
nothing either in Scripture (which John, being in the
Spirit, would know), or in the apostle's own experience
or discernment, that would enable him to solve the mystery this woman presented. I know the angel says:
"Wherefore didst thou wonder?" but it seems that this
question was a mild form of reproof that the apostle had
not turned at once to his angelic guide; for that guide
proceeds: "I will *tell* thee the mystery of the woman, and
of the beast that carrieth her."

We know that the true Church was a mystery hid in
God until revealed to the apostle Paul; and doubtless
John, like Peter *(II Peter 3:15, 16)* had studied those

marvelous letters of the Gentile apostle—that "less than the least of all saints," to whom God unfolded the heavenly character, calling, and destiny of the Church, as the Body and the Bride of Christ—to be caught up and presented to Him, "without spot or blemish or any such thing."

Now, behold! Here was *another* woman, the very antithesis of the true Church, unholy, profligate, hideous, shamelessly displaying "the things of her fornication," seated upon the beast that John must have instantly recognized from the former vision *(Revelation 13),* as the last great world-power, and now "full of names and blasphemy," and also *scarlet*-colored! It was then the Roman beast, filling the world with blasphemous wickedness. That scarlet was one of the colors of imperial Rome, we know from Matthew 27:28. They put a *scarlet* robe on our Lord, in mockery of His title as King.

But this woman is seen in both purple and scarlet (Christ was by Rome also arrayed in *purple*—Mark 15: 16, 20)! Purple was the Roman imperial color. The emperor was clothed in it: the senators wore a broad band of it, and the knights, a narrower band; so that this woman in John's eyes would be exercising all the power of the Roman Empire, though herself not crowned, not a queen, in her own right! Thus the mystery. Who was she? On her forehead was written the word "mystery," and "Babylon," and also the fact that she was a "mother of harlots" and also of "abominations" (false gods) for the whole earth. Furthermore, she was drunken with blood!—and that of the saints (before Christ) and "the martyrs of Jesus" (after His coming).

Babylon, the City, and Its Final Doom

Revelation 18

OUTLINE:

1. The second angelic announcement *(verses 1-3).*

2. The call to God's people to flee out of Babylon *(verses 4, 5).*

3. The final character of Babylon's sin—now become full—godless world-commerce *(verses 12-17, 23-b)*.

4. The mode of Babylon's final overthrow: catastrophic —in "one hour," and direct: from God's hand *(verses 8, 19, 21)*.

5. The "mourning" of earth's kings and merchants *(verses 9-11, 15-19)*.

6. The awful perpetual curse of desolation upon Babylon *(verses 2, 22, 23)*.

7. The cumulative guilt of Babylon: the blood of prophets, saints and all earth's murdered *(verse 24)*.

8. The solemn fact that her judgment was decided by the saints in heaven *(verse 20)*.

9. The unlimited joy of heaven over this final judgment of Babylon *(verse 20 and 19:1-5*—The four hallelujahs).

10. Babylon's people doomed to eternal flames *(19:3)*.

Before we proceed with this great chapter which reveals the sudden ending under divine wrath of the present world system, let us say a few words concerning the real meaning of the spirit of commercialism which has been seizing tighter hold every hour upon so-called civilization and will be the cause of its wreck.

THE CHARACTER OF COMMERCE

1. It is not of God—especially world-commerce, but is of man and of Satan.

2. God placed His nation, Israel, in a land where commerce with other nations was very nearly impossible. Palestine had no harbors. On the East and South were deserts; at the North, mountains with only a narrow "entering in." Jehovah expressly forbade the multiplying of horses, and also of silver and gold *(Deuteronomy 17: 16, 17)*.

3. North of Israel, the city of Tyre on the Mediteranean coast became the great maritime center of the earth and upon it was pronounced the terrible judgment of Ezekiel 26-28. Chapter 26, too, reveals Tyre's envy of Jerusalem as a place where the peoples of the earth

should resort and her desire to turn to herself in a commercial way, that gathering of peoples whom God meant to be instructed at Jerusalem in a spiritual way (as all the ends of the earth came to hear the wisdom of Solomon).

4. Israel's commercial dealings corrupted her both in the days of Solomon and Jehoshaphat. "Judah, and the land of Israel, they were thy traffickers (Tyre's): they traded for thy merchandise wheat of Minnith, and pannag, and honey, and oil, and balm" *(Ezekiel 27:17)*.

Zechariah closes his prophecy concerning the Millennium: "In that day there shall be no more a Canaanite (literally, trafficker) in the house of Jehovah of hosts."

5. International commerce:

a. Enables man to avoid as far as possible God's command to till the earth and to live by the sweat of his brow.

b. Tends to unify the humanity that God has definitely divided into nations, for the very purpose of covering the earth with the spirit of self-confidence and rebellion as before Babel *(Genesis 11)*.

c. Enables individuals, cities and nations to become unduly swollen with riches. It begets universal covetousness, which is idolatry—in that the man who has money, can be independent of God. Govett well says: "The opposition to the spirit of commerce which this Book of God shows, is very remarkable, especially as running in direct contrast to the avowed plans of rulers and peoples of our day. 'Cherish COMMERCE,' is one of the great admitted ends of statesmanship. But its effects upon the mind are generally productive of covetousness."

6. The nature of commerce is very simple. You take your products (generally by ships) where you can get the highest price; fill your ship there and again sail where you get the high price, and again load your ship at a low cost with wares desirable in other countries, and so on and on. Now this is not tilling the ground and living quietly. God hates it and will destroy it utterly. What God wants, is that each man live beneath "his own vine and fig-tree," "content with such things" as he has. "Big

business" is an abomination. It will be the ruination of the world.

7. "Business" is an excuse most common in the thoughts of men for not serving God (and yet shortly they will stand before God!) Millions of men really think that "business" has a real claim upon them.*

8. We see the wickedness of the spirit of commercialism both from the fearful power exercised by the Beast of Revelation 13, forbidding either selling or buying without "his mark" stamped upon the hand or upon the forehead, and also from chapter 18 of Revelation. It is atheistic; it is self-indulgent; it is self-confident: "I sit a queen."

9. The difficulties experienced by God's dear saints of all days on account of "business" claims is proverbial. The spirit of commercialism, which has seized upon the human race, is fast blotting out real human ties (home, church or country).†

---

*The correct reading of Romans 12:11 is found in the Revised Version:— "In diligence not slothful; fervent in spirit; serving the Lord; (referring wholly to diligence in *the spiritual life*, as see context)—rejoicing in hope; patient in tribulation; continuing steadfastly in prayer"; etc. "Business" is not in that at all.

†"In what, indeed, does the mightiest and farthest reaching power on earth now already center? A power which looms up in all lands, far above all individual or combined powers of church, or state, or caste, or creed? What is it that today monopolizes nearly all legislation, dictates international treaties, governs the conferences of kings for the regulation of the balance of power, builds railways, cuts ship-canals, sends forth steamer lines to the ends of the earth, unwinds electric wires across continents, under the seas, and around the world, employs thousands of engineers, subsidizes the press, tells the state of the markets of the world yesterday that everyone may know how to move today, and has her living organizations in every land and city, interlinked with each other, and coming daily into closer and closer combination, so that no great government under the sun can any longer move or act against her will, or without her concurrence and consent?

"Think for a moment, for there is such a power; a power that is everywhere clamoring for a common code, a common currency, common weights and measures; and which is not likely to be silenced or to stop till it has secured a common center on its own independent basis, whence to dictate to all countries and to exercise its own peculiar rule on all the kings and nations of the earth. That power is COMMERCE; the power of the ephah and the talent— the power borne by the winged women of Zechariah 5; the one with her hand on the sea and the other with her hand on the land—the power which even in its present dismemberment is mightier than any pope, any throne, any government, or any other one human power on the face of the globe.

"Let it go on as it has been going, and will go, in spite of everything that earth can interpose to hinder, dissolving every tie of nationality, every bond of family or kindred, every principle or right and religion which it cannot bend and render subservient to its own ends and interests; and the time must come when it will settle itself down somewhere on its own independent base, and where Judaism and heathenism, Romanism and Protestantism, Mohammedanism and Buddhism, and every distinction of nationality—English, German, French, Italian, Greek, Turk, Hindoo, Arab, Chinese, Japanese, or what not— shall be sunk in one great universal fellowship and kingdom of *commerce!*"— *(From Seiss; "On the Apocalypse" written in 1865.)*

We scarcely know how far we have drifted. Our fore-fathers were content with their living. They had domestic ties, "family reunions," quiet church affiliations, gladly worshipping in the same old church, generation after generation. They had deep, kind, loving patriotism.

But the forgetting of God is fast falling upon earth under the soul-stifling power of universal greed. Such delusive catch words as "a higher standard of living" have poisoned the streams of the life of the world. "Be ye free from the love of money; content with such things as ye have," said Paul. "We brought nothing into the world, for neither can we carry anything out; but having food and covering we shall be therewith content." "Godliness with contentment is great gain." Everybody wants to be rich—which damns its tens of millions! "Get up in the world." "Get on in the world!" What lies! What will-o'-the-wisps of Satan to be followed by folks whose feet shall shortly stumble into open graves!

10. Commercialism brings spiritual deadness and insensibility as nothing else does. Once consent in your heart that "business" has a claim upon you and your spiritual life begins to shrivel. For a man to do an honest day's work is not to yield to the claims that "business" makes upon humanity. God told us to work, to work with our hands, to do with our might what our hands find to do, to do the humblest tasks, even those of a slave, as unto the Lord. The thing called "business" has to be discerned distinctly by you if you are to understand the hideousness into which the whole world will leap, and alas, how shortly!

"Depression" is, I have no doubt, *an answer to prayer,* as was the famine in Ahab's idolatrous days an answer to Elijah's prayers. Civilization goes mad to get rich—anything to get rich! Now this simply means anything to gain *independence of God.* The Lord Jesus said, "Take heed, and keep yourselves from all covetousness: for a man's life consisteth not in the abundance of the things which he possesseth."

And God in His mercy has let men come to realize the deceitfulness of riches. "Have your hope," said Paul, "set on God, and not on 'the uncertainty of riches.' " The Lord Jesus said to His saints, "Lay not up for yourselves treasures, upon the earth . . . but lay up for yourselves treasures in heaven." What He meant by the right use of money, He shows in the parable (Luke 16) of the unjust steward, whose master commended as *wise*, the lavishing of that master's funds upon *others*, when the steward found he must give account. Then He said, "I say unto you, Make to yourselves friends by means of the mammon of unrighteousness; that, when it shall fail (as it will), they (those you have helped) may welcome you into the eternal tabernacles" *(R. V.)*.

> After these things I saw another angel coming down out of heaven, having great authority; and the earth was lightened with his glory. And he cried with a mighty voice, saying, Fallen, fallen is Babylon the great, and is become a habitation of demons, and a hold of every unclean spirit, and a hold of every unclean and hateful bird. For by the wine of of the wrath of her fornication all the nations are fallen; and the kings of the earth committed fornication with her, and the merchants of the earth waxed rich by the power of her wantonness.

"Another angel"—than that of chapter 17:7; not Christ, who is not "another" angel: He is *the* Angel of Jehovah. (See notes on Revelation 10:1.) Christ, the Lamb in heaven, has given this angel "great authority." (Christ Himself has all authority in heaven and on earth.) Nor is this angel to be confused with our Lord's second coming in Revelation 19:11-16. This angel's "glory" marks the greatness of the occasion.

The fact that this angel is additional to the one of chapter 17, is one of the proofs that the Babylon of chapter

18 is Babylon on the Euphrates rather than Rome (which is the mystery Babylon of chapter 17).

"Fallen, fallen, is Babylon the great." The double use of "fallen" emphasizes the fact which excellent expositors have found here—that of the *double* overthrow of chapters 17 and 18.

"A habitation of demons, and a hold," etc. Alford calls "hold" *(phulake),* "a place of detention, as it were, an appointed prison." This is the evident meaning, so that the city of Babylon on the Euphrates during the Millennium will be a jail of demons. Compare Isaiah 24:21-23; which is millennial also, and the judgment upon Edom, in Isaiah 34:13-15; also millennial. (Of course these conditions give way to the last judgment—when the earth is destroyed, in 20:11-15, and all lost beings are finally sentenced.)

"Kings . . . and the merchants." It is the last phase of Babylon, which is seen from Genesis 11 to Revelation; being first the city on the Euphrates which practiced idolatry and opposed God's city Jerusalem; then in "mystery"—the harlot on the seven hills of Rome, continuing Babylon's ancient trinity of father, mother and son, under Christian names; and finally, after the Church is raptured (4:1), the re-established world-capital at Babylon on the Euphrates, whose prophesied destruction *like Sodom,* has not yet taken place. Thus the human race would combine to set up Babylon, which becomes the center of commercial world-activity. Of Tyre, God wrote in Isaiah 23 that she was a "bestower of crowns, whose merchants are princes, whose traffickers are the honorable of the earth." While the nations rush to rebuild Babylon and it becomes the Beast's capital, then at last will be the full "power of her luxury" as described in Revelation 18:3 *(margin).*

> And I heard another voice from heaven, saying, Come forth, my people, out of her, that ye have no fellowship with her sins, and that ye receive not of her plagues: for her sins

have reached even unto heaven, and God hath remembered her iniquities. Render unto her even as she rendered, and double unto her the double according to her works: in the cup which she mingled, mingle unto her double. How much soever she glorified herself, and waxed wanton, so much give her of torment and mourning: for she saith in her heart, I sit a queen, and am no widow, and shall in no wise see mourning. Therefore in one day shall her plagues come, death, and mourning, and famine; and she shall be utterly burned with fire; for strong is the Lord God who judged her. And the kings of the earth, who committed fornication and lived wantonly with her, shall weep and wail over her, when they look upon the smoke of her burning, standing afar off for the fear of her torment, saying, Woe, woe, the great city, Babylon, the strong city! for in one hour is thy judgment come. And the merchants of the earth weep and mourn over her, for no man buyeth their merchandise any more.

"Come forth, My people, out of her."

While these words have a real application to the believer to come forth to Jesus outside the spiritual Babylon —ecclesiasticism, Nicolaitanism and the false promises of "mystery" Babylon in its various forms; yet the particular *interpretation* of the words is not to the saints, who will have been raptured before this call goes forth. The call to "come forth" from this great commercial Sodom of the last days—rebuilt Babylon, is evidently issued to those individuals living in or doing business in that capital of the Antichrist in the last days. In Isaiah 52:11 and Jeremiah 50:8; 51:6, 9, 45, we see that it will be especially Jewish saints and those attached to them that are warned; for they are bidden in Jeremiah 51:50 to "Remember

Jehovah from afar, and let Jerusalem come into your mind."

Now in Revelation 18:4-20 the "voice from heaven" of verse 4 is speaking. It is most solemn: the sure word of prophecy declaring to the opened ear a scene yet future with a vividness that makes it *live* before us!

> Merchandise of gold, and silver, and precious stone, and pearls, and fine linen, and purple, and silk, and scarlet; and all thyine wood, and every vessel of ivory, and every vessel made of most precious wood, and of brass, and iron, and marble; and cinnamon, and spice, and incense, and ointment, and frankincense, and wine, and oil, and fine flour, and wheat, and cattle and sheep; and merchandise of horses and chariots and slaves; and souls of men. And the fruits which thy soul lusted after . . . and all things that were dainty and sumptuous. . . . The merchants of these things . . . were made rich by her . . . she . . . was arrayed in fine linen and purple and scarlet, and decked with gold and precious stone and pearl! . . . So great riches. . . . And every shipmaster, and everyone that saileth any whither, and mariners, and as many as gain their living by sea, stood afar off, and cried out as they looked upon the smoke of her burning, saying, What city is like the great city? And they cast dust on their heads, and cried, weeping and mourning, saying, Woe, woe, the great city, wherein all that had their ships in the sea were made rich by reason of her costliness! for in one hour is she made desolate. Rejoice over her, thou heaven, and ye saints, and ye apostles, and ye prophets; for God hath judged your judgment on her. And a strong angel took up a stone as it were a great millstone and cast it into the sea, say-

ing, thus with a mighty fall shall Babylon, the great city, be cast down, and shall be found no more at all. And the voice of harpers and minstrels and flute-players and trumpeters shall be heard no more at all in thee; and no craftsman, of whatsoever craft, shall be found any more at all in thee; and the voice of a mill shall be heard no more at all in thee; and the light of a lamp shall shine no more at all in thee; and the voice of the bridegroom and of the bride shall be heard no more at all in thee: for thy merchants were the princes of the earth; for with thy sorcery were all the nations deceived.

We must remember that the Beast and his ten kings of chapter 17 made desolate the woman that sat on the seven mountains—Romanism *(17:9, 16)*. But the overthrow of chapter 18 is directly from God: *"in one day," "in one hour,"* *(18:8, 10, 17, 19)*. This overthrow is lamented by the kings of the earth.

Russia teaches us lessons here. For although she has burned churches and martyred priests and preachers, she is desperately seeking to build up *commerce,* to "industrialize" a whole nation in five years, to create markets by any means whatever! Russia would be self-sufficient, but for this curse of commerce that is filling the earth. Russia could close her harbors and have abundance to supply all her real needs, if her rulers were content to live in humble quiet. As far as she is able, she has destroyed religion, as the Antichrist will do in Revelation 17. But,— she desires *luxury.* And thus is she joined to Babylon in spirit.

If you desire to know the last and final form of iniquity, behold the two women of Zechariah 5 bearing an ephah, covered with a talent of lead. The woman, called Wickedness, sits in the ephah. "Whither do these bear the ephah?" asks the prophet, and the angel answers: "To build her a house in the land of Shinar: and when it

is prepared, she shall be set there in her own place."
Now Babylon is in that land of Shinar (Genesis 10:10).

Notice in Revelation 18:3, 11, 15, 23, "the merchants
of the earth," also "merchandise," (Greek "cargo"—showing these things will be carried by ships, as see verse 17).
Rome has no market and the Tiber has no harbor, to
speak of. Naming the articles of the cargo begins with
verse 12: "Merchandise of gold, and silver, and precious
stone," etc. Nearly thirty kinds are enumerated, and it
is all a story of luxury upon luxury! It must be pearls;
it must be *fine* linen; it must be *silk;* it must be vessels
of *most precious wood;* it must be *fragrant* spices; it
must be *wine* and olive oil; it must be *fine* flour; it must
be *slaves;* it must be things that are *dainty* and *sumptu-
ous.* This city must be "decked" in *fine* linen, *scarlet,*
gold, and pearls!

Now of course Roman Catholic dignitaries are seen
thus decking themselves (at great cost to the poor and
even to kings). But only the "clergy" and their retinues
do this. The people suffer *poverty.*

1. Over three years before the Babylon described in
Revelation 18, the Beast and his ten kings have destroyed
the harlot, the city on seven hills.

2. For over three years more, the Beast and the Man
of Sin *who denies all that is called God and is worshipped,*
will have full power on earth.

3. Rome's motto is "semper idem." She cannot deny
the Father and Son, as Antichrist does, and *exist.*

Therefore, it appears necessary to believe that the
Babylon of chapter 18 is not Rome, but the great commercial center, Satan's world-capital, which has always
been Babylon on the Euphrates.

It seems clear from Scripture that God will permit one
man publicly to "gain the whole world and forfeit his
life." And that God will also permit man's love for luxury and pleasure, and the money that secures it, to *run
full riot,* and set up an amazing world center of inconceivable grandeur and riches in the old place—Babylon.

Therefore in one day shall her plagues come, death, and mourning, and famine; and she shall be utterly burned with fire; for strong is the Lord God who judged her. And they cast dust on their heads, and cried, weeping and mourning, saying, Woe, woe, the great city, wherein all that had their ships in the sea were made rich by reason of her costliness! for in one hour is she made desolate. And a strong angel took up a stone as it were a great millstone, and cast it into the sea, saying, Thus with a mighty fall shall Babylon, the great city, be cast down, and shall be found no more at all.

We have noticed this, but it needs to be re-emphasized: "Mystery" Babylon was destroyed by *man's* hand—by the Beast and his ten kings. Literal Babylon with its minstrels, flute-players, trumpeters, craftsmen, "marrying and giving in marriage" *(verses 22, 23)*, will be overthrown, and in an instant, swallowed up into the bowels of the earth, and with a burning like Sodom and Gomorrah. The earthquake under the seventh seal of Revelation 16:19 was seen destroying Babylon, the great. *(Isaiah 13, 18, 19.)* And then the next verse, Isaiah 13:20, has never been fulfilled: for there *are* inhabitants there. The Arabians do pitch their tents and the shepherds make their flocks to lie down there; but when God destroys it finally, *there shall be no such thing.*

CHAPTER XVI

MARRIAGE OF THE LAMB
Revelation 19:1-10

Revelation 19 is *full*, with two tremendous events:

1. The marriage of the Lamb celebrated in heaven; and the marriage supper in heaven.

2. The advent of the Lord in the Great Day of Wrath, as King of kings; and the slaughter on earth, and the frightful "supper" connected therewith.

As the Day of Wrath at Armageddon is the most fearful, so is the marriage of the Lamb the most blessed and happy of all events that have occurred so far in creation.

Introduction—The Four Hallelujahs—(Revelation 19:1, 3, 4, 6)

Hallelujah is the Hebrew expression frequently occurring in the later Psalms and meaning "praise to Jehovah." The last five Psalms, 146-150 (R. V.) begin and end with this wonderful word, *hallelujah*. Others, like Psalm 106, set forth the spirit of millennial anticipation and praise, as does the shortest—Psalm 117. Only in these four verses of Revelation 19 does this mighty praise-word occur in the New Testament.

But this is what we would expect; for there is no place today (except in the life of individual saints who rejoice in the assembly, under the movement of the Holy Spirit) for this great word of high exultation unto God.

Because the Messiah when He came to Israel, although received by the wise men with exceeding joy, and gladdening the hearts of the poor shepherds, was rejected by Israel, and crucified; victory was postponed, and hallelujah can be uttered only by *faith* when the Church is filled with the Holy Spirit and becomes a prophetic testimony of *grace*. Personal hallelujahs can be given to God, but the triumph that brings the universal hallelujah to all holy things is yet in the future! Indeed, mercy and grace were too soon forgotten, and papal bondage entered into by the Church itself. The harlot Babylon rises—the woman drunken with the blood of the saints *(Revelation 17)*. It is not the time for hallelujahs.

Not until Babylon, the harlot, is completely overthrown, swallowed up in divine indignation, as we see in Revelation 17; and not until literal Babylon (Chapter 18) is completely gone, and all Babylonian things have disappeared forever, does hallelujah burst forth from all holy hearts.

Notice that the first two hallelujahs are drawn forth by Babylon's judgment:

> After these things I heard as it were a great voice of a great multitude in heaven, saying, Hallelujah; Salvation, and glory, and power, belong to our God: for true and righteous are his judgments; for he hath judged the great harlot, her that corrupted the earth with her fornication, and he hath avenged the blood of his servants at her hand. And a second time they say, Hallelujah. And her smoke goeth up for ever and ever.

Indeed, verse 4, including the third hallelujah, with the word "Amen" preceding it, may well be joined with the hallelujahs of verses 1 and 3, as expressing the utter consent of those most intimately connected with the divine throne—the twenty-four elders and the four living beings.

> And the four and twenty elders and the four living creatures fell down and worshipped God that sitteth on the throne, saying, Amen; Hallelujah.

There is now a call from the throne itself, for *universal* jubilant praise, such as it seems has never been issued before:

> And a voice came forth from the throne, saying, Give praise to our God, all ye his servants, ye that fear him, the small and the great.

Notice that this call is given to all whose warfare is over, for it is a heavenly scene.*

We now come to the mightiest verse of *response to God* in all Scripture:

> And I heard as it were the voice of a great multitude, and as the voice of many waters, and as the voice of mighty thunders, saying, Hallelujah: for the Lord our God, the Almighty, reigneth.

While all preceding hallelujahs have risen from relief at the overthrow of Babylon, this fourth hallelujah is a limitless expression of ecstasy at the reign of "the Lord our God the Almighty."

In our poor feeble spiritual experiences and aspirations, it is most difficult even to *imagine* the delight *in God* heard now in heaven. A great multitude—many waters—like mighty thunders: such is the voice!

The Marriage of the Lamb

Now, at last, we are coming to that inexpressible climax, that glorious event awaited by God the Father, and the Bridegroom, His Son; and the Blessed Spirit. Yes, and all holy beings, who like John (the Bridegroom's friend) can say, "this my joy therefore is made full." And so we read:

> Let us rejoice and be exceeding glad, and let us give the glory unto him: for the marriage of the Lamb is come, and his wife hath made herself ready.

---

*It is, we believe, evident that at the moment this great call comes for praise on the part of all God's servants and those that fear Him, the small and the great, there are still on earth, in great trouble, those whose warfare is not yet accomplished. Hear Luke 18:8, "When the Son of man cometh, shall he find *faith* on earth?" There will be those on earth who are really God's elect, but have not yet received faith. It will not be given until the first three verses of Isaiah 60 are fulfilled "Arise, shine; for thy light is come, and the glory of Jehovah is risen upon thee. . . . and His glory shall be seen upon thee. And the nations shall come to thy light." This is not until the Lord Himself is revealed in Jerusalem unto beleaguered Israel, until they "*look* unto him whom they have pierced." "Then shall appear the sign of the Son of man in heaven," which is His pierced Person, and they shall at last, like Thomas, believe because they have seen. Moreover the whole scene of Revelation 19:1-10 is heavenly, not earthly, and it precedes the coming of the Lord with His heavenly armies to destroy His enemies.

Let us reflect that this "marriage of the Lamb" has been the longed-for and looked-for event of age upon age. It is not necessary that this great event of blessing should have been continually referred to in Scripture to make it important. The virgin birth of our Lord is not frequently referred to, but of how vast eternal consequence!

> And it was given unto her that she should array herself in fine linen, bright and pure: for the fine linen is the righteous acts of the saints.
>
> And he saith unto me, Write, Blessed are they that are bidden to the marriage supper of the Lamb. And he saith unto me, These are true words of God. And I fell down before his feet to worship him. And he saith unto me, See thou do it not: I am a fellow-servant with thee and with thy brethren that hold the testimony of Jesus: worship God: for the testimony of Jesus is the spirit of prophecy.

Certain questions arise immediately concerning this great revelation of the marriage of the Lamb and the marriage supper.

1. When does this event occur? Evidently directly upon the overthrow of Babylon on earth; for the celebration of that judgment-event in Revelation 19:1-5 was immediately succeeded in verses 6 and 7 by the mighty praise attending the reigning of the "Lord our God the Almighty," which brings in the marriage.

2. Where is the marriage, with its attending marriage supper, celebrated? The answer can only be—in heaven; for the scene is wholly heavenly. No one can read verse 6 without coming to this conclusion.

3. What saints constitute "the bride, the wife of the Lamb"? *The Church!* See Ephesians 5:22-32.

In Israel as a nation the high priest was expressly forbidden to marry a "divorced woman" or "a widow" (Leviticus 21:10, 13, 14). Israel is spoken of both as divorced (Jeremiah 3:8) and as a widow (Lamentations 1:1; Isaiah 54:4). When Jehovah returns to Israel in millennium blessings, Isaiah 62:4, 5 will be fulfilled, as will 54:4, 5, etc., but it will be "Jehovah delighteth in thee, and thy land shall be married," for, "as a young man marrieth a virgin, so shall thy sons marry thee; and as the bridegroom rejoiceth over the bride, so shall thy God rejoice over thee." This is an earthly scene, and must be contrasted with the marriage of the heavenly Bride, the wife of the Lamb.

In Revelation 21:10, the angel reveals the wife of the Lamb to John, thus:

"He carried me away in the Spirit to a mountain great and high, and showed me the holy city Jerusalem, coming down out of heaven from God, having the glory of God." We read concerning the patriarchs, that they desired a better country, that is a heavenly; therefore, "God is not ashamed of them, to be called their God," for He prepared for them a city. Also, that Abraham "looked for the city," *with the foundations,* whose architect and maker is God. And in Galatians 4:26 Paul declares concerning Church saints that "the Jerusalem that is above is free, which is our mother."

This heavenly Jerusalem is seen in Revelation 21:24-27 to have come down to the new earth (upon a great and high mountain), with the "nations" walking amid the light thereof, and the kings of the earth bringing their glory into it—the gates never being closed, and admitting the holy inhabitants of earth freely.*

That Abraham, the patriarchs, and all who were given by God a heavenly hope, will share in the bliss of the New Jerusalem, appears scriptural.

---

*Those who teach that Revelation 21, 9, ff, goes back to the millennial order, before the last judgment and the new creation, claim that "nations" will not exist in the new earth. But these seem to forget Isaiah 65:-17, 18 as well as 66:22, where the creation of the new heavens and the new earth is connected with the perpetuation of the seed and the name of Israel. There are many prophecies setting forth the eternal perpetuity of that elect nation. And if of Israel, the elect nation, then also of other nations. Also, as seen in Revelation 21:26, "And they shall bring the glory and the honor of the nations into it." We know that the formation of nations arose out of a judgment—at Babel. But the establishment of Israel as a kingdom under David arose from the judgment upon Israel's rejection of Jehovah as their king! Our Lord's royal title lies in the covenant with David, the king, His father. The idea that nations will cease to exist does not seem to be borne out in Scripture. (See notes on Chapter 21.)

But that Abraham or any other Old Testament saint will form part of *the Body of Christ,* we cannot for a moment believe! The great mystery of the Church, His Body, committed to Paul in such a sense that he called himself *minister* thereof (Colossians 1:24-27), a ministry so very distinct, definite and exclusive as to call for the great passage of Ephesians 5:23, cannot be merely an opening up to Old Testament saints of a calling, character and privileges which they possessed and of which they did not know! That is unthinkable. No one was "baptized" into that one Body until Pentecost. When that Body, the Church, is presented by Christ to Himself "a glorious church, not having spot or wrinkle or any such thing," it will be composed only of the saints from Pentecost to the rapture.

4. Are the marriage and the marriage supper distinct? It certainly appears so, for in Revelation 19:9, you have those that are "bidden" to the marriage supper of the Lamb. These guests most certainly do not constitute the Bride. No bride needs an invitation to her own wedding!

In John 3:29, John the Baptist says, "He that hath the bride is the bridegroom: but the *friend* of the bridegroom, that standeth and heareth him, rejoiceth greatly because of the bridegroom's voice; this *my* joy therefore is made full." Now, here is a saint concerning whom the Lord Jesus testified: "Among them that are born of women there hath not arisen a greater." And yet he is not of the Bride. Nevertheless, he is at the marriage supper, for he is the friend of the bridegroom—a place of singular honor! In divine, sovereign arrangement, he is not of the Bride.

5. Who will be the guests at the marriage supper? Evidently not all the saints; otherwise, why the special blessing pronounced (verse 9) upon those that are bidden to the marriage supper?

I. The Prime Importance of This Marriage Scene

1. This event is the great delight of God, to which He has looked forward from all ages. It is a fulfilment of our

Lord's words of Matthew 22, "A certain king . . . . who made a marriage feast for his son." The relationship of the Father and the Son is one of infinite, eternal tenderness. All marriage joys of earth were planned by God and given to mankind in love that they might understand somewhat of heaven's feeling at this marriage; for, "love is of God."

Let us seek to enter, if we may, into the contemplation of that delight of the Father—"from whom every family in heaven and on earth is named" (Ephesians 3:14), when the time at last has come for His Son to "present the church to himself a glorious church, not having spot or wrinkle or any such thing"; for God the Father gave the Church to Christ. Read John 17: "I pray not for the world, but for those whom thou hast given me." There is no meditation so exalting as that upon the relationship and affections of the Persons of the Godhead, one to another.

2. This marriage is the great anticipation of Christ. Paul tells us the story in Ephesians 5—"Christ also loved the Church, and gave himself up for it." His love for the Church is immeasurable, unchanging, infinite. It is in the very nature of the case, peculiar love. Christ wept over Jerusalem, for there was, and is, a special tenderness of our God toward those to whom He was the Messiah, and over whom He will be King on David's throne. He had "compassion on the multitude" as He does today. He gave Himself a ransom for all. But His love for His Bride, the Church, is, as it must be, and that, eternally, a peculiar, particular, husband's affection, and that without measure!

3. This heavenly wedding is the great prospect of all holy beings. (We mean, of course, of all those in heaven; for this marvelous scene is wholly heavenly, as is evident.)

From the time in Revelation 5, when the Lamb takes the seven-sealed book of the kingdom, His actions as well as His Person have been the constant jubilant delight of heaven (Revelation 5:8-14; 7:9-17; 11:15). But now the climax has been reached. In an earthly wedding, especially a wedding of the favorite one of the house, how all the relatives and also the servants of the household are stirred! Now Jehovah God appointed and directed the first wedding, in Genesis 2, and our Lord's first miracle at Cana of Galilee celebrated with "the best wine" another wedding. But Ephesians 5:25, 31 and 32 proclaims that every marriage sets forth anew the relationship of Christ and the Church! It is, therefore, the height of holy joy to every heavenly being, this marriage of the Lamb!

4. To bring in this festal day in heaven, Satan's earthly system was overthrown.

This marriage could not be celebrated while the harlot Babylon, the false church, who pretended infamously to be the Bride of Christ, remained unjudged.

a. For the heavenly wedding must have peace and joy unmixed—all gladness, unmingled with jealousy or conflict.

b. Judgment of that which pretended to be Christ's Bride was absolutely necessary for such peace and joy.

c. Just as the triumph of holiness over iniquity is necessary for public peace, so indignation must give place to satisfaction of heart for such an occasion as the heavenly wedding.

d. Participation in God's holiness and holy judgment must be prior and preliminary to participation in His day of love toward His Son, and to that Son's absolute delight. Therefore, we read concerning the judgment of Babylon: "Rejoice over her, thou heaven, and ye saints, and ye apostles, and ye prophets; for God hath judged your judgment on her." The very beings who are now to enter into the festal joys of the marriage of the Lamb, whether they are guests or servants, are those who pronounced the judgment which God executed upon the shameless, earthly, Satanic bride-pretender. You remember that David's mighty wars had to precede Solomon's reign of peace and the Song of Songs of marriage joy.

5. Review the expressions of rapture with which all holy, heavenly beings celebrate this wedding.

First, "The voice of a great multitude saying, Hallelujah!" (Revelation 19:1). Then you have the four and twenty elders, and the four living creatures of verse 4, with "Amen, Hallelujah." Then comes the call from the throne: "Give praise to our God, all ye his servants, ye that fear him, the small and the great." Then follows the most mighty voice of heavenly acclamation in the whole Bible: "The voice of a great multitude" rises like "many waters" and "mighty thunders," saying, "Hallelujah: for the Lord our God, the Almighty, reigneth. Let us rejoice and be exceeding glad, and let us give the glory unto him: for the marriage of the Lamb is come, and his wife hath made herself ready." Through age on age, the heavenly hosts have burned with ever-increasing expectancy toward this culminating day of divine joy!

II. Identifying the Church as the Bride of Christ

1. The Church is the Bride—"The wife"—as seen in:

a. Ephesians 5:23-32. This passage compels this belief. In II Corinthians 11:2, Paul writes, "I am jealous over you with a godly jealousy: for I espoused you to one husband, that I might present you as a pure virgin to Christ."

b. The scene of Revelation 19 of the marriage of the Lamb is wholly *heavenly;* the Bride could not be, therefore, the earthly nation Israel.

c. Israel is both divorced and widowed. She will be Jehovah's restored wife in the thousand years; but not the heavenly Bride of Christ, the Son.

2. Fix in mind the difference between the marriage of the Lamb and the marriage supper of the Lamb. One is the occasion itself, the other the celebration by others than the Bride of the occasion. In the marriage, it is the wife; in the supper, the guests, that are in view.

III. The Marriage Bliss of the Lamb and His Wife

The bliss of the marriage of the Lamb is without limit. It is the PERSONAL DELIGHT of Him who created all things! No other love has the person-toward-person character of marital love. Parents love their children because they are their children. Brothers and sisters alike have a love of natural relationship. Friendships are based on common interests. But the love of bridegroom and bride is a delight each in the person of the other. This is why marital love is so often so wholly unexplainable! We say, "What did he see in her?" or, "Why did she choose him?" There is no answer but one—love. This love of Christ's for His Bride is the love that is "strong as death . . . a very flame of Jah," that "many waters cannot quench," of the Song of Songs (8:6, 7—margin).

Let us dwell upon the words, "Christ also loved the church and GAVE HIMSELF up for it." He values His Bride as Himself. And upon her, He lavishes His personal affection, without limit, constantly, and for evermore! For we read in Revelation 21, after the thousand years have passed, that she is still "as a wife adorned for her husband."

Here then is a marital love, a tenderness, an appreciation, and a delight, *that will grow for ever and for ever.* Oh, wonder of wonders, that such a record can be written! *Christ will never change* in His affections! What must the ages hold for the wife of the lamb!

And the love of that Bride, the wife of the Lamb, will correspond to that of her husband—*unceasing, increasing, for ever and for ever!*

Have you known a husband and wife whose love deepened as the years went by, whose satisfaction with each other was such as to keep them together constantly, of their own *mutual will;* whom neither "society" nor "business," nor outside pleasures could separate? Let such a happy marital existence be *a whisper to you of what*

Christ and the Church will enjoy more and yet more for evermore!

We no longer marvel at the effect upon John the Seer, as he views and tastes in the Spirit the ecstasy of this unutterable occasion. It is a sign of the overwhelming blessedness of the marriage of the Lamb and the festal supper thereafter, that this apostle, who had been on the transfiguration mountain; and had been filled with the Holy Spirit on the day of Pentecost; and had seen the glorious Son of God, and the heavenly throne itself; and all the wonders of the seals, the trumpets, and the vials; and who had heard the thunders of the heavenly hallelu-jahs—that he is now at last suddenly *so enraptured by the bliss* of the Church's coming marriage day that he falls to worship at the feet of the revealing angel!

IV. The Marriage Supper

In Psalm 45:1-5 we have a marvelous description of Christ's second coming as King. He is called "King of kings" in Revelation 19, and here in this Psalm, He is "the King"—"fairer than the children of men." His triumphant advent and victory over His enemies is por-trayed, and His personal majesty and beauty make a glorious and thrilling picture. God the Father is, in verses 6 and 7, speaking to Christ *(compare Hebrews 1:8, 9)*, "Thy throne, O God, is forever and ever . . . God, thy God, hath anointed thee With the oil of gladness above thy fellows." (Here the Bridegroom's companions are seen and then the Bridegroom's personal presence: "All thy garments *smell* of myrrh, and aloes, *and* cassia." Then the gladness and joy of the day to the Lord Himself: "Out of ivory palaces stringed instruments have made thee glad. Kings' daughters are among thy honorable women." (This is a scene, of course, after the Lord and His Bride, the Church, have come down to earth and inaugurated the millennial reign.)

"At thy right hand doth stand the queen in gold of Ophir."

And then this divine word to *her* in that glad day:

"Hearken, O daughter, and consider, and incline thine ear; forget also thine own people, and thy father's house" (the things of the first creation are left behind forever!).

"So will the king desire thy beauty."   ("The king," here, is, Christ, the Husband.)

"For he is thy lord; and reverence thou him."

"And the daughter of Tyre *shall be there* with a gift" —earthly gifts.

"The rich among the people (Israel) shall entreat thy favor"—that is, of the Queen, the Church, in the new Jerusalem, her home *(Revelation 21)*.

"The king's daughter within *the palace* is all glorious": that is, in the new Jerusalem which will be tabernacling *above* the earthly Jerusalem in the 1000 years; and afterward upon the new earth.

"She shall be led unto the king upon broidered work.

"The virgins her companions that follow her shall be brought unto thee.

"With gladness and rejoicing shall they be led:

"They shall enter into the king's palace."

The virgins, her companions, may be represented by the five wise virgins in Matthew 25. We see them again in the Song of Solomon, where the "daughters of Jerusalem" delight in the bride. But those "daughters" are not the bride. The beloved Shulamite, espoused by King Solomon, is the type of the Church as the Bride of Christ in that coming day *(Song of Songs 3:11; 6:8, 9)*. Here we find several companies: *First,* the Bride; *next,* the "guests" at the high festival in heaven; *then,* the "virgins" who enter the marriage feast of Matthew 25:10; *again,* those ready and looking for their Lord "when He shall return *from* the (heavenly) marriage feast," an evidently earthly scene. See the passage in Luke 12:35-40.

We know that some insist the five wise virgins represent the real saints, who are raptured up to the heavenly marriage feast; that the "foolish virgins" are not "known" by Christ, and so represent unsaved professors; and that this marriage feast the five wise enter (inasmuch as but one marriage feast seems to be described), may be the heavenly feast; and that the "ten virgins" parable is surely meant to instruct and warn all who profess to belong to Christ.

However, the festivities of our Lord's coming back to earth, described in Psalm 45 as following the Great Day of Wrath, certainly constitute a celebration as well as a prolongation of marriage bliss and joy, consequent upon the marriage of the King. The earthly and Jewish character of Matthew's gospel, together with the fact that the "ten virgins" scene is evidently connected with our Lord's return to earth and as "Son of man" (Matthew 24:37, 39, 44, and the opening word of Matthew 25, *tote*—"at that time"); considered in connection with the feast and the marriage of Revelation 19, which is not directly connected with Christ's coming, all make me believe that the "ten virgins" enter the celebration after the heavenly marriage and are thus connected with Psalm 45.

V. What Is the Bride's "Making Herself Ready"?

We read, "It was *given* unto her." The preparation for this marriage, "the supreme event for which the ages are waiting," is an absolute *bestowal of divine grace*. It is not, of course, *salvation,* since those who constitute the Bride were saved long before, while on earth. But it is a special *granting from God* to prepare herself for this great climax.

Again, to "array herself in fine linen, bright and pure: for the fine linen is the righteous acts of the saints." The King James version falls utterly short of the meaning, by translating the Greek plural word *dikaiomata,* which means "righteous things" or "acts" as if it were *dikaiosunee,* "righteousness." These bridal saints were declared righteous in Christ *when first they believed.* The bridal array for the wedding, is something absolutely different.

Garments are woven little by little; and thus were woven the materials for her, the Bride of Christ.

The Holy Spirit who indwelt the Church wrought what Paul calls in Philippians 1:11 "the fruits of righteousness, which are through Jesus Christ"; or, as in Ephesians 2-10, "We are his *workmanship,* created in Christ Jesus for good works, which God *afore prepared that we should walk in them.*"

Now, although for our service each one in the kingdom will "receive his own reward according to his own labor," yet all the works wrought through Jesus Christ by the Holy Spirit in and by the saints of the Bride will all belong alike to that holy Bride: for the whole Church is the Bride. Linen represents *manifested righteousness,* and this is *"fine linen, bright and pure."* It has that same "exceeding white and glistering" appearance as her Lord's raiment had on the transfiguration mount—of glory as well as purity.

In other words, the Church will appear, all of it, in raiment wholly befitting Christ, her glorious Bridegroom. She herself had no righteousness; Christ Himself is her righteousness and her standing. She is *one with Him.* But now all those blessed Spirit-led works, those "righteous acts" of the saints while on earth, are wrought to produce an array manifestly befitting the Bride, herself, without "spot, blemish or any such thing"—in this unspeakable scene!

VI. Exactly What Is the Marriage?

Is it not Christ's presenting "the church to himself a *glorious church,* not having spot or wrinkle, or any such thing," described so rapturously by Paul in Ephesians 5? We constantly read in Scripture (where alone we dare read here) of a man *taking* a wife unto himself. We get our attention, at an earthly wedding, fixed on the *ceremony:* forgetting that the real *marriage* is "this man *taking unto him* this woman" to be his wedded wife. The "ceremony" only proclaims and pronounces it; as the wedding feast only celebrates it. The perfect picture of Christ's taking the Church as His Bride is seen in Genesis 24, where Abraham would "make a marriage for his son." He sends Eliezer, his steward, to far Mesopotamia, to find and woo Rebekah by showing her the "things" of Abraham and Isaac (as the Holy Spirit shows us "the things of Christ"); and Rebekah says, "I will go." And then, the journey over, "Isaac *took* Rebekah; and she became *his wife;* and he *loved* her."

CHAPTER XVII

THE GREAT DAY OF WRATH

Revelation 19:11-20:3

I. The Coming to Earth of Christ as KING OF KINGS

And I saw the heaven opened; and behold, a white horse, and he that sat thereon called Faithful and True; and in righteousness he doth judge and make war. And his eyes a flame of fire, and upon his head many diadems; and he hath a name written which no one knoweth but he himself. And he is arrayed in a garment sprinkled with blood: and his name is called The Word of God. And the armies which are in heaven followed him upon white horses, clothed in fine linen, white and pure. And out of his mouth proceedeth a sharp sword, that with it he should smite the nations; and he shall rule them with a rod of iron; and he treadeth the winepress of the fierceness of the wrath of God, the Almighty. And he hath on his garment and on his thigh a name written, KING OF KINGS, AND LORD OF LORDS.

The passage before us, which includes Revelation 19: 11 to 20:3, may be divided as follows:

I. The coming to earth of Christ as KING OF KINGS, and Lord of lords *(Revelation 19:11-16)*.

II. The gathering of the birds to the "supper of God" *(Revelation 19:17, 18)*.

III. The overthrow of Antichrist and his armies *(Revelation 19:19-21)*.

IV. Satan bound for a thousand years *(Revelation 20:1-3)*.

I never heard a sermon on the Great Day of Wrath —did you? Yet the writings of the prophets are full of that very day!

The coming of the Day of Wrath is, as we have found, at the end of the *long-suffering* of God. For centuries of human sin God had *waited*. Even after He proceeds to preliminary judgments, He goes with *slow* steps, as we have seen in the seals, trumpets, and vials. Under these divine strokes, the earth, like Pharaoh of old, hardens itself into utter blasphemy "against God who had the power over these plagues." Now comes the Great Day of God, The Almighty *(Revelation 16:14)*.

We again solemnly urge every believer to study the Scriptures concerning this Great Day of Wrath. It is entirely separate and distinct from the last judgment of the Great White Throne.*

---

*Isaiah 2:12-21; 8:6-10; 24 entire; 30:27, 28, 30; 34 entire; 63:1-6; Ezekiel 32:5-10; Amos 5:18-20; Obadiah 15, 16; Micah 5:15; Nahum 1:2, 5, 6; Zephaniah 1:7, 14-17; Haggai 2:6; Zechariah 14:1-5, 16; Malachi 4, 1.

These are some of the passages of the prophets that look toward this terrible Day of the Lord, when He comes to tread His enemies under foot, according to the Father's appointment. Remove from your mind the thought of mercy in "that day of vengeance of our God." An evil and adulterous generation today hates the thought of judgment. Sin is sweet to them, therefore is the sword of Jehovah bitter. Like King Agag, its prophets and preachers simper to their scripture-ignorant hearers: "Surely the bitterness of death is past" (Samuel 15:32). But the next verse says, "And Samuel hewed Agag in pieces before Jehovah in Gilgal." The false prophets of this hour—all the shallow "advanced" college professors, the wicked well-poisoning modernist horde of lying preachers, the dead denominationalists, content to sit in cushioned pews and pay a fawning puppet to preach inanities that never reach men's consciences: yes—all the false prophets who cry, "Peace, peace," when God warns of the swiftly coming Day of Wrath; and all the Satan-drugged hosts of Christendom, content to hearken to them and lie down to sleep on the edge of the volcano of destruction: let them read such Scriptures as the above! But they will not. In the present day, Jeremiah 5:30, 31 is realized before our eyes: "A wonderful and horrible thing is come to pass in the land: the prophets prophesy falsely, and the priests bear rule by their means: and my people love to have it so: AND WHAT WILL YE DO IN THE END THEREOF?"

The forbearance of God is at last at an end. To prolong it would be to connive at sin! Therefore, God's holy hatred toward sin is unloosed, in all its "fierceness." He will send His dear Son, whom men despised, with the direct commission of utter vengeance! It will be a "winepress"—the bodies of men will be crushed. It is the winepress of wrath: "Who may stand in thy sight when once thou art angry?" It is the winepress of the fierceness of wrath—the words are terrible! And finally, it is "the winepress of the fierceness of the wrath of God the Almighty!" Ah, how feeble are words to portray the unloosed fury of that dreadful day!

I found a great nest of hornets one summer, built upon the cottage porch. I would have been glad to observe their workings from the room within. But no, they challenged my every approach. I had to go in and out of the house by a back door, and even then they were annoying and dangerous. There was no peace; there could be none. After several particularly grievous attacks by these deadly insects, I took a fishing pole, wrapped the tip of it round and round with several yards of muslin, which I tied carefully; then waited night-fall, when the hornets would all be in their nest. I soaked the cloth thoroughly with kerosene and lit it. Then I held that flaming pole beneath that hornets' nest with relentless determination. The insects rushed out to burning and death. I left not one! This earth will have become a nest of hideous hornets against God! And God will clear

1. The Day of Wrath is a *particular* and *distinct* event:

a. It is separated in *time* from the last judgment by a thousand years and a little more (Revelation 20:3, 7, 11).

b. Its *object* is entirely distinct and different from the day of judgment. The latter is to pronounce final and eternal destiny; "books" are opened; inquiries made; exact, judicial sentence pronounced. But the Day of Wrath, which precedes the thousand years' reign of Christ and His saints, is to get the earth cleared up for that thousand years' kingdom.

c. The last judgment comes on only *after* the present heavens and earth have passed away; but the Day of Wrath is an event *on this earth;* the embattled rebels being dealt with in Palestine!

2. The Day of Wrath has *specific characteristics:*

a. It is the *pent-up divine outburst of indignation,* of outraged holiness, majesty, love and truth! The earth will be filled with haters of God, blasphemers of His blessed Name, despisers of His Son. "Therefore saith the Lord, Jehovah of hosts, the Mighty One of Israel, Ah, I will ease me of mine adversaries, and avenge me of mine enemies." His sword shall drink its fill (Isaiah 34:5). "I will also smite and I will cause my wrath to rest."

b. God will thus *answer the prayers of all His saints* for the coming of His kingdom on earth—that His will may be done here as in heaven, where everything is subject to Him. Their prayers finally bring this answer!

All things opposing the establishment of that kingdom must be swept out of the way by the besom of destruction.

Let it be understood that no "moral suasion" whatever is connected with the setting up of the kingdom of God upon this earth. It will be a putting of Christ's enemies under His feet by the stupendous instantaneous exercise of power in wrath. The human will must be

them out! He will leave not one! Not one rebel will be spared (Matthew 13:41, 42). And Christ will strike first at Armageddon.

Gathered about Jerusalem will be "all the nations," in a battle line of 200 miles, from Edom to Carmel (Revelation 14:20; Isaiah 63:1-6). And how our Lord will "strike through kings," and tread down their millions, in that day! (Psalm 110:5, 6).

put down. The Millennium, or thousand years' reign, which follows the Day of Wrath, will be an iron-rod rule. It will be dashing in pieces like a potter's vessel absolutely everything opposed to the will of God on this earth. Rebellion will not be allowed to lift its head.

We must conceive of God as long-suffering, full of compassion, merciful, for wrath is His "strange" action. He postpones judgment for that reason; as we read in Isaiah 28:21: "Jehovah will rise up . . . He will be wroth . . . that he may do his work, his *strange* work, and bring to pass his act, his *strange* act." God is love; that is His name; but His wrath—when mercy is no longer left, when iniquity has filled up its cup—will be all the more terrible. The old proverb, "Beware of the anger of a patient man" illustrates this.

c. God would have His wrath SHOWN *and His power* MADE KNOWN. We know He will do thus *forever* upon the "vessels of wrath" described in Romans 9:22. Therefore, it should not surprise us that at the inauguration of the reign of His Son upon this earth, the fury and fierceness of the anger of God against the finally obdurate, hateful human rebels, who have allied themselves with God's old enemy, Satan, to oppose His dear Son, to keep Him out of His rights, to resist His taking the throne which He purchased with His Own Blood—will burst forth with unrestrained wrath toward His enemies, until they be utterly swept off the earth or entirely subdued.

d. The vast *riddle of permitted evil* will thus be resolved. Things will come to such a pass on this earth that only the intervention of God in wrath will satisfy the public conscience of holy beings.

e. Christ and the heavenly armies are themselves the *executors* in this terrible day of visitation.

3. Mark the four names given to the Lamb on that day:

a. "Faithful and True." By this name He is seen as the Sitter on the white horse, coming from the open heaven. This name reminds us of His earthly life of

faithfulness upon which God bases His exaltation—
(*Psalm 45* and *Philippians 2*). But He is coming now
in righteousness, not in grace. Before, He said He
came not to judge but to save the world; now,
He comes as judge. This great day reveals Him "making
war." Note this: later He will judge the nations, ruling
them with an iron rod, but this is the war of the great
day of God. The struggle will be brief; but remember it is not sessional judgment, but battle.

His eyes are now "a flame of fire";—not merely "like a
flame of fire" (as in Church days: *Revelation 2:18*). As
over against the ten diadems of Antichrist—how briefly
worn!—are "many diadems"—universal dominion—upon
His head.

b. The Unknown Name. It is "written," but He
alone knows it, for is He not God?

c. "The Word of God." Thus is He arrayed in
the blood sprinkled garments of vengeance, according to
the prophetic word. His retinue follow on white horses,
in fine linen, white and pure. It will include all the angels
(*Matthew 25:31*) *and all His saints* (*I Thessalonians 3:
13*). Whatsoever other principalities, powers, thrones,
dominions and "glories" may attend, there will be in-
fintely above all, *"his own glory, and the glory of the
Father" (Luke 9:26)!*

The "sharp sword" is His Word, His *voice*.*

d. Finally, the royal vesture, and the thigh of might,†
marked, "KING OF KINGS AND LORD OF LORDS." How
all earthly royalty and power collapses and withers at this
sight! We shall have occasion to trace further, in looking at the Millennium and its order, the might and glory
of the KING OF KINGS!

---

*Mark the seven occurrences of the words: "voice of Jehovah" in Psalm
29, with the instantaneous might of the effect—for this Psalm is millennial—when "He shall rule them with a rod of iron." This is "the
breath of His lips" that shall slay the wicked (*Isaiah 11:4*).

†The same "mighty One of Jacob," who comes having "KING OF
KINGS" written upon His thigh, in that Great Day of Wrath, to establish
His kingdom, touched Jacob's thigh on the night He wrestled with him
(*Genesis 32*), taking away his carnal strength! "For by strength shall
no man prevail"—"Power belongeth unto God!"

II. The Gathering of the Birds to the "Supper of God"

> And I saw an angel standing in the sun; and he cried with a loud voice, saying to all the birds that fly in midheaven, Come and be gathered together unto the great supper of God; that ye may eat the flesh of kings, and the flesh of captains, and the flesh of mighty men, and the flesh of horses and of them that sit thereon, and the flesh of all men, both free and bond, and small and great.

Flesh, flesh, flesh, flesh, flesh!—five times over! They chose to walk after the flesh spiritually and now their flesh must be devoured literally!

If you ask me how an angel could stand in the sun and speak to earth, I answer frankly, I do not know,—except that it *will* be done. I have often felt that men know little of astronomy, for all their vaunted discoveries. I am certain that they know little of the power of angels "the mighty in strength, that do God's commandments."

Now, behold, the frightful feast on earth,—the birds feasting on those who despised the invitation on high to the marriage supper of the Lamb; both feasts described in this one chapter! What a lesson!

The balance maintained by God in creation is a marvel. "I have created the waster to destroy," God said. If insect or animal pests increase to the point of danger, other creatures are on hand to devour them, which in turn must themselves be devoured, if necessary for man's preservation.

When our Lord described, in Luke 17:34, 35, the snatching away by the angels of those that "caused stumbling and practiced iniquity" in order that those "left" might share His kingdom (Matthew 13:41-43), the disciples inquired about this action, and the scene of it, in the words "Where, Lord? And he said unto them, Where the body *is* thither will the vultures also be gathered together" (Luke 17:37 R.V. margin).

Now we know that when the Lamb in wrath treads the battle line at Armageddon, absolutely millions upon millions pour out their blood in slaughter—even to the bridles of the horses!

This then, in Revelation 19, is a literal call to the birds which feed upon flesh, from all over the earth: *and they come!* It is a literal feast, awful though the scene may be. God's scavengers clean the land completely.

No interpretation is possible for this passage but the literal one: anything else is unbelievable, fantastic. And when we accept it as literal we see the necessity of it. God will not allow His Son's kingdom to begin with a plague, caused by the festering carcasses of slain multitudes.

III. The Overthrow of Antichrist and His Armies

And I saw the beast, and the kings of the earth, and their armies, gathered together to make war against him that sat upon the horse, and against his army. And the beast was taken, and with him the false prophet that wrought the signs in his sight, wherewith he deceived them that had received the mark of the beast and them that worshipped his image: they two were cast alive into the lake of fire that burneth with brimstone; and the rest were killed with the sword of him that sat upon the horse, even the sword which came forth out of his mouth; and all the birds were filled with their flesh.

The description of the great supper by the birds, precedes that of the slaughter of those upon whom they feed, as the closing words of this passage show.

What an array! "The Beast, (the Antichrist) and the kings of the earth" are "gathered together"—not only the Antichrist's allied ten kings, but, deluded by the three unclean spirits of Revelation 16:13, 14 "the kings of the *whole world*" are gathered together "unto the war

of the great day of God, the Almighty." We have already
noted that their headquarters will be at the valley of
Megiddo, called Armageddon, just southeast of Mt. Carmel in Palestine.

There is evidently on the part of these armies, a *knowledge* of Him against whom they are fighting. I believe
that when the heaven is "opened" and the Lamb upon
the white horse and His armies come forth, the scene
is visible from this earth. It is a direct warfare of hell
against heaven. Satan, cast with his millions of angels
out of heaven in his war against Michael and his angels
(chapter twelve), has brought up this false christ with
his false prophet and arrayed the millions of earth's mortals against Michael's Lord and all the hosts of heaven!
What supreme folly! The dragon could not prevail even
against Michael. Now he is trusting the puny arm of
flesh to defy the whole host of heaven, led by the Son
of God Himself! This is the *incurable insanity* of sin,
which wars away in spite of defeat after defeat, against
a holy God!

"The Beast *was taken,* and with him the false prophet."
Against the forward march of the KING OF KINGS there
can be no *struggle,* such as there was when the dragon
warred with Michael in chapter 12. How the beast shall
be "taken" we are not told: the King gives the order,
and immediately occurs the *arrest* of these hellish leaders,
the two men from the lost regions who had been permitted to return to earth to be the accepted leaders of a
Christ-rejecting humanity.

"They two" are cast *alive* into the lake of fire. The
word "alive" here signifies existence in a human body. It
is not only a state of conscious existence; but *life* in a
human body. (The Greek word translated here "alive"
occurs in Acts 1:3; 4:41; 10:42 ("quick"); 20:12; 25:
19; I Thessalonians 4:15, 17.) Our Lord's use of the
word concerning His own life after resurrection is seen
in Revelation 1:18 "I am *alive* for evermore"; in Revelation 20:4, it is used for coming to life in resurrection,

"they *lived,* and reigned with Christ." (These had spirit-existence before.)

Furthermore, this lake of fire into which the Beast and the false prophet are cast (first mentioned here: compare Revelation 20:10, 14, 15; 21:8) is the same as the *Gehenna* of which our Lord warned the Jews in Matthew, Mark and Luke and through the apostle James.*

This is proved by comparing Matthew 25:41 with Revelation 20:10.

It is of immeasurable importance just now, that believers should become established concerning the nature and eternity of future punishment; also as to the distinction of Sheol (Hades) from the lake of fire; and of the literal character of the latter.†

The fearful fact that these two men in human bodies *(Mark 9:43-48)* are found in the lake of fire *after* the thousand years *(Revelation 20:10)* and are to be tormented ceaselessly there forever, should sober all our thoughts. When sin becomes absolute, it will bring absolute punishment, and that eternal.

Note that the "rest" of this vast horde of millions gathered against Jerusalem are slain directly by Christ: "With the breath of his lips shall He slay the wicked" (Isaiah 11:4—a kingdom passage).

And now, as the closing scene of the present order, behold the millions upon millions of flesh-eating birds clearing away the carcasses of the rebels against God and against Christ! One vulture or two feeding on some fallen creature is a hideous sight to our eyes. What, then, will be this awful line of corpses, of two hundred miles, covered with countless hosts of scavengers! Re-

---

*See Matthew 5:22, 29, 30; 10:28; 18:9; 23:15, 33; Mark 9:43, 45, 47; Luke 12:5; James 3:6.

†J. N. Darby's tract on "Eternal Punishment"; F. W. Grant's book, "Facts and Theories as to a Future State"; Sir Robert Anderson's "Human Destiny" are excellent (although Mr. Grant yields to the common absurd cry that the *fire* of hell may represent something "more terrible." R. A. Torrey's words on hell, in "What the Bible Teaches," are true and searching. The best thing we have ever seen on the subject is the booklet, "Life and Death" by C. J. Baker, obtainable from Pickering and Inglis, London, England; and Moody Colportage Association, Chicago.

flect anew on what sin brings! This scene will come to pass!

IV. Satan Bound for a Thousand Years

And I saw an angel coming down out of heaven, having the key of the abyss and a great chain in his hand. And he laid hold on the dragon, the old serpent, which is the Devil and Satan, and bound him for a thousand years, and cast him into the abyss, and shut it, and sealed it over him, that he should deceive the nations no more, until the thousand years should be finished: after this he must be loosed for a little time.

This imprisonment of the great enemy is the closing scene connected with the Day of Wrath; and, we may say, the opening scene of the coming age—the Millennium.

1. How completely God has removed the enormous power of this fallen head of the cherubim *(Ezekiel 28:14)* is seen in the fact that *"an angel"* chains him—not even Michael, the archangel, is needed, but simply "an angel." What humiliation! The host of fallen *angels,* together with the *demons* and the world of *men,* during the preceding three and one-half years, had bowed to Satan; now "an angel" lays hold on him and fastens upon him a great chain! Again, as in Revelation 12:9—four names are designated: "the dragon"—that is, his hideous, *murderous* character before God; "the old serpent"—the ancient *deceiver of angels* first, and later of men; "the Devil"—the *slanderer (diabolos),* the accuser of the saints; and "Satan"—the great *adversary* of God, His Son and all His people.

2. He is bound for a thousand years, sentenced for this definite period—which, of course, will be the Millennium: we must remember that his presence and influence upon the earth will not in any sense be felt during that one thousand years! Praise God!

3. He is cast into the *abyss;* that is, the pit in the heart of the earth. Compare Matthew 12:40 with Romans 10:7; also with our notes on Revelation 9:1, 2. Afterwards he will be cast into the lake of fire, which is outside this earth entirely, when the present heaven and earth shall have passed away. The "shaft" to the abyss spoken of in Revelation 9:1 is *sealed.* He is shut within it—shut in his prison; giving relief to earth, release from all his deceits!

4. The fact that he must be loosed "for a little time after the one thousand years" should give us no surprise—for God would give the human race a final chance after Christ's reign, to *choose!* One thousand years with Christ and His saints over them in peace; then the decision: will they have *this* Man to rule over them? or will they choose the great enemy again? We shall see.

CHAPTER XVIII

SATAN BOUND, THE MILLENNIUM

Revelation 20:4-10

The Thousand Years' Reign

And I saw thrones, and they sat upon them, and judgment was given unto them: and I saw the souls of them that had been beheaded for the testimony of Jesus, and for the word of God, and such as worshipped not the beast, neither his image, and received not the mark upon their forehead and upon their hand; and they lived, and reigned with Christ a thousand years. The rest of the dead lived not until the thousand years should be finished. This is the first resurrection. Blessed and holy is he that hath part in the first resurrection: over these the second death hath no power; but they shall be priests of God and of Christ, and shall reign with him a thousand years.

I. What the Thousand Years' Reign Is

The thousand years' reign is the direct administration of divine government on earth for one thousand years by our Lord and His saints. Its earthly center will be Jerusalem and the nation Israel, though Christ and His saints will rule in heavenly resurrection bodies in the New Jerusalem and will take the place now occupied by angels (*Hebrews 2:5-8*). Satan, as we have seen, will be in the abyss during the thousand years; and his "host of the high ones on high" will be "prisoners gathered in the pit, and shut up in the prison" during that time (*Isaiah 24:21-23*).

Just as the affairs of the world at present are directly, though unconsciously, controlled by Satan and his host (under the permission of God, but interfered with from time to time by holy angels sent of God, as in Daniel 10), so Christ and His saints will rule during the thousand years; generally, doubtless, invisible to the eyes of men whom they control. Yet the glory of the Lord will be seen by all flesh *(Isaiah 40:5)* and most wondrously and constantly over the temple at Jerusalem *(Isaiah 4:5)*.

II. Object of the Thousand Years' Reign

1. *Looked at from God the Father's side:*

a. It will be the public earthly honoring of His Son just where men dishonored Him on this earth and at Jerusalem. It will be part of the literal fulfilling of such passages as Philippians 2:6-11: Christ became "obedient even unto death . . . wherefore also God highly exalted him . . . that in the name of Jesus every knee should bow."

b. It will be the carrying out of God's promises to His Son, and the prophecies concerning Him, to "give unto him the throne *of his father David*"—in Jerusalem *(Luke 1:32)*.

"Ask of me, and I will give *thee* the nations for thine inheritance, And the uttermost parts of the earth for thy possession. Thou shalt break them with a rod of iron; Thou shalt dash them in pieces like a potter's vessel." "Sit thou at my right hand, Until I make thine enemies thy foot-stool. Jehovah will send forth the sceptre of thy strength out of Zion: Rule thou in the midst of thine enemies" (Psalms 2 and 110). It will be God's setting His King (Christ) upon His holy hill of Zion, in restored Jerusalem.

c. It is the final divine trial of sinful man on this earth before the earth is destroyed. The trial of man began in Eden; it continued from the fall to the flood; it proceeded at the Babel dispersion; it was continued publicly, though on a limited platform, in Israel under the law; upon Israel's breakdown, power was given to the Gentiles, from Nebuchadnezzar on. Gentile rule having been abolished at Christ's second coming, Satan and his host being imprisoned, the trial of humanity continues for a thousand years, the question being, Does man *desire* God's righteous rule? God would have all eternity know that the human race, whose head was Adam the First, not only did not in themselves achieve a righteous and benevolent rule or government of themselves, but did not *desire* such a rule, when executed in all honor and glory under Christ the Last Adam's direction!

Men claim that they are seeking, evermore, a "perfect form of government"; but that they are not at all seeking such a government, but that they actually *hate* it, will will be evidenced by their instant revolt to Satan's banner when he is loosed for a "little season" after the Millennium. For we shall find the hordes of mankind rushing up to overthrow the righteous and benevolent reign of Christ at Jerusalem! The deepest sentiment of the natural heart *is enmity against God;* and this fact God will have brought out so thoroughly that there will never be a question again concerning the wisdom of taking governmental affairs out of unregenerate man's hands, and placing them absolutely in Christ's, who shares it with His saints.

d. It will be God's answer (so far as is possible before the *new* earth) of the prayers of His saints: "Thy kingdom come, thy will be done on earth as it is in heaven."

The Millennium will, of course, be a *mixed* state of things, in that, although curtailed greatly, both sin and death will be on earth *(Isaiah 65:20).*

2. *Looked at from Christ's side:*

a. He receives, after long patience, the kingdom of this this world which He has been constantly "expecting," there at God's right hand *(Hebrews 10:12, 13).* And He will reign in that righteousness which He has loved *(Psalm 45:6, 7).*

b. At last He will be able to confer upon the meek of the earth the place and inheritance He ever loved to promise them! They shall "inherit the land, and shall delight themselves in the abundance of peace" *(Psalm 37:11; Matthew 5:5).*

c. He will share, with that infinite generosity and gladness to which His infinitely gracious heart moves Him, all His kingly honors with His saints!

3. *Looked at from the saints' side:*

a. The Millennium brings the three classes of saints, (named in Paragraph III following) and also earthly Israel, into a state of indescribable blessedness! That iniquity is at last put down; righteousness enthroned, and a *beloved Redeemer* reigning—this fills the cup of joy for Christ's own!

b. The very physical changes made in the earth—the razing of the mountains, the elevation of the valleys, the changes in Palestine *(Zechariah 14:9,10)*, the blossoming of the desert *(Isaiah 35:1-7)*; the specially built "highway," and the way, called the "way of holiness," traveled only by earth's redeemed *(Isaiah 35:8-10)*, all these reveal a little of the loving care God will have taken for the comforts and joys of His earthly saints at that blessed time!

4. *Looked at from the side of the nations, the peoples of the earth:*

a. It will be a thousand years under an *iron-rod scepter. Unregenerate* man, having proved wholly unfit for "liberty," will find it forever removed from him.

b. Yet there will be *peace* at last among the nations—enforced certainly, but real.   The one who rode into Jerusalem at the triumphal entry "shall speak peace unto the nations: and his dominion shall be from sea to sea, and from the River to the ends of the earth" (Zechariah 9:9-11). This "Ruler," born in Bethlehem, shall be "great unto the ends of the earth.   And this *man s*hall be *our* peace" (Micah 5:2-5). This "child born," this "Son given" —"the government shall be upon his shoulder . . . his name shall be called Wonderful, Counsellor, Mighty God, Father of Eternity, Prince of Peace. Of the increase of his government, and of peace there shall be no end, upon the throne of David, and upon his kingdom. . . . The zeal of Jehovah of host will perform this" (Isaiah 9:6, 7).

c. All nations will be compelled to go up from year to year to worship the King, Jehovah of Hosts, and to keep the feast of tabernacles. Most of the people of the earth will be yet unregenerated: for, time after time, in the book of Psalms, we read that because of *the greatness of His power,* His enemies shall *yield "feigned obedience" (Hebrew, lie)* unto Him. The prophetic portions of the book of Psalms will then be fulfilled: for the Psalms are millennial, and primarily concern Israel and their Messiah-King.

For example, see the King coming (Psalm 45) with His Bride and His mighty ones; the remnant of Israel trusting through all the upheavals of mountains, islands, and seas of the tribulation time until the King comes to make "wars to cease" (Psalm 46); the jubilation of Israel over the arrival of the "great King over all the earth" to whom "the princes of the peoples are gathered together *to be* the people of the God of Abraham" (Psalm 47); and the glorious establishment of the temple on Mount Zion in Jerusalem delighted in by Israel, and wondered at by the nations (Psalm 48). *(Compare Isaiah 2:2-4.)*

5. *Looked at from the side of "creation":*

a. The creation was "subjected to vanity, not of its own will," but through Adam's sin, which involved even the *ground* in a curse *(Genesis 3).* It was God who thus subjected it, looking forward to the day "the creation itself also shall be delivered from the bondage of corruption into the liberty of the glory of the children of God" *(Romans 8:20-22).*

b. At the "revealing of the sons of God," at Christ's coming back to earth, this deliverance will be effected. The whole land of Israel, from the Euphrates to the Nile, will be completely delivered: "The wolf and the lamb shall feed together, and the lion shall eat straw like the ox; and dust shall be the serpent's food. They shall not hurt nor destroy in all my holy mountain, saith Jehovah" *(Isaiah 65:25).* Indeed, the following passage seems to indicate that *all the earth* will be delivered: "for *the* earth shall be full of the knowledge of Jehovah, as the waters cover the sea" *(Isaiah 11:9).* What a marvelous prospect! Habakkuk 2:14 tells us that it will be "the knowledge of *the glory* of Jehovah" that will thus fill the earth. Man, with his littleness, will at last be nothing;

"Jehovah alone will be exalted in that day" *(Isaiah 2:12-22)*—a passage that should be read often in these bragging days of puny man!

6. The Millennium will be the time predicted by our Lord in Matthew 5:18: "Till heaven and earth pass away, (which they do at the end of the 1000 years) one jot or one tittle shall in no wise pass away from the law, till all things be accomplished." All those infinitely wise, just, and kind provisions set forth in the ordinances, statutes, precepts, and judgments of the law given by Moses, will be put into effect. Israel, then an "all righteous" nation *(Isaiah 60:21)*, will have the law in their hearts—*loving* it, and in their minds—remembering it.

III. The Order of the Thousand Years

1. Christ will be here in person—King over all the earth. He will sit "a priest upon his throne" *(Zechariah 6:13)*. This is the fulfilment of the Melchizedek priesthood. Howbeit, it must be remembered that our Lord has a glorified body, while the saved remnant of Israel, and also, as I see it, the faithful Israelites raised when our Lord returns, will all have flesh and blood bodies—as earthly people.

2. While Christ Himself, as Israel's Messiah, will thus be King over all the earth, and be seen "in his beauty" at Jerusalem in the millennial temple (Isaiah 33:17, 22), yet it will be on the Sabbaths (after the "six working days") and on special feast days that He will thus be seen by Israel (Ezekiel 43:7; 44:2; 46:1-3) : but David himself will be the prince whom God will raise up from the dead for this high honor (Ezekiel 37:24, 25; 34:23, 24; Jeremiah 30:9; Hosea 3:5). We must not confuse in our minds this situation. We must believe the plain words of God. David is not the Son of David. Christ, as Son of David, will be King; and David, His father after the flesh, will be *prince,* during the Millennium. See Ezekiel 46:4-12—the special worship and walk of the prince.

3. The Church will reign with Christ in glorified bodies like His *(I Corinthians 6:2, 3)*. The Church, evidently, is the *first* class of the *three* mentioned in Revelation 20:4: "I saw thrones, and they sat upon them." There is no account of resurrection; for they were caught up at the end of chapter 3 of Revelation. (We do not believe that they are the twenty-four elders who are seen only in connection with the heavenly throne and the four living ones.) It will be remembered that the twelve apostles will sit on twelve thrones "judging" the twelve tribes of Israel *(Luke 22:28, 29)*. They will, it seems, in a beautiful way, be the connecting link between the heavenly Church and the earthly Israel!

The Church, in heavenly bodies *(real* bodies, of course, like Christ's), will not interfere with the earthly order of Israel any more than God's angels interfered with the Davidic kingdom in former days. *Judgment,* and not the mere execution of it, will belong to—be "given to"— the Church.

4. The *second* class seen in Revelation 20:4, is, "the souls of them that had been beheaded for the testimony of Jesus, and for the word of God." These are, evidently, the martyrs under the fifth seal of Revelation 6:9. They are not the Church. They are, we believe, the martyrs coming after the rapture of the Church and before the class last noticed. Also, the word "beheaded" indicates the revival of the Roman Empire method of execution. These martyrs now receive their resurrection bodies, for the words "they *live,*"* must refer to bodily resurrection, and to that only.

---

*Alford truly says, "If, in a passage where two resurrections are mentioned—where certain souls lived, at first, and the 'rest of the dead' lived only at the *end* of a specified period, *after* that first—the 'first resurrection' may be understood to mean a 'spiritual' rising with Christ, while the second means a *literal* rising from the grave, then there is an end of all significance in language, and Scripture is wiped out as a definite testimony to anything. If the first resurrection is spiritual, then so is the second,— but if the second is literal, then so is the first, which, with the whole primitive church, I do maintain."

Stuart says, " 'They lived' means they revived, came to life, returned to a life like the former one, *viz.,* a return to a union of soul and body."

Elliott says, "The resurrection spoken of *(here in Revelation 20:4)* corresponds in every case to the death out of which it was a revival."

Bengel says, "The first resurrection is a corporeal one. Therefore, the dead 'became alive' in that part in which they were dead or mortal, consequently in their body."

5. The *third* class who reign with Christ are "such as worshipped not the beast," which plainly identifies them as saints from The Great Tribulation time. They either pass through those awful three and one-half years, or are martyred. They receive resurrection bodies now to reign with Christ the thousand years.

Thus we are prepared for the great unfolding of verse 5: "The rest of the dead lived not until the thousand years should be finished." "The rest of the dead" are the lost, whose spirits are imprisoned in Hades, in the earth's center, till after the thousand years.

IV. The First Resurrection

1. We have been constantly told by our Lord and His apostles, as well as in Daniel 12, that there will be two resurrections of absolutely different character—one "of the just," and the other "of the unjust." Unto this glorious consummation — this "out-resurrection from among the dead"—Paul's whole spirit was eagerly striving. And it should be the daily, hourly anticipation of every Christian heart *(Philippians 3:8-11)*.

2. Those partaking in the first resurrection are called "blessed"—which denotes their state of grace from God; and also "holy"—which sets forth their separate character and walk when on earth. Over such, the second death is declared to have no authority *(exousia)*. The believer is not subject to judgment in the sense of endangering his eternity *(John 5:24 and 3:18)*.

Their reign partakes of the Melchizedek character of Christ's throne. The expression "of God and of Christ" is remarkable. Perhaps light is shed upon it by Revelation 1:6: "He (Christ) made us a kingdom, priests unto his God and Father." It is the business of priests to carry on for others "the things pertaining to God" *(Hebrews 2:17 and 5:1)*. This opens a wonderful subject!

And when the thousand years are finished,
Satan shall be loosed out of his prison, and
shall come forth to deceive the nations which

> are in the four corners of the earth, Gog and
> Magog, to gather them together to the war:
> the number of whom is as the sand of the sea.
> And they went up over the breadth of the
> earth, and compassed the camp of the saints
> about, and the beloved city: and fire came
> down out of heaven, and devoured them. And
> the devil that deceived them was cast into the
> lake of fire and brimstone, where are also the
> beast and the false prophet; and they shall be
> tormented day and night for ever and ever.

Here we see the Devil loosed after the thousand years
of imprisonment, and immediately rushing back to his
old task of deluding earth's inhabitants to that "war"
against God, to which the "enmity against God" of the
"mind of the flesh" was ever prone, but for which, during the thousand years, leadership was lacking.

"Over the breadth of the earth" the Satan-led hosts
come against "the camp of the saints" (the Church above
Jerusalem) and the beloved city—Jerusalem itself.

Now at last, the patience of God being exhausted, and
the malignity of man fully demonstrated, fire from God
descends and devours earth's wicked hosts: thus ending
forever the sinning human race!

Then we see the execution of the long prophesied
doom of the damned. Antichrist and his lieutenant will
have been in this fearful literal lake of fire and brimstone *alive* (*i.e.* in a human body) for 1,000 years (*Revelation 19:20*). They are seen, yet in torment. Now the
Devil, the great deceiver, is cast into this same literal
lake, into that "eternal fire which is prepared for the
devil and his angels," of which our Lord warned in
Matthew 25:41.

It is, therefore, most fitting, indeed *necessary*, that this
revelation of the appalling doom of Satan and his two
chief human agents should immediately precede the account of the casting into that same lake of fire of those
responsible creatures who reject their God—of all *choosing sin as their portion.*

CHAPTER XIX
THE GREAT WHITE THRONE JUDGMENT
Revelation 20:11-15

And I saw a great white throne, and him that sat upon it, from whose face the earth and the heaven fled away; and there was found no place for them. And I saw the dead, the great and the small, standing before the throne; and books were opened; and another book was opened, which is the book of life; and the dead were judged out of the things which were written in the books, according to their works. And the sea gave up the dead that were in it; and death and Hades gave up the dead that were in them; and they were judged every one according to their works. And death and Hades were cast into the lake of fire. This is the second death, even the lake of fire. And if any was not found written in the book of life, he was cast into the lake of fire.

1. The great white throne is not dispensational or governmental in any sense, but a final, personal, eternal assize.

This is evident from the fact that the whole present creation completely disappears before the Sitter upon this throne! It is also abundantly confirmed by the silence of those judged. They are not actors in any sense. Finally, the sentence from this throne is eternal.

Let us distinguish therefore the Great White Throne judgment from all those dealings with His enemies which God has heretofore had; as for instance, at Armageddon. Hitherto God's enemies, though vanquished, have been permitted the opportunity to oppose Him, even after such an iron-rod order as the Millennium. Eternal, final action has not been taken against those who remained unregenerate upon earth.

2. The Great White Throne judgment is not what we upon earth call a trial. Not one of the judged is asked a single question, for the facts are all in! And the "works," (upon which judgment must be based always) are all written in the "books." Thoughts also are known —even "the secrets of men," all have been recorded.

3. Only one inquiry is made—Is the name in "the book of life"? Judgment indeed proceeds: the "dead" are judged "out of the things which were written in the books, according to their works": for there are degrees of guilt. But THE DETERMINING QUESTION IN EVERY CASE WILL BE, IS THE NAME IN "THE BOOK OF LIFE?" We cannot emphasize too strongly that this judgment is NOT AT ALL A TRIAL; but a Great Public MANIFESTATION of FACTS SETTLED BEFOREHAND, and RECORDED.

Let us now proceed to examine this brief but truly stupendous account of the last judgment.

A Great White Throne.

Distinguish this from all other aspects of the divine throne; whether of Revelation 4 and Daniel 7, or of Isaiah 6, Ezekiel 1, I Kings 22:19, or Exodus 24:9-11.

Weigh each word: *Great,*—it is the Infinite before whom the finite must stand; *White,*—it is the unveiled, undimmed blaze of the divine holiness and purity and justice; *Throne,*—it is majesty unlimited, in which inheres utter right to dispose of the destiny of creatures. Before such a throne, creatures cannot stand; but they *shall* stand—even the lost!

Him that sat upon it.

We must, in view of John 5:22, 27, believe that Christ, the Son, to whom all judgment and the execution thereof has been committed, is the Sitter on this awful throne. But we cannot avoid the feeling that all the Persons of the Godhead are there! It is God as He is, in infinite, holy and eternal majesty; although unto Christ, because He is the Son of man, the actual judging and execution of judgment has been committed by the Father.

The simplicity of the description makes the scene indescribably awful. *Eternity* is involved therein! The
thought is appalling—to face the unapproachable LIGHT
of God's presence—UNFORGIVEN!

**From whose face the earth and the heaven fled away;
and there was found no place for them.**

It is no place here for impotent unbelief in its fearful-
ness to begin to plead that these plain words indicate
merely a purging of the earth by fire. Peter declares,
"The earth and the works that are therein shall be burned
up." Our Lord plainly says, "Heaven and earth shall
pass away." Paul declares, "The things which are seen
are temporal; but the things which are not seen
are eternal." And again, "Yet once more will I
make to tremble not the earth only but also the heaven.
And this word, "Yet once more, signifieth the removing
of those things that are shaken, as of things that have
been made, that those things which are not shaken may
remain. Wherefore, receiving a kingdom that cannot be
shaken, let us have grace." The "kingdom" referred to,
does not include the old material earth and the heavens,
which pass away, but our new bodies like Christ's, and
such dispensation of all things new which God shall
create after the old has forever passed away!

To hold on to this old earth when God says it will
"flee away" and "no place be found for it," is to become
first cousin of the pagan who holds the eternity of matter
in the past, and also is of one piece with the legality
that professes to be justified by faith but must hold on
to Moses as "a rule of life." The Reformation theology will not consent that our history was ended at Calvary, thus freeing us from the "bond that was against
us" forever. In like manner this same theology is afraid
to face eternity with no earth to stand upon and no
heavens to look to, but only the throne of God left! It
is thus unprepared for "the all things new"—even the
"all" of the material as well as the spiritual existence
of the new creation of Revelation 21. The Lord Jesus

came and "stood in the midst, the doors being shut," and said, "See my hands and my feet . . . handle me, and see; for a spirit hath not flesh and bones, as ye behold me having. . . . Have ye here anything to eat?" Only *faith* looks with joy (though mixed with astonishment) on such a scene. Only faith can receive such words as, "I saw a new heaven and a new earth: for the first heaven and the first earth are passed away." It is unbelief which says that the earth remains, although "its characteristics are changed by fire."

And I saw the dead, the great and the small, standing before the throne.

These, we believe, are all unsaved people:

1. In verse 6, we find (by implication) that the second death has *authority* (R. V. margin) over those not in the first resurrection: which would surely put them in jeopardy.

2. Our Lord definitely declares (John 5:24) that those hearing His words and believing Him that sent Him, *have* eternal life, and are *not coming into judgment,* but have passed *out of death into life.* "He that believeth on him, *is not judged*" (John 3:18).

3. With regard to eternal destiny, *only two resurrections* are known in Scripture. "The resurrection of life; and the resurrection of judgment" (John 5:29, Acts 24:15, Daniel 12:2).

That these "dead" have received their bodies when they stand before the Great White Throne, is evident from Revelation 20:5. For we know, from other Scriptures, that their spirits were existing in Hades all this time. And the words, "they lived" can then be applied to them only as to their bodies; just as the same words are spoken of the martyrs of verse 4, "They lived, and reigned with Christ." We know that certain of these martyrs' souls were seen under the altar at the opening of the fifth seal of Revelation 6:9-11 where they not only were conscious, but knew what was going on on the earth; but had not yet received their bodies.

And books were opened.

If judgment of any creature is to proceed, it must be according to what he has done—his "works." The works of those judged are evidently fully recorded. God will have a record even of the thoughts of every creature, whether its nature is clear to us or not—it will extend to the utmost particulars. At least, it will be in accord with the memory of the creature. It is a well-attested fact that every action and thought is recorded in the memory of man, however unable he may be to "recollect" a matter at will. In that day, God judges "the secrets of men," and men will know those secrets to be theirs, their very own *(Romans 2:16)*.

And another book was opened, which is the book of life.

The question arises, "What book is this?" Is it the "Lamb's book of life" of 21:27; 13:8 and 17:8? The answer is that only those who *belong to Christ,* given by the Father to Him, are saved. Only such are in *that* book!

Christ is seen in charge of this book in Revelation 3:5. If there are false professors who have "escaped the defilements of the world through the acquaintanceship *(epignosis)* of the Lord and Saviour Jesus Christ," who having known "the way of righteousness, turn back"; or rocky-ground hearers who "receive the word with joy" but have "no root," who "for awhile believe, and, in time of temptation fall away"; who "taste (but do not drink), the heavenly gift" (eternal life), and then "fall away"; then the thought of being blotted out of the "book of life," (seen also in Exodus 32:32, 33, Psalm 69:28), should not be in any wise a stumbling-block. Judas Iscariot was "numbered" among the twelve apostles, but "he fell away and went to his own place."

In Psalm 69:25-28, which Peter quotes in Acts 1:20 as referring to Judas, (and which the context shows includes those wicked in Israel who joined then in hating Christ): "Let them be blotted out of the book of life,

and not be written with the righteous." In these awful
words we see that though Christ "gave himself a ransom
for *all*," and "tasted death for *every* man,"—thus giving
to the whole race of mankind a potential place in the book
of life: yet this fact does not constitute them "written
with the righteous" eternally. In fact there is both the
"blotting certain out" from connection with "the book of
life," and the refusal to write them with "the righteous."
They had refused Him who is "the propitiation for the
sins of the whole world": so that they lose that potential
ransom-benefit all men had; and will never be "written
unto life." (See Isaiah 4:3 and Daniel 12:1.) It seems
plain that "the Lamb's book of life" contains only elect
names,—"Those found written in grace's book."

There is the mystery of the sin of man which chooses
to apostatize, but there is also the mystery of the grace
of God which preserves the elect.

God does not want any true believer to lack assurance
of eternal safety. Christ said: "I give my sheep eternal
life and they shall never perish." But let us insist on
that other mark of Christ's sheep: "They follow me."
If we are going on in our own way, then what right have
we to assurance? Remember the "seal" of the "foundation of God," in II Timothy 2:19: "The Lord knoweth
them that are his: and, Let everyone that nameth the
name of the Lord depart from unrighteousness."

> **And the sea gave up the dead that were in
> it; and death and Hades gave up the dead
> that were in them.**

Now Death holds the bodies and Hades the spirits of
the lost of the human race. Those drowned at sea are
not different from those dying in any other manner.
Death holds their bodies and Hades their spirits if they
are unsaved. Therefore, the dead who are in the sea,
appear not to be human dead. Satan, whose doom is
described in verse 10, was not a man, but was the
anointed one of the cherubim (Ezekiel 28). In the following passage from the prophet, we find two classes

of beings and also two distinct points of time: "In that day, (at Christ's coming to earth) Jehovah will punish the host of the ones on high, and the kings of the earth upon the earth. And they shall be gathered together, as prisoners are gathered in the pit, and shall be shut up in the prison; and after many days shall they be visited" (Isaiah 24:21, 22). This passage seems to teach plainly that Satan's host will be judged at the great white throne judgment—after the "many days" of the Millennium. Part of his host is the demons, who seem to be the disembodied spirits of a former creation. It has been believed by many excellent students of God's Word that the sea is connected with Satan's host. (See Pember's "Earth's Earliest Ages.")

And death and Hades were cast into the lake of fire.

This is a literal fulfilment of the prophecy in Hosea 13:14, "I will ransom them from the power of Sheol: I will redeem them from death: O death, I will be thy plagues: O Sheol, I will be thy destruction; repentance shall be hid from mine eyes." Death is personified because it has a personal character. We have elsewhere remarked that Death is more than mere dissolution, more than the separation of spirit and body. Because Death in Revelation 20:14 is said to be "cast into the lake of fire," it does not for a moment permit us to consider this awful lake as unreal. This monster, this first Death, is, together with that horrible jail, Hades, cast as things hateful to God into a place of eternal wrath. It is a guarantee to all holy beings that sin will never be allowed to invade God's new creation. (This passage is difficult. I know I have not sounded its depths. I would be thankful for further light upon it.) Of one thing I am certain: It is that this lake of fire and brimstone does not and cannot lose in the least, its *terrific literality*, from this or from any other passage!

They were judged everyone (Greek, ekastos, each) **according to their works.**

To translate this "every *man*," is to interpret, not translate. God said "each": which may apply to any, and must apply to every being who stands before that awful throne that day, whether man, angel or demon.

This is the second death, even the lake of fire.

The very brevity of this verse is one of the elements of its awfulness. The finality and eternity of this unspeakable doom—how they should be *preached* and *cried aloud* these days! It is not love, or faithfulness, to avoid them because they are such terrible facts. God described creation itself (Genesis 1:1) in seven Hebrew words. Here is described in ten Greek words, a doom that will never end!

For, inasmuch as this is the "fire . . . prepared for the devil and his angels," we need only to refer to verse 10 to see the state of those who will be cast into that lake of fire:

1. They are "tormented." This is consciousness and anguish.

2. It is "day and night"; that is God's description of ceaselessness.

3. It is "unto the ages of the ages," God's technical term (from Galatians 1:5 on), for unendingness, whether of God's own existence or the blessed reign and glorified state of His saints *(Revelation 22:5);* or the punishment of the wicked.

And if any was not found written in the book of life, he was cast into the lake of fire.

Let us mark certain facts here:

1. It is not the absence of good works in the book that dooms a person. It is the absence of his *name.* Only names, not works, are in that book!

2. It is not the fact of evil works. Many of earth's greatest sinners have their names in the Book of Life.

3. All whose names do not appear in the Book, are cast into the lake of fire.

4. All names there found in that day, will have been written before that day. There is no record of anyone's name being written into the Book of Life upon that day, but rather the opposite: "If any was not found written." How overwhelmingly solemn is this!

CHAPTER XX

THE NEW CREATION

Revelation 21:1-8

And I saw a new heaven and a new earth: for the first heaven and the first earth are passed away; and the sea is no more. And I saw the holy city, new Jerusalem, coming down out of heaven from God, made ready as a bride adorned for her husband. And I heard a great voice out of the throne saying, Behold, the tabernacle of God is with men, and he shall dwell with them, and they shall be his peoples, and God himself shall be with them, and be their God; and he shall wipe away every tear from their eyes; and death shall be no more; neither shall there be mourning, nor crying, nor pain, any more: the first things are passed away. And he that sitteth on the throne said, Behold, I make all things new. And he saith, Write: for these words are faithful and true. And he said unto me, They are come to pass. I am the Alpha and the Omega, the beginning and the end. I will give unto him that is athirst of the fountain of the water of life freely.

Three great passages, Isaiah 65:17; 66:22; II Peter 3:10-13 and the present Revelation passage, deal with this stupendous subject, the new creation. The definite and repeated statements that the old earth and heaven "flee away," "pass away with a great noise," and are "burned up"; together with the statement that "there was found no place for them," compel the conclusion that those who argue that these words indicate only a "cleansing by fire" and not actual eternal dissolution and disappearance, shrink from the *searching realities* of this subject. The word "create" is a solemn word to modify or trifle with! We know that *create* in

Genesis 1:1 cannot mean anything but the calling into existence of that which did not before have being *(Hebrews 11:3)*. And certainly Revelation 21:1 is just as new a beginning!*

The words, "Behold, I make all things new" must be taken literally. It is not that things are "changed" or "purified." The very *laws of material being* must be included in the new creation. Our Lord entered and stood in the midst, "the doors being shut," and said, "Handle me, and see; for a spirit hath not flesh and bones, as ye behold me having." And our bodies are to be like unto His. In Isaiah 65:17 God says, "I create new heavens and a new earth; and the former things shall not be remembered, nor come into mind." In the more than one hundred and twenty Bible occurrences of the word "create" or its cognates, I can find no hint of any meaning except *origination* of things. There is no thought of a former creation, changed or cleansed.

Furthermore, this Revelation 21:1 plainly discriminates the two creations, in that one must pass away before the other appears.

The matter thus lay also in the mind of our blessed Lord who said: "Heaven and earth shall pass away, but my word shall not pass away." To one of the simplicity of a child, all these Scriptures convey nothing else than the complete disappearance of a former creation

---

*The searching words of Govett need to be weighed here:

"Many will not accept the Scripture doctrine of utter destruction of the old globe. What the reason is, is perhaps hard to say, but most will with earnestness contend that the fire will only purge the world, not destroy it. Perhaps this is owing to the felt connection between the entire destruction of man's abode and the eternal suffering of the wicked. With some it arises from fancied scientific reasons: 'matter cannot be annihilated.' True, man cannot annihilate it, but cannot God? Did He not bring it into existence out of nothing? Can He not hurl it again into nothingness? This answer often brings out into view the fact that many do not believe in *creation;* they believe that God did *not* make all things out of nought. He only 'framed them out of pre-existent matter.' Such are indeed consistent: but they are opposed to the glory of God and to the testimony of His Word. Moreover, the apostle argues that the prophecy in Haggai foretells the final shaking of heaven and earth preparatory to their entire removal; in order that the new creation may supersede them *(Hebrews 12:26-28)*.

"If any further proof were needed, the words of the passage in Revelation 20:11 are evidently designed to furnish it. The result of the passing away of the heaven and earth is that, 'there was found no place for them.' How this can consist with their atoms being remolded and constituting the place in which the redeemer shall live, would puzzle the acutest to discover."

and the appearing by the Word of God of a material creation absolutely new. Even the resurrection of the body does not prove the eternal existence of matter already created. We read, "That which thou thyself sowest is not quickened except it die: and . . . thou sowest not the body that shall be, but a bare grain . . . but God giveth it a body even as it pleased him." The former grain was gone and dead. The germ of life (a profound and undying mystery!) sprang up.

It is certain that the redeemed will retain and possess forever the memory of that former sinful state in the first Adam out of which God in grace redeemed them; but that is no argument for the perpetuation of the old Adam—rather the opposite!

For this is the great mystery of the cross: that there God secured the transference righteously of His saints from that Adam in which they were born into the Last Adam and the new creation. Their guilt was put away, and they being identified with Christ, died with Him and thus were brought to an end as to their history in Adam the first.

Then God, having raised up Christ as the "first born from the dead," "made us alive together with Christ and raised us up with him."

Now before this history, we are called "separate from Christ, having no hope," etc. But God *now* says concerning us we are "God's workmanship, CREATED in Christ Jesus"!

That which is now true of us as spirits (for that which is born of the Spirit is spirit) will, when Christ comes, become true of us as to our bodies.

The fact that our Lord passed through doors, though in a body of "flesh and bones," reveals that He was in that realm where all things are new, even the *laws of existence and substance,* as well as of action.

We dwell on these things because this hanging on to the old creation, admitting only that it is to be *"cleansed by fire"*; this claiming that "pass away" does not mean disappear, but merely be "changed," and that God's statement that the "earth and the works that are therein" will be burned up does not carry its simple and full meaning, but means only the clearing off the earth of its present order, the marks of sin, etc.,—all this we cannot but associate with the desperate effort of the legalists to hold on to Moses. They will, for instance, acknowledge justification by faith; but they must have the law as the "rule of life." In other words, they will not consent to Calvary's being *the end of their history;* with *only Christ* to stand in and to glory in forever. Like Agag, they come whining, "Surely the bitterness of death is past."

But we cannot but feel the *power* of the words, "I create new heavens and a new earth"!

Creation unto new creation becomes thus the phrase that spans the Bible.

The first creation was the sphere and scene of what God calls "the first things." Sin, beginning in heaven and with the highest of the creatures, challenging the will of the Creator as the creature's highest good, came in to mar, ruin, and wreck the first creation. Now comes at last, based upon Christ and His work, a wholly new creation which will never pass away, and in which the apostle Peter announces that "righteousness will be *at home*" *(II Peter 3:13, Greek)*. Even the *temptation* to evil will be eternally absent, for every opportunity of rebellion against the rule of the Most High will have been thwarted, every such rebellion having been proved by experiment disastrous to the creature, as well as dishonoring to the Creator.

The Two Final Classes

He that overcometh shall inherit these things; and I will be his God, and he shall be my son. But for the fearful, and unbelieving, and abominable, and murderers, and fornicators, and sorcerers, and idolaters, and all liars, their part shall be in the lake that burneth with fire and brimstone; which is the second death.

While those who chose darkness and evil deeds are indeed seen in this final state, it is as eternally separated from holy beings, and under divine indignation (Revelation 21:8). There is no longer any danger of invasion, either from former evil, or from temptation or trial in any sense whatever to God's holy ones. Not only is evil no longer triumphant, as at present, and in the days of Antichrist, and even, though checked, during the thousand years' reign; but there is complete, deep, final rest from it! And will not that be a glad day!

And, be it noted, the only two classes seen in this final eternal order are those who *overcome,* and those *cast into the lake of fire.* The "overcomers," thus, are shown to be *all God's true children.* For all had the divine gift of *faith,* all were *begotten of God.* So we read in I John 5:4: "Whatsoever is begotten of God overcometh the world: and this is the victory that hath overcome the world, even our faith."

CHAPTER XXI

THE NEW JERUSALEM

Revelation 21:9-22:5

And there came one of the seven angels who had the seven bowls, who were laden with the seven last plagues; and he spake with me, saying, Come hither, I will show thee the bride, the wife of the Lamb. And he carried me away in the Spirit to a mountain great and high, and showed me the holy city Jerusalem, coming down out of heaven from God, having the glory of God: her light was like unto a stone most precious, as it were a jasper stone, clear as crystal: having a wall great and high; having twelve gates, and at the gates twelve angels; and names written thereon, which are the names of the twelve tribes of the children of Israel: on the east were three gates; and on the north three gates; and on the south three gates; and on the west three gates. And the wall of the city had twelve foundations, and on them twelve names of the twelve apostles of the Lamb. And he that spake with me had for a measure a golden reed to measure the city, and the gates thereof, and the wall thereof. And the city lieth foursquare, and the length thereof is as great as the breadth: and he measured the city with the reed, twelve thousand furlongs: the length and the breadth and the height thereof are equal.

1. It is a *literal city,* the materials, dimensions, appearance, appointments, inhabitants, divine glory and indwelling, and eternity of which are all distinctly declared.

2. It *descends from God out of heaven.* It is that *better country and heavenly* for which Abraham and the patriarchs looked. It is that *place prepared* for God's

saints. "He hath prepared for them a city" *(Hebrews 11:16)*.

3. It will be peculiarly *the home of the Church,* the Lamb's wife *(Ephesians 5:27-32);* others will be there, and many will have access *(Revelation 21:24-26);* but the Church will be as the wife in the home.

4. It will be *vast indeed:* a cube of at least fifteen hundred miles each way *(Revelation 21:16).* Much, indeed all, of our conception of that city must be in the realm of faith—along with that of our father Abraham, who "looked for the city which hath the foundations, whose architect and maker is God."

5. It will be *lighted directly by the presence and effulgence of God.* This is thrice stated:

a. In chapter 21:11, the city has "the glory of God" with a light (or luminary) in consequence "like unto a stone most precious, as it were a jasper stone clear as crystal";—this is its effulgence—its appearance from without.

b. Revelation 21:23—"no need of sun, neither of the moon, . . . for the glory of God did lighten it, and the lamp thereof *is* the Lamb." We are here *within* the city, walking "in the light of God," constantly conscious that Christ is the channel of all blessing to us. That *the Lamb is the lamp* is the secret and the source of the unspeakable blessedness of those who walk there! What a sense of redeemedness; of being beloved even as Christ, and of fathomless depths of eternal security!

c. Revelation 22:5—"night no more; and they need no light of lamp, neither light of sun; for the Lord God shall give them light: and they shall reign unto the ages of the ages." Note three elements here:

(1) No more dependence on creature or mediate light.

(2) The immediate light constantly from God, Himself.

(3) Their "reigning" thus *forever!* That "reigning in life," which began when they first believed *(Romans*

5:17) is now at last consummated; and is eternally perpetuated.

And he measured the wall thereof, a hundred and forty and four cubits, according to
the measure of a man, that is, of an angel.
And the building of the wall thereof was
jasper: and the city was pure gold, like unto
pure glass. The foundations of the wall of the
city were adorned with all manner of precious
stones. The first foundation was jasper; the
second, sapphire; the third, chalcedony; the
fourth, emerald; the fifth, sardonyx; the sixth,
sardius; the seventh, chysolite; the eighth,
beryl; the ninth, topaz; the tenth, chrysoprase;
the eleventh, jacinth; the twelfth, amethyst.
And the twelve gates were twelve pearls; each
one of the several gates was of one pearl: and
the street of the city was pure gold, as it were
transparent glass. And I saw no temple
therein: for the Lord God the Almighty, and
the Lamb, are the temple thereof. And the
city hath no need of the sun, neither of the
moon to shine upon it: for the glory of
God did lighten it, and the lamp thereof
is the Lamb. And the nations shall walk
amidst the light thereof: and the kings of the
earth bring their glory into it. And the gates
thereof shall in no wise be shut by day (for
there shall be no night there): and they shall
bring the glory and the honor of the nations
into it: and there shall in no wise enter into it
anything unclean, or he that maketh an abomination and a lie: but only they that are written
in the Lamb's book of life. And he showed
me a river of water of life, bright as crystal,
proceeding out of the throne of God and of the
Lamb, in the midst of the street thereof. And
on this side of the river and on that was the

tree of life, bearing twelve manner of fruits,
yielding its fruit every month: and the leaves
of the tree were for the healing of the nations.
And there shall be no curse any more: and the
throne of God and of the Lamb shall be therein:
and his servants shall serve him: and they
shall see his face; and his name shall be on
their foreheads. And there shall be night no
more; and they need no light of lamp, neither
light of sun; for the Lord God shall give them
light: and they shall reign for ever and ever.

6. It will be a *new city*—corresponding with a new
heaven and a new earth. Many have taught that during
the thousand years it will be suspended over the earth.
Many hold also that Revelation 21:8 is the end of the
progress of the Book; while 21:9 on through chapter
22:5 turns us back to millennial times. They compare
this passage with chapter 17:18, which describes in greater
detail the character and overthrow of Babylon the great,
although that overthrow really occurred in the preceding
chapter (16:19).

Those who hold that Revelation 21:1-8 describes the
eternal state while Revelation 21:9 to 22:5 reverts to millennial times, because we read in 21:24-26 that "the nations shall walk amidst the light thereof" the kings of the
earth bringing "the honor of the nations into it"—seem
to overlook several important points:

a. In chapter 21:3, where we read that the tabernacle
of God is at last "with men," we also read that "they
shall be his peoples" (Greek *laoi*). It is amazing to
find discerning men apparently almost wilfully translating the plural *laoi,* as if it were *laos.* Alford reads,
" 'they shall be his people': plural, because as in
verse 24, many nations shall now partake in the
blessed fulfillment of the promise." But for this very
reason he should have translated *laoi, "peoples,"* faithfully, that is, *literally: "peoples,"* not *"people."* Seiss,
even in his "revised text," reads, "God shall taber-

nacle with the men, or *mankind* (?) and they shall be his *people,*" etc. The Revised Version, which so many affect to despise, translates truly and plainly, "They shall be his *peoples,*" and thus prepares us to avoid the impossible assumption that 21:9 to 22:5 is a passage that reverts to millennial scenes.

b. We know positively that at least *one* nation and *one* seed, ISRAEL, will belong upon the new earth. In Isaiah 66:22 we read, "As the new heavens and the new earth, which I will make, shall remain before me, saith Jehovah, so shall your seed and your name remain." This is *eternity* for national Israel, and no escaping it! Because Isaiah 65:17, 18, which belongs to the new creation, has been confused with the millennial verses (20-25) men have rushed to the conclusion that all that Isaiah says concerning the new creation is millennial. But God says Israel's "seed and name" shall *remain,* in the new heavens and earth, that is, in that new order beginning in Revelation 21:1. But in this new order, we are distinctly told "death shall be no more," whereas, in Isaiah 65:20, "the child shall die a hundred years old."

Now, Israel is God's elect nation—elect not for the past, or even through the millennial age, but *forever.* Yet, if Israel be the elect nation, the existence of other nations is presupposed! You reply, "Were not nations the result of God's judgment at Babel?" They were, doubtless. But God, when He acts in grace, is evermore bringing good out of man's evil! When Adam sinned, Christ, as the Seed of the woman, was first announced. When Israel asked for a king, God, after Saul's rejection, brought in *David,* in whom He lodged the royal Messianic counsels for all time to come. When Israel crucified their Messiah—the highest act of sin— God brought forth "abundance of grace" through Him who "tasted death for every man."

At Pentecost, salvation was announced to every nation in its own tongue. Grace came to the nations without destroying or changing national existence, or even national individuality.

The prophet Zephaniah *(3:9)* indeed tells us of a coming day, when, saith Jehovah, "I will turn to the peoples a pure language, that they may all call upon the name of Jehovah, to serve him with one consent." The word "language" here is in Hebrew *lip,* as it is in Genesis 11:1. But that *national* existence will not cease, is shown clearly by verse 20 of the same chapter: "At that time will I bring you (Israel) in, and at that time will I gather you; for I will make you a name and a praise among all the *peoples* (plural!) of the earth."

c. Finally, the language of the first 5 verses of chapter 22 of The Revelation, and especially of verses 4 and 5, is just as eternal in its character as anything at the beginning of chapter 21. "The throne of God and of the Lamb shall be therein: and his servants shall serve him; and they shall see his face; and his name *shall be* on their foreheads . . . and *they shall reign unto the ages of the ages.*" Why should such statements be connected with a passage that is meant merely to go back and describe millennial conditions? That would be incongruous. Furthermore, it is not in keeping, we feel, for the Scripture to go back after the *last judgment* has been held, and *the new creation* has come in, to times before that last judgment and new creation!

7. The new Jerusalem is the *capital city of God*—the place of the divine presence and government of the universe. "The throne of God and of the Lamb shall be therein" (22:3). No other or further throne than this is described in the Word of God. As we have seen, various phases and aspects of the divine majesty have heretofore been exhibited in Scripture. Now it is "forever and ever." Note that it is "the throne of *God* and of the *Lamb.*" *Christ,* who delivered up the kingdom to God, yet shares that throne, as the One who redeemed these now blessed creatures unto God. The Redeemer abides in view of His people as the sacrifice and priest. In each view of the city,

the Lamb is named. Seven times does the word occur in connection with the new Jerusalem *(21:9, 14, 22, 23, 27; 22:1, 3)*.

God's Eternal Plan Was to Be "With Men"

His *"delight* was with the sons of men" *(Proverbs 8:31)*. Man was made in God's "image" and "likeness." Doubtless we will never know all that these terms mean! God was manifest in the flesh in Christ, the Son of man. Jesus, though crowned with glory and honor, remains man forever.

What the "delight" of God will be in this new earth "with men," and what their capacity for knowing God, and progressing in that blessed and only real knowledge, can be measured only by eternity, and the infinity of God Himself; which is to say, it is utterly without limit! Marvelous and yet reasonable fruit of "the redemption that is in "Christ Jesus," who "suffered for sins . . . that he might bring us to God." Note the words "with men," "with them," "with them"—three times in one verse (21:3). Pause now, and consider this long and well.

It is astonishing, and yet should not be so, that there is no mention after Revelation 21, of those blessed beings previously seen as accompanying the throne of God: cherubim, seraphim, living ones, elders: it is now simply "the throne of God and of the Lamb." Not that those others are not there. They are, and are in ecstatic, eternal delight that God is revealed at last as they could not as mere creatures ever know him: as the blessed One who is LOVE. Those beings knew His eternity, His power, His holiness, and His Glory; and celebrated these attributes constantly—as in Revelation 4:8-11 and Isaiah 6. But now God's heart goes fully out. He has, through infinite sacrifice, "brought many sons unto glory," to be "conformed to the image of his Son, that he might be the firstborn among many brethren." Not only to these, the "church of the firstborn," but to the various peoples of this new earth, His love is now, without limit, extended; and will be extended forever and ever. And in this will all holy beings find endless joy.

"LOVE IS OF GOD." We can scarcely write here for awe and wonder! How should her Creator say to the Bride: "Thou hast ravished my heart, my sister, my bride; Thou hast ravished my heart with one look from thine eyes." "Turn away thine eyes from me, For they have overcome me."

Oh, how little do we know our God! How small is our widest thought of Him! Do we not see this great Bible He has given us going right forward against all obstacles, over all mountains, through all valleys, yea, to Gethsemane and Calvary—to come to this sweet, eternal consummation, *that God may be WITH MEN, THEIR GOD?* that He may wipe every tear from their eyes, that He may banish into the far forgotten past, mourning, crying, and pain; and say, *"Behold, I make all things new"?* For GOD IS LOVE!

Let this thought overwhelm us as we turn to the closing chapters of The Revelation, that while God's lovingkindness is "over all his works," it is never said in Scripture that God LOVED any but *man!* John, who writes this closing book of God's blessed Word, cries, "We know and *have believed* the *love* which God hath *in our case.* God is love" *(I John 4:16).* Let us, too, know it and believe it; and thus enter by faith this glorious new creation scene; bending low under this weight of glory, though yet we tread this earth. Let us know this love that passeth knowledge, and, breathing the fragrant air of the city of God, walk daily through its gates of pearl and walk by faith its golden streets, *"giving thanks unto the Father, who made us meet to be partakers of the inheritance of the saints in light."*

NOTE ABOUT THIS HEAVENLY JERUSALEM

I. It is a Literal City.

II. Its Object and Destiny.

III. Its Relation to the New Earth.

IV. The Blessedness of Its Dwellers.

We do well to return again and again to Revelation 21 and 22, for it is the end of the pilgrim path. The more distinct the vision to the pilgrim of the beauty and glory of the city to which he journeys, the less the immediate environments of his journey attract him.

I. It is a Literal City

1. Because of the literalness of its description. If gold does not mean gold, nor pearls—pearls, nor precious stones —stones, nor exact measurements—real dimensions, then the Bible gives nothing accurate nor reliable. There is no one on earth who can assure your heart concerning the meaning of these "symbols"—if they are symbols! Nowhere in God's Word, for instance, is there any account of the "symbolism" of precious stones. Twelve such stones are found in the high priest's "four-square" breastplate *(Exodus 28:15-21)*: sardius, topaz, carbuncle, emerald, sapphire, diamond, jacinth, agate, amethyst, beryl, onyx, jasper—"inclosed in gold in their settings. And the stones shall be according to the names of the children of Israel, twelve . . . like the engravings of a signet, every one according to his name, they shall be for the twelve tribes." No one doubts that these were literal stones, nor do we doubt that God has a special reason for assigning to each tribe a peculiar stone. Some time it may be revealed what these stones mean, and whether they have any connection with the foundations of the New Jersualem; but to deny that they are literal stones in The Revelation, and to admit them as literal in Exodus, is not only absurd, but unbelieving.*

2. A second reason to consider the city a literal one, is, that child-like faith in reading the account always regards it as such. As the little girl asked her mother concerning

---

*There have been many interesting, though not always profitable, investigations and surmises concerning these precious stones. Perhaps the most instructive remark I have found is made by J. N. Darby (Synopsis, *in loc*):- "The precious stones, or varied display of God's nature, who is light, in connection with the creature (seen in *creation*, Ezekiel 28; in *grace* in the high priest's breastplate) now shone in *permanent glory*, and adorned the foundations of the city."

the preacher who said that our Lord's words in John 14, "I will come again," did not mean that He would come back in *person:* "Mamma, if Jesus did not mean what He said, why *didn't* He say what He *meant?*"

3. Abraham and the patriarchs "looked for a *city*"— not a state of mind! The sublime faith of Abraham led him to leave a city in the most remarkable civilization known on earth, and become a stranger and pilgrim, caring only for a cave in which to bury his dead; 'For he looked for *the city* which hath the foundations, whose architect and maker is God"! Abraham will be satisfied with nothing short of a *place,* such as he looked for. And God will not disappoint him!

4. In all other parts of the Bible, simple faith in God's statements is asked from man; why not then in Revelation 21, *of all places,* here *at the end* of God's book? "Wherefor do questionings arise in your heart?" the Lord asked, when He presented Himself in a risen body in the upper room. If reasonings and doubts of the reality and literalness of His body were excluded, *then,* when the human mind would *naturally* be astonished; how much less now can questionings and doubts be admitted as to the literalness of the marvelous city of Revelation 21, which is to be the *eternal home* of our Lord's *risen body,* and that of His saints in *glorified bodies* like unto His!

5. If the New Jerusalem is not to be taken literally, we can not claim that the millennial Jerusalem of Ezekiel 40-48 and Zechariah 14 can be literal. But to deny these is wholly to abandon faith in the accuracy of God's Word!

6. In this book of The Revelation, the former Jerusalem is literal *(11:8);* and also Babylon the Great *(18:10).* Indeed both Jerusalem (the "great city"), and Babylon, were the objects of the last fearful earthquake of Revelation 16:19. Just as the old *earth* which disappeared was literal, and the new *earth* which takes its place is literal and substantial, *so also must the New Jerusalem be.*

7. The unfolding of divine things in the Bible is pre-

cisely contrary to the idea that in order to have "spiritual-ity," material things must be left behind.

God was revealed to the patriarchs' faith without a defi-nite place of abode or habitation. Then, in the wilderness, the pillar of cloud and fire accompanied His visible dwell-ing-place, and both the tabernacle and the temple were so filled with His glorious presence, that, for the moment, the priests themselves, "could not stand to minister"! Also we are told that Jehovah *chose* Jerusalem, and Mt. Zion therein, because He loved it *(Psalm 87:2; 78:68; 132: 13, 14)*.

Then, so far from the progress of God's revealing Him-self to man taking on more and more ethereality, the con-trary is seen, for God "was manifested *in the flesh"* when Christ came! Immanuel is, *God with us:* i.e., *God present here,* in the Person of that babe of Bethlehem! This of course is what the Devil hates. "Many deceivers are gone forth into the world, *even* they that confess not that Jesus Christ cometh *in the flesh.* This is the deceiver and the antichrist" *(II John 7)*.

Even in the thousand years, the children of Israel are told: *"Thine eyes shall see* Jerusalem a quiet habitation . . . Jehovah will be with us in majesty . . . *thine eyes shall see* the king in his beauty; they *shall behold* a land of far distances." How beautiful these things to simple faith, and what a denial of the vagaries of those deluded souls who connect sin with matter as a necessity! The only log-ical "spiritualizers" that I know of are the Christian Scientists—which are neither Christian, nor scientific! The old Manichaean heresy governs millions who call them-selves Christian, though it is a Satanic lie, and pagan, and utterly anti-Biblical. The Bible leads on to *a literal and blessed home* of the redeemed, possessed of bodies like Christ's body—real and holy, incorruptible, immortal!

8. It is therefore wicked and harmful to permit our-selves to drift into that weak apprehension of future reali-ties expressed in many hymns, and much loose preaching and speaking of these days. What right have we to thoughts of "going to heaven," merely, concerning those

who "fall asleep"? God says they have departed to "be with Christ" (Philippians 1:23), or "to be at home with the Lord" (II Corinthians 5:8).*

It is sad to find, from a devoted pen like Cowper's:

> "Then in a nobler, sweeter song
> I'll sing they power to save.
> When this poor lisping stam'ring tongue
> *Lies silent in the grave!*"

How much better to sing:

> "When this poor lisping stam'ring tongue
> *Hath triumphed* o'er the grave!"

But it is even more distressful to hear real Christians using blinded, demoralized, worldly expressions concerning a believer's falling asleep: such as "he passed on," "he is gone into the unknown," etc.

Now while we may not be certain that the New Jerusalem is yet *opened* to the saints (for that event, perhaps, is reserved for Christ's second coming, and for His saints in *redeemed bodies)*, yet surely we should have that City constantly before us as a reality; and remember that those that have gone to be with Christ are simply swelling the great expectant throng, whose eager hope looks forward to that blessed day of glory and joy when they shall enter in through the gates into that ineffably blessed City!

Meanwhile, the saints are "with Christ." Paul, in II Corinthians 12, "was caught up into Paradise (to the third heaven) and heard unspeakable words, which it is not lawful for a man to utter."

Evidently he was given to taste the infinite joy of what is coming.

What a company is gathering yonder!

Some believe that the marriage of the Lamb will mark the Bride's entrance into that city.

---

*Paul says in II Corinthians 5:4, that the Christian's hope is not to be *unclothed*, that is, *disembodied*, but "clothed upon, that what is mortal" (mortal and immortal always being spoken of of the *body*) "may be swallowed up of life." He is simply *willing* rather than to be absent from the body, and to be at home with the Lord (*R.V.*). It might, indeed did, become Paul's lot. But it is not the proper Christian hope, which is the *redemption of the body* at Christ's coming.

At all events, remember that it is *a literal city* to which you are going. There cannot be anything else meant!*

II. Its Object and Destiny

It is the eternal dwelling place, "habitation," of God—Father, Son and Holy Spirit. Although only "God and the Lamb" are named, yet we know from the Scriptures, and from this very book of Revelation, that the blessed Spirit administers eternally that glorious state of which the Father is the Author and the Son the Source.

In other parts of Scripture, as we have noted before, various aspects of God's throne are displayed: in connection sometimes with the expression of His character, or being, as the Holy One; sometimes with the execution of His government; sometimes with the form of His perpetual worship—as in the progressive perpetual tenses of Revelation 4:9, 10.

But God's *home* is never spoken of until the New Jerusalem comes on the scene. Heretofore, it had been written: "Heaven is my throne, and the earth is my footstool" *(Isaiah 66:1)*. To Israel in the wilderness, through Moses, Jehovah had indeed said, "Let them make me a sanctuary, that I may dwell among them," and it was done. Yet he dwelt in thick darkness, and judgments had to be executed from time to time upon that unbelieving and wilful generation: so that finally, as we read in Ezekiel 8:6 (and in all the prophets) they drove Him away from His sanctuary—as they did afterwards His Son when He sent Him to them.

But now all is over. Redemption has been accomplished—the thing dearest to God's heart—that which for all eternity reveals Him as Infinite. God is love, and yet absolutely righteous; *the Lamb slain* and now risen and abiding in that city, becomes throughout the new creation the eternal proof and utterance of all God is!

---

*Alford well remarks: "As in our common discourse, so here with the evangelist, the name of the material city stands for the community formed by its inhabitants. But it does not follow, in his case, any more than in ours, that *both material city and inhabitants* have not a *veritable existence*. Nor can we say that this glorious description applies only to *them*" (and not to the literal city).

It will also be the capital city of the new creation, for we read, "the throne of God and of the Lamb shall be therein." Nor is any other center of the divine manifestation and government hinted at in this closing book of the things that are revealed. We are indeed told three times in The Revelation, that the New Jerusalem "cometh down out of heaven from my God" *(3:12; 21:2, 10)*. But this describes its double character from God—divine in its origin, and also heavenly. "It might have been of God and earthly; or heavenly and angelic. It was neither: It was divine in origin, and heavenly in nature and character." (Darby.) This perhaps is the full meaning of the words: "from God."

On the other hand, there remains this question: Is there to be a manifestation of the glory of God, and a seat of His government belonging to heaven, while this New Jerusalem, located upon the new earth, governs only the affairs of the new earth?

Several considerations lead us toward the conclusion that the New Jerusalem is God's one eternal resting place.

1. Immediately we see the new heaven and new earth and the New Jerusalem descending to the new earth *(21:1, 2)*, we are told, "Behold, the tabernacle of God is with men"—the former heaven and earth having disappeared. The object of the new heaven and earth is to bring about this—*that God shall eternally have His home* in this capital city of the new creation!

2. No other eternal habitation of God is seen than this of the New Creation's capital! Always before, God was in heaven and man upon earth. Now that this city has come down, created by God for His dwelling, we cannot conceive of His *real* presence and worship being elsewhere!

3. This heavenly city has *the glory* of God *(21:11, 23; 22:5)*. It is the home of Him who "dwelleth in light unapproachable." It is not that this city has glory given to it; it *has* God's glory: for He is there! The glory is the effulgence of His Being!

4. It also has the *throne* of God, and that "service" of 22:3, properly called priestly service, or spiritual worship —(*latreia: Hebrews 9:1; Romans 12:1; Philippians 3:3; Revelation 7:15*).

5. "They shall *see his face*." Here at last God, who is Love, reveals Himself to the saints of that blessed city *directly*. There is no temple, no form, no distance. This, therefore, must be the place of God's rest forever!

6. We need only to remember that the dwellers in the New Jerusalem "shall reign unto the ages of the ages" *(22:5)*. This could not be written of others than the inhabitants of the capital of the new creation!

III. Its Relation to the New Earth

In the thousand years' reign of Christ and His saints upon the old earth *(Revelation 20:46)*, Christ and His heavenly saints formed a "camp" above the old Jerusalem *(Revelation 20:9)*, and Gog and Magog, the hosts of earth, were led by Satan into its final rebellion against the reign of Christ and His glorified saints in the "camp" above Jerusalem, and the earthly Jerusalem itself, "the beloved city." It seems wrong to assume that the New Jerusalem has come down so that the nations "walk amidst the light thereof," as in the new earth *(Revelation 21:24)*. For, although Christ and His glorified saints will have taken over the control of affairs, such as angels now exercise *(Hebrews 2:5-8 R. V. margin)*, yet it is to the earthly Jerusalem and the nation of Israel that God will directly subject the nations of the earth in the Millennium (Isaiah 60; 61:4-9; but especially 4:5, 6). This is the glory of Jehovah revealed upon the earthly Jerusalem, and to it, during the Millennium. The effect of this unveiling of the divine glory in the thousand years is seen in Micah (7:16, 17): "The nations shall see and be ashamed of all their might. . . . They shall lick the dust like a serpent; like crawling things of the earth they shall come trembling out of their close places; they shall come with fear unto Jehovah our God, and shall be afraid because of thee." Psalm 72:9 declares: "His enemies shall lick the dust"! *"Kings, kings, kings,"* are men mentioned in the next two verses; while *kings* will lick the dust of Israel's feet, according to Isaiah 49:23. It is a day of *iron-rod rule;* of compelled subjection. The very atmosphere is different from that of Revelation 21; when, down to the new earth, wherein righteousness is at *home—(II Peter 3:13 Greek)* this New Jerusalem will come from God to be planted upon her eternal foundations, and to become the glad center of *attraction* unto the kings and nations of those happy days.*

It has impressed me more and more that the New Jerusalem will not be in sight of the old earth during the Millennium, which will be a highly judicial time—a time of military rule, the holding of a position already conquered. At the Millennium's beginning, peace and prosperity on earth will be conditioned on complete *subjection.* Consequently the heavenly saints constitute a "camp," evidently above the earthly Jerusalem. Upon that earthly city and upon redeemed Israel, the glory of God will be seen, Israel's twelve tribes being "judged" by the twelve apostles *(Luke 22:28-30)* including Matthias *(Acts 1:21-26).*

When the thousand years, and the last judgment are over, and the new heaven and the new earth have succeeded the old, then, and not until then, does the New Jerusalem come down *to* the new earth.

IV. The Blessedness of Its Dwellers

Of the blessedness of those who dwell in that eternal city of infinite beauty and delight, who shall speak! It is enough to repeat: "They shall see His face; and His name *shall be* on their foreheads."

---

*It has been well remarked by Govett: "That the eternal standing of the city is in question, I gather from 22:3: 'There shall be no more *curse.*' Now at the close of the Millennium comes the most fearful sin, and wrath of God, with the second death. Again, *entrance into* the heavenly city would not be possible during the Millennium; for then the city is only suspended over the earth. It does not come down upon it. To meet this difficulty, the holders of the opposite view translate Revelation 21:24-26, 'bring their glory *unto it,*' not *into* it. But this translation is unfounded, for, whenever a verb of motion capable of signifying penetration, or entrance into, a penetrable subject, such as a river, house, etc., is followed by the preposition *eis,* 'into'—there *entrance* is affirmed."

Of even the inhabitants of the new earth, though not of the new city, it is written: "The tabernacle of God is with men, and he shall dwell with them, they shall be His peoples, and God himself shall be with them . . . their God: and he shall wipe away every tear from their eyes; and death shall be no more; neither shall there be mourning, nor crying, nor pain, anymore: the first things are passed away."

But to *see His face,* and to be so wholly His in likeness that *His Name shall be on our foreheads*—what a destiny! It is even more eagerly to be anticipated, than the reigning eternally!

"THE JERUSALEM THAT IS ABOVE"

Jerusalem the golden,
  With milk and honey blest,
Beneath thy contemplation
  Sink heart and voice opprest:
I know not, O I know not
  What social joys are there;
What radiancy of glory,
  What light beyond compare!

For thee, O dear dear country,
  Mine eyes their vigils keep;
For very love, beholding
  Thy happy name, they weep:
The mention of thy glory
  Is unction to the breast,
And medicine in sickness,
  And love, and life, and rest.

O one, O only mansion!
  O Paradise of joy,
When tears are ever banished,
  And smiles have no alloy!
The cross is all thy splendor,
  The Crucified thy praise;
His laud and benediction
  Thy ransomed people raise.

O sweet and blessed country,
  The home of God's elect!
O sweet and blessed country
  That eager hearts expect!
Jesus, in mercy bring us
  To that dear land of rest,
Who art, with God the Father
  And Spirit, ever blest.

Bernard of Cluny—12th century.

Lo! what a glorious sight appears
  To our admiring eyes!
The former seas have passed away,
  The former earth and skies.

The God of glory down to men
  Removes His blest abode;
He dwells with men; His people they,
  And He His people's God!

Isaac Watts—1674-1748.

Jerusalem, my happy home,
  Name ever dear to me,
When shall my labours have an end
  In joy and peace, and thee?

When shall these eyes thy heaven-
    built walls
  And pearly gates behold,
Thy bulwarks with salvation strong,
  And streets of shining gold!

Joseph Bromehead—1748-1826.

For ever with the Lord!
  Amen, so let it be:
Life from the dead is in that word;
  'Tis immortality.
Here in the body pent,
  Absent from Him I roam,
Yet nightly pitch my moving tent
  A day's march nearer home.

My Father's house on high,
  Home of my soul, how near!
At times, to faith's foreseeing eye,
  Thy gates of pearl appear!
Ah! then my spirit faints
  To reach the land I love,
The bright inheritance of saints,
  Jerusalem above!

James Montgomery—1771-1854.

CHAPTER XXII

CLOSING MESSAGES
Revelation 22:6-21

We are now come to the closing words of this great book of prophecy, The Revelation; and, inasmuch as God ordered the arrangement of the books, they are also the closing words of the Bible.

We shall find exactly what we would expect to find: (1) The Lord giving His seal to the inspiration, authority, and absolute verbal accuracy of all things written in this book. (2) A solemn warning, therefore, against tampering in any way with its contents, either by addition or subtraction. (3) The bringing to the front finally, as was done in the closing books of the Old Testament *(Zechariah 14; Malachi 3 and 4)*, of that great event which is the chief subject of prophecy—the Lord's own personal return to earth.

> **And he said unto me, These words are faithful and true: and the Lord, the God of the spirits of the prophets, sent his angel to show unto his servants the things which must shortly come to pass. And behold, I come quickly. Blessed is he that keepeth the words of the prophecy of this book.**

The speaker here is Christ Himself *(Compare verses 10, 16, 18, and 20)*. In whatever manner the revealing angel is used to convey the utterances (as in chapter 19:9, 10, etc.), the author is the Lord, as is evident in the words "I come quickly"—thrice repeated in this passage—*(verses 7, 12, 20)*. Furthermore, the words "sent his angel" is not *"has* sent," as a reporting angel would speak accrediting himself, but the historical tense as of the sender, Christ, Himself accrediting the agent.

Perhaps no book of the Bible has been more neglected, despised, added to and subtracted from, than this same book of The Revelation. Therefore, both the faithfulness and truth of the Author are again and again announced, whether by saints *(15:3)*, or heavenly beings *(16:7)* or by angels *(19:9; 22:9)*. But, also, in an even more emphatic way, the *very words* of this great book are over and over sealed as "faithful and true": by God *(21:5)*, by the Holy Spirit *(1:10, ff)* and here in the closing chapter no less than *five times* by our Lord Jesus Christ Himself *(verses 7, 10, 16, 18, 20)*.

We naturally and necessarily connect the close of this great book with its beginning (22:6 and 1:1): "the things which MUST shortly come to pass." Also, we are bowed with awe at the title and actions of Deity in our blessed Lord. For in 1:1 it is Christ who "sent and signified by His angel"; in 22:6 it is "The Lord, the God of the spirits of the prophets sent his angel"; and He sets a final seal: "I Jesus have sent mine angel to testify unto you these things for the churches" (verse 16). Therefore, the Lord Jesus, the Eternal Word, was the direct Inspirer of the prophets! As He says also in verse 13, "I am the Alpha and the Omega, the first and the last, the beginning and the end," whereas in chapter 1:8 we read, "I am the Alpha and the Omega, saith the Lord God, who is and who was and who is to come, the Almighty." In this verse, as we have elsewhere noted, is gathered up all the revelations of God in the Old Testament: Adonai, Elohim, Jehovah, the Almighty. And "without robbery," nay with the calm of Deity, our Lord declares Himself to be all these, in this final chapter of the Bible! Blessed is the man who in his heart of hearts, like Thomas, cries: "My Lord and my God!"

Note now the first of the three phrases—"I come quickly" of this final chapter. How absolutely all things have been committed unto our Lord by the Father, and with what quiet assurance He announces His own personal coming as the climax of the thousand pages of the Old Testament and the three hundred pages of the New. We are overwhelmed as we behold! Ah, what blindness is theirs who know not the second coming of Christ—those to whom it means nothing. TO GOD AND HEAVEN IT MEANS EVERYTHING!

The word is startling: "Behold!" It occurs about two hundred times in the Greek Testament, and always announces what is striking and surprising (Matthew 1:20-23; 3:16; 21:5).*

Beginning at Revelation 1:7, "Behold" *(idou)* occurs in the Apocalypse 30 times, and at least seven of these are in calling attention to our Lord's coming, or in preparation therefor.

"Quickly." To the Lord, one day is as a thousand years. Therefore, to Him, His absence has not yet been two days long! We must learn to look at time as our Lord does; and in proportion as we surrender to His complete Lordship, we will be enabled to do this, and His coming will be to us an imminent thing. We will be saying with Paul, *"We that are alive, that are left* unto the coming of the Lord." "Quickly" *(tachu)* occurs seven times in The Revelation, and all but once *(11:14)* refers to Christ's actions. It means *the next thing on the program.* We cannot believe that those who would have the Church looking for the Antichrist and the Tribulation rather than for Christ Himself, are fulfilling His command to *watch*—the command given to ALL *(Mark 13:37).*

We do not need to remark, of course, that the vain promises, however honestly made by the great ones of the earth, whether in Russia, Italy, Germany or America, can in any wise modify God's specific word in I Corinthians 2:6: "The rulers of this age . . . are coming to nought." We are down in the end-time, the feet of the great image of Daniel 2. We are looking for the Lord from heaven to catch us up in the clouds, and, after the Great Tribulation, to descend with all of the heavenly hosts; and like the stone cut without (human) hands from the mountain, to strike and utterly destroy Gentile world-power. "Behold, I come quickly" is the Christian's watch-word; let the

*The best help in the study of the Bible is the *"Englishman's Greek Concordance,"* one volume (of the New Testament); and the *"Englishman's Hebrew and Chaldee Concordance,"* two volumes (of the Old Testament), published by S. Bagster & Sons, London. These volumes, although now somewhat expensive, are indispensable to one determined to find the real meaning of Scripture. EACH ORIGINAL WORD WITH ALL ITS OCCURRENCES may be seen at a glance with a full line from each verse quoted.

"slogans" of the uprising world-movements be what they may.

Now we note in verse 7 a blessing pronounced upon him that "keepeth the words of the prophecy of this book." The word "book" signifies The Revelation, and is used seven times in this last section (7, 9, 10, 18 [twice], and 19 [twice]). All readily admit that The Revelation is a *book;* also that it is a book of *prophecy.* But alas, how few *keep* (meaning, *"to guard as a treasure"*) the *words! "To tamper with the words of the prophecy of the book is to bring oneself under the divine lash" (verses 18, 19),* just as to treasure them brings a special divine blessing for *you.*

> **And I, John am he that heard and saw these things. And when I heard and saw, I fell down to worship before the feet of the angel that showed me these things. And he saith unto me, See thou do it not: I am a fellow-servant with thee and with thy brethren the prophets, and with them that keep the words of this book: worship God.**

For the second time *(19:9, 10)* John is overwhelmed. It is, we feel, in view of all that has preceded, and especially of the blessed announcement of the near coming of his Lord, that the Seer, overwhelmed, falls down to worship the revealing angel. Alas, our poor hearts turn perpetually to adore something short of God—the creature rather than the Creator.

The fidelity and humility of the angel abase and shame us. Though higher than man, he is a "fellow-servant" *(sundoulos)*—a word that wholly excludes independence, in which man *glories.* Note also how the angel remembers "the prophets," those faithful servants of God, and also that the angels themselves are "keepers of the words" of this book of The Revelation. Doubtless Michael and his angels derive their very courage for the terrific conflict of chapter 12 from the revelation of certain victory given through John the beloved. How wonderful are the ways of God! Let us lay close to our hearts the angel's words: "Worship *God.*" These words will search us out. Unless we are walking with God, other gods are holding our affections. The very glory of divine revelations may tend to turn our weak hearts away from adoration of the divine Person, Himself *(Compare Paul in II Corinthians 12:7).*

> And he saith unto me, Seal not up the words of the prophecy of this book; for the time is at hand. He that is unrighteous, let him do unrighteousness still (or yet further); and he that is filthy, let him be made filthy still: and he that is righteous, let him do righteousness still; and he that is holy let him be made holy still. Behold, I come quickly; and my reward is with me, to render to each man according as his work is. I am the Alpha and the Omega, the first and the last, the beginning and the end. Blessed are they that wash their robes, that they may have the right to the tree of life, and may enter in by the gates into the city. Without are the dogs, and the sorcerers, and the fornicators, and the murderers, and the idolaters, and every one that loveth and maketh a lie.

We have here: (1) The Revelation is an unsealed, open book. (2) The fact that its clear and awful revelations will not change those who choose wickedness, is not to hinder its teaching; it will bless the *godly.* (3) The *second* announcement of "I come quickly." (4) The second (and overwhelming) imprimatur of the Author of this book. (5) The blessedness of those that "washed their robes" in the blood of the Lamb *(see 7:14),* thus having the right to the tree and to the city.* (6) The six great classes of those eternally excluded from the city (compare the eight classes cast into the lake of fire in *21:8).*

1. Briefly, let us examine—*The Revelation unsealed.*

---

*The reading "do his commandments" is now generally agreed to be a false reading, and it would constitute a false ground of any divine favor, which is based on the work of Christ.

Daniel was told to seal up his prophecy: "O Daniel, shut up the words, and seal the book, even to the time of the end: for the words are shut up and sealed till the time of the end" *(Daniel 12:4, 9)*. But inasmuch as we are now in "the last time," "the last hour" *(I Peter 1:5; I John 2:18)* and "the ends of the ages" have come upon us *(I Corinthians 10:11)*, God gave this book of The Revelation to our Lord Jesus Christ for us, as John has told us in chapter 1:1, 2. This very reason of the nearness, the *next*-ness, the at-hand-ness, of its time is given by our Lord for letting this mighty book remain *unsealed* —that is, *open to* all who will believe it and are willing to search the Old Testament Scriptures—"the Scriptures of the prophets"—to gain the understanding of its scenes and language. What a rebuke to the negligence, the neglect, the sneering, ignorant arrogance, shown by most of Christendom toward The Revelation! Our Lord Jesus may declare it an open, unsealed, understandable book; *men* say it is filled with "unintelligible language" and "mystic symbols." Christ says: "Blessed is he that readeth"; *men* say: "Let it alone, you cannot understand it." Some day all these will give an account of their insolent, insulting attitude toward this holy, open book of plain prophecy, given by God to Christ for us, and *distinctly left unsealed*. And "the time is at hand" with which its mighty language deals! This word "at hand" *(Greek eggus)* is used thirty times in the New Testament. It is illustrated in Matthew 24:32, 33 (translated *"nigh," "near"*). Paul, looking for Christ, uses it in Philippians 4:5 "The Lord is at hand."

2. Verse 11 is generally regarded as a mere sentence of finality on the state in which any soul is discovered at the Lord's coming. But if we look carefully at its connection with the preceding verse, it would seem to be suggested by the words "Seal not up the words of the prophecy of this book." The terms "do righteousness still" and "be made filthy still" seem to have the same significance of a *life-choice,* which you find in Romans 2:12—"as many as *sinned."* The tense is the aorist, not

the perfect; and indicates the *choice of the man's life,* his *whole* life, viewed *as* a whole, so that we find in *Revelation 22:11* those who have made the final choice of unrighteousness and are *living in it.* The word "unjust" (R. V. "unrighteous") is made into a verb: "Let him keep-on-doing-unrighteousness" (for he has *chosen* it). Likewise, the one who has chosen righteousness, "let him keep on practicing *(poieo)* righteousness." Paul, indeed, plainly declares: "We (indwelt by Christ) are a sweet savor (fragrance) of Christ unto God, in them that are being saved, and in them that are perishing; to the one a savor (fragrance) from death unto (deeper) death; to the other, a savor (fragrance) from life unto life" (unto higher life). The fact is, that The Revelation of Christ and His Gospel damns rejecters the more deeply *(John 15:22-24).* Just so the unfolding of the terrible visitations, plagues and judgments of the book of Revelation moves most men to deeper rejection and hatred of God's truth. Witness the growing denial of eternal punishment in literal fire and brimstone, so undeniably asserted in The Revelation, but so desperately rejected by "modern" thought.

3. Our Lord connects the second, "Behold, I come quickly *(verse 12)* with that *individual reward* He retains in His own hand to bestow *personally:* "My reward is *with me."* No saint of either Old or New Testament has been rewarded finally yet. And the Lord will not commit even to Michael or Gabriel the giving of the reward for the least service rendered to *Him!* Precious thought! Be "always abounding in the work of the Lord, forasmuch as ye know that your labor is not vain in the Lord."

4. We have already noticed the first voice of Deity in verse 6 and have called attention also to the second in verse 13: "I am the Alpha and the Omega, the first and the last, the beginning and the end."

The fact of the absolute deity of our Lord Jesus Christ could not be more strongly affirmed. Everything stands or falls with this doctrine. Christ is "God before and after all; and filling duration."

5. In the simple words pronouncing "blessed" those who avail themselves, through faith, of the infinite, cleansing power of the blood of Christ, how much is wrapped up! Notice, it is not the declaration of the Judge in justifying the ungodly who believe, that is in question here (that is Romans); but it is the cleansing effect of the shed blood of Christ, fitting the believer's person to come to the tree of life and to enter the very home of God, the New Jerusalem. Faith, true faith, involves not only a righteous standing, but the removal of all defilement from the person of the believer: both justification and cleansing. Christ said: "Already ye are clean because of the word which I have spoken unto you"; or, as Paul writes in Colossians 1:12: "Giving thanks unto the Father, who made us meet to be partakers of the inheritance of the saints in light." To the weakest and humblest believer both of these things belong. The *right (exousia)* to the tree of life and to the city thus forever and ever rests on faith in the blood of Christ. How simple, yet how glorious!

6. Now as to those excluded: "the dogs"—unclean *(as Isaiah 66:3; Matthew 7:6);* cruel *(Psalm 22:16, 20; Jeremiah 15:3);* utterly profane *(Deuteronomy 23:18);* sin-loving *(II Peter 2:22);* to be guarded against by saints *(Philippians 3:2);* "the sorcerers"—direct dealers with the Devil and demons; "the fornicators"—those who have *chosen* this uncleanness; "the murderers"—those who chose hatred—violence and slaughter—(so far, sins against man). Now "the idolators"—those serving and worshipping the *creature,* thus hiding away from the Creator; "and everyone that loveth and practiceth *(poieo)* a lie"—those shutting out the truth of God, who hide in the darkness that they may love and do falsehood: who refuse to be made sincere before God.

What a list! Here, it is exclusion from the city where the blessedness will be. In 21:8, it was their judicial consignment to the lake of fire as banished from God, whose "tabernacle" was now *"with men."*

I Jesus have sent mine angel to testify unto you these things for the churches. I am the root and the offspring of David, the bright, the morning star.

How blessedly comforting that our Lord takes His *personal* name here at the close of the book! "Thou shalt call his name *Jesus*." As He lay in the lowly manger of Bethlehem, that name was given to Him. God, the Father, will see to it that at *that Name* every knee shall bow *(Philippians 2:10)*. But here He uses it in all the loving tenderness of old. In His announcing Himself as both the root and offspring of David, both His deity and His birth at Bethlehem are in view. He is both David's Lord and his son. And we are distinctly told by Paul that He was "born of the seed of David according to the flesh" *(Romans 1:3)*; we are to remember Him the *Risen* One as such *(II Timothy 2:8)*: "Remember Jesus Christ, risen from the dead, of the seed of David, according to *my gospel*." It is part of the Pauline revelation (for the twelve imparted nothing to Paul). Nevertheless, although His royal throne and kingdom come through David and are connected with Israel on earth, we have a nearer and more blessed revelation: "I am the bright, the morning star." Our Lord is coming, indeed, as the Sun of Righteousness to rise upon the darkness of this world and reign in the millennial kingdom. But it is yet "this darkness"; although "the night is far spent, and the day is at hand." Yes, the day is not here—but lo, the harbinger of the day, the Morning Star! It shines in the night, but it prophesies the coming sunrise. "The assembly *(ecclesia*—the Church) sees Him in the now far spent night as the Morning Star, recognizes Him, while watching for Him, according to His own Word, in His bright heavenly character—a character which does not wake a sleeping world, but is the delight and joy of those who watch. When the sun arises, He will not be thus known: the earth will never so know Him, bright as the (coming) day may be" *(Darby)*. If you have never seen the morning star, I beg you get up long before day some morning,

gaze upon it, and be taught what our blessed Lord means
or should mean to every real saint!

> And the Spirit and the bride say, Come. And
> he that heareth, let him say, Come. And he
> that is athirst, let him come: he that will, let
> him take the water of life freely.

The blessed Holy Spirit, during our Lord's absence, having in care all the spiritual needs of all the saints, knowing
all the counsels of God—and how they are connected with
our Lord's appearing—continually utters, *"Come."* He
breathes, *"Come"* toward Him who is awaiting the
Father's moment, there at God's right hand. Also, the
Bride, because she is the Bride—all the Church, all the
Body of Christ, not part of it—says instinctively and from
her heart, *"Come,"* to her Bridegroom on high.

There is also the exhortation to every uninstructed
hearer, who may read or hear read this great book of The
Revelation with its mighty consummation in Christ's second coming—he is exhorted to join the Spirit and the
Bride in inviting Him back: "Let him that heareth, say,
Come." And then, if any one is *athirst,* it is the same
old tender welcome of Matthew 11: "Let him come."

And, as if that were not wide or free enough, there is
this joyful final word from the Lord's own lips, "HE
THAT WILL, LET HIM TAKE THE WATER OF
LIFE FREELY." It is as if the Lord had said to His
beloved John, "Preach the glad tidings at the very close—
the water of life, the tree of life, the eternal home of God,
the New Jerusalem—offer them all things *freely."* The
Greek word "freely" is our dear old Greek word "dorean"
(Romans 3:24; John 15:25)—"gratuitously," "without a
cause *in us* why it should be given. We are all invited to
take this infinite, infinite boon—"the water of life." Oh!
may not unbelief shut any reader or hearer out from the
FREE GIFT of God, which is ETERNAL LIFE!

> I testify unto every man that heareth the
> words of the prophecy of this book, If any man
> shall add unto them, God shall add unto him

> the plagues which are written in this book:
> and if any man shall take away from the words
> of the book of this prophecy, God shall take
> away his part from the tree of life, and out of
> the holy city, which are written in this book.

Here is the most solemn warning in the whole Bible against tampering with the words of God. If judgment came upon the wicked king Jehoiakim (*Jeremiah 36*) because he cut out with his pen-knife and burnt the predictions of evil uttered by Jeremiah against Jerusalem, how much more awful will be the doom of those who add to or take from a book given by God to the Lord Jesus, who Himself, as it were, with His pierced royal hands, stamps it over and over, with the great seal of high heaven! And especially when that One to whom all judgment has been committed, warns us not to trifle with even its words! An old Puritan preacher used to say, "There are just two things I desire to know: The first, Does God speak?— the second, What does God say?"

Let anyone who considers detracting from the meaning of the words of The Revelation, or refusing to believe that these things written therein will literally come to pass, *and that shortly*, reflect carefully upon the words, "God shall add unto him the plagues which are written in this book: God shall take away his part from the tree of life and out of the holy city." Fearful thought!

Notice these phrases—all in this last chapter: "The words of the prophecy of this book" (*verse 7*); "The words of this book" (*verse 9*); "The words of the prophecy of this book" (*verse 10*); "The words of the prophecy of this book" (*verse 18*); "The words of the book of this prophecy" (*verse 19*); "Written in this book" (*verse 19*). Beware lest the jealousy of God burn like fire—for he has exalted his Word above all his Name (*Psalm 138:2*).

And then mark also: "I Jesus have sent mine angel to testify" (*verse 16*); "I testify unto every man that heareth" (*verse 18*); "He who testifieth these things saith" (*verse 20*).

Our Lord not only jealously guards the *Words,* but also announces *Himself as the Witness to the Words:*

He who testifieth these things saith, Yea: I come quickly. Amen: come, Lord Jesus.

This is now the third announcement by our Lord of His speedy return. The first *(verse 7)* was connected with our guarding as our treasure this book of The Revelation. The second *(verse 12)* was connected with the reward He personally is bringing to His servants.

But this third and last *announcement* is the simple one *of the* FACT. This renders it supremely important. It makes the second coming of Jesus Christ to this earth from heaven the great event of the future!

Christ's death on the cross was the foundation, making possible the fulfillment of all the counsels of God.

Again, the coming of the Holy Spirit at Pentecost was the next most important fact. For His coming, His descent, made effectual to us the salvation purchased at Calvary, and keeps back ("hinders") the manifestation of the iniquity of earth, and Satan's man of sin, until the Church, the Body of Christ, is caught away.

But all now awaits this transcendent event: His "coming again"—and "quickly"!

The word "behold" *(idou)* has given way to the Greek word of absolute affirmation *(nai);* "actually"—"for a fact"—"surely"—"certainly"—"*I am coming, quickly.*"

John, the beloved, replies for the whole Church, "Amen: come, Lord Jesus." No unwillingness to have God's will done on earth as in heaven possessed the heart of the apostle; no plans of his own, however earnest, held back the eager call of his heart to the Lord to come; no concern for those yet unsaved who might be near and dear, or for whom his soul was burdened, could for an instant invade the inner sanctuary of his soul where *he awaited his Lord from heaven!* And so should it be with us! In Revelation 1:7 God had spoken the first prophetic word of this book of The Revelation: "Behold, He cometh with the clouds," and, "Even so, Amen!" was the

Spirit's seal to this striking testimony, and now, at the close, John in glad inspiration, cries aloud to the Lord Jesus to come!

The grace of the Lord Jesus be with all the saints. Amen.

As you know, the Old Testament ends with the word "curse," for it is the warning given an earth whose future hangs upon that of Israel—upon the conversion of the remnant and upon the receiving of the preaching of Elijah (evidently one of the two witnesses of Revelation 11), just before Christ should return. The law could make no absolute promise, and so God's Word by Malachi ends, "Lest I come and smite the earth with a curse."

But now Christ has come and put away sin by the sacrifice of Himself. And, although the book of The Revelation has had to uncover the fearful rebellion of the earth, and the necessary and dire judgments of God; yet upon those who have believed, to His saints, the benediction of divine favor rests. Just as Christ lifted up His hands and blessed them over against Bethany, at His ascension, so all His saints are now—under His pierced, uplifted hands of blessing. Amen!

APPENDIX I

Hymns of Christ's singers through the night of the dark ages: For They Saw The Morning Star!

3rd Century—Clement of Alexandria: "Shepherd of Tender Youth" (earliest Christian hymn).

4th Century—Ambrose of Milan:
"The dawn is sprinkling in the east
Its golden shower, as day flows in;
Fast mount the pointed shafts of light;
Farewell to darkness and to sin."

5th Century—Claudianus Mamertus:
"Sing, my tongue, the Savior's triumph!"
Anatolius of Constantinople:
(a) "Fierce was the wild billow," (b) "The day is past and over."

6th Century—Gregory the Great:
"O Christ, our King, Creator, Lord!"
St. Hilary of Arles:
"Thou art the world's true Morning Star!"
Venantius Fortunatus:
"The royal banners forward go!"

7th Century—Andrew of Crete:
"Christian, dost thou see them?"

8th Century—Stephen of St. Sabas:
"Art thou weary?"

9th Century—Rabanus Maurass:
"Come, O Creator, Spirit Blest!"
Joseph of the Studium:
"Jesus, Lord of life eternal";
also, "Safe home, safe home."
Theodistus of the Studium:
"Jesus, Name all names above!"

10th Century—Metrophanes of Smyrna:
"O Unity of three-fold light."

11th Century—Hermanus Contractus:
      "Come, Holy Ghost, in Love!"

  Peter Damiani:
      "There not waxing moon, nor waning,
        Sun nor stars in courses bright;
      For the Lamb, to that glad city
        Shines an everlasting light."

12th Century—Unknown Author:
      "The strife is o'er, the battle done;
      He closed the yawning gates of hell;
      The bars from Heaven's high portals fell;
      Let hymns of praise His triumps tell!
        Hallelujah!"

  Adam of St. Victor:
      "Earth blooms afresh in glorious dyes;
      In Christ's arising all things rise;
      A solemn joy o'er nature lies;
        Alleluia;"

  Bernard of Cluny:
        "Jerusalem, the Golden."
  Unknown Author:
      "Fairest Lord Jesus" (The Crusader's Hymn).

13th Century—Thomas of Celano: *(Dies irae, dies illa!)*
      "May I find grace, O Lord, with Thee?
      So the thief upon the tree;
      Hope, too, Thou hast breathed in *me*."

14th Century—Unknown Author:
        "Jesus is the Name we treasure."
  Jacobus de Benedictus: (Stabat Mater)

  Mechtilde of Helffde:
      "If the world were mine and all its store
        And were it of crystal gold;
      Could I reign on its throne forevermore,
        From the ancient days of old,
      An empress noble and fair as day,
        O gladly might it be;—

That I might cast it all away:
Christ, only Christ for me!"
"For Christ, my Lord, my spirit longs,
For Christ, my Saviour dear:
The joy and sweetness of my songs
The whilst I wander here."

As the great truths of *grace* began to be recovered more fully, the "Song of the Lord" burst more and more fully forth; until the Reformers took down the Church's harps from the willows of the "Babylonian Captivity" of over a thousand years.

APPENDIX II

"Elders" are mentioned twelve times in The Revelation. That they are individuals and not a symbolic company, is evident, it seems to me, for several reasons:

1. The Revelation is an unsealed book. When symbols or signs are shown they are plainly said to be such: *e.g.,* chapter 12:1-3.

2. If the twenty-four elders are representative or symbolic, then the four living creatures must be also; but we all believe that four means four when applied to the living creatures; just as to the cherubim in Ezekiel 1.

3. The language used concerning the elders compels our belief that they are individuals. "One of the elders saith unto me" *(chapter 5:5)*. "One of the elders answered" *(7:13)*. "The twenty-four elders sit before God upon their thrones" *(11:16)*.

4. Any one who takes the first mention of these elders *(4:4)* as anything other than twenty-four individuals, must have thorough proof for it, and that scriptural and not conjectural. "I saw four and twenty elders sitting" is a very definite statement indeed! We have found no Bible proof they are other than twenty-four individuals.

5. We know from I Chronicles 24: 7-19 that the orders of the priests of Aaron's house were divided into twenty-four courses. In the following chapter, moreover, those who "prophesied" with harps, psalteries and symbols according to their service by the hands of the king were also twenty-four *(I Chronicles 25:9-30)*. Furthermore, the military forces under King David were marshalled "of every course twenty and four thousand." These changed month by month—twenty-four thousand monthly *(I Chronicles 27:1-15)*. Even before this *(I Chronicles 23:4)* we find twenty-four thousand of the Levites who were "to oversee the work of the house of Jehovah" (although in this case the twenty-four thousand were chosen out of thirty-eight thousand—verse 3).

Darby says, "The number 24 represents twice 12. One might perhaps see here the twelve patriarchs and the twelve apostles—the saints in the two dispensations." *(Coll. Writ. Proph. Vol. 11, page 22.)* This is better than to make them "represent" the *Church;* but it leaves them symbolic rather than actual elders.

We can only assume, not prove, that "the elders" are of our race at all. The cherubim are not; nor the seraphim nor the "chief princes" *(Daniel 10:13).* Because the term "elders" is so often mentioned (over 200 times) in Scripture, both in connection with Israel and the Church, many are willing to assume that the elders are human beings. But the elders do not testify of their own *salvation* at all: although they celebrate that of *others,* as in 5:8, 9 (R. V.).

Inasmuch as God had "elders" over His people *Israel,* and "elders" were also to be appointed in each *Church,* (Titus 1:5); and inasmuch as twenty-four seems God's governmental order, we do not see why it may not be that there are "elders" over God's creation; that they were created so; and they are twenty-four in number; and that just as the four *zoa* express in heading up, the four genera of God's creation,—beast, cattle, man and eagle (Revelation 4:7; Genesis 1:20, 24, 26), so these "elders" were created and associated by God with His government. When Christ, with His Bride, the Church, comes to reign in power, in Revelation 19, we hear no more of these twenty-four elders: for God then subjects *all* to the *Man:* Psalm 8 is fulfilled. The elders, as all other heavenly beings, have their place, but under Christ and the Church.

APPENDIX III

IDOLATRY: Especially the Worship of a Man by His Fellows.

1. *Definition:* Idolatry is man's placing a visible object of worship before his eyes to protect him from God, thus silencing his conscience that he may indulge his lusts. God's "invisible things are clearly seen" by all His responsible creatures. In idolatry, man deliberately "changes the glory of the incorruptible God for the *likeness* of an image of corruptible man," and of lower creatures—even to "creeping things" *(Romans 1:23)*. Idolatry is man's deliberate, determined putting away from the thoughts of the concept of the holy God, and choosing and "changing" therefore a concept that will not judge his *sin,* and the setting up an "image" of that concept, a "likeness," as an outward object with which the bodily senses may be occupied. This effectually excludes *God.*

2. *History:* Idolatry was unknown before the flood. The cherubim were placed at the gate of Eden, with "the flame of a sword." Thus was man kept from the tree of life, that he might not live forever in his sinful state; and thus, perhaps, was he restrained from that hideous insult to God which idolatry ever is, just as in Israel's case, "Israel served Jehovah all the days of Joshua, and all the days of the elders that outlived Joshua, and had *known all the work . . . that he had wrought for Israel"* *(Joshua 24:31)*. Not until after the apostasy that preceded the flood (and which the flood judged) do we find record of man's being permitted to throw off all knowledge by means of idolatry. Probably the earliest idolatry spoken of in Scripture is in the same chapter *(Joshua 24:2, 14)*.

From "beyond the river" (Euphrates)—that is, from Mesopotamia, more particularly from Babel (later Babylon), and still more definitely from the daring acts of Nimrod, the "mighty destroyer" whose wife, Semiramis, (one of the most able and wicked women of the human race) was, upon her death deified as "queen of heaven,"

do we trace the beginnings of *idolatry,* which eventuates
in Satan-worship by means of "the image of the Beast,"
seen in Revelation 13. From Babylon, idolatry extended
to every land, for Babylon became "a *land* of graven
images . . . *mad* over idols." "Babylon hath been a
golden cup in Jehovah's hand, that made all the earth
drunken: the nations have drunk of her wine; therefore
the nations are mad" *(Jeremiah 50:38, 51:7).* Idolatry
spread thence to every nation, and God was *blotted out
from man's knowledge.* Read Isaiah 44:12-20. God's sad
and awful *irony* concerning the idolator!

And see the obscene stories and idols of every "mythology," to show that it has always been as in Exodus
32 and Numbers 25.

3. Why man gladly makes a *god* of a fellow-man *(as
in Revelation 13):*

a. He can *see* a man, and "the invisible things of
God" (of whom he is afraid) are thus escaped. Especially is this escape from God easy if the man worshipped
be possessed of overwhelming power, dazzling greatness,
or mysterious wisdom.

b. Man *has* to do with the infinite—he *must:* "God
hath put *eternity* in man's heart"; "his everlasting power
and *divinity*" are clearly seen. Man wishes *himself* God.
He hearkened to Satan's "ye shall be *as gods, knowing,*"
in Eden. Men therefore, in their weakness, are avidly
ready to accept the claims of some other man in power
and position, and with *daring* enough to assert himself a
god. It is what every natural heart would like to be!

c. To worship man, thus gratifies and satisfies man's
pride. Men unknowingly worship their imagined *selves*
when they worship a fellow-man.

d. Conscience is thus escaped, for the blaspheming self-
deifier relieves his mind and heart as to God; not, of
course, in the way of *priesthood* (for God is hated and
banished, and the desire is to escape Him!) but in the
way of *presumption,* for if our man-god defies God and
is suffered, other men also can cast fear away—not independently, but leaning on their *idol!*

Thus is attained the *first great end* of idolatry—*release from "the glory of the invisible God"*: that glory being now exchanged for the "likeness" of the god man has chosen. This "likeness" is held in the idolater's mind; he forms his "images" after that "likeness."*

e. Those who thus deify man are set free to practice all "human" lusts. The "wheel of nature" may revolve without restraint. And this is the *second great end of idolatry.* The awful course of Romans 1:21-31 is repeated in all idolatry. The moment Israel could look on a *calf,* and say, "These be thy gods, O Israel," they were set free to "rise up and play"—which means obscenities that cannot be written! *God being thus blotted from the mind* by "the likeness of an image," *lusts were let loose.* The unholiest doings of the human race this moment are connected with *religion without God.*

4. It should be noted, solemnly, that God "gives up" idolaters to their idols. "They that make them shall be *like unto them."* See Psalm 115—a great lesson! The "covetous man, who is an idolater," also: the "likeness" he holds in his mind is *treasure;* the "image," gold coin, stocks, bonds. He becomes *like* a coin—metallic, hard, cruel, harsh. The 'likeness" held in the Romish mind is the (imagined) "queen of heaven"; the "image," pictures and statues of "the Virgin"; these Romanists also become like unto their Babylonian "goddess." To say the very least, their inner hearts are feminized, and lose the sense of the all-holy God; to say the most, they become so vile that they are the scandal of history. But ah, what

---

*This is the claim of all idolaters, that they "do not worship the idol, but the concept behind the idol." Paul tells us they "sacrifice to *demons,* and not to God" *(1 Corinthians 10).* And the awful hideousness of the idols they make reveals the true character of the demons they worship!

It should be remembered, however, that even the deepest idolaters, who have "refused to have God in their knowledge," yet "know the ordinance of God, that they that practice such things are worthy of death" *(See Romans 1:28-32).* The state of the heathen is wilful and guilty. Do not lose sight of this for one moment! The terrible calamities, for example, upon China, and the horrible degredation of India—what is it but the "indignation" of Jehovah, the *true* God, the *living* God, an *everlasting King,* pouring out upon idolaters His wrath *(See, carefully, Jeremiah 10:1-10).* It is like a flash of divine jealousy—it *is* that. See the eleventh verse of this chapter, the one Aramaic (or earth-language) in a whole Hebrew book: "Thus shall ye say unto them, The gods that have not made the heavens and the earth, these shall perish from the earth, and from under the heavens."

will Revelation 13 bring forth, when men take Satan's Christ so deep into their hearts that "they *worship the dragon*," because he gives his authority unto their darling, the *Man of Sin!*

5. The story of the Gentile powers shows:

(1) That authority in the hands of unregenerate man leads constantly to the assumption of divine prerogatives. For neither the conscience's fear of God, nor regard for the welfare of man, can stem the flood of nature's pride let loose by irresponsible power, when vested in man.

(2) That self-deification is able to destroy all good qualities. See Nebuchadnezzar in Daniel 3, or Darius in chapter 6 as examples of that constant exaltation of self to divine honors by Gentile kings, with which every reader of history is familiar; notably, in the Roman emperors, from Julius Caesar on. What streams of martyr-blood have flowed from refusal to offer incense to the Emperor! (Read "Foxe's Book of Martyrs"—a book every Christian parent should early read to his children.)

(3) That the spirit of self-deification can only eventuate, as in Revelation 13, in the open Antichrist of the last days. And you must be prepared, by Scripture study, for this, for it is already *stealing on the world!*

If you doubt this, see Lenin in Russia,—already held a god! Or Mussolini's daring and growing claims in Italy, and Hitler's in Germany. Or, sad to admit, the rush to grasp power, exalt self, and compel subjection at any cost of abandoned promises, and political, moral and domestic safeguards—*when the opportunity is given,* in the United States of America!

APPENDIX IV

BULLINGERISM

This teaching has been so fully answered, both in England and America, and its deadly dangers so fully worked out, that a discussion of it is practically unnecessary here. See, for example, the brief, but able and clear tract by Mr. W. Hoste of England: *Bullingerism* (Light and Liberty Publishing Company, Fort Dodge, Iowa). He also combatted Dr. Bullinger in England when he was yet alive. Also the various comments made by the Editor D. M. Panton in the magazine *The Dawn* (C. J. Thynne & Company, London); and those by Dr. James M. Gray in *The Moody Monthly* (Chicago). The recent righteously firm and unanswerable booklet *Wrongly Dividing the Word of Truth* (Loizeaux Bros., New York) by Dr. H. A. Ironside, is not being answered by Bullinger votaries,—except by *petitio principii*,—begging the question that their rejection of water baptism is correct, the *final* teaching of Paul; and that those who disagree with them are ignorant or cowards. They do not answer the arguments made against them; instead they accuse their objectors.

Consider, regarding Bullingerism:

1. It subjects Scripture to *rigid rules* of outline and interpretation invented by the human mind. It does lean upon "its own understanding," rather than upon the Holy Spirit.

2. It assumes, with unbelievable pride, that it knows "truth," of which the whole Church has been ignorant since Paul. In other times, when men really recovered *truth,* as at the Reformation, or in Wesley's or in Darby's day, a mighty work of the Holy Spirit accompanied the Word, which resulted in the conversion of thousands, and the real *edification in love* of God's Saints. Bullingerism causes divisions; ministers "questionings" and defeats unity. I have watched it for thirty-six years deceive, puff up, release from prayer and burden for souls, make men once

zealous to reach the lost compass sea and land to make one proselyte to "no water-baptism," "only prison epistles," "Gospels not for *us*," etc., etc.

3. Bullingerism is probably the most subtle of all the doctrines that lead, eventually, to that great denial of eternal judgment, which is sweeping the world. The "soul-sleep" that Bullinger taught "lets down the bars"; being direct trifling with God's plainest of words regarding the disposition He makes of both the saved and the lost at death: that the believer "departs to be with Christ," being "absent from the body he is present with the Lord"; and that the lost proceed, as did the rich man of Luke 16, *at once to Hades.* Bullinger says: "Hades,—we might call it *Grave-dom.* There is not a place where the rendering *grave* would not be appropriate" (for Hades). Now Matthew 16:18 at once proves this utterly false! Church saints' bodies have been buried in *graves* constantly; but Hades, the region at the earth's center (Matthew 12:40; Acts 2:27, R.V.), since our Lord's resurrection, has not admitted one saint into its gates: "The Gates of Hades shall not prevail against it" (the Church). I am persuaded that all Bullingerites are candidates for some form of denial of eternal punishment. There are those of California who teach that even *Satan* will be restored: making God, in Revelation 20:10, a liar! "Buy the truth and *sell it not!*"

The more a man knows who teaches vital error, the more dangerous he is. Especially is he dangerous if he holds some,—even a great deal, of truth; for, "a little *leaven* leaveneth the *whole lump.*"

When I was in England first, in 1899, it was my great blessing to be closely associated with the best Christians there. Mr. Bullinger was at that time writing very busily. But all those devoted Christians said, "He seems to be a brainy man, but *we do not trust him.*" How well his fruits have proved their discernment!

It is my firm belief that one of three paths will be followed by all Bullinger followers: a. They will be delivered from it by divine grace; or, b. They will become so occupied with endless discussions about "dispensational" distinctions and divisions, that they will become fruitless for God, either at home or abroad; or, c. They will go on to the logical conclusion of setting aside this Scripture and that, in accordance with their "dispensational" claims, to the position of the Knoch *(Concordant)* faction of California: who have even printed their (per)version of the Scriptures, to *gainsay the Words of God* concerning *eternal punishment.*

Imagine Martin Luther being told that his beloved *Galatians* and *Romans* (by which, under God, he shook Europe), "Those are not 'Church Epistles,'—they do not belong to *us."* I should not care personally to be the "dispensationalist" to tell Luther that! Or Rutherford— imagine telling him that the Church is not the *Bride* of Christ! (Have you read his *Letters?)* Or content John Bunyan with words and questions such as these? Or tell Whitefield, weeping over 20,000 souls in his mighty sermon on "Ye must be born again," that John's Gospel, where he got his message, is "not for us"? God gave him thousands of souls by that message, and no peddler of "soul-sleep" teaching could stand before him!

George Whitefield read through Matthew Henry's Commentary twice—on his knees! What this shallow age needs is a long, steady acquaintance with such as Matthew Henry,* and the Puritans, and Spurgeon, and Darby's "Collected Writings"—and even with John Calvin's 51 volumes of commentaries! But they, conceiving themselves dispensationally "beyond" these really great men of God,—will they read these works?

We trow not. They will, instead, be more and more occupied with the "air-tight-compartments" of the clever and heady *Companion Bible,*—because it makes people think they are advancing, in their Scripture "dividing," and dispensational distinctions, in divine things,—whether the Holy Ghost unifies in love God's saints or not; and *whether revival showers come or not!*

---

*Matthew Henry was *godly,* as were the Puritans; though both are servants of a legal theology, alas!

WHY THE CHURCH WILL NOT BE IN THE GREAT TRIBULATION

We mean by *The Church,* the Body of Christ, which includes all "born-again" people from Pentecost to Christ's second coming. "Ye are the body of Christ. . . . In one Spirit *were we all* baptized into *one* body, . . . and were all made to drink of *one* Spirit. Christ also loved the church, and gave himself up *for it;* that he might present the church to himself, a glorious *church* . . . one body and one Spirit, even as also ye were called in *one* hope of your calling." (I Corinthians 12:27, 13; Ephesians 5:25, 27; Chapter 4:4.) Note, that we do *not* mean by "The Church" the religious profession the world knows by that name; but the true Body of Christ only, which will be also His Bride.

We mean by *The Great Tribulation* that "time of trouble" on earth spoken of by Daniel, Jeremiah, and other prophets, and our Lord, and the Apostles, as so terrible in character that "there hath not been the like from the beginning of the creation which God created until now, and never shall be" (Mark 13:19). Its duration will be brief,—3½ years, or 42 months (shortened somewhat "for the elect's sake"); and it will immediately precede the Lord's return *to earth* to set up His kingdom *on earth,* as "Son of man" (Matthew 24:29; 13:41-43).

1. We know that the most of the Church *cannot* go through The Tribulation; for the vast majority of it, during the nearly two thousand years *has already gone to be with Christ,* to return with Him at His second coming. I wish we might let that sink deep into our hearts! Why should a small number at the end be subjected to a test and trial that the rest, even "carnal" saints, have entirely escaped? *(I Corinthians 8).*

2. We do not deny, but rather continually affirm, that the Church is always subject to suffering—indeed, that for Christ's sake we are killed all the day of grace long, accounted as "sheep for the slaughter" *(Romans 8).* Such instances, for example, as the Boxer martyrdom in 1900 and the Russian situation prove that the Church is

always subject to suffering; in fact, that is the program
for it: as witness the early martyrs!

3. It is only from *divine wrath,* not human, that we
affirm the Church of God to be absolutely and forever
delivered, and that not only from the "great day of
wrath" at Christ's second coming *(Revelation 19)* and
from the eternal wrath at the Great White Throne judgment *(Revelation 20);* but we also affirm that the Church
has no share in the woes that come directly from God's
indignation, which occur upon the Lamb's taking the
sealed book in heaven *(Revelation 5:1).* Now why do we
affirm that? Because the Church is under grace, under
eternal favor. I mean God's elect, those chosen in Christ
before the foundation of the world, sanctified by the
Holy Ghost, believing the truth. Those in Christ *HAVE*
their redemption, the forgiveness of all their trespasses.
They have been made meet already to be partakers of
the inheritance of the saints in light. They have not
been appointed unto wrath in any sense. They are not
of the world; they have been made alive together with
Christ, and raised up with Him and made to sit with
Him in the heavenlies, with an eternal outlook of kindness from His hand in Christ Jesus. All wrath for them
from God was forever over at the cross when Christ
cried, "It is finished!"

Now these are the facts about the Body of Christ—
not perfected saints only, but all the saints. There is no
exception. God will not and cannot turn from His acceptance of those in His Son. Wrath has passed over
forever for the Church. They have been fore-ordained
to be conformed to the image of God's Son. They shall
be so conformed so that Christ may be "the first-born
among many brethren." This is the plain declaration of
the God of all grace. This was a sovereign act of His
own, not contingent upon their response to it; but, on
the contrary, God Himself undertaking to work in them
both to will and to do of His good pleasure, and to perfect that which concerned them. It was of the carnal
Corinthian Christians that Paul said they should be confirmed unto the end, that they should be unreprovable

in the day of our Lord Jesus Christ. Let me emphasize
the fact that Paul calls them *babes* in Christ, saying, "Ye
are yet carnal." But Paul says God is going to confirm
them unto the day of Jesus Christ. Paul addresses this
epistle to "all that call upon the name of our Lord Jesus
Christ in *every* place." Therefore, it covers this whole
age, and it covers "carnal" Christians!*

4. We find also that Paul was sent by Christ to reveal
not only the Church's heavenly calling, and destiny, but
also to reveal that *Gospel* which belongs to this day of
salvation, the essence of the message of which is that
God was in Christ, *reconciling the world unto Himself
at the cross, not reckoning* to them their trespasses; and
hath *committed* to His saints of this "day of salvation,"
the *"ministry* of reconciliation" in such a sense that the
word of reconciliation has been "placed in us." That is
the meaning of the Greek word—God has *placed in us
the word* of reconciliation, the business of telling others
regarding reconciliation. Unto us this word belongs.
"We are ambassadors therefore on behalf of Christ, as
though God were entreating by us: we beg you on behalf
of Christ, be ye reconciled to God." That is the attitude
of the Apostle Paul, and of the saints of God of this
age, *the whole age long!* Nor is there any hint that it
has ever changed. It cannot change. The saints, as sinners, having found Christ, can do nothing but proclaim
Christ to others. So that no matter how much we may
be moved to arouse men by warnings of eternal judgment, *we must ever return to the message of the cross:*
of the grace of God. The Church has no other commission, and the Church is God's house and the pillar and

---

*If it be argued that some of God's own are on earth during the wrath-days
of The Great Tribulation, and therefore why not the Church-saints? the answer
is, that it is perfectly evident to a thoughtful reader of prophecy regarding
Israel, and especially the Psalms, that there will be souls who seek Jehovah,
(and that in times of great trouble) to whom the finished work of Calvary is
not yet revealed. Their consciences are not yet purged; the sense of sin and
even of divine wrath—the wrath upon Israel oppresses them: the "fountain for
sin and uncleanness" having not been nationally opened to Israel (Zechariah
12:11-13:1). Yet the saints of the Church cannot be meant here, for the blood
of Christ is declared to have so cleansed,—not only from guilt, but from "dead
works," the conscience of the believer that he serves gladly and freely the Living
God (Heb. 9:14; 13:15). The Psalms present the consciousness, not of an
Ephesian Christian, but of a godly Israelite longing for his Messiah's (second)
coming as Deliverer and King.

stay of the truth in this age. So long as she is on earth
we do not find any Scripture, any warrant for the idea
that God will have two witnessing bodies with different
messages on earth at the same time, one of present grace
and one of present judgment! Let us keep this carefully
in mind.

5. We find in Scripture that God may reveal to His
servants, as to Enoch, judgments in which they will *personally have no part.* See the Apostle Jude, wherein
Enoch prophesies of the Lord's second coming in wrath
upon the ungodly. But Enoch was translated, and never
saw that wrath. Though he knew about it, he did not
see it. It was revealed to Enoch that he should be translated. Enoch becomes, therefore, a type of the Church
which is to be translated from judgment, even as Noah
was a type of the Israelitish remnant that will go through
the judgment and come out into the new kingdom on
earth when the Lord Jesus returns. We need not be surprised, therefore, that the Lord has told His Church, by
the Apostle John especially, of the end-horrors which
they will not themselves enter, nor even see, except from
above. The *principles* of evil are on now—"the *mystery*
of lawlessness," *many* antichrists: but not the *manifestation, "the* Anti-Christ": *that* is *restrained.*

6. You remember the passage: "We that are left unto
the coming of the Lord shall in no wise precede them
that are fallen asleep." This great Thessalonian revelation proves at once two blessed things: *first,* that the
proper Christian expectation is to be alive when Christ
comes: *"We* that are alive," says Paul by the Spirit.
Second, that so far from there being any time of wrath
in store for believers alive when Christ comes, there will
be such a naturally expected advantage from being left
unto the coming of the Lord that a special revelation
was necessary to assure the Church that those fallen
asleep would not be behind, but should really rise first!
Now if a portion of the Church is to share the fearful
horrors of The Great Tribulation, the only cry of any
intelligent saint should be, "How much better to die in
the Lord and escape all this!" But God has as surely

put the hope of the rapture of *translation* into the breast of His instructed saints, as He put it into Enoch's breast. *"We* will together be caught up in the clouds to meet the Lord in the air." The Spirit *moved* Paul to write that. That is the hope which we ought all to share. "We shall all be changed in a moment," in "the twinkling of an eye" we shall be caught up. Now this is *the hope,* and this is written into the hearts of the saints.

7. C. I. Scofield very aptly calls attention to Christ's *new* promise given in John 14, "I go to prepare a place for you. And if I go and prepare a place for you, I will come again, and will receive you unto myself; that where I am there ye may be also." Now will you notice that this promise has absolutely nothing to do with the Son of man's work of setting up a kingdom on earth! It is a *new announcement.* It is the anticipatory announcement of the heavenly prospects of the Church of God. It is our Lord's first intimation to His saints of this special phase of His coming. Our Lord, on the Mount of Olives, you remember, had given them a view of the dispensation with special reference to His coming to earth in judgment *(Matthew 24 and Mark 13).* Our Lord there looks on the disciples as *Jews* (which they primarily were), and those passages must be read in the light of that fact.* For instance, in Matthew 24 the Lord Jesus says concerning The Great Tribulation, "There shall be great tribulation, such as hath not been from the beginning of the world until now, no, nor ever shall be." And in connection with that, "Pray ye that your flight be not in the winter, neither on a sabbath," because a Jew could only journey so far on the sabbath day by their custom *(Acts 1:12)* without breaking the law; and I want to remind you the Jews will not then be under grace. They will not yet know grace in that awful tribulation time that is coming. They will be in spirit under the solemn sabbath restrictions, as in Maccabean days. But Paul said to the Colossians, "Let no one judge you

---

*"The whole effect of Christ's coming, with regard to the Jews, to 24:31, then to all His servants till His coming, to 25:30; then to the nations preparatory to His kingdom, 25:31-46." *(Darby)*

in respect of a sabbath day, which was *a shadow* of the things to come; but the body is Christ's. You are not under the law, but grace." The folks who talk about the Church going through The Tribulation do not realize Church truth; they do not realize the *absoluteness* of God's grace. I say that kindly, but I say it with much emphasis. I cannot teach anything else, and be true to the Gospel of the Grace of God! The constant use of such words as "look for his appearing," "wait for God's Son," "love his appearing," in the Epistles shows how the Spirit kept this hope alive in the hearts of God's saints. It was the expectation of the actual appearing of the Lord Jesus, "I go, I will come, I will receive you unto myself!"

8. Now the Thessalonian saints were in danger, like those of today, of getting their eyes *off* the real hope of Christ's personal and imminent return, the hope of translation into the air, and *upon* conditions round about them. So Paul writes his Second Epistle to the Thessalonians, upholding their faith which he established in his First Epistle. Let us quote this most important passage. "Now we beseech you brethren, *in behalf of* (the preposition here in the Greek means "in behalf of" not merely "concerning"—it is a *plea for*); the coming of our Lord Jesus Christ, and *our gathering together unto him.*" (He wrote them about it in the First Epistle. Read I Thessalonians 4:13-18. Now he would exhort them to hold fast what he wrote them in the First Epistle.) "To the end that ye be not quickly shaken from your mind" (the mind that he got them in by writing the First Epistle— I Thessalonians 4—where he said, "The Lord himself shall descend from heaven with a shout, with the voice of the archangel, and with the trump of God: and the dead in Christ shall rise first; then we that are alive, that are left, shall together with them be *caught up in the clouds to meet the Lord in the air;* and so shall we ever be with the Lord. Wherefore comfort one another with these words"). Now note II Thessalonians 2:2 "Be not quickly shaken from your mind" (into which my First Epistle brought you) "nor yet be troubled, either by spirit

(either your own "feelings," or else an evil spirit, as in a false prophet) "or by word" (any wrong preaching or instruction) "or by epistle" (purporting to come from me) "as (teaching) that the day of the Lord is present."

Now it is not "the day of Christ" as in the old version. The Revised Version reads *day of the Lord*. But "is present" follows: as 1 Cor. 3:22; Rom. 8:38. That is, the great and terrible day when the Lord comes down *(Revelation 19)* with the armies of heaven to execute vengeance and set up His kingdom and tread His enemies under His feet. "Don't believe," says Paul, "the *day of the Lord* is now present." "Let no man beguile you in any wise"— (they will try it; they are trying it now). "For *that* day will in no wise be" (that day *of the Lord*) "except the *falling away* come first, and the man of sin be revealed" —Antichrist.*

against another. He pleads for the day of Christ—when we are caught up to meet Him: "Don't let anybody move you away from that hope!" Watch for it! *"We* that are alive," *"we* that are alive," *"we* that are alive!" That is God's inspiration—it is the Holy Ghost who puts that into your heart, believer! We that are alive, that are left—we shall all be changed in the twinkling of an eye. That is the hope of the Church. Paul pleads for that.

It is described by the Spirit as "our gathering together unto him," the rapture or translation into the air with which they had been told to "comfort one another." And he warns *against* their expecting to see the day *of the*

---

*There is a great deal of controversy over what is meant by "the falling away." The Greek phrase *(apostasia)* is an expression used just once in Scripture. In my judgment Church days are not meant here. In these days I know there is a great deal of falling away from the faith (1 Timothy 4); and Paul writes in his last epistle, II Timothy 3: "The days will come when they will not endure the sound doctrine." But that is not what the Spirit of God meant by "the apostasy." The falling away is, I am perfectly convinced, described in II Thessalonians 2 and Revelation 13. It is the whole world *falling clear away from God to worship the Devil,*—all except the elect, who were written in the Book of Life *from the foundation of the world.* It will be the elect of *that day*, not the Church. For the Church has nothing to do with earth things, having been chosen in Christ *before the foundation of the world!* God will always have His witnesses, His saints. There is coming an awful apostasy, a falling away of the human race to the god of this age. They shall worship the dragon because he will give his power to the wild-beast—Satan's burlesque of the resurrection. There is the reversal of everything that is divine. Satan has the place of God, and the Beast is Satan's Christ; and the False Prophet becomes an awful parody of the Holy Spirit. *Now that is coming!* And that, I think, is what God means by "the apostasy." Everything else is preliminary, is not the real *apostasy.*

Lord while on earth. Now look at that. Don't you watch for the day of the Lord. The apostasy is coming, but "we that are alive" are looking for Christ's coming for us. A temple of God has to be built by the returned Jewish nation, as we find elsewhere, and a great falling away from God to Satan, and the man of sin has to sit there, setting himself forth as God, before the *day of the Lord,* the great and terrible day, could take place. But *their* hope, the Church's hope, was being *caught up to be with Christ.* They were not to look for the other, the day of the Lord, although they were informed of it, as Enoch was informed of the wickedness that was coming. He looked for translation; and *by faith Enoch was translated!*

9. We find that The Great Tribulation is not once mentioned by *Paul* in *his epistles which govern the churches* (Romans to Philemon) nor in Hebrews; nor are the saints warned of it. The last days are indeed spoken of; perilous times were plainly in Paul's view, and the turning aside to Satan from the truth planted by him. But this brings us to emphasize again that the days of The Great Tribulation are quite another thing from a departure from the gospel of grace, or even from the inspiration of the Bible, as in modernism. If there had been the remotest possibility that the Church would see those *wrath*-outpourings, Paul would have warned them of it. But he speaks in exactly the opposite way. See his words to the Corinthians in I Corinthians 11:32, "chastened of the Lord that they might *not* be condemned with the world."

10. The 70th week of Daniel, lasting seven years, has two halves, *in neither of which the Church can be on earth.* There is no other place The Tribulation can come but in the 70th week of Daniel 9:27. Careful students of the Scripture are agreed about that. In this prophecy of Daniel we read that in the middle of that week, when three and one-half years are up, he (that is, that "prince," that last prince of the Roman Empire) "will cause the sacrifice and the oblation to cease." He will stop the

Jewish worship like Antiochus Epiphanes, his famous prototype of the time of the Greek reign of the Seleucidae, in the second Century before Christ *(Daniel 11: 29, 30; 1 Maccabees)*. This Antichrist, this last prince, however, will come and place *himself* there in the Jewish temple that they are going to build. Antiochus Epiphanes, in his rage because Rome turned him back from conquering Egypt, came to Jerusalem and "did his pleasure." He sacrificed a sow and strewed its broth in the Holy of Holies of their temple. Now this last Roman "prince" will do worse than defile. He will set *himself* forth there as God: and this is the thing that will make Israel desolate—"the abomination that maketh desolate." The word "abomination" in Scripture is God's word for a pagan god, or for a demon that is worshipped. There was the "abomination" Ashtoreth, of the Sidonians; and Chemosh, the "abomination" of the Moabites, and Molech, the "abomination" of Ammon. God calls these various heathen gods *abominations*. Now there is an *abomination*-thing to sit "where he ought not." When therefore ye shall see the abomination of desolation, which was spoken of through Daniel the prophet," *(Matthew 24)* sitting in a place he ought not, then let the remnant (of Israel) flee: Let him that is on the housetop not go down to take out the things that are in his house. For God will have given matters over to the enemy for the "hour," as He did in Gethsemane *(Luke 22:53)*. There is coming this 70th week of Daniel, in the middle of which it was prophesied by Daniel and by our Lord Jesus Christ, that the Antichrist would thus take charge of things. Now I said that neither in the first half of this week of seven years, nor in the last half could the Church be here. Why?

In Revelation 11 we see the first half of this 70th week. You will remember from your study of The Revelation that we come to Jewish things in chapter 11. John has to "prophesy again," and the scene is Jerusalem of the last days: "Rise and measure the temple of God, and the altar, and them that worship therein. And the court

which is without the temple leave without, and measure
it not; for it hath been given unto the nations: and the
holy city shall they tread under foot forty and two
months." This refers to the *last* half of the seven years.
The next verse refers to the *first* half, "And I will give
unto my two witnesses, and they shall prophesy a thousand two hundred and threescore days, clothed in sackcloth." Now 1260 days are three and one-half years exactly. Well, you say, it may be the same time as the
other in the preceding verse. Come to chapter 13 and
read of the last emperor, the Wild-Beast, the Antichrist.
You will find he "prospers and does his pleasure" for
forty-two months, but it is during the second, not the
first half of the seven years. I cannot believe that his
way is open, until the "two witnesses" are out of the way.
He does not fully get his "hour," with his ten kings,
until then *(Revelation 17:12).*

During the first half, Revelation 11, God's "two witnesses," clothed in sackcloth and operating at Jerusalem,
*preclude the possibility of the Church's presence and
testimony on earth.* How? First, the whole earth becomes subject to a testimony which is *not the gospel,* not
"the ministry of reconciliation"; and subject to two persons who are *not of the Church.* Here we have two
witnesses that are of God, of course, but not preaching
the gospel, nor grace, as does the Church. "And they
shall prophesy a thousand two hundred and threescore
days, clothed in sackcloth." This is Old Testament
ground. Let us quote their description and see.

> These are the two olive trees and the two
> candlesticks, standing before the Lord of the
> earth. And if man desireth to hurt them, fire
> proceedeth out of their mouth and devoureth
> their enemies; and if any man shall desire to
> hurt them, in this manner must he be killed.
> These have the power to shut the heaven,
> that it rain not during the days of their
> prophecy: and they have power over the
> waters to turn them into blood, and to smite

the earth with every plague, as often as they
shall desire.

I said that the whole earth becomes subject, under
these two witnesses, to a testimony which is not the gospel. You cannot change the gospel ministry—it is "God
so loved the world," "whosoever will." You cannot
change that; you cannot mix it up. If the Church is
here she must preach the gospel and that only. She must
preach the gospel of grace. For the Church to leave the
gospel of grace, salvation to poor sinners, and turn to
anything else is to desert her commission. Any preacher
who leaves this and turns for example to prophecy only,
or to any other "specialty," dries up. The Church of
God has a commission to go forth to every part of the
earth, preaching the gospel to every creature. You cannot change that commission. Just because you find cer·
tain "saints" in the tribulation-time, do not imagine they
must be the Church of God. That is to have the same
kind of a veil about you that some folks have about the
law of Moses. Because, for instance, God gave the Jews
a seventh day sabbath such people must turn the first
day of the week into a Jewish sabbath! But we cannot
change the true interpretation of Scripture. We will not
listen to those who would plunge the Church of God into
a place where it cannot be scripturally!

The whole earth, I repeat, becomes subject to a testimony which is not the gospel, and to two persons who
are not of the Church. The present days of "no difference" between Jew and Gentile in God's sight, are past
at that time, for the testimony has reverted to Jerusalem
and the prophets are of the Old Testament. And they
deal with a nation which does not even know Jehovah
their God, but speak of Him as the "God of heaven"
(Revelation 11:13). They do not even *know* Jehovah
any more. And they (these prophets) are clothed in
sackcloth—a wholly Jewish, Old Testament attitude.
Personally, I believe Elijah is one of them. The Lord
Jesus said, as also Malachi, that Elijah would return to

Israel before the "great and terrible day of the Lord" (*Malachi 4:5; Matthew 17:11*).

Further, they "smite the earth with every plague as often as they shall desire." Here we have grace ended and judgment beginning. The attention of the whole earth is wholly taken up by these "two witnesses," and consequently there is no place nor time for the Church or for a *grace* testimony. Really, Church saints present there would *hinder* God. God wants the whole earth then to listen to these witnesses at *Jerusalem*. Try to imagine how it will be! All the telegraph wires and radios fairly humming with news about these two terrible prophets that cannot be killed—no man can destroy them. They send out fire from their mouths upon any one who wants to kill them, and such persons shall die. They have (so the news will go) smitten this nation, that nation, from afar off, with plagues, shutting up the heaven that it does not rain, turning the water into blood. I'd like to know how you would have got along with the gospel down in Egypt when Moses was swinging out his rod over the Nile and turning it into blood, or when the frogs were hopping out. No place for the gospel there! *God was doing something else down in old Egypt, and as God dealt with Egypt so God is going to deal with this whole world.* And for people to say the Church is there is sad blindness. It's a lack of discernment of the purposes of God, of His grace, or of the position of the Church of God. God does not mix things. If God has "two witnesses" there clothed in sackcloth, and the whole world subject to them, and they smiting the earth with every plague as often as they desire, where is there place for "Whosoever will let him take of the water of life freely?" *That is over—something else is on.* God is laying the foundation at Jerusalem in "the remnant" of fear of Jehovah again. We must remember that God has a deep and solemn work to do in the Jewish nation, ere He can take Israel's side against the nations (as He will do when He comes to earth: *see Zechariah 12:14*). This nation Israel has lost the fear of God and given itself up to covetousness and to idolatry. Now God is going to take Israel's part as He did in Egypt against Pharaoh. Terrible plagues are about to fall on the whole earth; but judgment is beginning with God's people Israel. The *"sinners in Zion* will be afraid" at that time!

You remember that these two prophets of God are killed by the Wild-Beast, and through three and one-half days their bodies lie there unburied "in the street of the great city," and all nations come to celebrate this awful thing! The Lord's "two witnesses" are slain at "Jerusalem that killeth the prophets."

> **And from among the peoples and tribes and tongues and nations do men look upon their dead bodies three days and a half, and suffer not their dead bodies to be laid in a tomb. And they that dwell on the earth rejoice over them and make merry; and they shall send gifts one to another; because these two prophets tormented them that dwell on the earth** *(Revelation 11)*.

Where are the churches? They are not there! The people are occupied with *something entirely different.* "And they shall send gifts one to another; because these two prophets tormented them that dwell on the earth." The *whole earth* was in their hands for judging and tormenting. Where is the ministry of *reconciliation* in that day? Where are the ambassadors that were formerly pleading in Christ's stead to be reconciled to God? That day is gone! People with discernment see that. God is doing something else then: judgment is on. And Israel and the nations are involved in it—not the Church!

> **And after the three days and a half the breath of life from God entered into them, and they stood upon their feet; and great fear fell upon them that beheld them. And they heard a great voice from heaven saying unto them, Come up hither. And they went**

> up into heaven in the cloud; and their ene-
> mies beheld them.

Praise God, heaven can take folks up that the earth
cannot stand! "And they went up into heaven in the
cloud; and *their enemies* beheld them"—the whole earth
at *public* enmity with God! The Church of God has
gone away. Evil is now unrestrained.

> **And in that hour there was a great earth-
> quake, and the tenth part of the city fell;
> and there were killed in the earthquake seven
> thousand persons; and the rest were af-
> frighted, and gave glory to the God of
> heaven.**

No, as I said, Israel of that day do not yet know Him
as "Jehovah their God." The Jewish nation does not
know Him *today*. "They gave glory to the God of
heaven." That is His name outside of Jerusalem, in
Persia or in Babylon. See Daniel and Nehemiah.

11. Now let us look at another passage describing the
second, or last half of Daniel's 70th "week." Turn to
Isaiah 60:2: "Behold, darkness shall cover the earth,
and *gross darkness* the peoples." Now the expression
"gross darkness" is God's term for judicial blindness.
Darkness, in a certain way, covers the earth now; even
in "Christendom." Not "gross darkness," however, as
in this verse. See Jeremiah 13:15, where God describes
vividly this expression "gross darkness": "Hear ye, and
give ear; be not proud; for Jehovah hath spoken." Jeremiah is pleading with the nation of Israel who are sinning away their day of grace. "Give glory to Jehovah
your God, before he cause darkness, and before your feet
stumble upon the mountains of twilight. And, while ye
look for light, he turn it into the shadow of death, and
make it *gross darkness.*" "Gross darkness," therefore, in
the Hebrew, is God's description of a state of things
when there is *no light left*. Judicially God has withdrawn the light. "Behold, darkness shall cover the earth,
and *gross darkness the peoples.*" It will be a spiritual

darkness like the physical darkness of the ninth plague in Egypt; "thick darkness that may be felt" *(Exodus 10: 21)*. People forget that. They think the Church will be there; but that is because of their thoughtlessness. And I want to tell you something about those who say that. They very soon begin to minify God's great future purposes about *Israel*. They begin to grow blind to the power and vision of the Old Testament concerning the coming kingdom; and they lose sight of the Church's distinct and separate calling—distinct from Israel and all earthly things. God will still deal with Israel. God says if the order of the heavens can be changed, then His purposes concerning Israel "from being a nation before him forever" can be changed. God says He is going to make a covenant with them in the future and you have to believe that. And Israel means Israel, and Jerusalem means Jerusalem. When God's light "ariseth" after that "gross darkness" it will be on His *earthly* people. *(Read Zechariah 12:10-13:1.)*

In Isaiah 60:1 we read: "Arise, shine; for thy light is come, and the glory of Jehovah is risen upon thee:" This is a prophetic message about Jerusalem, *beyond* The Great Tribulation, when the Lord Jesus comes back. The glory of Jehovah will rise upon Israel: "For, behold, darkness shall cover the earth and gross darkness the peoples; but Jehovah will arise upon thee (Jerusalem) and his glory shall be seen upon *thee.* And nations shall come to *thy* light, and kings to the brightness of *thy* rising." Those that have read prophecy with the Spirit of God, know of what I am speaking. Oh, the awful darkness that is coming! People forget that; they think The Tribulation is just the wilful career of the last Roman emperor. Alas, far more, it's God-given *judicial blindness!* "Darkness shall cover the earth, and gross darkness the peoples." There is no way of escaping this. The Church is gone, or *gross darkness* would not, could not, be written of the world! As long as the Church of God is here you cannot write those words *"gross darkness* covers the peoples." God said to Lot, "Haste thee, for I cannot do

anything *till thou be removed."* Nothing in the way of
judgment. Abraham said to Jehovah, "Wilt thou slay
the righteous with the wicked? Shall not the Judge of
all the earth do right?" Earth will be given up to believe
the lie (for the definite article is before it) *(II Thessalonians 2).* There is no place for the "ministry of reconciliation" then whatsoever! The earth turns to Devil-
worship and knows it. Our Lord said, "When the Son of
man cometh" (as Son of man, note, by which name He
is coming back to reign *on earth)* "shall he find faith on
the earth?" And you cannot answer that by any other
answer than "No." You say, do you mean to teach that
there will be no one on earth when He comes back as the
Son of man, who has *faith? I mean exactly that.* Israel,
the remnant of Israel—God must pour upon them the
spirit of grace and supplication ere they "look unto him
whom they pierced." They must *see* Christ. They must
look on Him. "They shall see the sign of the Son of
man in heaven." Christ has said, "When the Son of man
comes (as the Son of man) will he find faith?" No. He
will find those that are *going* to have faith, but they have
to *see* first like Thomas. What an awful state, and what
a terrible thing for people to be teaching that the Church
is going to be here when God says there will not be faith.

12. We know certain things have to take place at
Christ's coming. There is the rapture, the translation of
the saints, the judgment-seat of Christ when each saint
comes before the Lord to have his works examined and
to be rewarded. And afterwards comes the presentation
of the Church to Himself, "a glorious church not having
spot or wrinkle." Then comes the marriage in heaven of
Revelation 19. That all takes *time.* And yet these folks
would have us believe that that is all just an instant's
work at the second coming! But from the time He
comes for the Church in the air, has them all judged
there for their works, gives them their rewards, and then
presents them to Himself in that wonderful day of the
marriage of the Lamb *(Revelation 19),* until He comes
on down with them and the armies of heaven, God gives

us no dates whatsoever. But Scripture shows there will
be at least seven years between His coming *for* His
Church and His coming *with* them. Because, as we saw
in Revelation 11, the two witnesses fill the first half, and
the Wild-Beast the latter half of the closing seven years
of "Gentile times"; and in neither half are the Church
and the Gospel of Grace possible!*

13. Now, again, let me ask a few questions. Why
should a heavenly company, already made meet to be partakers of the inheritance of the saints in light, be asked
to "await their Lord from heaven," unless His *imminent
coming* be really their *hope?*

Again, what spiritual result is secured by giving up
the hope of the imminent return of the Lord? Are those
who give up this doctrine the more stable and steadfast
for it? Are they more filled with the Spirit?

Does the doctrine of the Church going through the
tribulation give joy? God's word says, "Hope deferred
maketh the heart sick." A dear friend of mine said publicly to me many years ago that he had abandoned the
hope of the imminent coming of the Lord. I went to
see him the next day and talked earnestly for hours with
him. I finally said, "Mr.—, how did you come to give
this hope up?" He told me that he had promised a friend
to re-examine the Scriptures in the light of certain arguments against Christ's imminent coming for the whole
Church. "I read the New Testament from the viewpoint
of those *arguments,*" he said, "and one day I got down
on my knees in my own parlor, weeping bitter tears, and
gave up a hope that had been very dear to me." I said,
"Mr—, do you expect me to give it up because you did?
God gave me this same vivid hope years ago, and it was
more wonderful than the experience of my conversion by
far, and I cannot give it up." A friend told me recently
that when she believed in a *partial* rapture she actually
hoped to *die,* so as to "depart and be with Christ," and

*The Lord says in Matthew 24:29 that "immediately" after the tribulation
the sun should be darkened, and He would come in glory. But at the close of
the 1260 days of the "two witnesses," other things entirely happen!

be *safe*. Legalism is at the bottom of all this post-tribulation talk.

Again—is zeal for souls increased by giving up the imminent hope of the Lord's coming? In a trip around the world I found the most earnest missionaries were expecting Christ *vividly,* and not looking to go through the tribulation. The most earnest seekers of souls I know are those that believe that Christ may come for His Church at any time.

Again—why do the post-tribulationists keep claiming that men who held Christ's imminent coming while on earth, made some statement to them, "just before death," declaring the opposite?

Robert Cameron, of *Watchword and Truth,* whose later life was largely a proselyting campaign for post-tribulationism, used to claim that Dr. Brookes, of St. Louis, had given up this hope "before he died, in an interview with him!" But both the last books and the later associates of Dr. Brookes deny this. Others claimed that Prof. W. G. Moorehead gave it up, etc., etc. Someone told me that R. A. Torrey weakened. *I challenged him.* He could produce no proof whatever! Mrs. Torrey, when told that a Canadian magazine had claimed that her husband had given up the hope of Christ's imminent coming for the *whole* Church, was much distressed, and wrote the editor to publish her denial of such a false report. (Which request that journal has never granted. Why?) A certain church paper published a letter from a western woman saying, "Poor old Blackstone, who wrote 'Jesus Is Coming!'—he has got to be over ninety and he is still *holding on to the same old ideas.*" Well, praise the Lord! She claimed that Dr. Scofield, "if he could only come back would be one of the first to revise all his ideas." When alive, did Dr. Scofield have to resort to a woman to prove Scripture to him? Nor could he be so faithless to the vision God had given him as to "revise his ideas."

Again—why do people claim to be teaching the truth when they are dividing the saints? The post-tribulationists are propagandists that are not publishing the *glad tidings* of Christ's second coming. They are seeking to turn away those who have received these tidings as the great hope of their life, to *their theory concerning* it.

Again—who have been the teachers and preachers of Christ's imminent coming? We have such men as John Darby, who was probably the greatest interpreter of Scripture since Paul, with such early Brethren as C. H. Mackintosh, J. G. Bellett, Wm. Kelly, and the rest, a marvelous coterie. Then you have C. H. Spurgeon. It is idle to claim that he was not *looking* for Christ's coming. He split no hairs such as the post-tribulationists do, but boldly and constantly proclaimed the second coming of Christ as *an actual and a daily possibility.* D. L. Moody was a wonderful witness to any truth God revealed to him; and his sermon on "The Second Coming of Christ" is a classic. He was looking for the Lord's coming. George C. Needham, beloved Irishman; Wm. E. Blackstone, whose life has been to *look for his Lord;* James H. Brookes, a mighty warrior, now with the Lord; A. B. Simpson, of whom Moody said, "Everything he says reaches my heart." All these were *looking* for Christ's appearing. It was the *hope of their lives.* H. M. Parsons, of Toronto, now with Christ; and Dr. Weston, yet in Toronto, faithful witnesses alike. Grand old I. M. Haldeman, of New York, as well as J. Wilbur Chapman, now with Christ. A. T. Pierson, of wonderful penetration in the meaning of Scripture; A. J. Gordon; George E. Guille—lately among us, now with Christ, devoted, gentle, sane, yet a *contender* for Christ's *imminent coming;* our Brother Ironside, whose praise is among the real churches of Christ; Lewis Sperry Chafer at Dallas; A. C. Gaebelein, of New York, Editor of *Our Hope,* perhaps the most persistent, faithful witness for over fifty years to the imminent return of our Lord for all His saints, that the Church has had in America.

To these names should be added that of James M. Gray, late President of the Moody Bible Institute of Chicago and Editor of the Moody Institute Monthly.

In the pages of the latter, Dr. Gray has often borne witness to the teaching of Holy Scripture that the translation of the Church which is the body of Christ shall precede the tribulation. See particularly the issue of August, 1931, page 583. See also his books, *Prophecy and the Lord's Return, My Faith in Jesus Christ, The Teaching and Preaching That Counts,* and chapter 10 of *Bible Problems Explained.*

Then there are the godly (and there are many) among the Holiness people, and also the Pentecostal people, those who seek to live a life of prayer and praise continually. Where do you find such saints aligned? They are all looking for the *blessed hope;* and they believe it can be in their day or they would not be looking for it. Where can the post-tribulationists find such witnesses as these? It has cost very much along every line of sacrifice for these witnesses to hold fast the *imminent hope of Christ's coming,* and along with it the infinitely precious doctrines of *grace* (for the two go always together).

Then there are a host of faithful witnesses to Christ's *imminent* coming, in Great Britain, Scandinavia, the mission fields, and Australasia.

Mr. George H. Pember of England (now with Christ) was one of the most honest men in writing that I have ever read, as well as a very able man, author of several books. But Mr. Pember was *forced by the logic of his position* to claim that the Body of Christ was not the whole Church at all, but just *certain surrendered folks!* And that arouses the query in our minds, What people have been surrendered enough to be in the Body of Christ? And, who is going to settle it? As we have said, the Corinthians were the Body of Christ, and they were *carnal* Christians. Mr. Pember gives a little over half a page of one large book to the whole subject of divine sovereign election, and claims that it does not concern salvation at all! Well, brethren, you cannot be rid of Spurgeon, Darby, Edwards, Calvin, Luther, Augustine, or Paul, as easily as that!

14. The final and unanswerable argument that the

Church cannot be in The Great Tribulation is revealed in our Lord's own outline of The Revelation: Chapter 1:19. Here we have: First, "The things which thou sawest," (the vision of Christ among the churches in chapter 1). Second, "The things which are," (the letters to the seven churches with their plain outline of the Church's history in chapters 2 and 3). Third, "The things which shall come to pass after these things," (the rest of Revelation, from chapter 4, onward).

In both the King James and Revised Versions an utterly inadequate translation is given of the last phrase of this divine outline. The Greek expression is *meta tauta.* "*Meta*" is a Greek preposition meaning "after"; "*tauta*" is a neuter plural pronoun meaning "these," or "these things." To translate this phrase "*meta tauta*" by the adverb "hereafter" is not to translate it at all! That is shown in chapter 4:1, where this remarkable phrase *meta tauta* both opens and closes the verse—a remarkable thing!* Let us read this verse:

> "After these things *(meta tauta)* I saw, and
> behold, a door opened in heaven, and the first
> voice that I heard, as of a trumpet speaking
> with me, one saying, Come up hither, and I
> will show thee the things which must come
> to pass after these things" *(meta tauta)*,—that
> is, *after* Church things.

a. No one would dream of translating *meta tauta* at the *beginning* of this remarkable verse by "hereafter." It would make no manner of sense. We *must* translate it, "after these things I saw."

b. But the use by the Spirit of God of this *same phrase* at the *end* of this verse compels us to believe that

---

*Liddell and Scott say *meta* with the accusative of place signifies "after, or next after;" and of Time, "after, next to;" and of Rank, "next to, next after." Winer (the dean of Greek grammarians, says *meta* with the accusative signifies *after* in regard to *time*, and is the opposite to *pro*, "before."

Thayer wholly agrees: "*Meta* with the accusative denotes sequence, i. e. the *order* in which one thing follows another; a. in order of Place—*after, behind*; b. in order of Time—*after*." Thus among some thirty instances of the phrase *meta-tauta* which he adduces, see examples in Luke 17:8; Acts 7:7; John 5:1; and then all the occurrences in The Revelation: 1:19; 4:1 (2); 7:9; 9:12; 15:5; 18:1; 19:1; 20:3.

the things set forth after 4:1 happened just as really after the things of the preceding chapter as the vision of 4:1 happened after those of chapters 1, 2 and 3.

The messages to the seven churches have been formally and fully closed at the end of chapter 3 and what *follows* these Church things is given from chapter 4, onward.

Indeed, as all commentators have recognized, we have in Revelation 1:19, a three-fold division answering to the past, present, and future; and, as Govett remarks, "The last division of the Book begins on the completion of the first two, *and not till then.*"

But we find The Great Tribulation not in the first three chapters, but beginning in Chapter 13:1. Now the Lord *said* this would occur *after the things* of chapters 1-3.

We repeat finally that a weak grasp of the real character and scope of divine grace; failure or refusal *to accept Paul as the revelator to the Church of God;* and consequently dimness of view of the character, security and coming glory of the whole Church, and a lingering legalism that does not perceive that our Lord in the sermon on the mount was speaking as the Great Prophet of Deuteronomy 18, backing up Moses, and *speaking to Israel, just as really as Moses on Sinai did, and not to the Church of God at all, which was yet future (Matthew 16):*—I say, all these elements enter into the deadly untruth that the saints of the Church are subject, any of them, to the wrath-time of The Tribulation.

Let the members of the Body of Christ remember that they are *one with their Head,* that judgment is past and only glory is beyond. That, however much men may distress them (for "in the world ye shall have tribulation,") The *Great* Tribulation, the "time of temptation that is to come upon the whole world" shall not touch them! "Because thou didst keep the word of my patience, I also will keep thee from the hour of trial that is to come upon the whole earth to try them that dwell upon the earth."

Let us beware of confusing the *Bema,* or "judgment-seat of Christ" after the Church is caught up, with divine judgment for *guilt,* as such. Christ *bare* our sins on the cross, with their entire guilt, and put it all away forever. "To them that wait for him (all His Church) he will appear a second time, APART FROM SIN, unto SALVATION." Remember, "They that are CHRIST'S, at His Coming."

15. Another proof the Church *cannot* be on the earth during the last half of Daniel's 70th week—the Great Tribulation, is seen in *the character of our warfare.* "We wrestle against the principalities and the powers *in the heavenly places*" (Eph. 6:12). But Satan and his whole host are cast altogether out of heaven, in Rev. 12,—*before the beginning* of the Great Tribulation! Then *warfare* in the "heavenly places" will be closed. The Church of necessity will have been removed from the warrior scene. Then *earthly* conflict,—"the time of *Jacob's* trouble," will begin (Jer. 30:7).

It must be most carefully noted that that warfare, which Church-saints carry on now in "the heavenlies" against Satan and his host, is *transferred to Michael and his angels,* in Revelation 12! And the result of the expulsion of Satan and his angels from heaven is announced in the words: *"Neither was their place found any more in heaven * * * he was cast down to earth, and his angels were cast down with him."*

Note now the facts that make it impossible that the Church should be on earth after Satan is cast down:

(1) The "Great voice in heaven" of Rev. 12:10 proclaims a *new state of things,* essentially opposite to the present time: *the salvation, power and kingdom of God COMES: with the authority of His Christ* in *execution,* as not before. While the Church was on earth "wrestling" with the "principalities and powers in the heavenlies," she suffered with Christ, but Christ now speaks with a "Get thee hence, Satan!" that banishes him utterly from all heavenly position whatever!

(2) The *accusations* before God of Satan are thus ended. That peculiar position of "Accuser," which is so fully shown in our Lord's words to Peter: "Simon, Simon, behold, Satan obtained you (plural, all of them!) to sift you as wheat; but I made supplication for *thee* (so in danger from self-confidence) that thy faith fail not,"— is now *over*. When Satan is "cast down," all his accusing work is past, thank God! while the saints, whom he "accused before God," are found in the heavens, from which he has been cast out.

(3) The *"heavens"* are called to *"rejoice"* (XII:12)— *and those who "are tabernacling in them."* (Compare "the camp of the saints" (XX:9). These are evidently, it seems to us, *the Church saints,* and *all the saints* who have *"overcome Satan" because of the blood of the Lamb, and because of the word of their testimony,—loving not their lives even to the death."*

(4) The *object* of Satan's rage when cast down is,— not the Church, but "the Woman that brought forth the Man-Child,"—that is, *Israel,* which, after the Rapture, represents God on earth. The Church, being heavenly in calling and destiny, has *disappeared from the scene!* Otherwise she, being "the fulness" of Christ Himself, because His very Body (Eph. II:22-23) would be more the object of Satan's attack than Israel: because Satan is more jealous of her! But she is *above,*—in the heavenlies, where Satan's place is *no more found!**

---

*If it be objected that we ourselves are now on earth, and yet carry on a warfare "in the heavenlies," and that therefore Satan can carry on such a conflict, even after being "cast down to earth"; the answer is simple: the saints are *in Christ,* they share His risen life, and their walk and warfare is by the indwelling Spirit "sent down from heaven,"—so that they are constantly and actually connected with heaven, in a Risen Christ!

Satan has no such connection,—no connection whatever *with heaven,* when once he is cast out of it. He is as much an "earthly" power as any earthly monarch. Having, indeed, still a spirit's ability to "walk up and down the Earth (Job I), and terrible power and energy,—yet he is no longer capable of *heavenly* warfare. This is evident at once in his impotence in Rev. 19:19-20:3; where his false Christ and his armies gather "to make war" against Him that sits on the white horse, *but make no war at all!* They are at once "taken," and cast into the lake of fire, *with no power of battle at all!* And Satan himself makes *no fight with angelic power,* as before in heaven, but is "bound," and "cast into the abyss!" (Rev. 20:1-3).